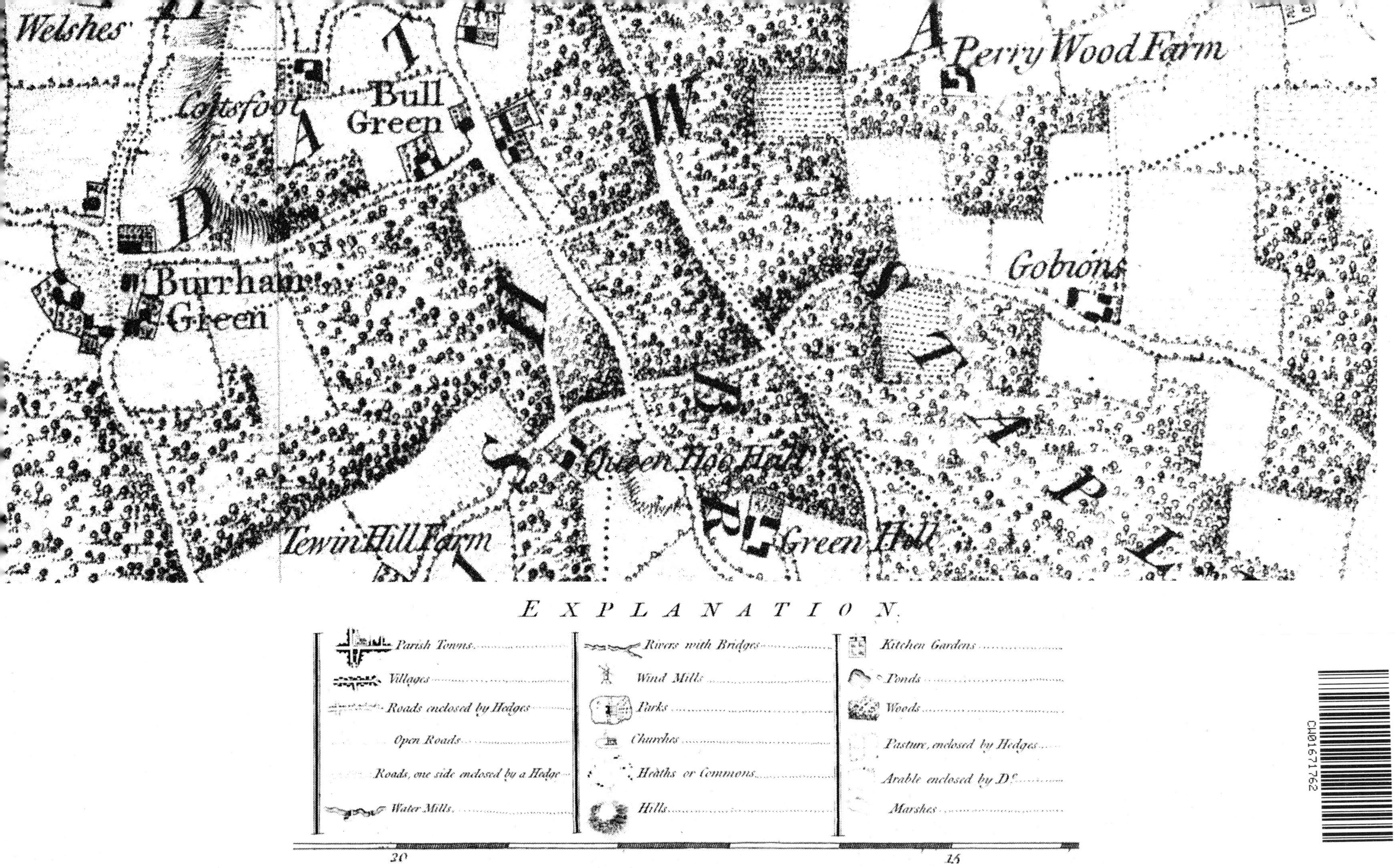

An extract from *'A Topographical Map of Hartford-Shire'* by Andrew Dury and John Andrews, 1766. Published by the Hertfordshire Records Society 2004

A HISTORY
OF
DATCHWORTH

Wendy Prowle and Jane Walker

Datchworth Parish Council
2014

Published in 2014 by
Datchworth Parish Council
Datchworth, Hertfordshire

Cover Design: Ian Walker

Front cover	Top pictures: Datchworth Green *c.*1936 and 2014 Lower pictures: Burnham Green *c.*1950 and 2014
Back cover	Datchworth Church 2014 from a painting by Shirley Ashby
Front endpaper	from *A Topographical Map of Hartford-Shire* by Andrew Dury and John Andrews, 1766 (re-printed by Hertfordshire Record Society 2003)
Back endpaper	Datchworth parish in 1839 based on the tithe map (HALS: DSA4/34/2)

ISBN 978-0-9509512-1-8

Printed and bound by Triographics Printers Ltd.
121 London Road, Knebworth, Herts. SG3 6EX

Contents

Illustrations

Images have been acknowledged where appropriate. Where special permission has been granted, the originator or copyright holder has been listed within the caption of the image in the book. Otherwise, the originator has been listed below in brackets. If no acknowledgement has been given, these images or designs have usually been provided by ourselves.

Illustrations

Illustrations

Conventions and Abbreviations

Conventions

Dates

Until 1752, 25 March was the start of the New Year. Following an Act in the reign of George II in 1751, the first day of 1752 was 1 January. In this volume, there are several documents that pre-date this 'new style dating' and where this has occurred, the date has been modernised to avoid confusion, for example, 3 March 1716 has been written as 3 March 1717.

Money

Old pence to new pence: 3d = just over 1p; 6d = 2.5p and 12d =1s =5p

Shillings to pounds:

s	£
1	0.05
5	0.25
10	0.50
20	1.00

Land measures

Hide: approximately 120 acres; said to be an area of land that could be ploughed in one year using one plough with a team of eight oxen, sufficient to support a family.

Virgate: a quarter of a hide

Councils

Parish Council: where 'the parish council' is mentioned, it refers to Datchworth Parish Council

District Council: Hertford Rural District Council was formed in 1894 and consisted of 15 villages, one of which was Datchworth. This was abolished under the Local Government Act 1972 and on 1 April 1974, it was merged with six other district councils to become East Herts District Council. In most cases in the book, when referring to either of these councils, we have simply referred to them as the 'district council.'

County Council: where 'the county council' is mentioned, it refers to Hertfordshire County Council

The Hertford Mercury

The *Hartford* [*sic*] *Mercury* newspaper was founded in 1772 and has, over the years, changed its name no less than eleven times, finally becoming the *Hertfordshire Mercury* in 1986. In most cases in the book, when referring to this newspaper, we have simply referred to it as the '*Hertford*' or '*Hertfordshire*' *Mercury*.

Use of square brackets and spelling

Occasional editorial explanatory notes have been given in square brackets
Examples: illegible writing: Thomas Gouge [? Goose]; obsolete units: [3 roods = ¾ acre]

In cases where extracts have been quoted from documents, the original spelling has been maintained.

Abbreviations

ARP: Air Raid Precautions
EEA: Elementary Education Act
HALS: Hertfordshire Archives and Local Studies
HTML: HyperText Markup Language; a computer language
ICT: Information and Communications Technology
MC: Military Cross
NVQ: National Vocational Qualification
PCC: Parochial Church Council
PTA: Parent Teacher Association
RE: Religious Education
VCH: *Victoria County History*
VE Day: Victory in Europe Day. 8 May 1945; official announcement of the end of Second World War
VJ Day: Victory in Japan Day. 15 August 1945; the eventual surrender of Japan
WAS: Welwyn Archaeological Society

Significant Dates

Early history time line (not to scale)

2000 BC	800 BC	AD 43	AD 410	AD 860	AD1066
Bronze Age→	Iron Age→	Romans	Saxons	Danes	Normans

Some important events: eleventh to the seventeenth century

	Year(s)	Event
Middle Ages	1086	Domesday Book
	1348	Black Death
Tudor England	1534	Henry VIII breaks with Rome; start of English Reformation
	1536	Start of Dissolution of the Monasteries
Stuart England	1642-51	English Civil War
	1649-60	Commonwealth with Oliver Cromwell
	1660	Restoration of the Monarchy

Reigning monarchs and their dates

Years of Reign	Monarch	Years of Reign	Monarch
1066-1087	William I	1553-1558	Mary I
1087-1100	William II	1558-1603	Elizabeth I
1100-1135	Henry I	1603-1625	James I
1135-1154	Stephen	1625-1649	Charles I
1154-1189	Henry II	1649	Charles II
1189-1199	Richard I	1649-1660	Commonwealth
1199-1216	John	1660-1685	Charles II
1216-1272	Henry III	1685-1688	James II
1272-1307	Edward I	1688-1694	William III & Mary II
1307-1327	Edward II	1694-1702	William III
1327-1377	Edward III	1702-1714	Anne
1377-1399	Richard II	1714-1727	George I
1399-1413	Henry IV	1727-1760	George II
1413-1422	Henry V	1760-1820	George III
1422-1461	Henry VI	1820-1830	George IV
1461-1483	Edward VI	1830-1837	William IV
1483	Edward V	1837-1901	Victoria
1483-1485	Richard III	1901-1910	Edward VII
1485-1509	Henry VII	1910-1936	George V
1509-1547	Henry VIII	1936	Edward VIII
1547-1553	Edward VI	1936-1952	George VI
1553	Jane	1952-	Elizabeth II

Preface

In 2011, a discussion took place at a parish council meeting that involved an ever increasing list of residents requesting a copy of *Five Hide Village,* written in 1984 by Tom Beachcroft and Wally Emms. Three further editions of the book had been printed, the final one being in 1995, all of which had long since sold out. As the book had been typed on a word processor, the printers advised that additional copies would be very expensive unless it could be reproduced in digital format.

Work eventually started in December 2011, when the book was re-typed in digital format and the following eighteen months was spent updating the material and photographs. However, by July 2013, it was realised that, as so much new and varied information had come to light, much of the material in the book was to change so drastically that it may no longer be recognised as *Five Hide Village*. After more discussions with the parish council, it was concluded that a completely new history book should be published, leaving *Five Hide Village* in its original form in recognition of Tom and Wally's work.

Apart from using Hertfordshire Archives and Local Studies (HALS) for much of the research, the invention of the World Wide Web has proved to be a useful tool for accessing new material and providing the key to related information. However, on the contrary, some research has been inhibited by the introduction of the Data Protection Act 1998, which has prevented access to some particular material from the last hundred years.

At the end of some of the chapters, extracts from residents' memories have been included which were the result of interviews that took place in the 1960s. These memories have recorded residents' views of village life in Datchworth from the early twentieth century and are available to read in Datchworth Museum. The names of those interviewed are listed beside the extracts. The interviewers were Jim Terry, Margaret Scott, Jean Steer, Denis Shepherd, Mrs B Shepherd, Mrs Thody, Miss A Wheatley and Mary Poole

The year of the publication of this book is significant in that 2014 is the 30th anniversary of the publication of *Five Hide Village*. Compiling and composing this new volume has been challenging and sometimes frustrating but nevertheless it has been immensely enjoyable, particularly as so many contributions both verbal and written have come from the villagers themselves.

Wendy Prowle and Jane Walker, 2014

Acknowledgements

Five Hide Village was the first book to be written about the history of Datchworth and reflects the result of considerable research carried out by the late Tom Beachcroft and Wally B Emms. It is with gratitude that we acknowledge this valuable source of material which has helped us in our task in producing this new volume. We should also like to express our thanks to Datchworth Parish Council, the copyright holders and publishers, for giving us the opportunity to write this book and for its continuous support.

During our research we used a variety of sources including Datchworth Museum, books, websites and private collections. There were numerous other organisations and the most productive was Hertfordshire Archives and Local Studies (HALS). We should like to thank the archivists and staff at HALS for their interest and untiring help. The retiring County Archivist, Susan Flood and her successor, Chris Bennett kindly gave us permission to reproduce images from HALS for which we are grateful.

Efforts have been made to place events in Datchworth in their historical context and where this has occurred the text has been read by people with appropriate expertise who have provided constructive and invaluable comments. Special thanks in this matter go to Dr Alan Thomson, Eileen Wallace and Alan Ruston. Dr Heather Falvey has been a great help in sorting out many major and minor conundrums and has given her professional advice on several of the early chapters. In the later stages of the compilation she kindly read through a printed manuscript and her comments enabled us iron out a number of last minute details. We greatly appreciate her continuous support.

Graphic designer Charlotte Tebbutt has produced several maps throughout the book with which we are delighted and thanks also go to Ian Walker for his help with many of the images, some old and some new. Jane Dodson has had the unenviable task of proof reading the entire text and has raised many important points in so-doing. We are particularly appreciative of this contribution.

Over the past two to three years, many local residents have provided a great deal of interesting material and some have generously invited us into their houses, all of which has helped enormously in the production of this book. In addition, other people have contributed from outside of the village, in some cases from organisations such as Welwyn Archaeological Society, Hertfordshire Constabulary, Hertford Museum and the CPRE (Campaign to Protect Rural England). Archivists from Hertfordshire Scouts and Girlguiding Hertfordshire have also been helpful. There are so many ways in which people have contributed and, apart from those already mentioned, we feel the best way to thank everyone is to list all the names as shown below. We apologise for any inadvertent omissions.

To those who are Datchworth residents, our thanks:

John Alden
Steve Arnold
Shirley Ashby
Fran Attrill
Claire Austin
Jean Austin
John & Kathy Barnes
Nick Bateman
Adrian & Claire Bennett
Julian & Karen Carter
James & Fizzy Chambers
Lesley Chambers
Tony & Anne Charles
Nick Collingridge
Les Davis
Annie Dexter
Barbara Edwards
Wally Emms
Anthony & Sue Flind
Geoff Gilbert
John Glanville
Simon Goddard
Leslie Goldsmith
Susan Haslam
Denise Gray
Sarah Hewitt
Pam Hill
Chris Hills
Doreen & Clive Hodson Smith
Clew Hughes
Ron & Sarah Hulman
Peter Hyne
Tony Jackson
Bob & Thora King
Peter Large
Julian Leach
Gill Lines
Ann Little
Jessie Little
Viv Marshall
Sara Miller
Steve & Jackie Nash
Denise Nee
Nina Nettell
Brian Packman
Frank Pearman
Mary Poole
Rosemary Sherwood
Lydia Somerville
Malcolm Tebbutt
Cameron Thompson
Will Topping
Alan Tyler
Chris Wilkins
Joy Wilkins
John Wright

To those who are from outside Datchworth, our thanks:

Dorothy Abel Smith
Ralph M Abel Smith
Margaret Ashby
Les Brownsell
Frank Brittain
Michael Clark
Pauline Conolly
Ian Curley
Diane Day
Roy Falder
Wendy Farrier
Keith Fitzpatrick-Matthews
Annette Glenn
Ken Griffin
Colin Heathcote
Kris Lockyear
Nik Pringle
Jean Riddell
Tony Rook
Jo Simson
Mary Underwood
John Wallace
Mary Willatt
Andy Wiseman

Finally, our sincere thanks must be given to our families who have been very patient and somewhat neglected over the past two years or so.

1. The First 1000 Years

An Anglo-Saxon Charter dated 15 May 969 recorded that King Edgar gave land in Datchworth to St Peter's Church, Westminster Abbey. This entry is the earliest known mention of Datchworth which at the time was spelt Decewrthe. The name was a combination of two Old English words, 'Dece' which was derived from the name of a man called Dæcca and 'wrthe' meaning enclosure; so Datchworth meant 'an enclosure belonging to Dæcca'. The ownership of this land, described as being 'five hides', was later confirmed by King Edward in 1065.

The enclosure implied in the name may have referred to an area which was once enclosed by a moat, fragments of which are still visible. It has been estimated that the moat originally enclosed an area of about six acres that later included the church and a manor house. A church would almost certainly have been built following King Edgar's grant, most likely of wood. Following the Conquest, many churches were rebuilt in stone and, indeed, the present church dates from the twelfth century. A manor house was built in 1728, and again, probably replaced an earlier structure of which no records have been found. No date has been given for the moat, it may have been Anglo-Saxon or earlier or it may simply have been a form of barrier to keep cattle in and other beasts out.

The Belgae and the Romans

Long before Datchworth was a parish, evidence suggests that there was earlier habitation in the region, some within the parish boundary of today and some close by. As with so many archaeological finds, prior knowledge, perseverance and luck all contribute towards discovery.

A well documented Roman road runs through Datchworth Green running east-west from Colchester to St Albans, part of which is visible on the map (Figure 1) labelled 'Watton Road'; however, Lionel Munby, in his book *The Hertfordshire Landscape,* has suggested that the road was originally an Iron Age route. Lying on this route, Datchworth is roughly halfway between known Iron Age settlements that were at Braughing and Welwyn. These were associated with the Belgae tribe that came from Northern France and after which Belgium was named. The Belgae, called the Catuvellauni by the Romans, invaded Britain from about 100 BC.

Local archaeologist, Tony Rook and his team have been diligent in their excavation activities and have discovered many Belgic and Roman remains particularly in the Welwyn area. It is not altogether surprising that certain items of Belgic and Roman origin have been found near to and within Datchworth parish.

Chapel Wood, north of Watton Road, is named after an early thirteenth century chapel, the remains of which were found by the Welwyn Archaeological Society (WAS) in 1975. A second building may have been a hermitage.

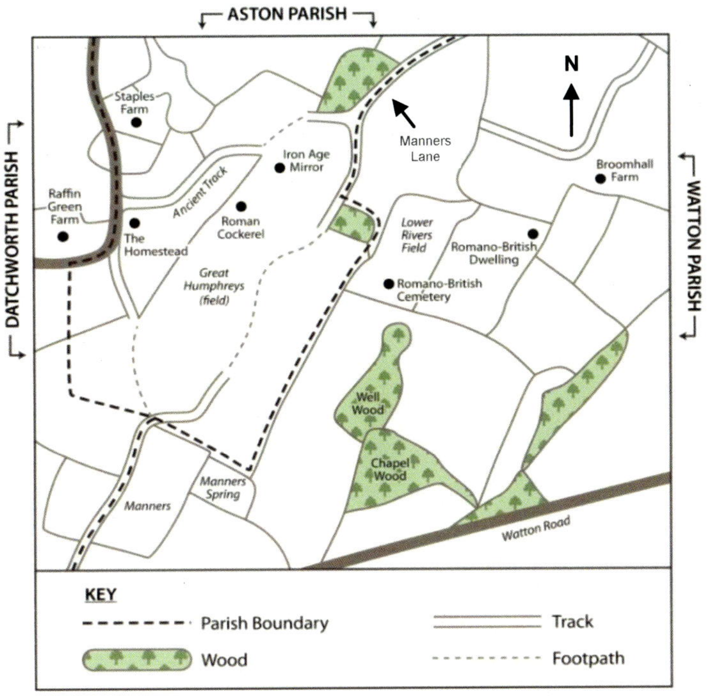

Figure 1: Archaeological sites to the east of Datchworth Parish (Designed by Charlotte Tebbutt)

Iron Age burial sites

In the late summer of 1975 field walkers discovered a cremation cemetery in Lower Rivers Field and in the summer of 1976 the site was excavated by WAS. Although the material had been badly damaged by ploughing, there was enough to identify several skeletons which were probably of both sexes and certainly of all ages, the youngest being a four-year-old child. It was concluded that this was most likely to have been a civilian burial site rather than a military one.

The location of an associated settlement was not known at the time of these discoveries. However, John Wallace of Broomhall Farm found a stamped rim sherd [fragment] of an amphora [wine jar] near the farm. This find prompted the British Museum to sponsor a dig in the area. Some native and Roman pottery was found, sufficient to suggest a Romano-British dwelling but there were no apparent conclusions about the size or nature of the site. Work is continuing in this area.

In May 1979, while walking in a field called Great Humphreys, John Wallace found another significant item. This time it was a bent and distorted piece of metal which he recognised as being of some archaeological importance. He contacted Tony Rook, who identified it as the plate of a Belgic mirror. Unfortunately the handle of the mirror was missing. After the harvest, a team from WAS searched the area using various metal detecting devices but to no avail. However, in September 1980, using more sophisticated detectors the handle was discovered about 20m from where the mirror had been found. The completed mirror is now at the British Museum.

More excavations in Great Humphreys uncovered the remains of a cremation burial near the site where the handle was found. Known as the Aston burial, it consisted of a shallow pit containing remnants of two pottery vessels and some bones in a heap. Results from the burnt bones analysis suggest that the individual may have been female. It is thought that the mirror could have come from this site.

In this same field not far from The Homestead, Raffin Green Lane, other excavations by WAS revealed a ditch, about 8m across and 2.5m deep, dating back to just before the Roman occupation. The material nearest the top was of the Roman era and included a delightful bronze cockerel and further down there was Belgic pottery. Deeper still at least 18 infant burials were found that were from the Roman period. The skeleton of one of them can be found in Datchworth Museum.

Figure 2: Belgic mirror (Replica owned by John Wallace)

Figure 3: Bronze cockerel (Replica owned by John Wallace)

Welch's Farm

A study of Datchworth parish boundary shows a curious loop in the region of Welch's Farm (Figure 4). The following discoveries go some way towards explaining this strange shape.

In the summer of 1968, a North Sea Gas pipeline was laid from Welwyn to Widford that passed near to Welch's Farm. Tony Rook, alert to the fact that something interesting might be dug up, spent the summer with his team pursuing the diggers. They were rewarded when archaeological remains emerged. A substantial Belgic settlement was identified and the findings were recorded in articles by Tony Rook in the *Hertfordshire Archaeological Review.*

Points A, B and C on the map (Figure 4) mark sites where sections of boundary ditches were found. The direction of each ditch coincides with the direction of the parish boundary at those points.

It was observed that at two places, A and C, the preferred route of the parish boundary follows the ancient ditch rather than the outskirts of fields called Pollards and Great James's. Tony Rook has suggested that when the parish boundaries were planned, the Iron Age features were respected rather than the edges of the fields.

Later, Perry's Grove Ditch was found which is in line with the ditch at A and is visible today. This was discovered after the main gas pipe excavations had been completed. Described as probably late Iron Age, it is listed as a Scheduled Ancient Monument.

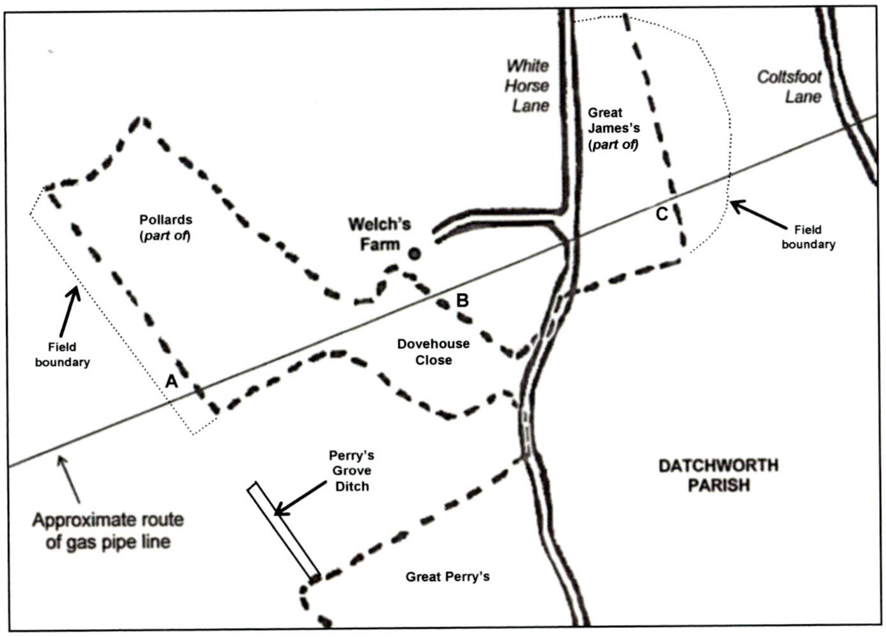

Figure 4: Belgic ditches near Welch's Farm discovered during the building of a gas pipe line in 1968 (---- = parish boundary)

Iron Age ditch on Datchworth Common

Figure 5: Datchworth Common, showing crop marks and a farm track leading from Bragbury End Lane. (Tony Rook)

In the dry spring of 1997, Tony Rook was invited by Harry Bott of Benington Lordship, to fly over some agricultural land to view the unusual nature of some of the crop germination where some areas were darker than others.

These dark patches indicated hidden underlying ditches and pits. The photograph, looking roughly south, has revealed clear crop marks on Datchworth Common, which is to the west of Bragbury End Lane. These show a rectilinear ditched enclosure with some patches in the middle. These were thought to be ploughed-out chalk pits.

Frank Pearman gave permission for further investigation to take place and a few local children joined the team to help extract such items as Belgic pottery. Some Roman tiles were also found in a depression 3m across which was situated at the point where the chalk pit meets the left hand section of the Iron Age ditch.

Saxon times

The beginning of the fifth century marked both the final departure of Roman legions and the Anglo-Saxon invasion of England from Northern Europe. Over the next two centuries while Roman culture slowly decayed, Saxon settlers established themselves in tribal groups bringing a different language (Old English) and new customs. The main tribes associated with Hertfordshire were the Hicce in the north from which the name of Hitchin is derived, the Brahingas of the Braughing area and the Waeclingas who were centred at Verulamium, close to St.Albans. The last two had chosen abandoned large Roman towns as their estate centres. One group close to Datchworth was the Beningas, 'dwellers on the River Beane' and gave its name to Benington and Bengeo.

These tribes belonged to kingdoms that were involved in many wars during the Middle Saxon period (600-850). Hertfordshire, as it is today, lay partly in Mercia (tribes of middle England) and partly in Essex (east Saxons). A boundary between these two kingdoms finally settled somewhere in East Hertfordshire. By this time Christianity had reached England (597) and Hertfordshire was divided between the dioceses of Lincoln and London. Tom Williamson, in *The Origins of Hertfordshire*, has observed that the boundary between these dioceses ran roughly north-south and passed through the western border of Braughing parish and may have coincided with the border between Mercia and Essex mentioned above.

In the second half of the ninth century, invasion by the Danes caused more disruption creating yet another frontier. A treaty was made between the leader of the Danish army and King Alfred. The conventional theory is that the chosen dividing line ran along the course of the River Lea. By 918 Alfred's successor, Edward, had conquered the Danes and during this campaign he built two forts in Hertford, one each side of the River Lea. It was at about this time that the shire of Hertford evolved, which is first mentioned in the *Anglo-Saxon Chronicle* in 1011. The borders of Hertfordshire sometimes follow physical features such as the Rivers Lea and Stort in the east; however other boundary features are not so clearly defined.

Datchworth Parish

It has already been mentioned that Saxon tribes had estates centred on places like Hitchin. After the conversion to Christianity a 'minster' or 'mother' church was built in each centre from which priests travelled to outlying areas to spread the Word. In time, this system become impractical, and these large Saxon estates fragmented into units that emerged as parishes. The outer boundary of the original estate probably followed topographical features such as watersheds between rivers; however, where fragmentation occurred there were sometimes irregular kinks and shapes in parish boundaries. These may be explained by the need to circumvent a physical feature like an odd shaped field, hillock or even a tree. In the case mentioned near Welch's farm above, the chosen route followed part of a Belgic ditch.

It is thought that Welwyn, with its minster, may have been the estate from which the parish of Datchworth evolved in 969 when King Edgar granted land in Datchworth to Westminster Abbey. Once a parish was established, a church was built often by the local lord close to his manor house. All Saints' Church, Datchworth, situated close to the site of Datchworthbury manor house is a typical example of this arrangement.

2. Domesday Book and Datchworth

According to the *Anglo-Saxon Chronicles*, at Christmas 1085, William I was in Gloucester with his councillors discussing the threat of invasion from Denmark. He wanted to have a report of available financial and military resources in the event of such an invasion. This is one of the reasons put forward to explain why he commissioned a survey to assess the taxable value of all the land and at the same time, to discover who owned what and, in particular, what were his royal rights. The Chronicles describe his action as follows:

> He then sent his men over all England into each shire, and had it made out how many hides of land there were in the shire; what the king had himself in land, and in livestock on the land; what dues he had from property each twelve months from the shire; also ... how much land his archbishops had, his diocesan bishops, his abbots and his earls, ... what and how much each man who was holding land in England, in land, in livestock, and how much money it was worth ... all the documents were brought to him afterwards.

The 'inquest', as it was also called, was likened to 'the Day of Judgement' in the sense that it spared no-one. Thus, when eventually a book was compiled, it became commonly known as Domesday Book although it was originally called the 'King's Roll' or the 'Winchester Roll'.

The country was divided into seven regions or 'circuits' mostly containing five 'shires'. Hertfordshire was in a group with Middlesex, Cambridgeshire, Bedfordshire and Buckinghamshire. Three or four commissioners were assigned to each circuit. Most shires were in the charge of an earl and a 'shire reeve', or 'sheriff', both of whom were responsible to the king and it was probably the sheriff who bore the burden of organising the collection of the data from each 'hundred'.

At the time of Domesday, Hertfordshire was divided into nine hundreds; these later became eight. Shires were originally divided into hundreds in the tenth century, each hundred being 100 'hides'. However as a result of changes some hundreds, for example Broadwater where Datchworth is situated, contained well over 100 hides at the time of Domesday. Traditionally, it was thought that the name of the hundred was that of its meeting-place, but this may not always have been common practice. In the case of Broadwater, the name was taken from what was originally a little hamlet, now absorbed into Stevenage, which lies on the boundary line between the parishes of Knebworth and Shephall.

Information for the survey was almost certainly collected orally, possibly by the reeve of each manor, who then presented his findings under oath at the hundred court. The data was checked by a jury consisting of four Englishmen and four Frenchmen and then was taken to the shire court where more checks were made under the commissioners' supervision.

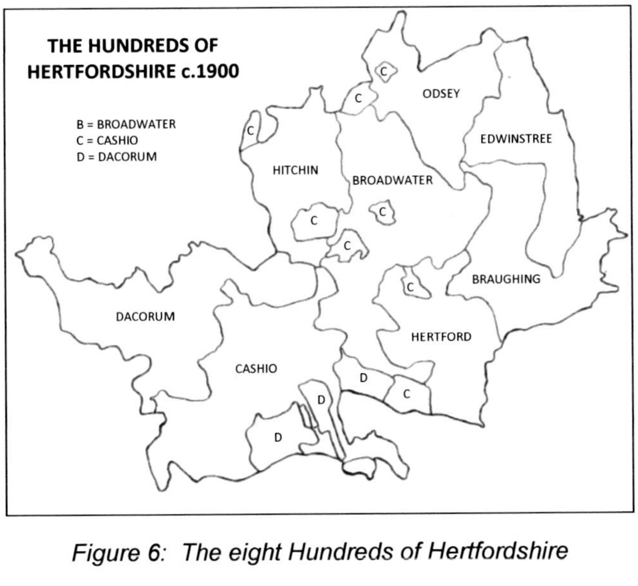

Figure 6: The eight Hundreds of Hertfordshire

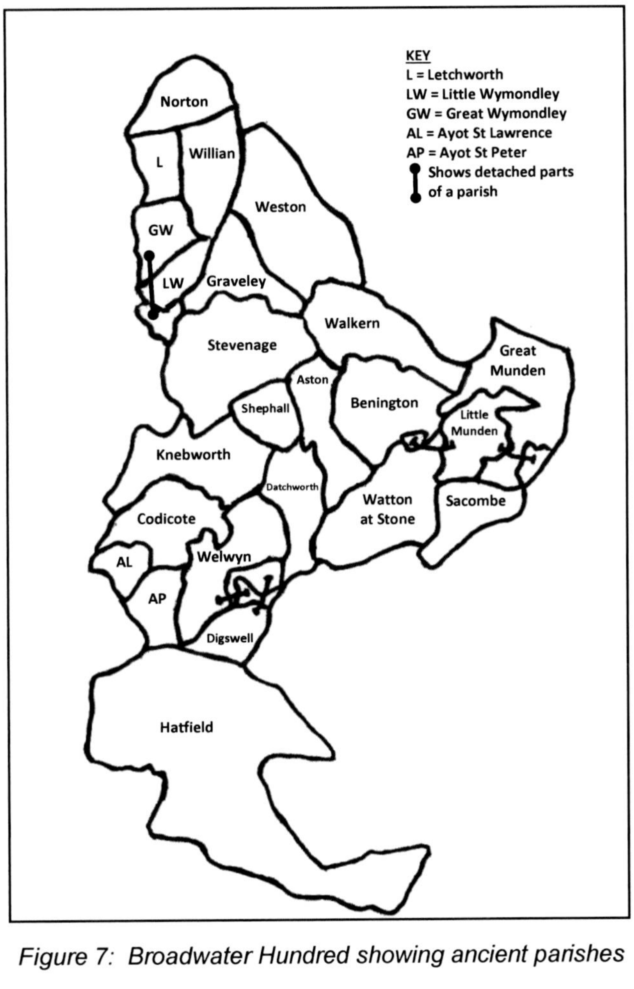

Figure 7: Broadwater Hundred showing ancient parishes

The survey started in 1086 but was abandoned following William's death in 1087 and was never completed. The task was so immense that there may not have been time to check every detail and probably available resources dictated that only disputed matters found their way to the courts. In these cases it was sometimes necessary to send an impartial representative to revisit a town or village to resolve such issues. All the information was recorded in Latin and eventually was compiled into two volumes, both of which are at the National Archives at Kew. Domesday Book was arranged according to the shires or counties and within each shire the land was listed by tenants. The king's lands came first, then those granted to the church, followed by those of the chief barons.

The text of each entry in Domesday Book has been translated, in Datchworth's case by Hertfordshire's John Morris (Figure 9). Datchworth is described as having a total of 'five hides', a hide being a unit of taxation for King William's purposes. Before the Conquest a hide was reckoned to be an area of land that could be ploughed in one year using one plough with a team of eight oxen, sufficient to support a family. The terrain and quality of the land dictated its size, so that a good, arable hide was smaller than a hide of inferior quality. It is difficult to fix the area that one hide represented but it is often taken to be about 120 acres. Even an 'acre' was not clearly defined; it was an area that could be ploughed by a yoke of oxen in a day, so the actual size was arbitrary.

Datchworth had roughly 600 acres of taxable land in 1086, but the parish covered a much larger acreage than that. In a survey dated 1829, it was estimated to be nearly 2,000 acres. Even when allowing for the inaccuracy of the 1086 estimate, much of the land must have been woodland, waste or other un-cultivatable areas.

About 20 years had gone by since the Norman Conquest and much of the land had changed in tenancy and value. These important elements of the survey are reflected in the replies to questions relating to land occupation and value before 1066, just after 1066 and in 1086. The other details were to do with, for example, peasant labour, workable land and woodland measured according to the number of pigs it could support.

Under the system of feudal tenure the king granted lands to tenants-in-chief in return for various services, usually military. The tenants-in-chief likewise granted lands to *their* tenants (sub-tenants). Knights were originally the fighting men at the Conquest who were rewarded with grants of land. They were expected to give 'knight service' in return.

King ↓
Tenants-in-chief (bishops, abbots, barons) ↓
Lesser tenants ↓
Knights ↓
Freemen ↓
Unfree peasants (villeins, borders, cottars) ↓
Slaves

Figure 8: The feudal hierarchy

A freeman could hold land that could be inherited, provided that he paid a fixed rent and carried out a few services. Of the unfree peasants, 'villeins' [or 'villagers'] were the most numerous. They occupied and could farm land, commonly about 30 acres. This was in exchange for services to the landowner usually about three days' work each week. Villeins owed their lords military service, but could avoid it by paying a fee. They could not move from the manor without obtaining permission from their lord.

Many borders and cottars had only a little land, barely enough to support a family and so were often obliged to do paid work. Slaves were the property of the lord and had no land.

At first sight, the entries appear to indicate that land in Datchworth originally comprised of four manors, the largest manor belonging to Westminster Abbey. However, on closer inspection, 'Land of the Archbishop of Canterbury' was originally part of the manorial holdings of the Abbot of Westminster. The origin and subsequent history of the other two portions is more obscure and it is suggested in the *Victoria County History for Hertfordshire* that these two parts were eventually absorbed into Datchworth Manor.

The holders of these two small sections of land had their own distinctions. Peter of Valognes, William I's nephew, was granted lands by his uncle in other counties besides Hertfordshire, where he was sheriff. In total he held 30 hides in Hertfordshire including several half virgate holdings such as Datchworth, the largest holding of 10 hides being that of Benington which was his residence.

Geoffrey of Bec, was notable for having two men-at-arms as sub-tenants. Knights were highly trained and were expected to be available for campaign duties for 40 days in the year. At other

Datchworth in Domesday Book

Translated entry in Domesday Book	**An interpretation**
Land of the Archbishop of Canterbury	**Tenant in chief of the King**
Archbishop Lanfranc holds 1 hide in Datchworth and Ansketel from him. Land for 2 ploughs. In lordship* 1 plough. 3 Villeins with 2 smallholders have 1 plough. Meadow for ½ ox; woodland, 50 pigs.*	Ansketel, a sub-tenant holds 1 hide; land for 2 ploughs* of which, 1 plough in lordship* and 1 plough for the villeins and smallholders. Land to support half an ox; woodland enough to support 50 pigs
Value 30s; when acquired 20s; before 1066, 60s.	Value of land: before 1066, 60s; just after conquest, 20s; 1086, 30s
Aelfric Black held this land from the Abbot of Westminster before 1066 but could not separate it from the church, as the hundred testifies; but for other lands he was Archbishop Stigand's man.	Aelfric Black, a Saxon lord, held this land from the Abbot of Westminster before 1066, did not have the freedom to sell because it was tied to St Peter's Church. Archbishop Stigand had been archbishop of Canterbury from 1052 until 1070. He died in 1072.
Land of the Abbot of Westminster	**Tenant in chief of the King**
In Datchworth the Abbot also holds 3 hides and 1 virgate. Land for 3 ploughs, in lordship 2 hides; 1 plough there. 6 villeins have 2 ploughs, 2 cottars. Meadow for ½ plough; pasture for the livestock; woodland, 50 pigs.*	The Abbot holds 3¼ hides: land for 3 ploughs of which, 1 plough in lordship and 2 ploughs for the villeins. Cottars (cottagers) had a little land. Small amount of meadow (½ plough); woodland enough to support 50 pigs
The value is and was 40s; before 1066 60s.	Value of land: before 1066, 60s; just after conquest, 40s; 1086, 40s
This manor lay and lies in the lordship of St. Peter's Church.	This manor [ie Datchworth] was part of the manorial holdings of Westminster Abbey
Land of Geoffrey of Bec	**Tenant in chief of the King**
In Datchworth 2 men-at-arms hold 2 ½ virgates from Geoffrey. Land for 1 plough; it is there, with 3 villeins.	Men-at-arms (sub-tenants) who held land in return for military service. Land for one plough for the **3 villeins**
The value is and was 12s 8d; before 1066, 20s.	Value of land: before 1066, 20s; just after conquest, 12s 8d; 1086, 12s 8d
3 freemen, King Edward's men held this land, they could sell.	This was pre-1066. It has been suggested that these **3 freemen** were demoted to **villeins** by 1086 (mentioned above)
Land of Peter of Valognes	**Tenant in chief of the King [Peter was Sheriff of Hertfordshire in 1086]**
Peter of Valognes holds ½ virgate in Datchworth and Robert from him. Land for 2 oxen, but they are not there.	½ virgate would represent about 15 acres with a potential use for 2 oxen.
The value of this land is and always was 6s.	Value of land: before 1066, 6s; just after conquest, 6s; 1086, 6s
Alstan, Aelmer of Benington's man, held this land; he could sell.	Aelmer was a Saxon Lord

Notes: * 'In lordship' = part of manor not held by tenants but kept for the lord of the manor
* 'plough' = plough + 8 oxen
* 1 virgate = a quarter of a hide

Figure 9: Datchworth's entry with an interpretation.

times they might be called upon for castle garrison duties and were paid in cash or kind, or perhaps in land. Interestingly, of the twelve knights in the shire, Geoffrey controlled [was lord to] ten of them. Seven of these knights were at Bengeo, near Hertford. These knights and the two in Datchworth may have been allotted some land in return for manning Hertford Castle.

The number of 'ploughs' gives an indication of how much arable land was available. For some villages it is stated that there is land for a certain number of ploughs but they are 'not there' showing that the potential of the land was not being fulfilled. This was the case for Peter of Valogne's half virgate which had the potential use for two oxen. However, Datchworth's other entries seem to indicate that that land was being cultivated to its full capacity. The mention of a fraction of a plough is puzzling until it is realised that a plough included a yolk of eight oxen that pulled it, so the meadow for '½ plough' above was probably too small to need a full yolk.

Much of the ploughing would have taken place in the open fields where some form of crop rotation would have taken place. A three course system existed much later and was probably the continuation of what was happening at the time of Domesday. Typically, in the first year, one of the open fields might be sown with wheat or rye, then in the following year it could be barley, oats or legumes and in the final year the field would be left fallow. So, in any particular year, for example, one open field would be fallow, the second could be sown with wheat and a third might have a barley crop.

Although Domesday Book gives a picture of the village at a moment in history, as a population survey it is incomplete, since only heads of households were listed. A measure of Datchworth's population at the time is not obvious but can be estimated to allow for women or children, who were not tax-worthy. There were twelve villeins, two borders and two cottars. Most would have had a family, possibly extended to an older generation and so a multiplier of five is probably appropriate. The knights have been omitted as their families were likely to have been elsewhere. This would give a population estimate of 80 for Datchworth in 1086. Others could have been omitted, for example the clergy or lords of the manor, so Datchworth's population may have been higher.

3. Famine, Plague, Tax and Revolt

Domesday Book represents a useful point from which to compare subsequent events. The population of Hertfordshire, for example, in 1086, has been estimated at about 30,000. Nearly 220 years later, this figure had more than doubled to 69,000 and then dropped sharply to 37,000 over the following 70 years. These figures are derived in turn from the 1307 Lay Subsidy, and the 1377 Poll Tax, a tax of 4d per head of the lay population aged over 14 years. These dramatic changes in population numbers had a profound effect on the structure of life in rural settlements.

Parish	Number of lay people	Total tax per parish		
Watton	48	£5	6s	11d
Stevenage	60	£4	12s	10d
Benington	43	£4	6s	4d
Welwyn	35	£3	18s	8d
Walkern	35	£3	13s	6½d
Digswell	21	£2	14s	3½d
Knebworth	26	£2	13s	6d
Aston	39	£2	8s	10½d
Datchworth	**22**	**£2**	**3s**	**9¼d**
Tewin	15	£1	7s	4d
Shephall	10		19s	11d
Bramfield	16		19s	9½d

Figure 10: 1307 Lay Subsidy Tax return

The 1307 Lay Subsidy was a tax on lay people on moveable property rather than on land. It was calculated as a fraction of goods such as cattle and household items. Figure 10 shows the information for Datchworth and surrounding parishes in descending order of the total tax collected. The lord of the manor often paid the largest tax in the parish and in the case of Datchworth, this was Henry Melksop who paid 12s 8½d. The minimum payment was usually about 7d.

From Domesday to about 1300, favourable weather conditions allowed good harvests, sufficient to support the increasing population but eventually subsistence levels were threatened, particularly among the less well-off. To alleviate the shortfall, waste land at the edge of woodland was reclaimed to grow more food, an activity that was called 'assarting'. However, this came at a price in the form of extra rent demanded by the lord. Villeins were beginning to pay cash instead of providing services to the lord, who was then obliged to hire labourers to do the work.

Soon after 1300, a series of wet and cold summers in 1313-1314 and 1317-1321 delivered a severe shock to the agricultural system and the rural inhabitants. Both crops and livestock suffered badly resulting in famine and disease. These events marked the beginning of the decline in the population which, of course, accelerated at the arrival of the Black Death in England in 1348. Population rates did not start to recover until about 1500.

Local records during this period are limited but some national surveys provide an opportunity to compare parishes according to their wealth. One of the earliest after 1086 was a survey in 1291 to assess the ecclesiastical wealth of England enabling King Edward I to collect a 10% tax on clergy's income. Another survey was completed in 1341, just before the arrival of the Black Death, which was an assessment of the agricultural value of each parish rectory. J E Cussans in *History of Hertfordshire* gives the figures for 1291 and a few from 1341.

The depreciation in value in the intervening 50 years was explained as follows: 'The circumstance of much of the arable land being uncultivated', no doubt as a direct result of the bad weather conditions and poor harvests. However, values given in 1534, at the Dissolution of religious houses, reflect recovery in most cases.

The Black Death

The Black Death reached Hertfordshire early in 1349 when in Codicote 59 people died and their names were listed in the court record for 19 May 1349. The number for Datchworth is unknown, but the rector, Walter Maunsel, succumbed on 6 June 1349 and was replaced two days later by John Cagon, who resigned soon after, on 5 July 1349, and may have been another victim. Datchworth was, at the time, in the Deanery of Hertford, part of the Lincoln diocese, and was mentioned in 'The registers of John Gynewell, Bishop of Lincoln, 1349-1350'. Others that

PARISH RECTORY	Value in 1291 assessment for tax			Value in 1341 agriculture value before Black Death			Value in 1534 at dissolution of religious houses		
Stevenage	£26	13s	4d				£33	6s	8d
Benington	£20	0s	0d	£11	5s	0d	£19	0s	0d
Walkern	£18	13s	4d	£6	18s	4d	£20	1s	10½d
Welwyn	£16	13s	4d	£8	0s	0d	£21	0s	0d
Watton	£15	6s	8d				£19	8s	6½d
Aston	£11	6s	8d				£26	11s	8d
Knebworth	£8	0s	0d				£13	1s	10½d
Tewin	£7	6s	8d				£14	0s	0d
Datchworth	**£6**	**13s**	**4d**	**£4**	**4s**	**6d**	**£14**	**13s**	**4d**
Digswell	£6	13s	4d				£7	4s	2d
Shephall	£5	6s	8d				£9	5s	10d
Bramfield		13s	4d				£11	6s	8d

Figure 11: Valuations of the parish rectory

suffered nearby were the rector at Watton-at-Stone in April, four clergy in Bengeo and Hertford in July and one each in Stapleford and Hatfield in August.

In the parish of Bramfield, 22 land-holders died, but, allowing for the young, the very old and those without land, the death toll was probably nearer to 80. This was believed to be about 75% of Bramfield's population. In 1428, some 80 years later, the village was not completely depopulated but there was no-one liable to pay taxes. By 1534 this number had recovered dramatically (Figure 11). Although the Deanery of Hitchin only lost two of its clergy, it is said that the plague was so severe in the town that one of the streets was named Dead Street, a name that survived for 500 years, until it was renamed Back Lane, and then it was changed again to its current name of Queen Street.

One effect of the Black Death was that it changed the running of the manors which had become severely depopulated. Lords continued to demand either services or payments from surviving villeins but the latter were in a position to bargain and many refused to perform services. Hired labourers were in short supply and so could demand higher wages or move to find more remunerative work elsewhere. The gap between villeins and freemen was reduced and many became 'yeoman farmers'.

The Peasants' Revolt

In 1351, parliament tried to turn the clock back and restore the old system of control by enacting the Statute of Labourers. However, manorial lordship was in disarray so this attempt failed and coupled with more Lay Subsidies and Poll Taxes, resentment built up among the peasant population. There was widespread refusal to pay the Poll Tax of 1380 and this sparked the Peasants' Revolt of 1381.

Riots spread through the country and in many counties, including Hertfordshire, legal documents and court rolls containing tax records were destroyed. In Kent, Wat Tyler lead a procession of peasants with a petition for the king demanding, among other things, the abolition of feudal customs. Amidst considerable violence in London, Richard II made promises to meet the rebels' requests but later retracted them. Wat Tyler and others were killed.

In Hertfordshire in the late fourteenth century St Albans Abbey, a large landowner, was subjected to many disturbances and riots from the townspeople objecting to their servile obligations. In 1381, news of events in London quickly spread to St Albans and men in Cashio Hundred, part of the Liberty of St Albans, were caught up in rebellious activities similar to those in London. Although no record has been found of Datchworth men being involved, representatives from Codicote and Shephall, both part of Cashio Hundred, supported the insurgents in St Albans.

Despite the apparent failure of the Revolt, there were some positive results for the peasantry: for example, the Poll Tax was not levied again and manorial dues became less burdensome.

4. Land, Status and the English Civil War

The Reformation and the Dissolution of the Monasteries

In Europe in the early sixteenth century, Martin Luther and others were challenging the doctrines of the church producing the seeds of Protestant Reformation. The English Reformation was accelerated by events surrounding Henry VIII's marriage to Catherine of Aragon and her failure to produce a male heir. Henry's wish to divorce his wife was forbidden by the church, so he sought permission from the Archbishop of Canterbury. Eventually, an annulment was granted in 1533 against the wishes of the Pope and Henry married Anne Boleyn. This led England to break away from the Roman Catholic church and Henry was declared Supreme Head of the Church of England by The Act of Supremacy in 1534.

English monastic houses, many of which were extremely wealthy, continued to be loyal supporters of the Pope. Henry now had the power to shut down (or 'dissolve') these monasteries and exploit their wealth. The Dissolution of the Monasteries began in 1536 when smaller ones were shut and ended in 1540 with the larger, wealthier ones being closed. Many buildings were demolished and treasures confiscated by the Crown.

At the time of the Dissolution, church land in Datchworth was in the hands of the Abbot of Westminster until the abbey was converted into the seat of a bishop in 1540. The bishopric of Westminster was suppressed by Edward VI in 1550 and joined with the bishopric of London, the change being confirmed by Queen Mary in 1554. It was at this time that most former monastic lands were purchased by secular landlords, creating a new situation for both land-owners and tenants.

Land and status

By this time the customary tenure of many villeins had been converted to copyhold. This was a form of tenure whereby a tenant held a copy of the court roll that recorded his or her possession of the holding. Initially, copyholders still provided some services to the lord, but by the sixteenth century these were replaced by money payments, in addition to entry 'fines' and an annual rent. The status of many copyholders was that of a 'husbandman', that is, the tenant of a slightly smaller holding than a yeoman.

Freeholders, on the other hand, always had a higher status than villeins, although they might hold the same amount of land. The former held land without having the burden of obligatory services to the lord and by the sixteenth century, many had the status of 'yeomen'. From 1430, freeholders, aged between 21 and 70, with land worth 40 shillings a year, had the right to vote and from 1696, results of such elections for knights of the shire were published in poll books. Freeholders could have more than one vote if they held land in more than one constituency.

A Hertfordshire poll book exists for an election held on 31 December 1697. The candidates were Ralph Freeman, a Tory, and Robert Cecil, a Whig, a complicated term which, in the late seventeenth century, included an element of anti-Catholicism. The table below shows the way Datchworth men voted. The Hertfordshire poll amounted to 2,188. Ralph Freeman won his parliamentary seat with a total of 1,311 votes.

Mr Freeman	Mr Cecil
Joseph Turner	John Dale
John Whittenbury	Francis Bigg
Robert Holwell	Michael Ray
Stephen Uncle	John Nicholls
Thomas Shortridge	Steven Uncle
John Mitchell	Thomas Gouge [? Goose]
John North	Robert Peck
John Kundall [? Randall]	Robert Kiddall
	Thomas Kimpton
	Thomas Cater
	William Pennyfather

The year 1696 was significant for another reason; it was the year in which parish constables were obliged to present a list of candidates who were eligible for jury service at the Quarter Sessions. All men between 21 and 70 with land worth £10 or over were in this category and Figure 12 shows the list of those in Datchworth who were eligible in 1699.

Datchworth residents	Absentee landlords	
Joseph Turner	Sir William Lytton	Knebworth
Thomas Goose	Henry Widdrington	Hertford
Daniel Nash	Mr Thomas Mitchell	Codycote
James Faulknor	Mr Richard Mitchell	Codycote
Mr Robert Kidall (attorney)	Mr William Wallis (lord of Datchworthbury Manor)	Wormleybury
	Mr Edward Medcalfe	Chesson [? Cheshunt]
	Mr Joseph Cramphorn	Sawbridgeworth
	Mr Thomas Adams	Walkon
	Edward Penifather	Wellin
	William Penifather	Wellin
	John Whittenbury	Brandfield [Bramfield]

Figure 12: List of copyholders and freeholders for 1699 (calendar of Quarter Sessions)

Daniel Nash in Figure 12 was probably the 'onely son' mentioned in Daniel Nash's will which is an example of a yeoman's standing with regard to property (Figure 13, followed by the will's transcription).

The will reveals that Daniel had a house and land in Datchworth that he left to his son, Daniel, with the proviso that his widow, Ann, had a room in the house: 'the chamber over the hall' which is mentioned in the inventory of Daniel Nash's goods on his death in 1683 (Figures 14a and 14b).

His daughter Mary inherited a house in Green End, Little Munden, with £40 and another daughter, Martha, was left ten acres of land in Bench Croft, Watton. The children could not inherit until they were 21 years old.

Reference to his 'brother', William Mills, probably referred to his brother-in-law.

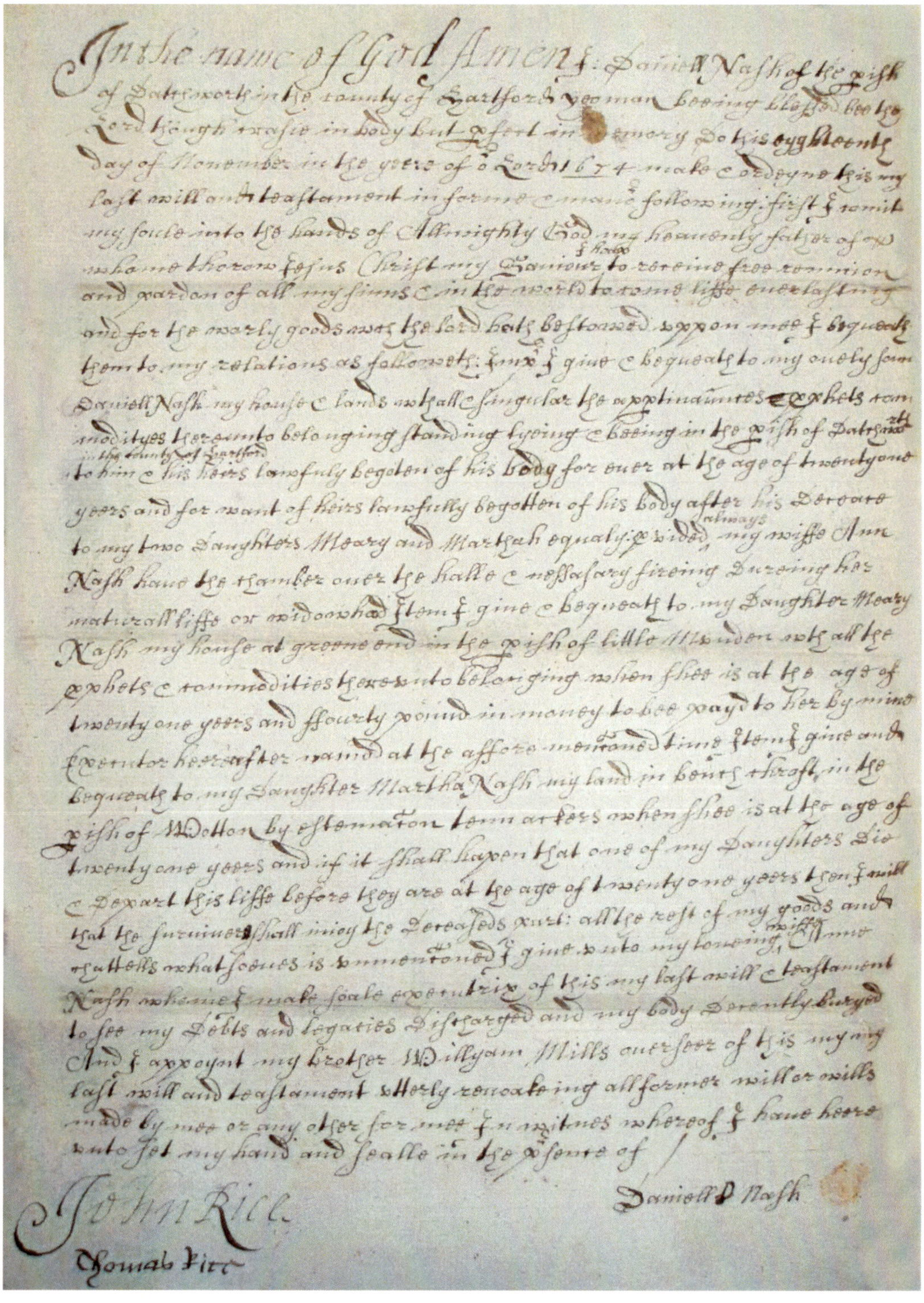
In the name of God Amen. I Daniell Nash of the parish of Datchworth in the county of Hartford yeoman being blessed bee the Lord though weake in body but perfect in memory doe this eyghteenth day of November in the yeere of our Lord 1674 make & ordayne this my last will and teastament in forme & manner following: first I comit my soule into the hands of Almighty God my heavenly father & whome through Jesus Christ my Saviour I hope to receive free remission and pardon of all my sinns & in the world to come life everlasting and for the worldly goods wch the lord hath bestowed uppon mee I bequeath them to my relations as followeth: Imp: I give & bequeath to my onely son Daniell Nash my house & lands wth all & singular the appurtenances & profits comodityes thereunto belonging standing lying & being in the parish of Datchworth in the county of Hartford to him & his heirs lawfully begotten of his body for ever at the age of twentyone yeers and for want of heirs lawfully begotten of his body after his decease to my two daughters Mary and Marthah equally devided, always my wiffe Ann Nash have the chamber over the halle & nessesary fireing during her naturall liffe or widoowhood. Item I give & bequeath to my daughter Mary Nash my house at greene end in the parish of little Munden wth all the profits & commodities thereunto belonging when shee is at the age of twenty one yeers and fforty pound in money to bee payd to her by mine executor hereafter named at the afore mentioned time. Item I give and bequeath to my daughter Martha Nash my land in bench croft in the parish of Watton by estemation tenn ackers when shee is at the age of twentyone yeers and if it shall happen that one of my daughters die & depart this liffe before they are at the age of twentyone yeers then I will that the survivor shall injoy the deceaseds part: all the rest of my goods and chattells whatsoever is unmentioned I give unto my loveing wiffe Ann Nash whome I make soale executrix of this my last will & teastament to see my debts and legacies discharged and my body decently buryed And I appoint my brother William Mills overseer of this my last will and teastament utterly revokeing all former will or wills made by mee or any other for mee In witnes whereof I have heere unto set my hand and sealle in the presence of

Daniell D Nash

John Rich

Thomas [illegible]

Figure 13: The will of Daniel Nash, yeoman, 1674
(HALS: 96HW55)

Transcription of the will of Daniel Nash, yeoman.

THE WILL OF DANIELL NASH
(18 – 11 – 1674)

In the name of God Amen I, Daniell Nash of the p[ar]ish of Datchworth in the county of Hartford **yeoman** beeing blessed bee the Lord though crasie in body but p[er]fect in memory Do this eyghteenth day of November in the yeere of o[ur] Lord 1674 make & ordeyne this my last will and teastament in forme & manner following:

first I comit my soule into the hands of Allmighty God my heavenly father of whome thorow [through] Jesus Christ my Saviour \I hoope/ to receive free remicion and pardon of all my sinns & in the world to come liffe everlasting and for the warly [worldly] goods which the Lord hath bestowed uppon mee I bequeath them to my relations as followeth:

Imp[rimis] I give and bequeath to my **onely son Daniell Nash** my house & lands with all & singular the app[er]tinances p[ro]phets commodityes thereunto belonging standing lyeing & being in the p[ar]ish of Datchworth \in the county of Hartford/ to him & his heirs lawfully begoten of his body for ever at the age of twenty one yeers and for want of heirs lawfully begotten of his body after his Deceace to my two Daughters Meary and Marthah equaly: p[ro]vided \always/ my wiffe **Ann Nash** have the chamber over the halle & nessasary fireing Dureing her naturall liffe or widowhood

Item I give & bequeath to my **Daughter Meary Nash** my house at greene end in the p[ar]ish of little Munden with all the p[ro]phets & commodities thereunto belonging when shee is at the age of twenty one yeers and Fourty pound in money to bee payd to her by mine Executor hereafter named at the afforementioned time

Item I give and bequeath to my **Daughter Martha Nash** my land in bench chroft in the p[ar]ish of Wotton by estemacion tenn ackers when shee is at the age of twenty one yeers and if it shall hapen that one of my Daughters Die & Depart this liffe before they are at the age of twenty one yeers then I will that the surviver shall injoy the Deceaseds part: all the rest of my goods and chattels whatsoever is unmencioned I give unto my loveing \wiffe/ Anne Nash whome I make soale executrix of this my last will & teastament to see my Debts and legacies Discharged and my body Decently buryed

And I appoint my **brother Willyam Mills** overseer of this myne last will and teastament utterly revoakeing all former will or wills made by mee or any other for mee In witness whereof I have here unto set my hand and sealle in the p[re]sence of

Daniell Nash

John Rice
Thomas Rice

Daniel Nash's Inventory with a transcription

Daniel Nash's largest asset was 'mony upon bond', a loan which the executor would presumably have to recover. This was a large amount of money and worth more than double all his other assets of which the next most important were his crops and animals. The inventory includes ten acres of standing corn, a modest amount for a yeoman, but he may have had other land such as pasture, meadow or fallow in addition.

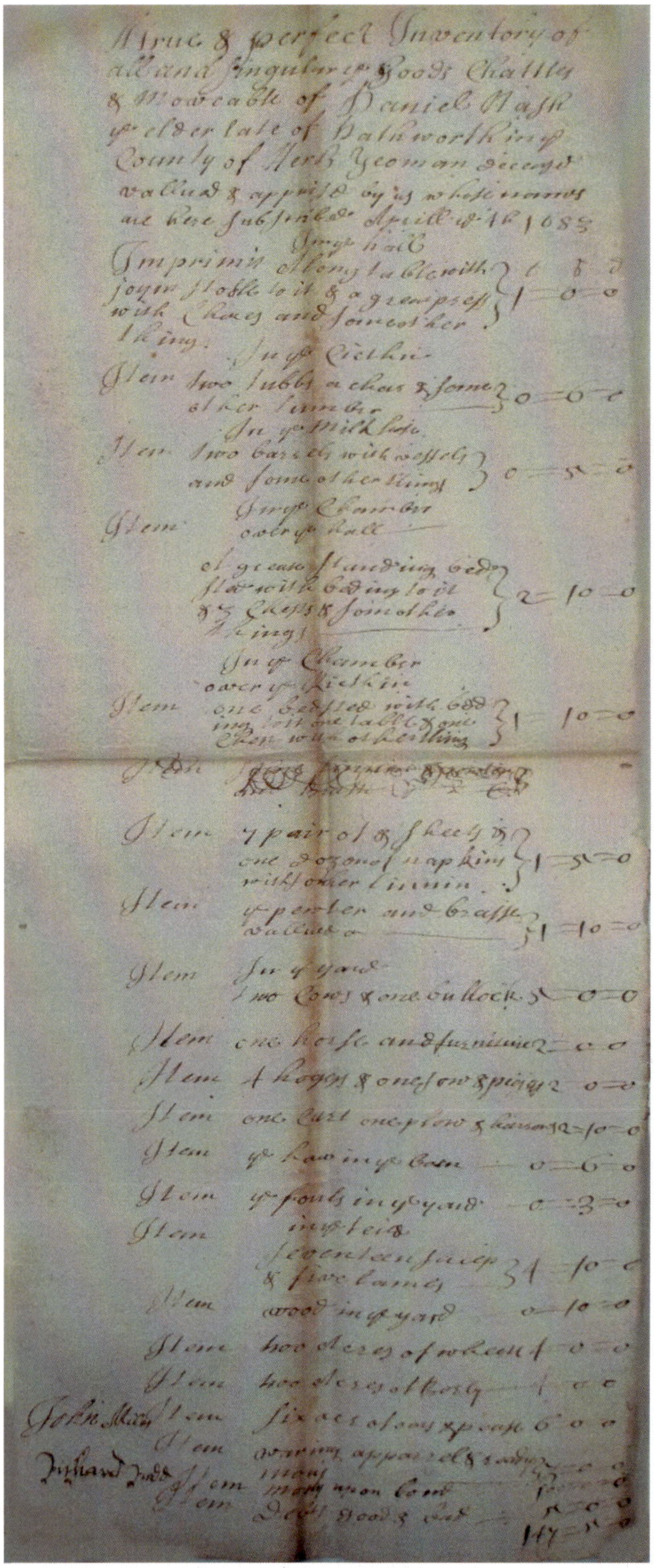

Figure 14a: Daniel Nash's inventory of goods at his death in 1683; valuers and appraisers in the margin on the left: John Miles and Richard Rudd (HALS: 96HW55)

	A true & perfect Inventory of all and singular the goods Chattles & Moveable of Daniel Nash the elder late of Datchworth in the County of Herts Yeoman Deceased valued & apprise by us whose names are here subscribed Aprill the 4th 1683	£	s	d
	<u>In the hall</u>	£	s	d
Imprimis	A long table with joynt stodle [stool] to it & a greate press with Chares and some other things }	1	0	0
	<u>In the Cicthin</u>			
Item	two tubbs a char & some other lumber }	0	6	0
	<u>In the Milkhse</u>			
Item	two barrels with vessels and some other things }	0	5	0
	<u>In the Chamber over the hall</u>			
Item	A greate standing bedsted with beding to it & 3 Chests & some other things }	2	10	0
	<u>In the Chamber over the Kicthin</u>			
Item	one bedsted with beding to it one table & one chest with other things }	1	10	0
Item	7 pair of & sheets & one Dozen of napkins with other linnin }	1	5	0
Item	The pewter and brasse valued as }	1	10	0
	<u>In the yard</u>			
Item	two Cows & one bullock	5	0	0
Item	one horse and furniture	2	0	0
Item	4 hoggs & one sow & piggs }	2	0	0
Item	one Cart one plow & harrows }	2	10	0
Item	the hay in the barn	0	6	0
Item	the fouls in the yard	0	3	0
	<u>In the feild</u>			
Item	seventeen sheep & five lambs }	4	10	0
Item	wood in the yard	0	10	0
Item	two Acres of wheat	4	0	0
Item	two Acres of Barly	4	0	0
Item	six acr[e] of oats & pease	6	0	0
Item	waring apparrel & ready mony }	3	0	0
Item	mony upon bond	100	0	0
Item	Debts good & bad	5	0	0
		147	5	0

Figure 14b: Transcription of Daniel Nash's inventory

Building

The new era of independence following the end of monastic dominance gave rise to an increase in building activity, sometimes in inappropriate places. In the thirty-first year of Elizabeth's reign (1589) such happenings gave cause for alarm. This was clearly indicated by the wording of a statute relating to the erection of cottages: '... great inconveniences caused by erecting & building of great numbers of cottages, which are daily more and more increased in many parts of the realm...'.

Later in the same statute, it was stated that all new cottages should have enough land to support a family, namely at least four acres; the penalty for contravention was £10. This law was primarily to prevent people getting a legal settlement in a parish by coming from another parish and then living in a cottage without sustainable land for a year. This became a burden to the parish to which they had moved because these people would need to be supported by the parishioners.

In the Quarter Sessions rolls, there are reports of several Datchworth residents who were challenged over this. In 1630 and 1631, both Samuel Unckle and Edward Gable, both labourers, were charged with newly erecting a cottage 'without laying thereto four acres of freehold land'. In 1654 Thomas Tyler was indicted for the same offence followed in 1656 by Cecily Head and in 1657 by George and Cicely Haunt. A variation was provided by Barnard Riddall, a labourer, who, in 1637, had 'converted a barn into a cottage without laying four acres of freehold land thereto'.

Another section of the 1589 Act stated that the penalty for 'allowing more families than one in each building' was 10s per month. In 1636 a complaint was brought against Christine Rudd, a widow of Datchworth, saying that she had 'received as inmates for two months William Lawrance and Mary his wife.' In the same year Edward Gabell, senior, was charged with 'harbouring' Robert Smith as an inmate. The Act was eventually repealed in 1775.

Apart from these contraventions, acceptable houses were built in this period and details of those that have survived are found in Chapter 12. In those earlier days, Datchworth parish consisted of a collection of scattered hamlets with the church at its centre. The layout is very similar today except that its recognised centre has shifted to Datchworth Green.

In 1636-7 the Plague arose in Hertfordshire and all the parishes including Datchworth appointed watchers and searches to ensure it did not spread. The magistrates responsible for implementing these measures in Datchworth and other parts of Broadwater Hundred, were Sir John Boteler of Watton, Charles Caeser of Bennington, William Lytton of Knebworth and William Priestly of Hatfield who were aided by two high constables, George Hakes and John North.

English Civil War

In the 1630s Charles I tried to rule without Parliament and to collect Ship Money from inland counties who had never paid it before. In 1636 the people of Datchworth had to collectively pay the Exchequer £18 7s 8d, a significant sum compared with the £72 paid by Hitchin, with many more inhabitants. Having tried to collect the money annually for the following three years there was a virtual tax strike in Hertfordshire by 1640.

In 1642, Charles was still short of funds to support his military activities. Parliament would not co-operate and his frequent clashes with Parliament continued until his disastrous entry into the House of Commons, where he attempted to arrest five MPs who had already escaped. This was the final spark that enflamed the Parliamentarians and war was declared after six months of failed negotiations and both sides raising arms.

Sequestration

In urgent need of funds and supplies, the Parliamentarians sought out Royalist sympathisers ('delinquents') with large estates. These estates were 'sequestered', owners banished, property and goods seized, timber felled and, in some cases, estates let to raise cash. Locally, Arthur, 1st Baron Capel of Hadham owned land in Walkern and as a Royalist found his name on the 'delinquents' list. Sir John Harrison who owned Balls Park was treated in the same way. Sir John's house was stripped bare of its contents, worth about £500. However, since Sir William Lytton, who owned land in Datchworth, was a Parliamentarian, his estate was not sequestered. John Gamon was lord of Datchworthbury manor at this time, but his affiliation is unknown.

Delinquent clergy were also sequestered and replaced by substitutes. In 1643, the incumbent of Datchworth church, Richard Newman, was labelled a Royalist delinquent and as such had his benefice sequestered. A report of his activities appears in the *Journal of the House of Commons*, vol. 2, dated 30 September 1642:

> Resolved, upon the Question, That Mr. Newman and Mr. Burdett, of Bury, shall be forthwith sent for as Delinquents, for dangerous Expressions uttered by them, in Sermons they preached at Bury: .....Notes were taken, and attested

> by Three several Witnesses, as appears by the Report from the Committee for Informations.

In effect he was banished from the church and Parliament replaced him first by Simon Peck and then by Thomas Stacey. In these circumstances wives of sequestered clergy were normally allowed one fifth of the revenue from the church as some compensation for loss. In 1650, the living at Datchworth was said to have been worth £85.

In *The History of Hertfordshire* by J E Cussans, a footnote throws light on the complications arising from being a pluralist rector:

> On the 18th September, 1645, a Committee of parliament sitting at Hertford was ordered to inquire why Mrs Newman, from whose husband the living had been sequestered, should not receive a portion of the profits of the rectory for the support of herself and children. On the 7th May, 1646, Mr Peck was released from making any payment to Mrs Newman, as he had himself nine children, and 'that the said Mr Newman is likewise sequestered from the rectorie of Hamerton being esteemed to be worth neere £120 a year'.

In the end, Mrs Newman gained from the decision because her right to one fifth of church income would be based on £120 rather than £85.

Troops in Hertfordshire

Hertfordshire's proximity to London made it an ideal temporary stopping place for the army during the Civil War. Hertfordshire was one of the five original counties that constituted the Eastern Association that provided an army for the Parliamentary cause. The Association was established in 1642. In August 1643 Edward Montagu, Earl of Manchester, was appointed commander of the army and was responsible for the conscription of soldiers. It was the task of the already overworked village constable to select out suitable candidates for the militia, however, no record has been found relating to conscripts in Datchworth.

The militia had to be accommodated, particularly during times when there was little in the way of wartime activity, often during bad weather. This could be just an overnight stay or for up to three months at a time. In the winter of 1644, troops were billeted (called 'free quarter' in contemporary documents) all over Hertfordshire.

A list of 'free quarter' repayments dated 6 March 1645 shows that troops were billeted in Datchworth at this time and the parish had claimed a total of £22 14s 4d in compensation for expenses incurred. These men belonged to units lead by three officers whose expenses were as follows: Captain Crowe, £3 19s 4d, Captain Dandy, £11 15s 4d and Colonel Fleetwood, £6 19s 8d, who was to become Oliver Cromwell's son-in-law in 1652. The breakdown of their expenses are not known, but typically, it would depend on the number of men, how long they were billeted and whether or not there were horses to cater for. Claims were also made for property that was stolen or damaged. Men from these officers' units were not exclusively billeted in one parish but were often scattered around in other parishes. This was the case of Captain Crowe, whose men were spread between Datchworth, Tewin, Digswell and Walkern amongst others.

Cromwell's name appears in several parishes, but the largest claim made in his name was in Hatfield, £48 14s 4d. It is not clear whether this indicated a large unit for a short period or a smaller unit for a longer time. The nearest either he or his men came to Datchworth was Stevenage, where his expenses amounted to £1. The Cromwell Hotel is a reminder of his connection with Stevenage: this was originally a farmhouse wherein resided John Thurloe, who became Cromwell's secretary in the 1650s.

Reports of a different kind exist in the Quarter Sessions records which illustrate other ways in which Datchworth was touched by these military events. In July 1645 there was an order that William Warne, a maimed soldier, 'shall have some present relief' and later, in January 1646, he was 'to receive a yearly pension of 40s'. In 1648, Alice Hale, widow of William Hale 'who lately died a soldier ... in the service of the State, should receive 2s 6d weekly for the relief of herself and her five children from Mr Mead treasurer for Maimed Soldiers'.

The Commonwealth and the Restoration

Cromwell's New Model Army, created in 1645, brought success to the Parliamentarians at the Battle of Naseby, where the Royalist army was defeated. Charles's cause did not recover from this defeat and eventually, on 1 January 1649, he was tried for treason. The charge against him was that he 'out of a wicked design to erect and uphold in himself an unlimited and tyrannical power' with the intention 'to rule according to his will', and also 'to overthrow the rights and liberties of the people of England'. The court judged him guilty and he was executed on 30 January 1649.

The monarchy was replaced by the Council of State for the Commonwealth and Cromwell was appointed its Lord Protector in 1653. During the next five years England was effectively under military rule and subjected to stern Puritan ideals. By the time Cromwell died in 1658 he was unpopular, partly because taxes were too high and the Puritan lifestyle was deemed to be unnecessarily restricting.

The monarchy was restored in 1660 and on his return from exile in France Charles's son was crowned Charles II on 23 April 1661. Sequestered landowners returned to their estates and clergy were restored to their previous incumbencies. In Datchworth, Richard Newman was reinstated by Arthur Capel, 1st Earl of Essex who was, by this time, patron of All Saints' Church.

The Restoration of the monarchy in 1660 brought a relaxed air to the country celebrating the end of Cromwell's Puritan regime and a subsequent period of anarchy. However, religious rumblings were not over. Although Charles II was outwardly Anglican, he had Catholic sympathies and when he was succeeded by his brother, James, a Catholic, there was public alarm. The fear that there would be another succession of Catholic monarchs increased even more when a son was born to James II in 1688. James's daughter Mary, a Protestant, was thus no longer heir to the throne. By this time she had married her cousin William of Orange, grandson of Charles I and at the news of the newborn son, William and Mary were secretly invited to invade England by a group of English Protestants. In November 1688 they landed in England, accompanied by a suitable force. News of the invasion spread quickly causing many members of James's army to defect to the Protestant cause. James, in defeat, fled to France in late December 1688. The way was then clear for William and Mary to succeed to the throne and they were crowned on 11 April 1689.

In the ensuing years, religion was subject to two more landmarks that had lasting effects. In 1689, the Act of Toleration allowed non-conformists to have the freedom of worship and the Act of Settlement in 1701 ensured that no Catholic or Catholic spouse could be enthroned. Various non-conformist sects had existed since the sixteenth century and the first English Baptist church is thought to have been built in 1612 in London. Details of non-conformity in Datchworth and the erection of Baptist chapels are given in Chapter 11.

5. Law and the Creation of the Parish Council

Frankpledge and the medieval courts

In medieval times, law and order was generally a local affair and villagers were aware of the customary rules. Originating in Anglo-Saxon times, order was controlled to some extent by a well established system of self-regulation called 'frankpledge'. Under this system, a settlement would be subdivided into groups of ten households called 'tithings'. Each tithing consisted of roughly ten males aged between 12 and 60; lords, knights and clergy were exempt. The tithing was expected to take responsibility for the behaviour of the group and a 'tithingman' was elected to represent the tithing at the 'manor court'. By the thirteenth century 'freeholders' were released from this obligation because land was reckoned to be sufficient pledge for good behaviour. The 'view of frankpledge' involved a biannual meeting at the 'hundred court', presided over by the sheriff to ensure that all eligible men were on a tithing list.

At the first sign of law-breaking, an alarm was sounded and the 'hue and cry' ensued. Members of the tithing had to ensure that a miscreant was captured and taken to the local manorial court, the 'court leet', for minor offences or to the hundred court for more serious cases. If the perpetrator failed to attend the court the tithing could be liable for a fine.

Typical cases were that of affray, failing to clear out ditches, attempting to enclose a piece of common land or failing to supply the required number of days work to the lord. 'Assizes of bread and ale' regulated prices of both commodities in line with the price of wheat, barley and oats. Giving false measures would also be liable for punishment.

At the time of Domesday, Datchworth's tithings would probably have come under the control of Peter of Valognes. He was the high sheriff of the shire and would have presided as chief magistrate over the 'hundred court' twice yearly for special cases. In general the hundred court was held once a month and its main duties were administration of law and the maintenance of the frankpledge system. A 'hundred', apart from being roughly 100 hides, was the collective term for ten tithing's or 100 households and Datchworth was part of the hundred of Broadwater.

Co-existing with the hundred courts was the 'shire court'. This met twice a year and was also presided over by the sheriff as the king's representative and chief administrator. The shire court's main functions were to oversee the hundred courts within its shire and to deal with more serious cases that could not be dealt with at the hundreds. Its functions were eventually undertaken by the county court in 1867 and the county council in 1889.

Datchworth was one of thirteen villages in Broadwater hundred that had the 'right of gallows' which meant that the lord could confiscate the property of a hanged felon; however, it is not known whether Datchworth had its own gallows. Robert Trow-Smith in *A History of Stevenage* quotes a case concerning a Datchworth resident. Reported in the Stevenage court roll of 1405, Thomas Nattok of Datchworth was brought to the shire court at Hertford for an unknown offence, 'was indicted and was convicted and is hanged'. His goods and chattels were forfeited to the bailiff of Westminster, listed as one brass pot, value 2s 6d and one brass platter, value 9d.

Entries in Doomsday Book show that manors were well established by the time of the Norman invasion; however, it was probably not until the end of the twelfth century that manor courts were held. These courts were presided over by the lord of the manor who held jurisdiction over his tenants although it was the steward who took control of the proceedings. The courts were held every three weeks or so by the lord to enforce the manorial customs and laws, exact dues, deal with petty offences, and resolve a variety of disputes concerning such matters as property rights and damage. All villeins had to attend, absentees were fined, freemen only attended annually unless they were involved in a dispute. Matters relating to minor crimes were mainly dealt with in the manor courts and more serious cases would go before the hundred court.

Unfortunately the earliest records found relating to the manor courts of Datchworthbury and Hawkins Hall only date from the late sixteenth century, by which time the lords held court mainly to deal with tenancy transfers and to collect fines and dues. At the start of each court session the names of those present were read out and each pledged loyalty by proclaiming 'homage' to the lord. Business proceeded and the hearing was recorded in the 'court rolls', a practice started sometime in the thirteenth century; Figure 15a shows a typical entry for Datchworth in 1768 and a map (Figure 93) illustrates the division of Datchworth's two manors in 1866.

Judgement at the medieval courts was harsh. It depended not upon evidence but on trial by ordeal – 'the judgement of God'. For knights this would have been trial by combat. An ordeal that involved trial by fire was reserved for freemen where the accused was made to hold a heated iron bar or pluck a stone out of a cauldron of boiling water. If, two or three days later, the skin on the victim's hand still showed signs of burning

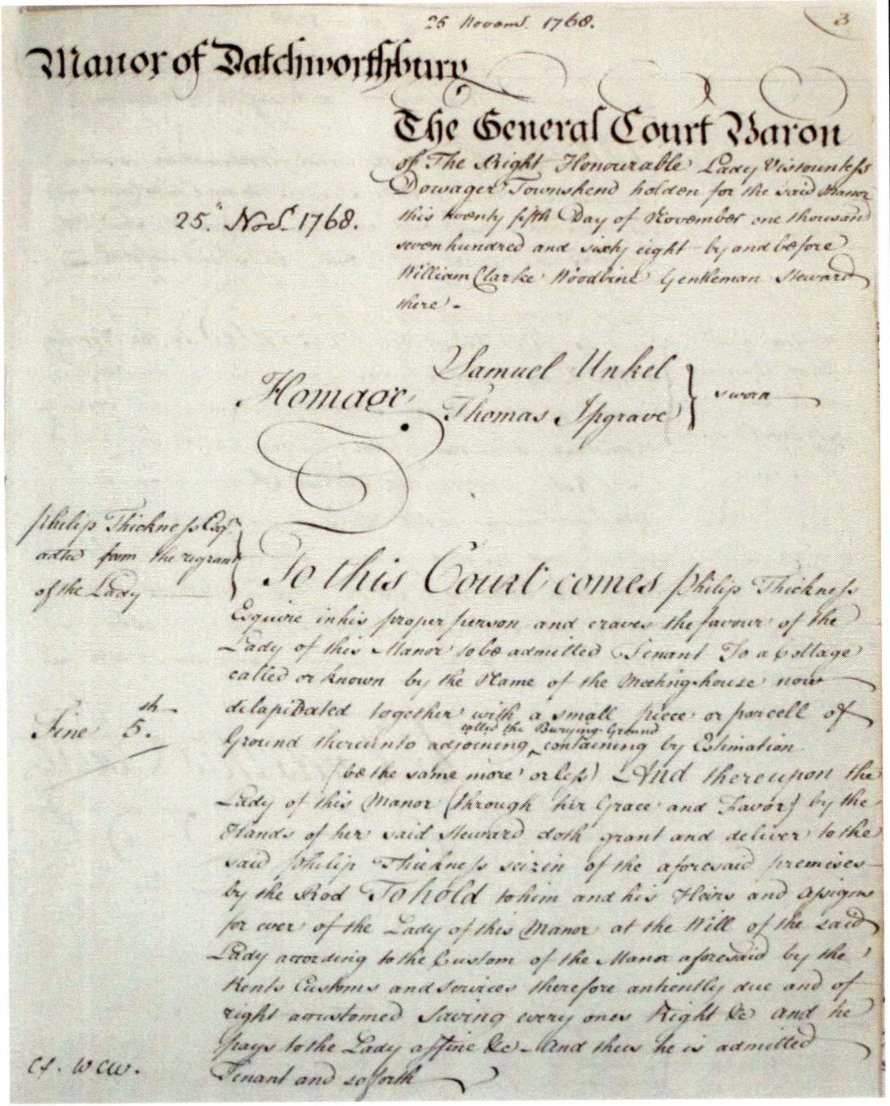
25 Novemb. 1768.

Manor of Datchworthbury

The General Court Baron

of The Right Honourable Lady Viscountess Dowager Townshend holden for the said Manor this twenty fifth Day of November one thousand seven hundred and sixty eight by and before William Clarke Woodbine Gentleman Steward there.

25. Nov. 1768.

Homage Samuel Unkel, Thomas Ipgrave } sworn

Philip Thickness Esq adtted from the regrant of the Lady

Fine 5 sh.

To this Court comes Philip Thicknesse Esquire in his proper person and craves the favour of the Lady of this Manor to be admitted Tenant To a Cottage called or known by the Name of the Meeting house now dilapidated together with a small piece or parcell of Ground thereunto adjoining called the Burying Ground containing by Estimation (be the same more or less) And thereupon the Lady of this Manor (through her Grace and Favor) by the Hands of her said Steward doth grant and deliver to the said Philip Thicknesse seizin of the aforesaid premises by the Rod To hold to him and his Heirs and Assigns for ever of the Lady of this Manor at the Will of the said Lady according to the Custom of the Manor aforesaid by the Rents Customs and Services therefore antiently due and of right accustomed Saving every ones Right &c and he pays to the Lady a fine &c And thus he is admitted Tenant and so forth

Figure 15a: An entry in Datchworthbury court roll of 1768 showing Philip Thicknesse's application for the tenancy of the Meeting House [near Pettits] on Datchworth Green.
Note in margin: 'Philip Thickness Esq ad[mit]ted from the regrant of the Lady' '[Entry] Fine 5 sh[illings]'

(HALS: D/EL2281)

25 November 1768

Manor of Datchworthbury

The General Court Baron

of the Right Honourable Lady Viscountess Dowager Townshend holden for the said Manor This twenty fifth Day of November one thousand seven hundred and sixty eight by and before William Clarke Woodbine Gentleman Steward there.

Homage Samuel Unkel, Thomas Ipgrave } sworn

To this Court comes ***Philip Thicknesse*** *Esquire in his proper person and craves the favour of the Lady of this Manor to be admitted Tenant To a Cottage called or known by the Name of the* ***Meeting house*** *now dilapidated together with a small piece or parcel of Ground thereunto adjoining\called the Burying Ground/containing by Estimation*

………… (be the same more or less). And thereupon the Lady of this Manor (through her Grace and Favor) by the Hands of her said Steward doth grant and deliver to the said Philip Thicknesse seizin of the aforesaid premises by the Rod To hold to him and his Heirs and Assigns for ever of the Lady of this Manor at the Will of the said Lady according to the Custom of the Manor aforesaid by the Rents Customs and Services therefore antiently due and of right accustomed Saving every ones Right etc and he pays to the Lady a Fine etc and thus he is admitted Tenant and so forth.

Figure 15b: Transcription of Philip Thicknesse's application

then guilt was assumed; however if no mark remained then the accused was considered to have 'God on their side', and thus proved to be innocent.

Villeins were subjected to trial by water whereby the accused was thrown into a pond with his hands and feet tied together. If the victim floated, he was guilty and would be severely punished, if he sank, then he was innocent.

In 1215 the Pope decreed that clergy should not participate in trials by ordeal. The power of the church was such that, without its support, trials by ordeal diminished but were not formally abolished until the nineteenth century. They gradually withered away and were replaced by the system of 'trial by jury' that had already been well established. In 1154, Henry II introduced the concept of 'common law', a term still used today. This would standardise hundreds of years of local custom so that it was 'common' to all the people. Although juries of local people had existed since Saxon times as providers of information, under this new system they had the power to decide on guilt. Judges were sent from London to assist in local trials and relay the system of common law to all parts of the country according to chosen 'circuits' such as particular groups of counties.

This formed the basis of the 'assize system' introduced in 1215 where 'circuit judges' from the 'King's Bench', that is the court in Westminster, travelled twice a year to their allotted region to deal with serious crimes at the shire venue; in Hertfordshire this was Hertford Castle. The arrival of the circuit judges was a spectacular affair with lots of pomp and ceremony.

In the mid fourteenth century all judicial duties of the courts were taken over by the Justices of the Peace (JPs), leaving the manor and hundred courts with only administrative, tenancy and civil functions to deal with.

As with the shire court, the responsibilities of the hundred courts declined further with the establishment of the county court in 1867. Its powers were then extinguished completely with the formation of Hertfordshire County Council in 1889, who took over all administrative duties. Although the hundred courts had no administrative or legal role after this date, they have never been formally abolished.

The powers of the manor courts began to decline in the seventeenth century and in 1660 feudal tenures came to an end, leaving the manor with only the right to hold court for property transfers and the collection of revenues, fines and rents from the lord's property. The passing of the Law and Property Act in 1922 meant that courts could no longer be held for the transfer of copyhold tenure and eventually, in 1926, this change was effected to freehold tenure. Technically, manorial courts can still be held today because they have never been formally abolished, but they would have no real business left to transact.

Justices of the Peace

In Hertfordshire the first commission for 'Keeping the Peace' was granted in 1327 by Edward III, a system designed particularly to keep the peace in unruly areas. In 1361 the 'keepers of the peace' were given the title of 'Justices of the Peace' by Edward III and in due course were appointed in every county.

Under the Act of 1361, JPs met four times a year to deal with local matters. These meetings became known as 'Quarter Sessions' and cases were generally heard before a bench of two or more JPs with a jury. From 1461, the responsibilities undertaken by JPs gradually increased dealing with such offences as riot, assault, theft or poaching with sentences that could include transportation, imprisonment or whipping.

The whipping post in Datchworth remains to this day and was last used in 1665 when two vagabonds were whipped but the stocks, which were situated near the whipping post, were 'removed by local inhabitants' in February 1899.

By the seventeenth century the workload of the Quarter Sessions was reduced by the introduction of the Petty Sessions court which was presided over by two or more JPs. It dealt with minor offences such as poaching, minor theft, assault and drunkenness. Crimes that were subject to capital punishment or life imprisonment were administered by the King's Bench at the Assizes, whose jurisdiction was eventually assigned to the High Court of Justice in 1873.

Examples of cases involving Datchworth people include:

> May 1606, Richard Stacey and Thomas Ralsey, Datchworth labourers, were convicted of stealing a 10d pair of sheets from George Kimpton, they confessed and were whipped.
>
> April 1621, Thomas Jones, a labourer of Datchworth, had been convicted of larceny after burgling the house of William Payne, the parish clerk, and stealing 40 pieces of tin value £5, a cloak 10 shillings and a hat 4 shillings. Thomas was hanged.

October 1677, Cicely Hans, widow, was convicted of 'threatening to be the death of Elizabeth Bar'. Cicely was sent to Hertford gaol.

In 1773, William Russell of Datchworth 'bought poison in Stevenage and put it in the food of a man and woman at Bramfield'. William was hanged.

Other examples of Datchworth people at Quarter Sessions and Assizes hearings can be found in Chapter 17.

The vestry and local constable

The 'vestry' was the governing body of the parish and met in the church vestry from which it took its name. Originating sometime in the fourteenth century its function was to manage ecclesiastical affairs which were carried out by churchwardens. An important duty was to maintain the general running of the church, financed by a church rate. This was a tax on householders that was based on the value of property at an agreed amount in the pound. Other duties included ensuring that parishioners attended church and reporting any non-attendance or other offences to the bishop.

The sixteenth and early seventeenth centuries marked an increase in the vestry's duties. In 1555 an Act was passed that required the annual appointment of a 'Surveyor of the Highways', who was responsible for calling upon local people to maintain their roads. The Poor Laws of 1597-1601 stated that two rate-payers must be elected annually to serve as overseers of the poor. The nominees had to be approved by the local JP and the main duties of the elected candidates were to collect poor rates and administer their distribution. The vestry was also eventually responsible for appointing the local constable.

An extract from the vestry records for the years 1711-1717 (Figure 17) shows that the position of 'overseer of the poor' was the most consistently recorded. Although in theory, all four appointments were elected annually from rate-payers in rotation, it is clear that some carried on for more than one year. In Datchworth, the surveyor of the highways was known as a 'stonewarden'.

Figure 16: The whipping post on Datchworth Green (1965)

The local constable

As previously mentioned the appointment of the parish constable eventually became the responsibility of the vestry but the office of constable has changed in meaning over the centuries. Initially, in the twelfth century, it was a military position of high rank where the main duty was to command the army. At that time, village law and order was still maintained by the frankpledge system where a tithing man regularly reported events to the manor court. It was from this tithing man that the village constable evolved and so, originally, he was responsible to the manor and appointed by the manor court. Gradually, as the power of the manor declined, the constable became an officer of the parish and was elected annually by his fellow rate-payers on a rotation basis. However, it was not until the Parish Constables Act in 1842 that the power to appoint the constable was formally transferred from the manor to the parish. This continued until the Parish Constables Act of 1872 when the vestry's power to appoint constables was abolished.

As part of dealing with petty crimes, the constable was responsible for the stocks, the whipping post and the village lock-up and when required he escorted prisoners to the appropriate court. He also had to collect county rates and national taxes such as the poll tax, land tax and hearth tax.

Year	Churchwarden	Overseer of the poor	Constable	Stonewardens
1711	John Bassett sen	Thomas Coulson	John Bassett jun	Thomas Kimpton & Daniel Mardell
1712	John Bassett	Thomas Coulson	John Whitfield	Thomas Kimpton & John Flindell
1713	John Bassett	Daniel Crawley	John Whitfield	
1714	John Bassett	William Blindall		
1715		Thomas Goose		
1716		Rowland Mardell		
1717	John Bassett	John Whitfield		

Figure 17: Extract from vestry records 1711 - 1717

At times when soldiers were needed, he raised the local militia. The checking of weights and measures and the supervision of ale-houses were also on his list. Other duties included attending to the poor and the provision of poor relief, organising apprenticeships for pauper children, ensuring parishioners attended church and dealing with itinerants and beggars, which often included executing whipping. He also had to impound stray animals and even had to take care of the parish bull.

Constables were unpaid but in 1612 they were empowered to claim for expenses out of the parish rates. Under the County Police Act of 1839, JPs were enabled to establish police forces in their counties and this led to the Hertfordshire County Constabulary Force being set up in 1841. According to the Parish Constables Act 1842, the parish constables were under the supervision of a high constable who was paid from the county rates but the role of parish constable could be voluntary or paid. Datchworth's first high constable, in 1842, was Thomas Pennyfather, who was one of two constables responsible for Broadwater Hundred and was paid a salary of £9 per annum. As well as Datchworth, Pennyfather was also responsible for the parishes of 'Welwyn, Digswell, Little Ayott, Ayott St Lawrence, Knebworth, Aston, Watton, Saccombe, Totteridge, North Mimms and Hatfield'.

In addition to the high constable at county level, local constables could be employed in each parish. In January 1842, at the Quarter Sessions, where high constables were appointed, it was stated that the chief constable 'had not been able to appoint the local constables', and there are no records to show who were the first constables for Datchworth. However, by 1845 parish constables had been appointed and those for Datchworth were John Watson and John Lawrance. At this time there was a high turnover of constables for several reasons. Apart from the annual appointment of two parish constables at a Special Petty Sessions, many were dismissed for drunkenness and so had to be replaced. The parish constables were usually people of quite high standing in the parish, for example, John Watson was a farmer at Bulls Green Farm and John Lawrance was a carpenter and employer. In subsequent years other farmers that were appointed included Edmund Carpenter of Datchworth Green and Richard Fensom of Burnham Green Farm. Other tradesmen included carpenters, linen drapers and thatchers.

By 1851 the local constable's occupation was listed as 'parish constable' and therefore may have been a paid position by this time. By 1871 the constable was given a house to live in, which, until the end of the nineteenth century, was a cottage at Hoppers End. In 1901 constable John Worbys lived at Bridgefoot Cottage as did John Robinson, William Birch and constable Cowling who succeeded him. In 1911 William Birch was awarded the Coronation Medal which was given to police officers on duty in London on King George V's Coronation Day and ultimately attained rank of sergeant before retiring in 1919. In 1921 when the first council houses were built in Bury Lane, one of these was allocated to the parish constable.

In 1938 Robert Wallace sold an area of land, 75ft by 100ft, (opposite the village hall) to the county council for the purpose of building an official police house. In 1950 the house was transferred to the Hertfordshire Police Authority. It consisted of a sitting room, kitchen, three bedrooms, a scullery, bathroom and office. The building ceased being used as a police house in 2002, after the retirement of Datchworth's last parish constable, Jim Lamb. It was sold to a property developer who subsequently transformed the house into an attractive five-bed property, which is now 97 Datchworth Green.

Figure 18: The police house at Datchworth Green. The single storey room on the left of the house was the constable's office. (2001)

The militia

Figure 19 shows an example of one of several militia lists that are available at Hertfordshire Archives and Local Studies (HALS). The Militia Act 1757 required constables to draw up a list of able-bodied men aged from 18 to 50 years; the upper age limit was reduced to 45 in 1762. A ballot was then held to decide which of these men should be called upon to serve or they could be replaced for a fee of £20.

Once enlisted a man would receive 28 days armed training and could serve for a period of three or four years anywhere in Britain.

Some men were exempt from enlistment, including: clergymen, licensed teachers, Quakers, united brethren, medical men, soldiers, sailors, fathers of three or more children (born in wedlock) under the age of ten years and constables.

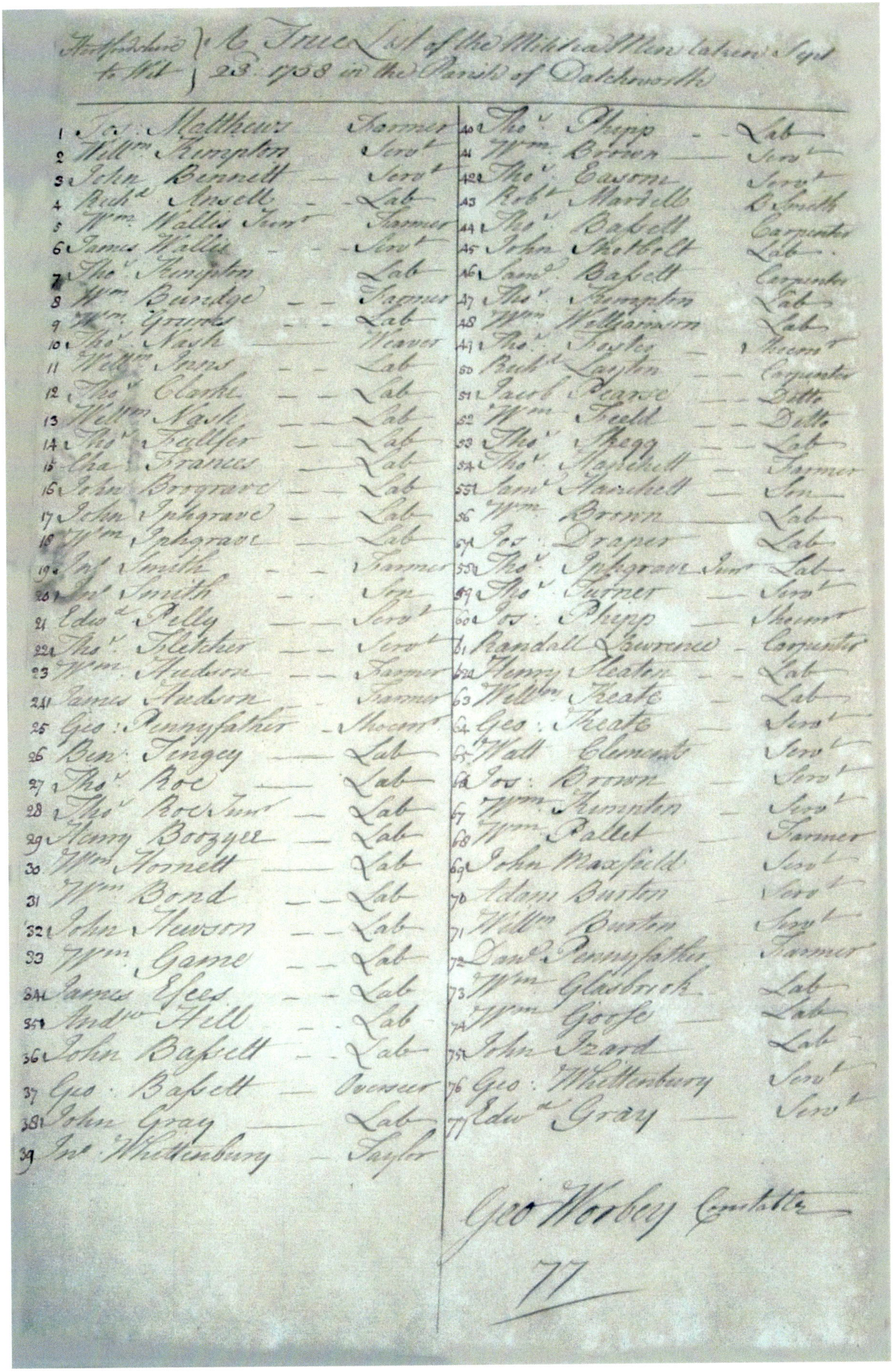

Hertfordshire } A True List of the Militia Men taken Sept
to Wit } 23. 1758 in the Parish of Datchworth

1 Jos: Matthews — Farmer
2 Willm. Kimpton — Servt
3 John Bennett — Servt
4 Richd. Ansell — Lab
5 Wm. Wallis Junr. — Farmer
6 James Wallis — Servt
7 Thos. Kimpton — Lab
8 Wm. Burridge — Farmer
9 Wm. Graves — Lab
10 Thos. Nash — Weaver
11 Willm. Innes — Lab
12 Thos. Clarke — Lab
13 Willm. Nash — Lab
14 Thos. Fullfer — Lab
15 Cha: Frances — Lab
16 John Brograve — Lab
17 John Iphgrave — Lab
18 Wm. Iphgrave — Lab
19 Jno. Smith — Farmer
20 Jno. Smith — Son
21 Edwd. Pelly — Servt
22 Thos. Fletcher — Servt
23 Wm. Hudson — Farmer
24 James Hudson — Farmer
25 Geo: Pennyfather — Shoemr.
26 Ben: Tengey — Lab
27 Thos. Roe — Lab
28 Thos. Roe Junr. — Lab
29 Henry Boozyee — Lab
30 Wm. Hornett — Lab
31 Wm. Bond — Lab
32 John Hewson — Lab
33 Wm. Game — Lab
34 James Efees — Lab
35 Andw. Hill — Lab
36 John Bassett — Lab
37 Geo: Bassett — Overseer
38 John Gray — Lab
39 Jno. Whittenbury — Taylor
40 Thos. Phypp — Lab
41 Wm. Brown — Servt
42 Thos. Easom — Servt
43 Robt. Mardell — B Smith
44 Thos. Bassell — Carpenter
45 John Shatbolt — Lab
46 Saml. Bassett — Carpenter
47 Thos. Kimpton — Lab
48 Wm. Williamson — Lab
49 Thos. Foster — Shoemr.
50 Richd. Layton — Carpenter
51 Jacob Pearse — Ditto
52 Wm. Field — Ditto
53 Thos. Shegg — Lab
54 Thos. Marchell — Farmer
55 Saml. Marchell — Son
56 Wm. Brown — Lab
57 Jos: Draper — Lab
58 Thos. Iphgrave Junr. — Lab
59 Thos. Turner — Servt
60 Jos: Phypp — Shoemr.
61 Randall Lawrence — Carpenter
62 Henry Heaton — Lab
63 Willm. Keate — Lab
64 Geo: Keate — Servt
65 Walt Clements — Servt
66 Jos: Brown — Servt
67 Wm. Kimpton — Servt
68 Wm. Pallet — Farmer
69 John Maxfeild — Servt
70 Adam Burton — Servt
71 Willm. Burton — Servt
72 Danl. Pennyfather — Farmer
73 Wm. Glasbrook — Lab
74 Wm. Goose — Lab
75 John Izard — Lab
76 Geo: Whittenbury — Servt
77 Edwd. Gray — Servt

Geo Worbey Constable

77

Figure 19: A militia list dated 1758
More than 250 years later the names Nash, Shadbolt & Draper are still in the parish.
(HALS)

Exemption from service was also granted on the grounds of infirmity or poverty, as it was thought that if such men were called to serve, their wife and children would have to be provided for out of the poor rates.

Militia lists are a rich source of information giving names of most of the able-bodied males and also their occupations. In the example of 1758 (Figure 19), it is perhaps not surprising that, assuming 'Lab' stood for 'agricultural labourer' the overwhelming source of employment was derived from the land, in this case showing nine farmers, two farmer's sons and—thirty-six labourers. Servants were next with seventeen entries. There were six carpenters, three shoemakers, a weaver, a tailor and a blacksmith. The overseer was also listed.

The creation of the parish council

By the end of the nineteenth century, the vestry had been relieved of most of its administrative functions. The county council was formed in 1889, taking on the responsibility for all civil administration at county level. A few years later, under the Local Government Act 1894, district councils were created, who then transferred all civic duties of the vestries to the new parish councils.

The office of 'parish clerk' was a position that was transferred in name from the church to the council but changed its function from a religious role to a secular one.

Originally the parish clerk, sometimes called the 'church clerk', was appointed by the minister, not by the parishioners. He assisted in religious services and his ability to sing was an important attribute because part of his duties included taking part in responses to the minister and singing psalms. In the eighteenth century, he was also expected to awaken sleepy members of the congregation by using a long pole to tap the miscreant on the head. There were occasions when the parish clerk deputised for the minister at church services but could only undertake baptisms, marriages and burials after being raised to major orders as a deacon.

Once the parish council was established, they were empowered to appoint a clerk, thus preserving the continuity of the title, although any connection with the church was severed. In addition to dealing with all administrative and financial tasks, the main responsibility of the modern day clerk is to ensure that the business of the council runs efficiently in accordance with the law.

The first parish council election for Datchworth took place on Tuesday 4 December 1894 and was held in the school. The rector, Reverend John Wardale, was voted chairman, together with five councillors: John Chapman (farmer), William Lawrance (timber merchant), John Smith (blacksmith), David Gaddie, junior, (farmer) and W. Strange (agent).

Its first proper meeting was held on 3 January 1895. Mr Beswick was appointed clerk at a salary of £2 per annum; this was increased in the April of the same year to £17. This initial meeting was controversial, as the chairman's right to make a proposition was disputed and this led to business being held over. Matters that were deferred related to whether or not to appoint a highway surveyor, the right of those on parish relief to benefit from the parish charities and when the gift of bread from the Gamon Charity should be distributed. The proposal that 'householders and voters' should be allowed to attend meetings was passed. However, by the end of that month, George Little had been appointed highways surveyor at a salary of £12 per annum, although this position did not last long as this responsibility was soon taken over by the county council. The parish council thereafter acted only to bring the county council's attention to highway problems.

Some Datchworth residents recalled the condition of the roads in the village at the beginning of the twentieth century:

> Raffin Green Lane was once gated with three gates. (Norman Pearman)
>
> In 1926 there was still a gravel road along the green. The road to Watton was little more than a cart track with grass down the middle.
> ('Peg' Newman)
>
> The roads were in better order than today because one man had his own stretch of road and took pride in its appearance and upkeep. (Bill Nash)

Various road widening schemes occurred between the two wars but Datchworth Green was not included in these plans until 1965, when a kerbed path was also added. Brookbridge Lane was widened in 1969.

The parish council subsists on a precept (the annual request to the district council for money from the council rates) to run parish affairs. The first recorded precept, in 1897, of £20 was to be 'signed and delivered to the overseers'. Today (2014) this figure is around £24,000.

Figure 20: An overgrown Datchworth Green with a horse and cart travelling along the narrow road. The cherry tree avenue has just been planted. (c.1935) (Datchworth Museum)

Following the Local Government Act of 1894, councils could provide land for allotments and this was one of the earliest items discussed by the newly formed parish council in February 1895. Residents in the part of Datchworth parish that used to be in Knebworth were given the opportunity to have allotments in a field at the back of dwellings in Station Road. An appeal was made for applicants and seven people responded.

Many matters were discussed in those early meetings, some that went on for many years and required public involvement, including the fight for pure water, various sewage schemes and excessive housing developments. These topics are described in more depth in later chapters. Some examples of other items discussed at the meetings are given below.

Pound House pond

At the meeting of February 1895 it was agreed to fill in the pond at Pound House, opposite the school. However, at the Annual Meeting of 1 April 1895, William Lawrance, councillor and owner of the three cottages nearby, opposed the filling in on the grounds that 'it has been a water supply for the neighbourhood for hundreds of years – but its present state devalues my property'. The previous decision was cancelled and the matter did not arise again until 1924, when the council attempted to get the lord of the manor (Abel Henry Smith) to repair the fence and walls around the pond. The reply that came stated that 'the late Reverend Wardale, being very distressed at the way this source of drinking water was contaminated by cattle manuring in the pond, walled in the waste, with the lordship's permission, using concrete with which he (Reverend Wardale) had been experimenting and as Datchworth now has an up-to-date supply of drinking water the lordship saw no reason for anyone to maintain the wall'.

Later, on 9 June 1933, Mr Clarke, the owner of Pound House, wrote to the council saying that he wished to exclude the public from the pond and its green and implied that the council had no jurisdiction over the land. The council disputed this, but on 10 July 1934 the access gate was said to be wired up. The council objected and resolved to watch this gate from time to time.

In 1936, Mr Clarke made two further attempts to gain rights over the land, both of which were refused. Later, in 1961, Mr Temperley, a councillor, who lived in Pound House, requested the right to enclose the land without full right of title. The parish council agreed to this in August of that year and sold it to him for £200 provided that he did not build on it.

Corresponding with Royalty

Along with the day to day matters of providing a service to the parish, on occasions, events from further afield were also dealt with. These included matters involving the Royal family as shown in the following quotations from the minutes:

> 31st Jan 1901
>
> The Chairman in a sympathetic speech made reference to the death of Her Late Majesty the Queen and in proposing a vote of condolence to the King and Royal Family and the German

Emperor put a resolution to the Council (the members standing) that the following be forwarded to the Home Secretary and the German Ambassador. This was seconded by Mr Smith the Vice Chairman and Carried unanimously:

> The Rt. Hon. G.J. Ritchie Esq. M.P.
>
> Sir,
> At a meeting of the Datchworth Parish Council held here this evening, I was desired to communicate to you the following resolution:
>
> That the inhabitants of Datchworth, Herts, through the Parish Council most respectfully and dutifully tender their sincere condolence to His Majesty the King and the Royal Family, on the overwhelming loss they and the nation have sustained in the death of our beloved and revered Queen of ever blessed memory. We also most dutifully and humbly offer our respectful congratulations to His Majesty The King on his accession and are quite sure the lustre and purity of the Throne, the honour of the Empire, and the privileges and liberties of his subjects, will be safe in His keeping and we pray God he may live long to reign over a contented and prosperous people.
>
> I remain, Sir
> Your Obedient Servant,
> W. Strange,
> Chairman of Parish Council

22nd May 1902

An Annual Meeting was held to arrange the celebrations for the Coronation of King Edward VII. After some discussion it was agreed that a Voluntary Subscription List should be opened in the parish and that a dinner be given to adults and a tea to children and a committee was formed to carry out the arrangements. The following address was sent to the King:

> At a meeting of the Parish Council of Datchworth in the County of Hertford, it was unanimously carried by Acclamation that on the auspicious occasion of your Majesty's Coronation on June 26th 1902 the inhabitants tender their dutiful congratulations, and sincerely trust that you with your consort our beloved Queen Alexandra may for many years be blessed with health and happiness and may continue to reign in peace and prosperity over the loyal subjects of a united Empire. In token of which we individually subscribe our name to this Petition of which we humbly beg your indulgent acceptance.

1st May 1911

A Public Meeting was held to consider schemes for celebrating the Coronation in the parish of Datchworth of King George V. A Fund was started for sports and tea for adults and children and not more than £30 to be expended and any surplus to be donated towards a fund for a Parish Room.

Boundary changes

Since its formation in 1894, the council has been faced with proposals to alter its parish boundary on four occasions. At a meeting on 6 June 1910 a proposal was debated that involved removing parts of Datchworth and Welwyn and adding them to Knebworth parish. The council was told that if adopted, the area of the parish would fall from 2,018 acres to 1,554 acres, the population would be almost halved by dropping from 953 to 595 and the rateable value would change from £3,347 to £2,208. The council voted to accept the proposal and no public meeting was held.

This boundary change was implemented on 1 April 1911. Datchworth had, in fact, handed back to Knebworth land it had acquired in 1822. A milestone near the crossroads at Station Road in Knebworth is a reminder of the 89 years that this land was in the parish of Datchworth. The stone is Grade II listed and still stands in Knebworth today.

Figure 21: Datchworth milestone erected in the mid nineteenth century. (2014)

Under the New Towns Act of 1946, parts of Datchworth parish at Hooks Cross and Bragbury End could be absorbed by Aston and Stevenage. This plan was opposed by the parish without success and was eventually implemented on 1 April 1953 by the Boundary Commission.

Another boundary change occurred on 1 April 1964 between Tewin and Datchworth which brought Burnham Green Village Hall into the parish.

About 30 metres north-north-west of Burnham Green Village Hall stands a boundary stone. It was erected in 1830 at a cost of £2 1s to settle a four year boundary dispute between Tewin and Datchworth residents. The stone was eventually erected to mark the spot where the four parishes of Datchworth, Tewin, Digswell and Welwyn met. It is made of white freestone and was inscribed with the initials of the four parishes. The stone is now Grade II listed but unfortunately is so weathered that the inscriptions are no longer legible.

Figure 22: Grade II listed boundary stone at Burnham Green.

In 1983 the Boundary Commission unsuccessfully attempted to annexe Welche's Farm to Welwyn, and in 1990 a claim by Tewin to take over part of the parish at the south side of Burnham Green Road was successful, which moved the boundary away from its ancient line of Hawkins Hall manor. Both these latter proposals were strongly opposed by the parish council.

A map (Figure 93) shows the boundary in 1866 and Figure 81 shows the boundary line as it is today.

Village Greens

The upkeep of Datchworth's greens has occupied the council almost continuously throughout the twentieth century and beyond. In the early days, it was deemed sufficient to use them as grazing areas but this untidy waste land led to parishioner complaints. Allowing farmers to cut the grass and offering hay to traders provided partial solutions, until eventually on 6 November 1947 the first contract was let to Brown Brothers to cut Datchworth Green at £8 10s 0d per annum. Also, local farmer and councillor, Charles Pearman, and later his son Norman, cut the grass, free, two or three times every year and from May 1963, a local pensioner, Mr Webb, was employed to cut the verges at £20 per annum, all in addition to the main contractor. In 1979, this contract amounted to nearly £4,000 and standards had fallen below those expected by many parishioners. As a result, the parish council decided to buy its own equipment and employed a groundsman, Jack Nash, thus eliminating the contract work. In its first year it cost £3,800 incorporating much more work and to a higher standard. In 1983 the labour force was doubled when Joe Buckridge was employed as an assistant groundsman, for a short time, to be followed by Matthew Hankey.

Eventually, Jack Nash retired but it was difficult to find a permanent groundsman to replace him. This, along with increasing machinery costs and more competitive tendering for the grass cutting led the parish council to return to a contractor. Therefore, in 1990, Kirkham Contracting, a Tewin based contractor, was taken on to do the job. More than 20 years later, and after regular tendering for competitive pricing, Stuart Kirkham is still looking after the village greens and verges today.

There were other problems related to the greens that included keeping gypsies away, preventing encroachment and controlling trespass. In addition, the ponds, which were the source of water in the early days, had to be kept clean and free from contamination from wandering animals. It was said that the main pond on Datchworth Green was five feet deep and one of the three at Painters Green nearly four feet deep. Eventually, the ponds became unnecessary for the main supply of drinking water, so those in public areas were filled in.

The coming of the motorcar presented yet another complication. This was the use of Datchworth Green by vehicles to reach the cottages at its west side, an activity that the council had strongly opposed for many years. Eventually a recognised track from the main road was consented to and when the sports pavilion was built on its present site, an extension to the track to form a roadway of a width of ten feet was authorised.

The drainage of Datchworth Green has been tackled from time to time and is a continuing problem for the parish council. In fact, the earliest record is of work sanctioned by the vestry in February 1863 when six acres of it were drained by Dan Gray of Welwyn, laying pipes three feet deep to the pond on Datchworth Green at a cost of £30 7s 6d. Mole drains were put in between the wars and in the 1970s these were added to by the sports club. In 2011 more drainage works were carried out at the west end of the green adjacent to the sports pavilion and further work was required alongside the access road in 2013.

On a number of occasions, the parish council has been able to provide financial assistance to village organisations. For instance, in May 1975 they authorised a loan of £300 to the village hall committee to enable them to purchase some land so that the new hall could be built, that was followed later by a further loan of £1,500 to pay the hall's debts. The council then made provision for an annual grant to be paid to the hall committee to contribute towards maintenance costs. The sports club has also benefitted by similar interest free loans, including one of £4,000 in 1982 when repairs and resurfacing to the tennis courts was necessary.

The council has also provided the parish with four play areas: Nutcroft, Datchworth Green, Burnham Green and the Turkey Farm. Many thousands of pounds have been spent providing equipment and ensuring that regulation standards are maintained. The provision of the Turkey Farm recreation ground in 1975 stands out as being one of the council's proudest projects.

The responsibilities of the parish council have multiplied as a result of the regular increase in local government activities outside the parish, so expanding the membership from eight to ten in 1976 must have been a great help.

Figure 23: Turkey Farm recreation ground (2014)

Following is a list of chairmen of the council since it came into being:

1894 – 1897	Rev. John Wardale, parson
1897 – 1905	William Strange, land agent
1905 – 1906	John Smith, blacksmith
1906 – 1907	Rev. Andrew Amos, parson
1907 – 1909	William Strange, land agent
1909 – 1910	Rev. Henry Fulford, parson
1910 – 1915	R.M. Munro
1915 – 1916	Herbert R. McMullen
1916 – 1922	Arthur Freer
1922 – 1930	Rev. Benjamin Reed, parson
1930 – 1932	Stanley Sturmer
1932 – 1943	Capt. A.E. Illingworth, J.P.
1943 – 1947	James L Little, farmer
1947 – 1961	A. (George) Facey, smallholder
1961 – 1973	Norman C. Pearman, farmer
1973 – 1978	William C. Sharman, retired chartered engineer
1978 – 1983	John H. Alden, marketing manager
1983 – 1987	Walter B. Emms, retired civil servant
1987 – 1991	Vivien M. Marshall, cytologist
1991 – 1994	Henry Burns Rouse, retired bank manager
1994 – 1999	Brian Woodget, principal university lecturer
1999 – 2001	Dean Goodman, planning officer
2001 – 2004	John Austin, funeral director
2004 – present	Christopher Wilkins, analyst programmer

1929	First female member (Mrs E Gregory) joined the parish council
1931	First time the chairman was elected from the parish councillors
1947	First polled election
1987	First female chairman

6. Agriculture and Farms

Early farming practices

Datchworth today is only just agricultural, in the sense that most wage earners depend on another occupation for their livelihoods. As with most of the world, its background is based on agriculture and this chapter goes into the detail of that background: the early field systems, the developments in equipment and how the workforce and ownership changed.

The open field method of farming, developed by the Saxons, was well established at the time of the Norman invasion and continued in some places until the eighteenth century. Open fields were composed of many small strips of land that were farmed by the tenants of the manor, each strip being an acre or so. Chapter 2 briefly explains the three-field system, whereby one of the open fields would be sown with a designated crop and a second open field nearby would be sown with a different crop and a third would be left fallow. Ideally, a tenant would have strips scattered over each of the three open fields harvesting crops from two of them while the strips in the third would be left fallow. The quality of the strips would vary according to their position in the open field, so some years the yield might be better than others. Open fields are often called 'commons' derived from the fact that they were farmed 'in common' by the tenants; they all had to do the same thing at the same time.

In Hertfordshire, the three-course crop rotation system was widely used. Crops were sown at different times and the land that had been fallow was ploughed ready for wheat or rye to be sown in the autumn. The preparation or tilling of the soil in this case led to this crop being called the 'tilth' crop. Barley, oats or peas would be sown on the stubble or 'etch' as it was called, from the previous autumn that had been ploughed in. These two crops were described in Datchworth as 'tilt' and 'edge' crops. Each of the open fields would be rotated in this manner ending with a year when the land was left fallow.

In Datchworth this rotation system was still being used in the early eighteenth century as described in Reverend William Hawtayne's tithe and glebe account book written between 1711 and 1747. A 'tithe' was an ancient obligation of all parishioners to pay one tenth of their annual produce to the parson (see Chapter 15 for details about both 'tithe' and 'glebe'). In 1715 John Whitfield, a tenant of Hoppers End Farm, had almost 13 acres of 'tilt' crop, nearly 28 acres of 'edge' crop and 10 acres of fallow. His land consisted of several fields elsewhere in the parish as well as some strips in the open fields.

Two of the three old open fields are clearly marked on the Datchworth 1839 tithe map in the northern part of the parish called Sliding Dale Common and Datchworth Common. Bragbury Lane marks the boundary between them. Travelling down this lane, Sliding Dale Common would have been on the left and Datchworth Common on the right, still known as 'The Common' today. Originally they had different names: Sliding Dale Common was once called Cundall Common and Datchworth Common had the former name of Chibden (or Chipden) Common. These older names are the ones generally found in contemporary documents. For example, in Hawtayne's tithe record, John

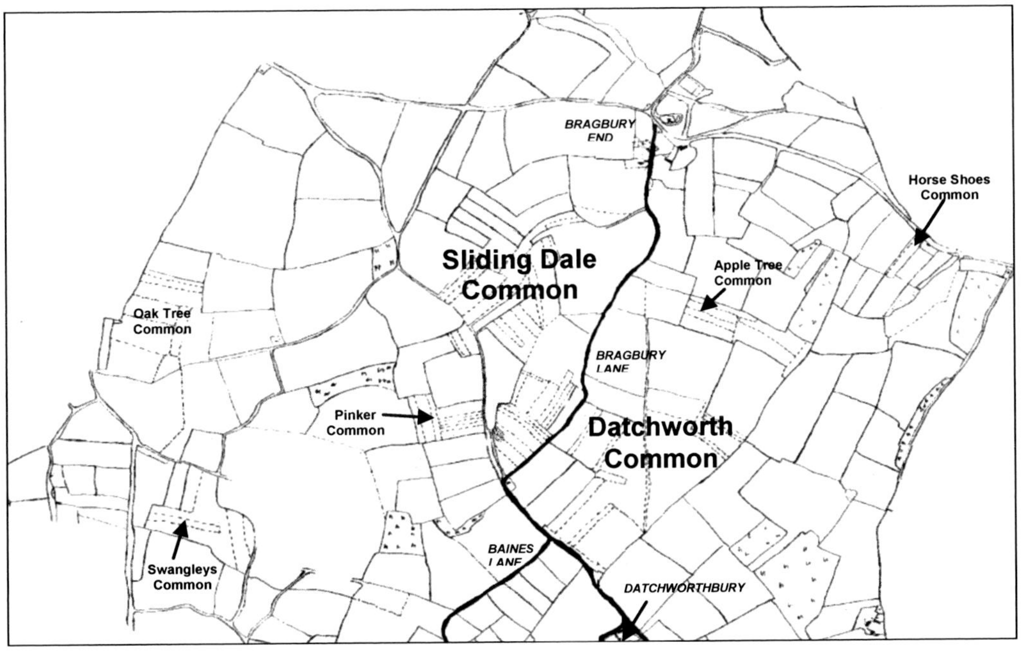

Figure 24: Part of the 1839 map published after the 1838 Tithe Award. It shows the northern part of Datchworth parish where fragments of strips are visible in the open fields.

Whitfield was said to have 'a piece in Cundall Common', 'a piece' being the usual description for a small strip of land in the open fields.

The location of the third field is not clear but details from a document relating to the sale of the Little House at Painters Green in 1749 provide a clue. The details include descriptions of some land, for example, there is 'a piece of ground in the Common Field called Chipden ... called Feakes Shott ... 1½ acres'. By 1839 this piece of ground was called 'Fig Shot' which is an illustration of how names were often spelt as they sounded. This strip and the others that are mentioned in the sale document are summarised below.

Common	Areas of strips
Chipden: 3 strips	1½ acres; ½ acre; ½ acre
Cundell: 2 strips	3 roods; ½ acre and 20 poles
Pinksworth: 1 strip	½ acre

[Note: 3 roods = ¾ acre; 20 poles = $^5/_8$ acre]

'Pinksworth' may have been part of Pinker Common suggesting that the area to the west of Sliding Dale was probably the third area of open fields.

In Datchworth, strips were often consolidated by private agreement between landowners. In many other parishes it took an Act of Parliament to achieve the equivalent. Only one Act in 1867 was required to enclose the last remaining strips in Datchworth. Land was allotted to individuals, such as William Blake, in lieu of strips in the open fields. As an example, on behalf of Blake, Abel Smith, junior, (1830-1898) gave permission for a plot called Four Acres to be exchanged for seven strips of land distributed between Sliding Dale Common and Pinker Common. In a similar way, Abel Smith acquired all the remaining strips of land.

Crops and livestock

In the autumn of 1983 a group of local people led by Lionel Munby transcribed and analysed 72 wills and 25 inventories of Datchworth and Tewin residents dating from between 1496 and 1696. Munby wrote a comprehensive summary of the group's findings, a copy of which is in Datchworth Museum along with copies of some of the wills that were studied.

His section on agriculture revealed that mixed farming was universally adopted during the period but evidence from the wills and inventories showed that the balance between crops and livestock varied according to the prosperity of the farmers. The richer farmers concentrated on produce for the market and favoured grain over livestock; whereas for a farmer who was growing for his own consumption, stock dominated crops. All crops mentioned in the 'Early farming practices' section above appeared in inventories. An example is illustrated by that of Thomas Kimpton, yeoman of Datchworth, dated 27 February 1648. It included barley and peas stored in the chamber over the milkhouse and in the wheat barn he had a store of wheat, rye, oats and hay. He also had 18 acres of wheat 'on the ground'.

All farmers represented in this group of wills had cattle but only the better off had horses. Six of the richer farmers had milk houses and nine people had equipment for milking and cheese making. Sheep were widely owned but, again, prosperity governed the size of the flock. In his will of 1529, Thomas Pennyfather of Datchworth bequeathed a cow and ten sheep to each of his five daughters and an unborn child. His only son, Thomas, was bequeathed two oxen and two horses in addition to his father's house and land.

According to Arthur Young's report published in *General View of the Agriculture of Hertfordshire* (1804), turnips and clover were often being used as crops on land which would otherwise have been fallow. Sheep fed on these crops producing a valuable fertiliser as a by-product. Turnips also provided food for animals during the winter that hitherto would have been slaughtered. Also by 1804 many farmers used a four or five year rotation system and in several cases they avoided the fallow year altogether. Young had interviewed several landowners while compiling his report and the nearest to Datchworth was Mr Whittington of Knebworth who, on lighter soil, rotated crops such as turnips, barley, clover and wheat but on clay still used a three year rotation including one fallow year.

Hawtayne's tithe records of the early eighteenth century give a rough idea of the quality of the crops harvested. In 1716 tithes for tilth crops, such as wheat or rye, were paid at 4s per acre and etch crops of barley or oats were at 2s per acre. In 1804 Arthur Young recorded that the tithe for Datchworth was given as 5s per acre which, at the time, was higher than that of Datchworth's neighbours Knebworth, 3s, and Welwyn, 3s 9d.

During the eighteenth century, the national population grew to such an extent that imports were needed to supplement home-grown supplies of grain. These were halted during the Napoleonic Wars (1803-1815) and grain prices soared, causing farmers to prosper but poorer people to suffer.

Imports were restored in 1815 but under the control of the first of the Corn Laws, which set home grown corn prices at a high level, before imports were allowed. Large landowners benefited but smaller ones suffered under the burden of such high prices, so the law did little to alleviate the plight of the poor. Several adjustments were made but matters did not improve. This was the situation in 1838 when the population in Datchworth was about 580, roughly double that of 100 years earlier.

Following the Tithe Commutation Act of 1836, land surveys were made nationally to assess the amount of arable land that was liable to tithe and identify the names of the tithe owners. These surveys were referred to as 'tithe awards' and consisted of a map of the parish and a book containing a tithe apportionment list of landowners and tenants and their fields. Under this Act, all tithes were commuted to cash. This procedure was completed for Datchworth in 1838 and the associated map was printed in 1839. A summary of all the land in Datchworth was written at the front of the book, giving a total area of nearly 1,923 acres, broken down as follows:

Description of land	Acres	Roods	Poles
Arable land	1,527	-	9
Meadows and Pastures	200	-	-
Woodland	97	3	38
Roads and Waste	63	-	36
Gardens belonging to houses	10	3	15
Glebe belonging to Rector	23	3	16
Total areas	1,922	3	34

[Note: 1 pole = 30 ¼ sq. yds: 40 poles = 1 rood: 4 roods = 1 acre = 0.405 hectares]

Arable land accounted for about 79% of the total area of Datchworth, with meadow and pasture being just over 10% - which illustrates the dominance of crop growing at the time.

The Corn Laws were repealed in 1846 and, following the re-introduction of imports, reasonable calm was restored in the agricultural world for both growers and consumers. However, in the 1860s imports from America posed a serious threat to British wheat production. Unfortunately, this coincided with a series of wet summers and poor harvests in the 1870s and 1880s and the net effect was disastrous for farmers. The Great Agricultural Depression lasted from 1875 until the onset of war in 1914.

Some farmers converted from arable to beef and dairy produce but others were reluctant to make such changes and many farms were left vacant. During this period several Scottish livestock farmers migrated to England. Local farmer, John Wallace, mentioned his own grandfathers as examples of this trend in his account entitled *Farming in Hertfordshire Past and Present.* In 1876 his paternal grandfather moved to Hertfordshire, first to Mardon Hill near Tewin, then taking on Swangleys Farm in 1886 followed by Mardleybury Farm in 1993, both on the Lytton estate, where he established a dairy herd and grew potatoes. The proximity of London had more than one benefit: it was a convenient market for produce and a source of cheap horse manure that arrived by train to Knebworth to fertilise Wallace's potato fields.

Some recovery in arable farming took place during the First World War and was maintained until about 1920 when all farmers suffered once again until subsidies were introduced in the 1930s. By the 1950s there were many mixed farms growing crops with dairy and beef herds being raised but since then the picture has changed. The efficient use of fungicides and fertilisers has allowed crop yields to improve dramatically and, currently, there are only a few beef cattle to be seen locally and there are no dairy farms.

Crop rotation still occurs to combat a nasty fungal disease called 'take-all' that attacks the roots of some crops, particularly wheat. Sowing wheat for more than two successive years reduces the yield drastically, whereas barley is not so severely affected. Crops such as oilseed rape and field beans act as a means of clearing a field of take-all so are often planted as part of a four-fold rotation such as: wheat, wheat, barley and rape.

Arable farming, mechanisation and employment

From early days, occupations associated with agriculture dominated rural employment. Apart from the farmer himself, there would be amongst others, a hayward who oversaw hay-making and ensured that hedges were impenetrable, a cowherd in charge of milking cows and their calves and a ploughman who was responsible for everything to do with crops as well as the maintenance of his plough. Farm hands, both

Figure 25: A Hertfordshire farm wagon (Five Hide Village)

male and female, were needed year in year out typically, in summer, working from 5am to 8pm and many of them slept and ate in the farmhouse. In the 1861 census Henry Campkin of Datchworthbury had a shepherd and an agricultural labourer in residence.

Harvest: reaping and binding

Figure 26: Two-handled scythe (at Datchworthbury Farm)

The summer months were the busiest time of year with haymaking and the harvest. In the sixteenth century, wheat, for example, was harvested with a short handled sickle where the stems were cut part-way down leaving strong stalks to be used for thatching. This tool was superseded by the scythe that had a larger blade and a long pole with two projecting handles. The reaping team often consisted of about five labourers; the men wielded the scythes and the women collected and bound the sheaves that would then be put together into 'stooks'. A team such as this was reckoned to complete about 2 acres per day. The stooks were taken to the homestead and built into ricks ready for threshing.

In 1831, the manual scythe was replaced by the horse-drawn reaper. Originating in America, it was displayed at the Great Exhibition of 1851 and soon became widely used in Hertfordshire on larger farms. In 1872 the 'reaper-binder' was invented. Often just called a binder, it cut grain and bound it into sheaves. Although these machines were available, not all farmers adopted them and traditional procedures were commonly used up to the 1930s and later.

Threshing

Threshing corn was usually a winter activity and was originally done using a flail that consisted of a long pole with a shorter heavy stick swinging from it; men often worked in pairs. In the late eighteenth century, threshing mills driven by horses that walked in a circle were introduced, but were not always an efficient method. In 1804 Arthur Young reported that 'Mr Blindel' of Welwyn, who may have been a descendent of Datchworth Blindells (or Blindalls) had a mill driven by four horses. Having spent £100 on the equipment, he tried it and managed to thresh 50 bushels of wheat in a day which was meagre compared to the 125-150 bushels produced by a superior model elsewhere in the county.

These mechanical threshing devices developed rapidly in the early nineteenth century, eventually being driven by steam. They were regarded by farm labourers as a threat to their employment, leading to riots in 1830 when threshing machines were burnt or smashed up.

Threshing machines travelled between farms first towed by steam traction engines and later by tractors. On arrival at the farm the towing vehicle was transformed into a power machine that drove the thresher using belts and pulleys.

Eventually, in the late nineteenth century, machines for combining, reaping and threshing

Figure 27: Massey Harris combine harvester 1950. Driven by Norman Pearman with Jimmy Little to his left. Standing in the field on the left is Charlie White and Art Stokes on the right. (Datchworth Museum)

Figure 28: Frank Pearman's combine harvester being driven by Kevin Morris 2011.

Figure 29: Standard bushel
(at Datchworthbury Farm)

Figure 31: Scales, probably Victorian.
(at Datchworthbury Farm)

evolved, the earlier ones being horse-drawn by 30 or so horses or mules. It was in the 1930s that the engine driven combine harvester was first introduced. Datchworthbury Farm had its first one in 1944. Imported from America, it arrived in a crate containing the constituent parts. All hands got to work to assemble the machine and were a bit bemused when they found that there were several parts left over but to their relief the harvester worked. Every time something went wrong, the 'spare' parts were investigated and were often found to have some practical use after all.

Figure 30: Sack lifter
(at Datchworthbury Farm)

The threshing machine routine was still being used in Datchworth in the late 1950s in spite of the existence of the combine harvester which eventually took over completely. Originally grain was measured by volume rather than weight and every farmyard would have had a standard 'bushel' as a measure. According to Jim Andrew, in a Birmingham Museum pamphlet written in the late 1970s 'at Hertford, wheat is sold sometimes by the bushel of 8 gallons ...and ... sometimes by weight, varying from 62 lbs [28 kg]'. A weighing machine exists at Datchworthbury Farm that will accommodate weights up to 3 cwt (150 kg) and also a hand operated sack lifter that was used to hoist sacks onto the scales.

Ploughing

Following the harvest, ploughing was done by oxen or horses towing a plough. Oxen, also called bullocks, could manage to haul heavy ploughs on clay soil but horses were faster particularly on lighter soil. Oxen were specifically mentioned in Datchworth in 1529, according to Thomas Pennyfather's will and the inventory of Thomas Kimpton of 1659 included two bullocks. Arthur Young reported in 1804 that Mr Whittington of Broadwater, Knebworth, had 16 oxen that he used in teams of four. Following enclosure, fields became smaller and horses were favoured because oxen were unsuitable and by 1840 were hardly used. Mr Little of Moat Farm had seven or eight horses on his farm in the 1920s, as remembered by resident 'Peg' Newman.

By the 1850s, steam traction engines were in use for ploughing where they sometimes worked in pairs with one located at each side of a field. They had cable drums underneath and the plough, connected to a steel hawser, was dragged between the two engines across the field. The

Figure 32: A Fowler traction engine: with ploughing cable drum under its boiler. (Five Hide Village)

hawser gradually unwound from one cable drum and was wound up on the other.

It may have been one of these steel cables that was found in Brookbridge Lane during the road widening in 1969. The workmen tried to remove it but it was so long that it proved to be impossible and so they reburied it. This all occurred near to 1 Brookbridge Lane where it is likely that some of this cable lies under the garden.

It is not known whether anyone in Datchworth owned a traction engine but census records for the village show that George Shelford, who lived in a cottage at Hoppers End, was a traction engine driver from 1881 to 1901, as was George Nutting of Datchworth Green in 1901 and 1911.

Steam traction power continued to be used into the 1930s despite the fact that motorised tractors came onto the market at the beginning of the twentieth century. During the Second World War food shortages and rationing led to pastures being ploughed up in favour of arable crops following the 'dig for victory' campaign.

Figure 33: Early tractor-driven plough (at Datchworthbury Farm)

Sowing

Once the land had been roughly ploughed, seeds could be sown. Before mechanisation a worker would walk across the ploughed field scattering the seed which was then covered with soil by harrows. Women and children often did the weeding and children were also employed as bird scarers, using a sort of wooden clapper. In 1701, Jethro Tull invented his famous seed drill and Nigel Agar in *Behind the Plough* remarks that it was becoming widely used in Hertfordshire by the 1830s but was not regarded as a threat to employment.

Initially, harrows were brushes made from hawthorn that were dragged across the ground, but by the sixteenth century they were made out of timber frames with wooden tines. In the eighteenth century these tines were replaced by metal teeth and eventually by discs in the nineteenth century. Typical of many, Daniel Nash's inventory of 1683 (Figures 14a and 14b) lists his belongings 'in the yard' where he had one cart, one 'plow' and harrows.

Domestic produce: allotments

In his book *The Local History Companion,* Stephen Friar suggests that modern allotment holders are 'the descendents of the medieval villein, who cultivated strips of land in the open field and enjoyed common grazing rights in return for manorial service'. Enclosure awards of the eighteenth and nineteenth centuries deprived peasants of these small holdings of land and in compensation they were provided with an allotment of ground sometimes attached to their cottages.

Self-sufficiency was an important element within the Erection of Cottages Act, 1589. This stated that all newly built houses must have at least 4 acres of land attached, sufficient to support a family. Prior to this law, people had the right to build on common land provided that they built something adequate in a day, but having achieved this, invariably they were unable to support themselves and as a result appealed to the parish for help. Parishes were finding this situation an ever increasing problem and this Elizabethan law was a means of trying to alleviate it.

Brian King, in *A Brief History of Allotments,* suggests that the real start of the allotment movement was in the mid 1760s. In *The Gentleman's Magazine* of that period prominent landholders and clergy were discussing the positive features of allotments. It was agreed that keeping an allotment would provide useful occupation for the unemployed and so reduce the burden on poor relief funds and it would also diminish the likelihood of crime. The recommended size was a minimum of 2 acres, half that stated in the 1859 Elizabethan law. These early ideas were slow to develop because there was opposition particularly from farmers.

One of the first Acts was in 1782. It allowed overseerers of the poor to appropriate up to 10 acres of waste ground to be used by the poor to grow produce, although this was not a legal requirement. The next piece of legislation was the Select Vestries Act of 1819 that authorised churchwardens and overseers to purchase up to 20 acres of land (increased to 50 acres in 1831) for use as allotments that could be let to unemployed parishioners. In 1832 the size of each allotment was to be between a quarter of an acre and 1 acre. Once again, this was met with a lack of enthusiasm by farmers who thought that farm workers would use valuable time and energy tending their plots instead of labouring on the farm.

It was not long after these Acts that tithe awards were made. Datchworth's tithe award in 1838 provides information about the number and size of gardens that were in the village at the time, some attached to dwellings, others standing alone. Out of 53 cottages listed, 38 had gardens ranging in size from eight poles [a twentieth of an acre] to over half an acre, with an average of just under an eighth of an acre. There was a 'Garden Field' of nearly 1½ acres near some dwellings in Burnham Green Road all owned by Lawrence Lucas and let to John Moore. Adjoining Hopkyns Hoo there was 'Garden Mead' of 2 acres. Parish officers owned a small piece of land named 'Garden' at Burnham Green rented by Ewington where a poor house once stood.

In addition there were nine pieces of ground labelled 'garden' distributed widely round the parish owned by different people usually at the side of a road. Amounting in total to roughly an acre, they appear to be pieces of waste ground that had been cultivated, the largest being nearly a quarter of an acre, the others being considerably smaller.

The next Act of importance was the Enclosure Act of 1845. It stated that field gardens of not more than a quarter of an acre must be made available to the labouring poor to compensate for loss of rights to common land. Strips of land in Datchworth's open fields were still being consolidated at this time, so some may have benefited from the 'field garden' system.

The Local Government Act of 1894 empowered new councils to provide allotments for residents. This was the subject of discussion at one of the earliest parish council meetings on 14 February 1895. Part of Datchworth parish was still in Knebworth at the time and included houses on the west side of Station Road. It was behind these houses that some land was being made available for allotments and a request was made for applicants. Seven people had responded by the meeting a month later; all seven were identified as living in 'Knebworth Station Road' in 1901. It was suggested that the plots should be two poles wide and ten poles deep amounting to an eighth of an acre at a rent of 5s.

The culmination of all these Acts with others was the Smallholdings and Allotments Act of 1908. This made it a legal requirement for councils to provide allotments if there was sufficient demand. At least six parishioners had to make requests in writing and councils had to recover costs by way of charging a fair rent. This Act is still in force today and the official wording for the size an allotment plot in Datchworth is as follows:

Each plot = 15 yards x 10 yards (5 poles/rods)
with 2 ft paths
NB. 1 pole/rod = 5.5 yards
(pole/rod sq. = 30.25 sq yards)

After the First World War, vegetables were scarce and expensive. Men returning from the war had no work to go to and the national applications for allotments amounted to 7,000 per week. The Land Settlement Facilities Act 1919 was especially designed to assist these men.

At a parish council meeting on 21 April 1920, the subject of allotments was on the agenda again. An area at Bridgefoot (Brookbridge Lane) described as being a 'new allotment field' (just over two acres) was to be sold by Abel Henry Smith (1863-1930) and the parish council was asked if it would like to secure this piece of ground for allotments (Figure 128). If agreed, the county council was to be contacted and informed that the suggested purchase price would be £100. The parish council would then rent the land from the county council for £8 per annum which would be recouped from the allotment tenants at 10s per 20 poles [one eighth of an acre] and 5s per 10 poles.

Other allotments existed at Hollybush Lane in the field opposite plot 298 (Figure 36). It is not known when these were formed but they were certainly there in 1881 as shown on an Ordnance Survey map of that year. There were 23 plots on the 'Allotment Gardens' as the field was labelled, 12 in one half and 11 in the other, the two areas being divided by a pathway running down the middle of the whole field. This was called 'Four Acres' in 1838 but by the 1920s, was partially taken up by the gravel diggings. On 22 February 1924, the parish council reported the receipt of a complaint from the estate office at Woodhall Park regarding the proximity of the gravel pit to these allotments. It seemed that no-one would take allotments adjoining the gravel pit and road 'owing to the insecurity of tenure as the gravel pit is being worked in that direction'.

In July 1928, once again allotments were discussed. A letter from Mr Hornett of Holly Bush pointed out that the allotment field was to be sold and requested that the parish council should apply to the county council to buy it in order that the holders may retain their plots. The parish council replied that 'as there were still plots available at Brookbridge Lane they therefore could not see their way to further an application for allotments to the county council at this time'. However, Hollybush Lane allotments survived and were still flourishing in the early 1950s as remembered by Geoff Gilbert. He lived in the cottage in plot 298 (Figure 36) and used to go over to the allotment field at the weekends to earn a few pence fetching and carrying. These allotments closed in the mid 1950s and Geoff's parents went on to rent part of the field to keep poultry for a few years. The field still exists and is now used for grazing.

Following a reduction in demand during the 1930s, applications increased again during the 'dig for victory' campaign in the Second World War. At Burnham Green, Phyllis Smalley's memory is as follows: 'The men of the village all had allotments, as most families were large. The allotments were always referred to as 'garden field' and really came into their own during the 'dig-for-victory' campaign during the Second World War.'

The allotments at Brookbridge Lane closed in 1968 when the land was sold to a property developer for new housing. There were no allotments in the village for the following thirteen years until plots were provided in the Turkey Farm recreation ground in 1981. These were charged at a rent of £5 per annum for five poles and were called 'leisure plots' by the parish council, rather than allotments in order to avoid various legislative complications and to enable the council to have greater control over the terms of use of the plots. Out of the initial 27 plots that were provided, only 20 remain today but all continue to be in use and now provide a popular hobby rather than a necessity to survive.

Employment changes

In the early days, all farming activity was labour intensive and kept a high proportion of the rural population in employment. A Datchworth militia list of 1758 (Figure 19) shows that of the 77 men on the list, 47 were farmers or farm labourers but these figures do not include men over 50, teenagers under 18 and women. The population at the time was about 300, so assuming that all agricultural workers on the militia list had wives that worked on the farm, roughly a third of Datchworth's population were involved in agriculture.

Information about employment on the land has been derived from Datchworth census data from 1841 to 1911 (Chapter 9) and summarised in Figure 34. The results reflect some of the national changes in farming already mentioned. Percentages have been calculated on the basis of the working population (i.e. omitting 'scholars', 'infirm', 'paupers' etc) and show that agricultural workers represented about a third of the population, until 1901 when the effects of the depression and mechanisation started to take hold.

In 1871 and 1911 Datchworth agricultural employment figures are comparable with national figures. The proportion of the national workforce employed in agriculture continued to decline. In 1930 it was nearly 8%, in 1950 it had dropped to 5% and by 1990, it was only 2%.

Year of census	1841	1851	1861	1871	1881	1891	1901	1911
Working population	406	491	469	443	437	490	500	880
Agricultural workers	135	167	171	121	133	152	113	120
Proportion of the working population in agriculture	33%	34%	36%	27%	30%	31%	23%	14%
Some national figures for employment in agriculture	-	-	-	22%	-	-	-	12%

Figure 34: Summary of agricultural employment figures in Datchworth (census returns 1841 to 1911)

Datchworth farms

The history of Datchworth farms has been considered from several aspects namely ownership, tenancy, size and the location of the 'homestead', the hub of farm. The first three considerations are subject to change but the fourth usually remains fixed as long as the associated farm continues. Many smaller farms were often absorbed into a larger estate, for example Painters Green Farm was usually associated with Hawkins Hall and Hoppers End Farms.

The farms divide themselves roughly into two groups, those that survived long term and those smaller ones that disappeared in the final quarter of the nineteenth century. In some cases, land near the village centre was used for housing development and in others, ownership or tenancy of a few acres became no longer viable.

The following is a brief description of the farms in Datchworth. Most of them have been described in some depth in Chapter 12 from the point of view of the farmhouses. Much of the information has come from a survey of 1829, the 1838 Datchworth Tithe Award and census data. The farms have been referred to using 'plot numbers' from the 1829 survey (Figures 36 to 39) where possible.

Datchworthbury Farm (Figure 36)

Datchworthbury Farm (plot 284) was bought by Samuel Smith of Woodhall Park on 27 January 1802 and consisted of the old manor house, which was called Datchworth Lodge in the sale details, and land amounting to about 190 acres. This included fields around the manor house and church and all the land where Foldingshott and Raffin Park are today and some of what is now Datchworth Common, on the east side of Bragbury Lane. There were also about 12 acres of strips from the open fields either side of Bragbury Lane. The farm remained in the ownership of the Smith family until 1920 when Abel Henry Smith sold it to Jeremiah Inns who was involved in gravel extraction in Hollybush Lane. Inns died in 1945 and two years later Charles Pearman, who was the tenant of the farm at the time, purchased the freehold from Jeremiah's estate.

Figure 35: Arthur Stokes working a horse and hay rake in Church Field (1941). (Datchworth Museum)

Earlier tenants of the farm included Henry Campkin, from at least 1829. He was still there in 1851 and by then the farm consisted of 330 acres. This acreage remained unchanged during the tenancy of Campkin's son, Henry, who took over the farm in 1864 and remained there until at least 1881. At the time he was living there with his wife, son, four daughters and two domestic servants. In the 1890s James Talbot took on the tenancy and lived there with his wife, two sons who worked on the farm, two daughters who were dairy workers and a general domestic servant. Talbot died in 1913 and Charles Pearman took over the tenancy before purchasing the freehold in 1947. The farm, now consisting of 600 acres of mainly arable land, has been in the Pearman family ever since.

Pound House, Pound Farm cottages and Smiths Croft (Figure 36)

Pound House (plot 297) at Pounds Green had several fields in Baines Lane and other pieces of land in Datchworth Common and Sliding Dale Common. The total acreage was about 77 acres and was farmed by the tenant Isaac Webster whose son took over in 1841 and eventually moved to Hoppers Hall to farm Hoppers End Farm. The land that Webster farmed at Pounds Green was jointly owned by Henry Abingdon and Abel Smith, senior (1788-1859). Unfortunately, it is not clear as to who took over this land after 1841.

One of the cottages at Pound Farm (plot 298) in Hollybush Lane was the homestead of a small farm in 1838 owned by Joseph Holdstock. He had about 4 acres near the cottage and a further 7 acres in Baines Lane that he let to Isaac Webster. In 1841, according to the census, Holdstock was living 'near Holly Bush Cottages' and was described as a wheelwright. It wasn't until 1861 that he had the description of 'farmer of 14 acres' living at 'Ivy House, Pound Green'. Most of the land in Baines Lane is now built on and privately owned, but one field remains next to Bragbury End Lane and is used for crops.

Smiths Croft (plot 360) contained a cottage and a substantial black barn and in 1838 was occupied by the tenant Edmund King. In the 1841 census Elizabeth King, Edmund's widow, was in occupation and she remained as farmer until at least 1861. The lane has a reputation of having 'no name' because it has changed several times over the years. Local resident Geoff Gilbert knows it as 'Granny King's Lane' and remembers the heap of rubble that was originally the cottage.

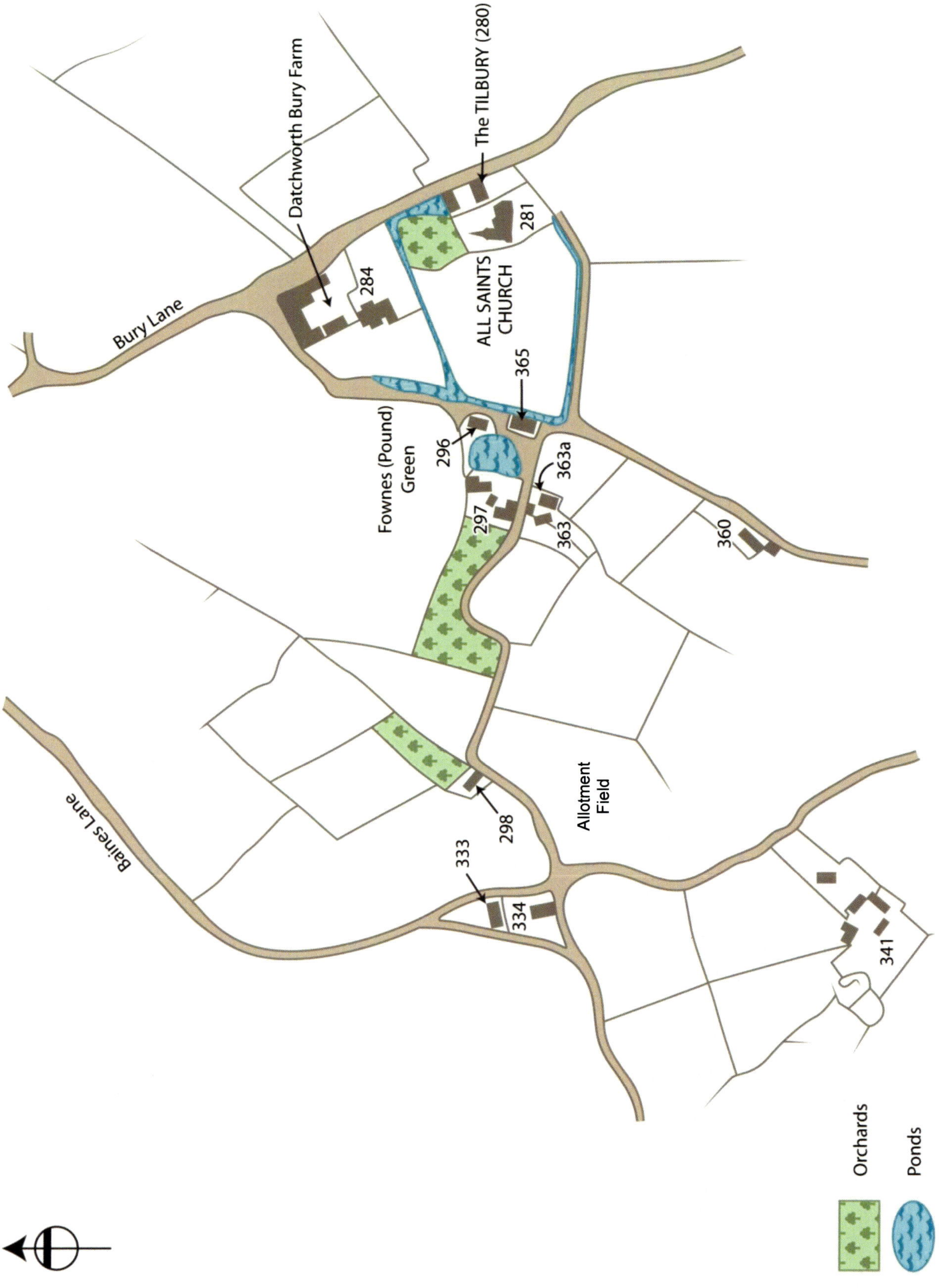

Figure 36: The church, school and rectory area in the 19th century; numbers refer to 1829 references opposite (Designed by Charlotte Tebbutt)

Plot References to Figure 36

1829 Survey PLOT NUMBER & DESCRIPTION	1829 OCCUPIER	1838 Tithe Award DESCRIPTION	1838 OCCUPIER (OWNER)
CHURCH, SCHOOL AND RECTORY AREA		**CHURCH, SCHOOL AND RECTORY AREA**	
280 Public House (old Tilbury)	William Smith	**Tilbury public house**	William Smith (Parish Officers)
281 Churchyard	Rev. Edward Bunting	**Church Yard**	Rev. Edward Bunting (Glebe)
284 Homestead (Datchworthbury)	H. Campkin	**Datchworthbury Homestead**	H. Campkin (Abel Smith)
296 Cottage (Poor House)	Overseers of Datchworth	**Cottage etc**	E. Darton (Parish Officers)
297 Homestead (Pound House)	Isaac Webster	**Homestead**	Isaac Webster (Abel Smith)
298 Cottage	George Burgess & Thomas Henchant	**Homestead**	Joseph Holdstock (Joseph Holdstock)
333 Cottages (Holly Bushes)	Joseph Ipygrave, James Graves, James Nash & Thomas Burgess	**Four Cottages**	James Warren & Others (James Coleman)
334 Cottage (Hollybush House)	George Skegg	**Cottages**	Joseph Mardell (H. Campkin)
341 House (old Rectory)	Rev. Edward Bunting	**Rectory**	Rev. Edward Bunting (Glebe)
360 Cottage	Edmund King	**Homestead**	Edmund King (Abel Smith)
363 Cottage	Thomas Mardell & William Hanchent	**Cottage**	Thomas Mardell & William Hanchent (Execs of William Pennyfather)
363a Cottage	William Harrington	**Cottage**	Joseph Liles (Robert Hill)
365 Charity School	Overseers of Datchworth	**'School House'**	Parish Officers (Parish Officers)

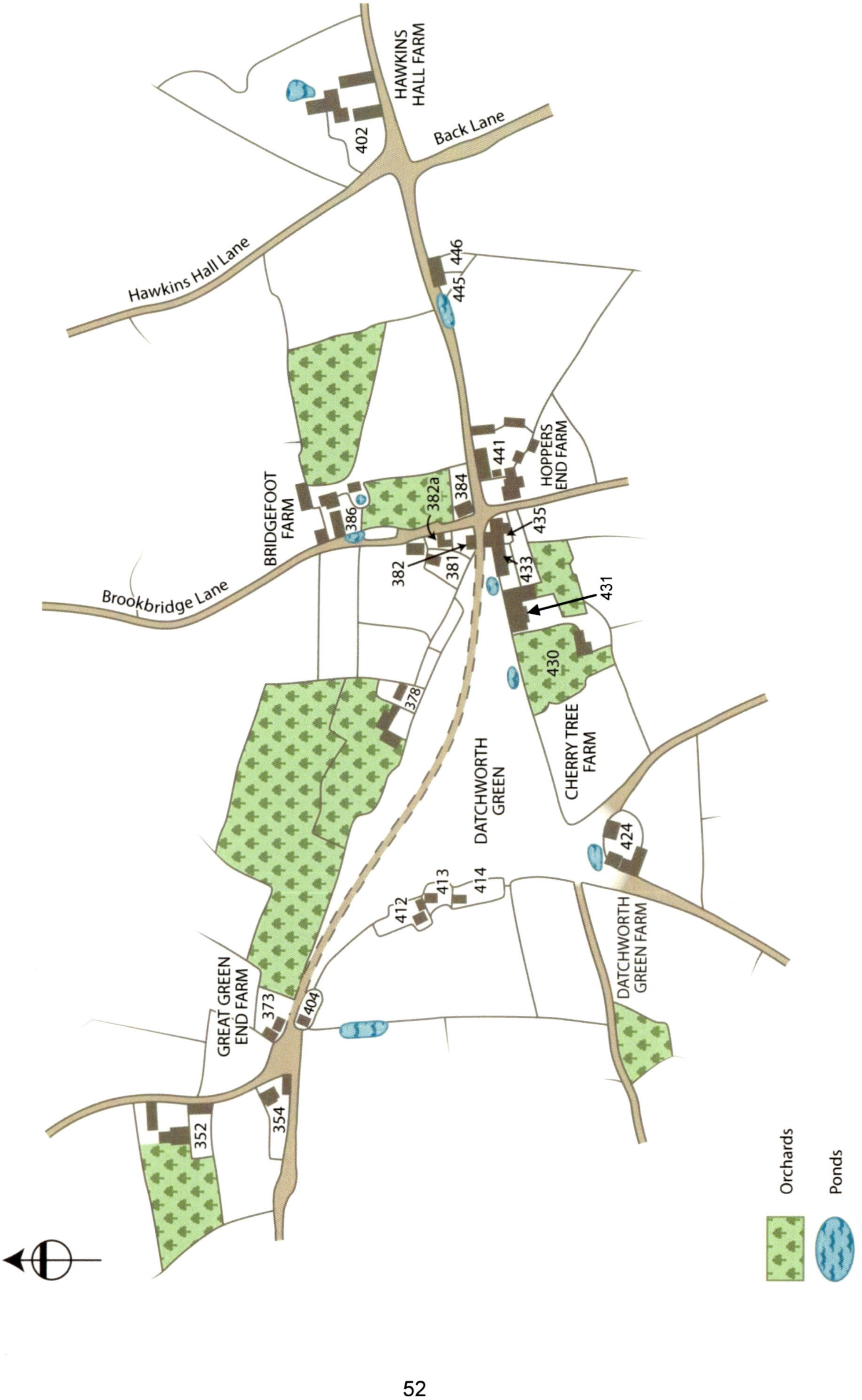

Figure 37: Datchworth Green and Hawkins Hall in the 19th century; numbers refer to 1829 references opposite (Designed by Charlotte Tebbutt)

Plot References to Figure 37

1829 Survey PLOT NUMBER & DESCRIPTION	1829 OCCUPIER	1838 Tithe Award DESCRIPTION	1838 OCCUPIER (OWNER)
DATCHWORTH GREEN		**DATCHWORTH GREEN**	
352 Homestead	William Pallett	**Homestead**	Henry Campkin (Abel Smith)
354 Cottage (Farrins)	Joseph Phipps & Joseph Hyrons	**Homestead**	George Barker (William Phipp)
373 Cottage (formally Green End cottage)	Charles Fletcher	**Cottage**	Jeremiah Gregory (Jeremiah Gregory)
378 Cottage (Pettits)	John Lawrence & Henry Barker	**Cottages**	John Lawrence (William Lawrence)
381 Cottage	William Page	**Cottage**	William Page (Abel Smith)
382 Cottage (4 Datchworth Green)	John Fletcher, Mary Lawrence & Elizabeth Hanchant	**Cottage**	Widow Lawrence and C. Fletcher (Execs of William Pennyfather)
382a Cottage	Unoccupied	**Cottages**	John Fletcher & Joseph Row (Charles Chappell)
384 House (Tilbury)	Mary Pennyfather	**House**	Edward Carpenter (John Allen)
386 Homestead (Bridgefoot)	Charles Chappell	**Homestead**	William Smith (Charles Chappell)
402 Homestead (Hawkins Hall Farm)	William Shippin	**Homestead**	William Shipping (Samuel Heathcote)
404 Cottage	Leonard Darton	**Cottage**	Leonard Darton (Jeremiah Gregory)
412 Cottage (Rose Cottage)	Thomas Field	**Cottage**	Widow Field (Abel Smith)
413 Poor House	Overseers of Datchworth	**Cottage**	Thomas Hunt (Parish Officers)
414 Cottage (now Green End & Cobweb Cottages)	William Lawrence	**Garden (& cottage)**	William Lawrence (William Lawrence)
424 Homestead (Hopkyns Hoo)	Thomas Page	**Homestead**	Joseph Holdstock (Thomas Horne)
430 Garden (& cottage) (Cherry Tree Hall)	Charles Chappell	**Orchard (& cottage)**	Charles Chappell (Charles Chappell)
431 Homestead (Cherry Tree Farm)	Charles Chappell	**Homestead**	Charles Chappell (Charles Chappell)
433 Cottage	William Fletcher	**Cottage**	William Fletcher (William Fletcher)
435 Cottage (Blacksmith's)	Joseph Holdstock, Mary Hanchant & William Ansell	**Blacksmith's shop etc.**	Holdstock & Others (Mrs Bassett)
441 Homestead (Hoppers Hall)	G.W. Wilson	**Homestead**	Robert Ray (Samuel Heathcote)
445 Cottage	William Whittenbury	**Cottage**	Samuel Webb (Peter Lovett)
446 Cottage	Thomas Balk	**Cottage**	Thomas Baulk (Peter Lovett)

The lane of 'no name' leads from the school towards Rectory Lane and has also been known as Black Barn Lane, named after the large black barn that stood about 250 yards down the lane. Unfortunately the barn blew down during high winds in 1990. Nowadays, the lane is usually called School Lane, given its proximity to the school.

In the early nineteenth century, the land associated with Smiths Croft amounted to about 15 acres and was composed of fields around the homestead as far as Hollybush Lane and a few fields on which Wheatcotes was built.

Smiths Croft was originally copyhold land that belonged to Knebworth Manor. Abel Smith, junior, was admitted tenant to the property on 14 February 1860. An 'enfranchisement' document of 22 January 1862, allowed Abel Smith to convert this land from copyhold to freehold for a fee of £70 12s 4d. The schedule included several pieces of land in Sliding Dale Common amounting to about 9 acres, together with two fields adjoining the cottage of about 5 acres, so the total area was still about 14 acres but slightly differently distributed. The property was in the occupation of William Chalkley at this time. From 1871 onwards there is no further mention of this smallholding.

The glebe (Figure 36)

The glebe was partly situated in the four fields adjoining the rectory (plot 341) with an area of about 15 acres. In 1838 these fields were under the control of Reverend E S Bunting who was rector at the time. He also had another 9 acres distributed around the open fields which were farmed by Isaac Webster and William Chalkley. About 100 years earlier, Reverend William Hawtayne was renting these small strips of land at roughly 4s per acre.

Glebe land was provided by the lord of the manor soon after the church was founded and was a valuable source of income for the incumbent. Once established, glebe land remained intact until such time as an Enclosure Act or other agreement caused it to disappear. The last Enclosure Act in Datchworth was in 1867 but this did not involve glebe land. The glebe, as a source of income, was still being referred to in *Crockford's Clerical Directory* until the mid-1930s but stopped at about the same time that tithes came to an end following the Tithe Act of 1936.

Hawkins Hall and Hoppers End Farms (Figure 37)

Hawkins Hall and Hoppers End Farms (plots 402, 441) have been linked with each other and with Painters Green Farm (Figure 39) on several occasions during their history. In 1657 Ralph Pennyfather bought all three farms and thereafter there were many changes of ownership where the trio were often treated separately. They were eventually reunited in 1880 when they were sold by Samuel Heathcote to Abel Smith, junior, along with Bridgefoot Farm (see below).

In 1838, Hawkins Hall was owned by Samuel Heathcote and was occupied by William Shippin whose family were tenants until at least 1881. The land in 1838 amounted to nearly 58 acres but at the 1851 census this was listed as 126 acres. This apparent increase is explained by the fact that Heathcote had land in neighbouring Watton and other parishes. The 1911 census records show David Gaddie, aged 88, as the head of the household whose son, William, was by then the farmer. In 1920 William Gaddie purchased the freehold along with 128 acres of land and two cottages at Datchworth Green from Abel Henry Smith.

In 1715, according to Reverend William Hawtayne's tithe accounts, Hoppers End Farm was in the possession of Mr Hawkins, brewer in London and in the tenancy of John Whitfield. Hawtayne listed the fields that amounted to about 50 acres for the purposes of collecting tithes in Datchworth parish. At the sale of Hoppers End Farm in February 1718, when Hawkins sold it to John Wellins another London brewer, the property was described as 'all situate and being in the parishes of Datchworth, Watton, Tewin, Wellwyn, Aston, Digswell' and amounted to about 121 acres.

Just over 100 years later, in 1838, Hoppers End Farm had 68 acres in Datchworth and belonged to Samuel Heathcote. Once again a realistic view of the size of the land holding can be found from the 1851 census where it was said to be 120 acres, accounting for land in other parishes. Isaac Webster, whose father had lived and farmed at Pound House, was the tenant and remained so until 1881. By this time Hoppers End Farm was owned by Abel Smith, junior. It continued as a working farm until 1947 and in 1956 was bought by Mr Higgs of Hawkins Hall Farm who kept most of the land and sold Hoppers Hall with 7 acres of land.

Bridgefoot, Cherry Tree, Datchworth Green and Green End Farms (Figure 37)

Bridgefoot Farm (plot 386) was owned by Rowland Mardell from about 1715 when the farm consisted of about 41 acres according to tithe records. In 1838, Charles Chappell of Cherry Tree Farm was the landlord and let the farm to William Smith, which by then was 33 acres of land mostly on the east side of Brookbridge Lane which has now been built on. The orchard next to the homestead accounted for 2 acres. Another field was called Nutcroft from which the housing development in that area gets its name. William Smith also had the tenancy of the Tilbury public house beside the church (Figure 36 plot 280) until it was sold in 1837 and in 1841 he was listed as 'publican' at the Three Horseshoes (Tilbury) near Datchworth Green. Bridgefoot Farm was another property that became part of the Smith family holding in Datchworth. As mentioned earlier, in 1920 Abel Henry Smith sold one of the fields in Brookbridge Lane to become allotments for a time, before the land was eventually built on.

Cherry Tree Farm (plot 431) was owned by Charles Chappell in the early nineteenth century and had 18 acres of land, including two orchards and Cherry Tree Field. Although the homestead was close to Datchworth Green, there were two farm cottages (plot 430) which were converted into one dwelling by Robert Wallace in 1930. The land stretched alongside the footpath that leads from Datchworth Green to Govers Green. Chappell was described as 'farmer' in 1841 but there is no further record of him or subsequent farming at Cherry Tree. The position of the old homestead is where other buildings have been erected at a later date, the earliest, the Coach House, being in the mid-nineteenth century. This suggests that sometime in the 1840s the farmhouse was demolished. Also, on the same site, two cottages (15 and 17 Datchworth Green) were built in the early 1930s.

Datchworth Green Farm (plot 424) was also known as Pages Farm for a time and was recorded as such on Bryant's map published in 1822. At a sale in 1832, it was in the occupation of Mr Thomas Page so could have been named after him or his family, but, in the sale details, it was given the formal name of 'Datchworth Green Farm' and the area of land was 47 acres. In the 1838 tithe award, Thomas Horne was the owner and it was occupied by Joseph Holdstock and his wife Pheba. There were 25 acres of the land in Datchworth, 6½ acres adjoining the homestead which is now called Hopkyns Hoo and the rest in the field which is now occupied by a rugby pitch south west of the sports clubhouse. The extra acreage in 1832 probably stretched into Welwyn parish and had hardly changed by 1851 when the total area was given as 50 acres. By then, it was in the charge of Pheba Holdstock and ten years later her daughter Sarah was the tenant with her brother John, who was a blacksmith.

Green End Farm (plot 373) was also known as Great Green End Farm. Earliest records go back to 1584 when it was sold by Edmund Bardolf to Edward Gable and was described as 'a cottage, orchard, garden, 3 crofts and a mead [meadow], 4 acres'. Four Acres was the name of the meadow behind plots 412 to 414. In 1767 it was purchased by Philip Thicknesse when it was listed as a 'messuage called Green End and 18 acres.....' along with the same description of land as that of nearly 200 years earlier. When Thicknesse sold the farm in 1777, it also consisted of an additional two farm cottages, one being plot 404. The other was next to Green End messuage but was no longer in existence when the 1838 tithe award was carried out. In 1838, the farm was owned by Jeremiah Gregory when the land was still as stated in earlier years and, as well as Four Acres, included the larger portion of the orchard beside plot 373 and fields to the north towards Church Field and west to Brookbridge Lane, amounting to a total of about 19 acres. By 1841, Jeremiah Gregory was listed as an annuitant [pensioner] and although his sons were all listed as agricultural labourers, there is no further mention of Green End Farm.

Bulls Green and Moat Farm (Figure 38)

Bulls Green Farm (plot 538) was owned by Thomas Campkin in 1838 and contained about 9 acres of fields in Datchworth along Bramfield Road. The parish boundary between Datchworth and Tewin passes through the middle of two of these fields, Wood Field and Haldings, so that in the tithe award the acreage of only 'part of' these two fields has been given. John Watson was the tenant in 1851, with a holding of 50 acres reduced to 20 by 1861. It was still a farm in 1911, with Ernest Welch and his wife in occupation with two gamekeepers as lodgers.

In 1838, Moat Farm (plot 459) belonged to William Campkin, son of Henry Campkin of Datchworthbury and contained about 8 acres in Datchworth between Govers Green and Bulls Green. The majority of the farm's land was in the parishes of Watton and Tewin. William Pennyfather, father of William Pennyfather of Coltsfoot, was listed as the farmer of Moat Farm in 1841 but died in the November of that year passing the tenancy to his nephew, Thomas Pennyfather, who was still there in 1851. At this time, the size of the farm was stated as 150 acres, most of which was in Watton parish. In 1861, given as 165 acres, it was taken over by Henry Campkin junior, another son of Henry Campkin, who eventually moved back to the Bury when his father died in 1864.

In 1877 Moat Farm was part of a deal made between Earl Cowper of Panshanger and Abel Smith, junior, of Woodhall Park that also involved Coltsfoot Farm. They exchanged about 250 acres of land of which Moat Farm was a part and it came into the hands of Abel Smith and still belongs to the family today.

Figure 38: Burnham Green and Bulls Green in the 19th century; numbers refer to 1829 references opposite (Designed by Charlotte Tebbutt)

Plot References to Figure 38

1829 Survey PLOT NUMBER & DESCRIPTION	1829 OCCUPIER	1838 Tithe Award DESCRIPTION	1838 OCCUPIER (OWNER)
BURNHAM GREEN		**BURNHAM GREEN**	
498 Public House (White Horse)	Thomas Lawrence	**Public House**	Edward Perry (John Marshall)
500 Poor House	Overseers of Datchworth	**Garden**	S. Sutton (S. Sutton)
501 Cottage	William Godfrey & Thomas Lawrence	**Four cottages**	William Hubbard & Others (Edward Terry)
504 Cottage	William Bennett & John Brownsell	**Cottage**	Widow Bennett (Execs of William Pennyfather)
504a Cottage	John Ewington	**Cottage**	John Ewington (Execs of William Pennyfather)
505 Garden (& cottage)	Daniel Bennett	**Cottage**	Daniel Bennett (Execs of William Pennyfather)
508 Homestead (Burnham Green Farm)	James Warner	**Homestead**	John Moore (Lawrence Lucas)
519 Cottage	Thomas Hills	**Cottage**	Benjamin Shadbolt (Lawrence Lucas)
520 Cottage	Daniel Warner	**Cottage**	George North (Lawrence Lucas)
522 Garden (site of poor house demolished *c.*1770)	William Shaw	**Garden**	John Ewington (Parish Officers)
523 Cottage	Thomas Maize	**Cottage**	Thomas Maize (Lawrence Lucas)
524 Cottage	Joseph Burton	**Cottage**	Joseph Burton (Lawrence Lucas)
531 Cottage (Club Cottage)	Robert Skegg & Henry Ray	**Cottages**	Robert Skeggs & James Shadbolt (Lawrence Lucas)
531a Cottage	William Shaw	**Cottages**	John Farr & Widow Shadbolt (Lawrence Lucas)
BULLS GREEN		**BULLS GREEN**	
459 Homestead (Moat Farm)	Jane Campkin	**Homestead**	William Campkin (William Campkin)
461 Cottage	William Darton	**Cottage**	William Darton (Richard Jepps)
463 Public House (The Horns)	Samuel Westwood	**Horns public house**	Joseph Lawrence (Messrs Lucas)
474 Homestead (Coltsfoot)	William Pennyfather	**Coltsfoot Homestead**	William Pennyfather (Abel Smith)
484 Homestead (Rats Castle Cottage)	William Pennyfather	**Cottage**	John Brownshill (Execs of William Pennyfather)
538 House (Bulls Green Farm)	Martha Shadbolt	**Homestead**	Thomas Campkin (Thomas Campkin)

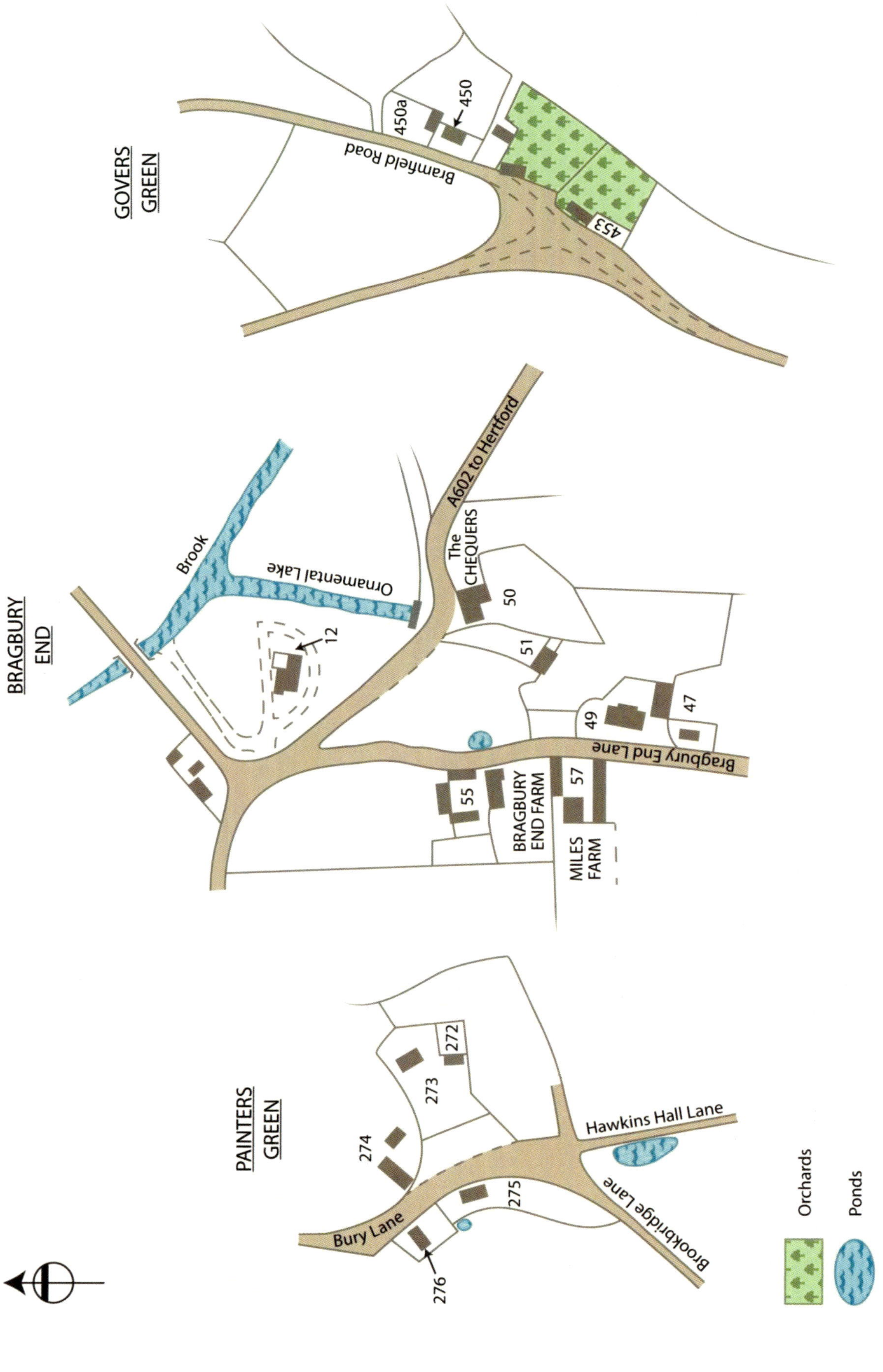

Figure 39: Painters Green, Bragbury End and Govers Green in the 19th century; numbers refer to the 1829 references opposite. (Designed by Charlotte Tebbutt)

Plot References to Figure 39

1829 Survey PLOT NUMBER & DESCRIPTION	1829 OCCUPIER	1838 Tithe Award DESCRIPTION	1838 OCCUPIER (OWNER)
PAINTERS GREEN		**PAINTERS GREEN**	
272 Cottage	Thomas North & Francis Brothers	**Cottages**	Thomas North & Francis Brothers (Samuel Heathcote)
273 Cottage	William Ipygrave	**Cottage**	William Epgrave (Elizabeth Brinkley)
274 Cottage (Innisfree)	John Shore	**Cottages**	John Shore (Samuel Heathcote)
275 Cottage (The Little House)	Joseph Harrington	**Cottage**	Charles Chappell (Joseph Harrington)
276 Cottage	John Bland & John Hale	**Cottages**	John Bland & Others (Abel Smith)
BRAGBURY END		**BRAGBURY END**	
12 Homestead (Bragbury House)	John Green	**House**	John Green (John Green)
47 Pasture	Robert Pallett	**Cottage**	George Nash (Abel Smith)
49 Homestead	Robert Pallett	**Old orchard**	William Chalkley (Abel Smith)
50 The Chequers P.H.	William Handley	**Public House**	Elizabeth Handley (Messrs Christie & Cathrow)
51 Cottage	Samuel Maynard	**Cottage**	Samuel Maynard (Samuel Maynard)
55 Homestead (Bragbury End Farm)	Robert Pallett	**Homestead**	William Chalkley (Abel Smith)
57 Miles Farm	Unoccupied	**Homestead**	William Chalkley (Abel Smith)
GOVERS GREEN		**GOVERS GREEN**	
450 Cottage	Benjamin Smith & Joseph Row	**Cottage**	B. Smith & John Row (Ben Smith)
450a Cottage	William Webb	**Cottage**	William Webb (Ben Smith)
453 Cottage	James Redd	**Cottage**	James Redd (William Campkin)

Coltsfoot Farm (Figure 38)

Coltsfoot Farm (plot 474) was another of Samuel Smith's acquisitions. Inherited by his son, Abel, it comprised about 170 acres in 1838. William Pennyfather was tenant followed by his son Daniel until sometime in the 1870s. In 1877 the farm changed ownership from Abel Smith, junior, to Earl Cowper of Panshanger. It may have been at this time that Philip Franklin became tenant who was still there in 1881 when the land holding was given as 282 acres. The Franklins remained tenants until 1919, when the Desboroughs of Panshanger sold Coltsfoot to Thomas Franklin. It remained in the Franklin family until 1994 when a substantial amount of the property was sold to Mr Goldsmith of Welch's Farm and so Coltsfoot's life as a farm came to an end.

Burnham Green Farm (Figure 38)

Burnham Green Farm (plot 508) consisted of land in Datchworth, Digswell, Tewin and Welwyn. The homestead itself was in Datchworth along Burnham Green Road. In 1838, it was owned by Lawrence Lucas and the tenant was John Moore. In 1861, the tenant was Richard Fensom when the farm consisted of 52 acres. The following year it was purchased by Earl Cowper who later leased it to Elizabeth Franklin of Coltsfoot Farm. Eventually it was sold as part of the 1919 sale along with Coltsfoot, mentioned above, when the Desboroughs of Panshanger sold all of the outlying parts of the Panshanger estate. Unfortunately the homestead, cottages and most of the farm buildings no longer remain but its pond that was within the grounds of the homestead is still evident.

Bragbury End Farm and Miles Farm (Figure 39)

Bragbury End Farm (plots 55 and 57) was initially part of the estate of Bragbury house, until 1717 when the farm was sold to Edward Harrison of Datchworthbury manor. In 1801, it was sold by Lord Townshend as a separate concern from Datchworthbury. By 1838, the farm was owned by Abel Smith, senior, whose tenant was William Chalkley. There were 292 acres, mostly in the northern section of both Sliding Dale and Datchworth Commons. Although the census returns for 1841 to 1861 include several entries for 'Braggers End', 'farmer' as an occupation does not appear. The first such mention is in 1871, when Noah Chalkley was farming 265 acres, which, according to *Kelly's Directory*, was at Bragbury End Farm. In 1881, he is mentioned again and living in a farmhouse not at Bragbury End but somewhere near Hooks Cross. In 1912 the farm was sold by auction and was described as having 247 acres in the parishes of Datchworth, Aston and Shephall, of which 235 were within Datchworth. It was purchased by Major Arthur Bonfoy St Leger, a major in the service of the King's Royal Rifle Corps and also a JP for Huntingdonshire. Samuel Wallace, farmer, took on the tenancy. The land continued as a farm until 1976 and after an application for a change of use was approved in February 1977, it became the Roger Harvey Garden Centre.

Raffin Green Farm

Raffin Green Farm is on the eastern edge of Datchworth parish and when it was bought by Samuel Smith in 1802, it had land in the adjoining parish of Aston including 9 acres of strips in 'Raffin Common Field', making a total of 246 acres. It also had parts of the farm that strayed in and out of Datchworth parish as a result of small changes in the parish boundary. At the time of the 1838 tithe award, Mrs Wadsworth was the tenant of the farm, which by then was a considerable size. She rented just over 138 acres from Abel Smith, senior, and a little over 216 acres from Elizabeth Barbara Bulwer Lytton, which was almost Mrs Lytton's entire holding in Datchworth. Taking land in Aston into account she must have had at least 450 acres.

Various members of the Wadsworth family kept about 250 acres of the original farm and it was this land that John Chapman took over sometime before 1871. The Chapmans were still there in 1911 but by 1914 the tenant was John Inns, whose brother, Jeremiah, had purchased the farm along with Datchworthbury from Abel Henry Smith in 1920. Both Inns brothers died in the mid 1940s and Charles Pearman purchased the freehold of the two farms in 1947. In 1951 Pearman sold the farmhouse to Jimmy and Jean Clarke with land amounting to 39 acres in the parish of Datchworth, including Great Bury Wood, which is about 13 acres. Their daughter and son-in-law, Felicity and James Chambers, live there now where they keep poultry and use some of the land for grazing.

Swangley's Farm

Until 1883, Swangley's Farm was in a detached part of Knebworth parish, as shown on the Datchworth 1839 tithe map (back endpaper), but on 24 March 1883, there was a boundary change that brought Swangley's Farm into the parish of Datchworth. So in 1871, when Charles Boyce was at the farm (of 411 acres at the time), he would have been a Knebworth parishioner until the change in 1883. In 1886, Samuel Wallace took over the farm, having recently moved from Scotland. He was still there in 1911 when another boundary changed occurred that transferred Swangley's Farm back to Knebworth. At that time, Wallace was living there with his wife, three of his five sons and his daughter. He also had two domestic servants and fourteen farm servants residing at the farm.

Residents' memories:

Reg Chalkley: Datchworth Green was used by various farmers for grazing. At Raffin Green Farm, at harvest time, each man kept his own barrel of beer in a shed. This made them late home, so instead the boys used have to take drink to their fathers at lunch time and after school. We boys also used to go scaring the crows in the fields with a sort of wooden clapper board.

Katie Russell: I moved to Datchworth in 1920 as a land girl, I only had my uniform, no civilian clothes. I lodged at Cherry Tree Farm and worked at Moat Farm [Bulls Green] for 25s a week, my rent was 12s. I remember that Nutcroft was a big poultry farm run by Mr Glover.

Arthur Arnold: The Turkey Farm site, before it was a turkey farm, had been cultivated and given special weed treatment, so that after two years it provided turf for Wembley Stadium and Tottenham Hotspurs Football Club. This really spoilt agricultural land by removal of topsoil.

'Peg' Newman: Directly after harvest, dung was spread on the land; very little artificial fertilizer was used, mostly it was natural manure. Dung heaps ten feet high known as 'dungles' were piled up at various points. There was one outside the cottages at the Post Office end of the green. Truckloads of horse manure were brought from London brewers who were still using horses. In the 1920s, plough horses were much in use rather than tractors. At one farm, for instance, there were six plough horses and one faulty tractor. Mr Little had seven or eight horses on his farm. Vincent's of Luton ran very well known horse sales. A good farm horse would fetch up to 140 guineas. You could see as many as 100 people at work in a field at once on such jobs as picking potatoes. For years I made twice weekly cart trips to Hertford with a load of potatoes. Gypsies were really useful at certain times and would be allowed to put their caravans on the fields as agreed by the farmer concerned.

Louie Cubbage: I remember steam ploughing beginning in the village.

Mr Tyler (Burnham Green): Farm labourers were paid 15s per week and cowman or foreman 16s. To get rid of men, they were taken to market and hired out to other farmers. Hay would be taken to London, the driver had to sit suspended on the side of his horse as he was not allowed on the hay itself because he would be too far from the horse. The harvest would be followed by 'harvest-home', that was when we farm labourers borrowed Palmer's cart and go to Hertford and the villages and tour around suppliers, seed merchants and farriers etc. to collect our annual perks – they were called largesse.

Phyllis Smalley (Burnham Green): There were four working farms in the village and I remember fetching the milk from Burgess's farm every day for 2½d a pint, I also fetched the milk for a lady who gave me a halfpenny for going. In the summer, we used to spend our time down the fields watching the corn being harvested. When the corn was being cut, rabbits and hares would run from the field, the farmers would shoot them and often he would give us one to take home for mum to make a rabbit stew. Many women were employed doing potato picking, then after the fields were cleared by the farmer 'us kids' all went prodding the field for any left. The men of the village all had allotments, as most families were large. The allotments were always referred to as 'garden field' and really came into their own during the 'dig-for-victory' campaign during the Second World War.

Mrs Payne: We got milk from Bury Farm at 1d a quart. You could also get cream, eggs and buttermilk.

Bernard Reynolds: In those days Stevenage and Welwyn Garden City were of no consequence to Datchworth as the new towns did not exist. Hertford was the major nearest town where the farmers would go and stop for a few drinks with the proceeds of their sales.

Jimmy Little: Back Lane was used for herding flocks of turkeys from Norfolk to London markets, taking a couple of months at a time.

Norman Pearman: There were no buildings between Church Cottage and Painters Green, where there were four cottages belonging to Deards and were occupied by Pearmans [no relation], Pitmans and Gibbs. Another two cottages there belonged to Raffin Green Farm.

7. Services: Gas, Electricity and Water

The chief sources of information for this chapter are the minutes from parish council meetings and the memories of previous village residents. Some of the early recollections of villagers can be found at the end of the chapter.

The supply of fresh water was an ongoing problem that was discussed at parish council meetings starting at the council's formation in 1894 and continuing for the next 25 years or so.

Gas

In the *London Gazette*, dated 24 November 1911, the Welwyn, Knebworth and District Gas Company was advised that, in order to gain authority to 'distribute, supply and sell gas' to Datchworth and ten other parishes, an application had to be made by 23 December 1911. This was granted and on 24 January 1912 Datchworth Parish Council was approached regarding a proposal for a gas supply, which was manufactured at Welwyn Gas Works. The council agreed to this and a gas holder was built on land at the junction of White Horse Lane and Robbery Bottom Lane. The holder was eventually removed and the land sold in 1954.

Initially the gas supply was limited to the area around Datchworth Green stopping short at the crossroads. Burnham Green also received gas from Welwyn but by a different route. Bulls Green did not have gas installed until the mid 1980s which, by that time, would have been natural gas. Some people had to pay to have gas piped to their houses and those who chose not to pay are still without a mains gas supply. Dwellings in Baines Lane and the surrounding area are also without gas.

Electricity

The supply of electricity to Datchworth parish was a gradual affair governed by the rate at which sub-stations were built, the first of which was in 1926 at Burnham Green on land rented from Edward Elsmore. In 1929 the centre of the parish benefited from the next supply that was on land owned by JW and J Inns at Painters Green. In 1930 Bulls Green was the third area to be supplied – this was from a station that was erected on land rented from Mary Howitt. A fourth sub-station was provided in 1934 at Govers Green. These installations continued to be built and by 1982 there were 18 sub-stations supplying the parish.

Street lighting was another matter that frequently appeared on the parish council agenda. The first light to be erected was a single gas lamp at Datchworth Green crossroads in 1937, which was eventually removed in June 1956. In January of that year there was a proposal that 28 lamp posts should be erected along Datchworth Green. A public meeting was held to discuss this matter and the scheme was met with unanimous disapproval, the view being that this sort of lighting was unnecessary in such a rural area and so the proposal was rejected. Since then, lighting has been included in the planning approval of some building schemes as a ruling from the district council.

Fresh Water

Until the early twentieth century Datchworth residents were still obtaining their water from dipping buckets into the ponds on the greens. There was endless trouble with impure water; waterborne diseases, such as diphtheria, were commonplace. Some more fortunate residents were able to obtain their water from wells; however, most of these were on private property.

A report in the *Hertford Mercury* in 1853, by the medical officer, describes the poor state of the water in Datchworth:

> There were no less that 76 'nuisances', dangerous to health in the single parish of Datchworth. The places where 'nuisances' existed were Bulls Green Lane, Burnham Green, Datchworth Green, Hooks Cross and Hollybush cottages. The nuisances include stagnant and offensive ditches, privies in a filthy state close to the cottages and pig sty's, heaps of dung, filth etc immediately adjoining the dwellings. There is everywhere a great want of well or spring water and the inhabitants generally used, for all purposes, pond water, which looked very bad, is extremely filthy and the drains run into it. There is scarcely a well in the parish, even the baker makes his bread of pond water, which he filtered before using it.

The medical officer went on to say that he had served several notices on Mr Jephson (steward to Abel Smith, senior) who had abated 'some' of the nuisances, and that he would now bring the problem to the knowledge of the landlords and serve notices to the other owners of the premises on which the nuisances existed.

Figure 40: The cast-iron standpipe on Datchworth Green with the whipping post, newly planted copper beech tree, blacksmith's forge and weather-boarded cottages in the background. (1935)

(Datchworth Museum)

Under the 1878 Public Health Act parishes were compelled to provide 'wholesome water within reasonable distance of every home'. This matter was raised at a parish council meeting in July 1895 following the condemnation by the Welwyn sanitary inspector of an open pond that served as the water supply for Burnham Green.

Although local residents had been told that the pond was not fit for use they carried on drawing water from it as it was 'that or go without'. The decision was made by the parish council to ask Mr Lawrance to clean all the ponds immediately. Councillors also discussed the options of having a well dug or having a pump and filter fixed to the ponds.

In 1897 a letter was sent to the district council asking the medical officer to produce a report on the state of the ponds in the parish. The medical officer, Dr Turner, duly replied that 'the water supply was insufficient in quantity and of doubtful quality and that steps should be taken to provide a wholesome supply'. He later outlined a scheme to the district council which would cost £1,500, whereby the water would be taken from a deep well at Burnham Green by an oil-engine driven pump and piped to most of the parish. This would serve some 127 houses, of which seven were large, four public houses and six farms. This scheme was rejected by the district council.

At a parish council meeting in October 1897 the rector, Andrew Amos, was criticised for misrepresenting the council at meetings in the district council offices. He spoke out against the scheme to use an oil-engine, as he believed the village could be sufficiently supplied at little expense by good rainwater tanks. Here is a section of Reverend Amos' speech to the district council:

> When nature supplied us with good rainwater from above it certainly seemed a waste of power to let it sink 100ft into the ground and then drawn it up again. Calcutta, Bombay and no doubt many other cities in the tropics were supplied with rainwater, collected in tanks during the rainy season. Rome we know was supplied with river water brought from great distances in aqueducts. They could not have read their bibles with any attention without noticing the frequent mention of cisterns and pools, what were these for but to collect rainwater? Jerusalem was mainly supplied with rainwater. What was good enough for King Solomon was quite good enough for the good people of Datchworth.

The parish council then suggested a wind-pump to raise water from the deep well (210ft) at Bury Farm and pipe it to Pound, Painters, Govers and Datchworth Greens, at an estimated cost of £839; this idea was dropped as well.

Further schemes were proposed and abandoned, but in the interim, in 1904 Reverend Amos arranged to lease the well at Bridgefoot from Abel Henry Smith for 1s per annum, for the use of the general public. The following report was put in the parish magazine:

> Reopening of the Bridgefoot well to those who are in need of drinking water, is we think a great gain to the village. It is hardly open to doubt that water from the open ponds was not very good, and various schemes were not beyond the paper stage. The opening of this well will at least give people the opportunity of getting good water; a chance they had not before.

In 1908, a report on the situation of the water supply in Datchworth was released by the water sub-committee of the district council. It states:

> Partly supplied from High Welwyn. The Holly Bushes: These cottages have rain water tanks; fairly good supply. Two cottages (owner Mr. Wallace) have theirs from pond passed thro filter. The houses about the school have their water from a well supplied from roofs of school and houses, also a deep well at the Bury Farm (a fair supply). The houses abutting on Green and rear thereto are supplied, some from tanks, others from ponds on Green. The principal one required to be cleaned out. In this parish a scheme to supply all the outlying parts would be a costly matter, but most of the worst supplied places might be much improved by the individual owners.

By 1909 Knebworth had piped water, so Datchworth parishioners living in the Station Road area (shortly to be annexed by Knebworth) were on a piped supply. Elsewhere in the parish, 29 houses were using piped water but over 100 were still using ponds or wells.

Finally, in November 1913, a resolution was passed by the district council for an agreement with Welwyn District Council, to supply water in bulk to Tewin and Datchworth (of between 8,000 and 14,000 gallons a day) at a price of 10d per 1,000 gallons for the first 8,000 and 3½d for every 500 over 8,000 gallons. In June 1914, a tender from William Willson & Co (Newcastle) Limited for £3,228 was accepted, of which Datchworth would pay £2,120. This brought water to stand pipes strategically located but not piped into houses.

Figure 41: The demolition of Burnham Green water tower in 2004. It was located where part of Tebbutt Court has now been built.

In March 1915 it was agreed that Bramfield would also be included in the scheme. The water would come via Harmer Green to a water tower at Burnham Green and then on to Bulls Green, Coltsfoot Farm, Datchworth Green, Painters Green and Hawkins Hall. Work was finally completed in November 1915 and a Mr Spooner was appointed the 'collector of water rates' at a salary of 4% of the annual amount collected.

Most houses now drew their water from the stand pipes which was considered a luxury compared to using the ponds and wells; however, the standpipes had the disadvantage of freezing during bad weather, despite attempts to lag them with straw and sacking.

The new water mains included a number of hydrants for fire fighting purposes. The necessary standpipes and hoses for them were purchased in 1923 at a cost of £21 18s 6d and council members were called upon as volunteer firemen. Nevertheless, when Hawkins Hall caught fire in March 1927, it was found that the hoses were not long enough and in any case the hydrant key was missing. After this unfortunate episode, the parish council resolved to form Datchworth's own fire brigade. The fire engine was initially housed in the barn at Buckridge's shop but when this was wanted for the manufacture of munitions, during the Second World War, it had to be moved. A timber extension was specially built onto the coach house across the road and this served as the new accommodation for the fire engine.

When the parish's second batch of council houses was built in Bury Lane in 1928, fresh water was piped to interior taps. This led to much disgruntlement amongst the tenants of the earlier council houses, built in 1921, as although the mains ran past their doors they were still using a standpipe and buckets.

In 1953, work started on a new water tower at Bulls Green to bring water from Aston. This was completed in 1956 and during the construction, the contractors were respectfully asked not to test pipes on Mondays when more water was used. The new supply was expected to save £800 in purchased water. This improvement led to the abandonment of the standpipes, the last of which, situated outside the Baptist chapel on Datchworth Green, was removed in 1964. Nearby, was the last cottage to be connected to the mains in early 1963.

Sewage

Methods of sewage disposal in the parish were primitive, there were external privies with buckets and some had cesspits. There are houses in Datchworth that still use the latter system today. In 1935, a tanker was used to pump out the cesspits and a rather crude sewage disposal plan was accomplished by running the sewage along trenches from which it soaked into the land.

Some more opulent houses had an 'earth closet'. These were situated in a separate building from the main house. It consisted of a metal container in which dry earth and ashes would be added to excreta having a deodorising effect. The mixture would eventually dry out and then be used as fertiliser. Raffin Green Farm still has an earth closet in its grounds and the eco-house (see Chapter 14) uses the earth closet system today.

After the Second World War there was a rapid increase in the number of houses being built in the village with attendant problems of the disposal of sewage and waste water. It was only then that action was taken to provide most of the parish with mains drainage, using pumping machinery that was installed near 62 Datchworth Green. In 1970 the drains were rearranged to carry the foul water directly to Woolmer Green and so the pumping station was no longer needed.

Residents' Memories

Mrs Payne: We could get lovely soft water from the well, near where the old manor house was. Granny used to fetch it in a little bucket. She used one of those wooden things to balance two small buckets. The school got water from a well behind the school house. My granny supplied the children's drinking water, from a bucket hung on the wall round the school. A coal cart came round with bags – 10d a hundredweight bag [50 kilos]. If they had any left over after a day's trip they let my granny have some for 9d a bag.

Mrs Joys: We got the water most days from the pond which used to be on the green. It had four or so steps down into it. We filled the bucket, let the sediment settle, strained it through a clean muslin cloth into a bowl to get rid of tadpoles and wriggly things, then boiled it and drank it. Dad went to the well or spring on a Saturday, if he wasn't working. He took the water barrow. The well was near houses in Brookbridge Lane at Bridgefoot and the spring was in the fields on the left of Watton Road, it was covered with a big wooden board to keep it clean.

Louie Cubbage: We had a well in our garden. Once I saw the cat fall in, but our neighbour got it out with a bucket. We had an earth toilet, one between two houses, which was emptied once or twice a year. I remember the day that Hawkins Hall farmhouse was burnt.

The fire broke out about 8 pm. A four-horse-drawn fire engine came from Welwyn, operated by hand. This was in 1927.

Mrs M. Nash: Water was taken from water buts, wells and ponds. I remember the water from the well at the rectory being drawn by a pony going round in circles.

Ethel Durston: For water we had a well in the garden for four houses. Later a tap was installed to be used by eight houses. The school toilets emptied into a pond. In 1912 the whole village caught diphtheria; all but our eldest sister were in the Isolation Hospital in Hertford.

Bernard Reynolds: We lived at Datchworth Green and used to collect water from the well and emptied our slop buckets in one of the ponds accepted by neighbours for that purpose. The smell was less noticeable in the winter when the water was frozen.

Reg Chalkley: Datchworth Green was used by various farmers for grazing. There were five ponds, one the drinking water and another, called 'puppy pond', was used by people to throw 'swill' etc. in. In about 1914 it was a very dry summer and water was rationed. Jim Draper took the water cart around the village, one bucket of water was allowed per house.

Mr Tyler (Burnham Green): Burnham Green was open common land with cattle, sheep, horses and geese grazing. It had seven ponds on or near it. One had a pump connected which was the only water supply until mains fitted around 1911. The water tower was built during the First World War.

Jimmy Little: When a fresh water supply came there were several large taps with lion faces. They were located by the chapel, by the Page's house [Tudor Lodge], near the whipping post, Bridgefoot [Brookbridge Lane] and Painters Green. They were apt to freeze up during the winter. In the main firewood had to be bought, not collected. Forresters controlled the woods and cutting of firewood, but rotten wood could sometimes be collected free.

Mrs Skeggs: Ovens were a rarity, we cooked over open fires, in pans and bowls.

Phyllis Smalley (Burnham Green): In 1927 we moved across the road to the new council houses in Welwyn parish, where there was cold running water and a bath. It had a big brick copper in the bathroom and a fire had to be lit to heat the water, which had to be bucketed from the bath for our washing and baths – Friday nights only in those days. Previous to this water was fetched from the water pump outside the row of farm houses. It had a large lion head and a handle was pumped up and down and the water came from the lion's mouth. In winter a fire was lit, usually of newspaper, to thaw the tap. Our house had gas lighting and a gas cooker with a 1d meter, but most of the cooking was done by a coal fire range in the living room. Electricity came much later.

8. Two World Wars

First World War

A total of 65 Datchworth men joined the forces in the First World War, out of the adult male population of about 150. According to a report in the *Hertfordshire Mercury* newspaper, Datchworth farmers struggled to find labour during the war. There was an expectation that women might be willing to help in the fields but this was not forthcoming. This added weight to the argument that some farmhands should be allowed exemption from conscription. Before a farm worker could be released from military service, his employer had to make an application in support of the worker at a military tribunal. There were examples of this procedure in Datchworth. On 29 July 1916 George Little of Moat Farm attended such a tribunal on behalf of Thomas Wade, a ploughman and at the same hearing there were four of Mr Pearman's labourers from Bury Farm. All five of the men were given temporary exemption.

Farmers were still hard-pressed to find enough labour, particularly at harvest time and it was then that they engaged the help of school children. The children also worked in the school garden that had been converted for food production. Details of the school in wartime are given in Chapter 13.

Datchworth parish council minutes have only one record directly relating to the First World War. In September 1914, in response to a scheme proposed by the County Relief Commissioners, the parish council formed a committee that consisted of George Little, Reverend Dyer and the district councillor to 'deal with any disasters arising in consequence of the war'. This committee would have been aware of the threat of attack by Zeppelins that regularly flew over Hertfordshire on their way to London. According to *Five Hide Village*, an anti-aircraft detachment had been set up opposite Shippin's Farm (now demolished) close to Datchworth's boundary and its presence with its searchlight and guns would have been known to the 'war committee'. This unit was too far away to have witnessed what happened on 13 October 1915. The pilot of a Zeppelin had lost his way and mistook the River Lea for the River Thames and bombed Hertford thinking that he was attacking London. This incident, though some way from Datchworth, must have been newsworthy at the time.

Other minutes throughout these years seemed rather trivial in comparison to national events and to a great extent it appeared that life carried on almost as normal in the village. Issues raised included the poor state of the roads, ponds and stiles, the council's fight to have a finger post erected at the crossroads and residents complaining about the postal delivery. The council campaigned successfully on behalf of the residents for a second delivery to be extended to outlying parts of the village including Raffin Green, Bulls Green and Coltsfoot. Villagers were also complaining that 'the postman was being late and not reaching Datchworth until 8.50am causing considerable inconvenience'. In response to this complaint the postmaster at Stevenage replied that 'as the postman's usual time for Datchworth is 8.40am I cannot see that there is much cause for concern therefore this matter will not be taken any further'.

Between the Wars

Smallholdings for ex-servicemen

Servicemen returning from the war were faced with the prospect of finding employment. As part of a movement entitled 'homes for heroes', the Land Settlement Act of 1919 required county councils to make land available for ex-servicemen. This Act was a development of the Smallholdings and Allotment Act of 1908 under which county councils had already bought or leased land to be used as smallholdings. The 1919 Act made the distinction that 'preference will, in the first instance, be given to those applicants who have served in H M Forces'.

By 1920, in Hertfordshire, 619 applications by ex-servicemen were made for smallholdings. Applicants had to attend an interview at which they were expected to verify their service record and assure the council of their ability to cultivate the land. A suitable rent would then be agreed for successful candidates.

Locally, in July 1919, at Burnham Green, just over 28 acres were bought by Hertfordshire County Council from Lord Desborough for £700. This land included what used to be Burnham Green Farm but by then was in the hands of Mrs Franklin of Coltsfoot Farm. Following the sale, Mrs Franklin was given until 29 September 1920 'to quit'. The first tenants were Messrs E and H W Shadbolt of Burnham Green.

Fields on the northern side of Burnham Green Road are part of this land and were subsequently bought by Leslie Goldsmith of Welch's Farm, who grew strawberries and other soft fruit for a time. It has changed hands again and is now used for grazing.

Another applicant for land was described as follows: 'Mr William Tyler of the Plough, Datchworth who has served in HM Forces, applied for 20 acres of land at Datchworth or at Burnham Green together with a cottage. The applicant is

30 years of age and is a grocer and pork butcher. He appears to have had previous experience with regard to the cultivation of land'. The sub-committee recommended that he should be provided with land in 'one the above districts'.

Sporting activities

Figure 42: The ladies cricket team and the old cricket pavilion in the background.

The cricket team was re-formed in 1921 and initially matches were played in a meadow behind Cherry Tree Hall. Eventually the venue for matches was transferred to Datchworth Green after a reasonable surface had been prepared. This involved a considerable amount of work as the ground was still used for grazing at the time.

Other sporting activities in the 1920s included quoits in the Tilbury orchard and at the Horns public house. Bowls and croquet were played on the rectory lawn and Datchworth formed its first football team in the 1920s.

The greatest achievement between the two wars was definitely the 'village green improvement scheme' in the mid 1930s. The parish council took on the challenge of, what was described as, 'the conversion of a green into a national fitness and recreational centre' and was thought to be the first project of its kind in the country. The scheme included the drainage and maintenance of the green, a children's playground and a small cricket pavilion on the south side of the green. Also in 1935 as part of the scheme, as well as in commemoration of King George V's Silver Jubilee, the avenue of cherry trees were planted along the green, grass tennis courts were laid and a copper beech tree was planted at the far east end of the green, in front of the coach house, which is still there today. On 18 May 1937 the new green was officially opened by Viscount Hampden, Lord Lieutenant of the County and President of the Village Green Improvement Society.

Figure 43: Cherry Tree Avenue, Datchworth Green (c.1960) (Datchworth Museum)

However, just as life was improving for the people of Datchworth, on 3 September 1939 Britain declared war once again.

Second World War

Unlike the First World War the Second World War apparently had more of an impact on Datchworth life, although business still went on almost as normal according to the parish council minutes. There was correspondence with the county council concerning its request to erect street lighting in the village, to which the parish council continued to object and correspondence regarding the district council's proposal to build 42 council properties in the village. The tennis club also carried on as usual, as seen from a number of letters that were written to the parish council between 1941 and 1943, in its quest to be allowed to use Datchworth Green courts on Sundays. The parish council unanimously refused this request 'so as not to disturb the peace and quiet', and even after a public meeting was held the decision remained unchanged.

Village parishioners became involved in the war effort in a number of ways. Some Datchworth men eligible for military service were exempted on the grounds that they were needed for agricultural work. School children were employed once again to work in the fields and in a number of other ways described in Chapter 13.

The Women's Institute worked on allotments as part of the 'dig for victory' campaign, but despite the reputed lack of food resources the parish council struggled to fill vacant allotments at Brookbridge Lane. At the start of the war there were six plots unused, of which four were eventually taken but in March 1941, the council resolved to ask James Little, farmer, to remove and plough the vacant plots.

The Women's Institute organised jam-making groups, knitting groups and cooking classes for the women of the village in order that 'the best be

Figure 44: Ladies at Pound House knitting for the forces in the 1940s.

made of the food resources available'. Knitted garments and clothing for troops were also made by a group of women that formed a Church Needlework Fund.

In addition Datchworth church formed a 'Youth Service Squad' that continued until Christmas 1941. It raised money for several organisations such as Beaverbrook's War Weapons Fund, Prisoners of War Fund, Comforts for the Forces Fund and the Red Cross.

Amy Buckridge's tea rooms at Datchworth crossroads were taken over by Nivea Cream (which later became Smith and Nephew Ltd), where adhesive dressings were put on reels. Later a lathe was installed for the making of a variety of different parts for munitions.

At Bulls Green garage, Leslie Howitt serviced War Department lorries and the RAF employed his engineering expertise to make bomb carriages for Lancaster bombers. One of these was used as a 'cart' at the garage for many years after the war. He also modified 200 American Thompson sub-machine guns (or 'Tommy' guns as they were called) to conform to army requirements for the Dieppe raid in 1942.

Datchworth Home Guard moved to Bulls Green garage in 1942, having previously been based at the village hall. Other places in the village were used as reporting points for the Home Guard such as the village hall, the cricket hut on Datchworth Green, 'Buckridge's barn' (behind the village shop) and the local public houses.

Figure 45: Datchworth Home Guard in the early 1940s with the old Datchworth Village Hall in the background.

As with the rest of the country, Datchworth had its Air Raid Precaution (ARP) organisation. The control centre was set up at Cherry Tree Hall. Under the direction of the ARP warden, the village was divided into sections each containing a volunteer fire fighting group. The warden also had to ensure that lights could not be seen from any of the houses at night. The following article was put in the parish magazine in September 1939 which illustrates the warden's frustration with the residents:

> A.R.P.
>
> I made an unofficial inspection of Datchworth during the recent Black-Out and my observation shows that the Village has still failed to become Raid conscious.
>
> People went to bed not troubling about the Black-Out because it took place after their usual bed time, but some forgot it when they had to get up to see to the baby or perhaps get a drink.
>
> Well these folks showed by their lights where Datchworth stood on the map, and if there had been any enemy about, Datchworth would have caught a packet.
>
> One house was completely lit up when I arrived, and to identify me the people turned on an outside light, which would have given them away to the enemy for miles.
>
> Will all you good folks please get into your heads that you may be responsible for the death of yourselves or your friends if an emergency comes and you do not screen your lights as required by the Home Office.
>
> WALLER CHURCH
>
> (Air Warden).

In 1938, a year before the war started, dug-out shelters were provided at the school. Then, in 1940, air raid shelters were built on Bulls Green and Burnham Green. Also, an emergency food store was kept at the Hornbeams on Burnham Green Road.

Although Datchworth suffered little from air raids, it proved to be in a vulnerable position towards the end of the war, when it was subjected to bombing by V1s and V2s. These unmanned devices were launched from the Dutch coast and directed towards London, but some deviated to the north of London and landed in Hertfordshire.

V1 flying bombs, otherwise called 'doodlebugs', flew at low altitude and had an audible approach, hence their other name of 'buzz bombs'. They

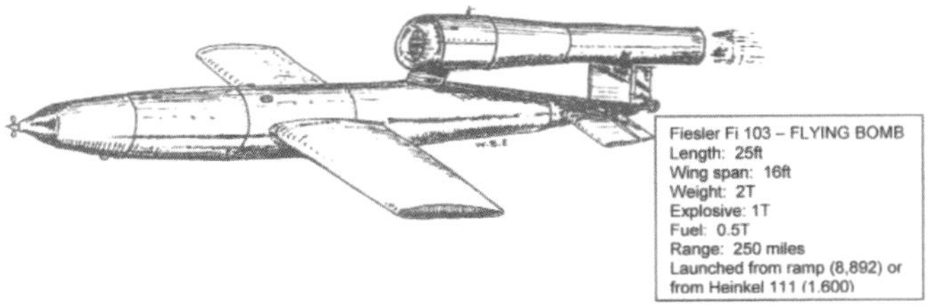

Figure 46: Sketch of a Flying Bomb (V1)
(Sketch by W.B. Emms)

continued on their crudely directed path until the engine stopped which was the warning to people in the area that the bomb was about to land. V2 bombs, however, were rockets (inter-continental ballistic missiles) that were propelled to a great height and descended at high speed giving no indication of their imminent arrival.

A V1 dropped on Bulls Green Nurseries on 23 August 1944 only 25 feet from the owner, Mrs Facey, as she stood in the conservatory at the back of her house. Fortunately she was unhurt. The damage caused to surrounding properties by this incident was considerable, including the entire west end of Rats Castle Cottage. A V2 rocket fell and exploded at Sedge Green behind Hopkyns I loo where damage was caused to the thatched roof and windows were broken at Cherry Tree Hall.

Mr Towler, headmaster of Datchworth school, recorded in his diary that on 8 January 1945 a V2 rocket fell on 'Fir Grove' in Swangleys Lane, just outside Datchworth parish. However, it was near enough to have caused damage to property in Baines Lane and to Jubilee Cottages in Bragbury End Lane and to have broken windows at Pound House, Bury Farm and the church.

The last but one V1 that fell on British soil landed on the sewage works near Mardleybury Farm, Woolmer Green, at about 9.00 am on 29 March 1945. The final one landed in open countryside at Iwade near Sittingbourne in Kent.

The War Memorial

The war memorial in the churchyard was designed, sculptured and erected by F Brook Hitch of Harleyford Road, Vauxhall. The funds were raised by local subscription including contributions from the Girl Guides and school children. It was consecrated on 4 October 1919 and on the same day, the first wreaths were laid by two young girls to commemorate Datchworth servicemen who lost their lives in battle. Dorothy Ware's wreath was from the parish and a second wreath from the school children was laid by Bertha Hornett. There are 17 names of Datchworth men inscribed on the memorial, thirteen from the First World War and a further four were added in 1945 after the Second World War. For more information see Appendix 1.

The names of men killed in the First World War were: Stanley William Arnold, John Bennett, Reginald Campkin, William Ellis, Charles William Francis, Thomas Griffin, William Hipgrave, John Lisles, Arthur Medhurst, Herbert Scales, Walter Shadbolt, Albert Tyler and Cecil Tyler.

The four names added after the Second World War were: Robert Francis Brownsell, Leonard Cranwell, Herbert Mark Miller and Roy Frederick Benson Temperley

Figure 47: War Memorial erected in 1919 (2013)

Residents' Memories

Phyllis Smalley (Burnham Green): When the war started in 1939, most of the young men of the village either joined the forces or were called up. I myself joined the ATS, stationed mostly on Salisbury Plain where I was a clerk and Physical Training instructor. I married and returned home in 1945. On Remembrance Sunday we walked to Tewin, then marched behind the British Legion to the service at the war memorial, which was observed on the 11th November at 11am and 1 minute's silence was kept.

Bernard Reynolds: During the war, my father had to be up at four in the morning to ride his bicycle 18 miles to work every day. On Saturdays there were dances in the village hall near Farrins slaughterhouse, often to a four piece band.

Bill Nash: During the First World War, I remember seeing a regiment of troops marching through Datchworth. Mounted troops were often going through the village.

9. Population, Employment and Local Business

Population

A useful source for estimating population figures can be found in diocesan visitation records, where the number of 'families' or houses is listed for each parish. Datchworth is fortunate because these survive for 1563 and for the first quarter of the eighteenth century and are published in *Hertfordshire Population Statistics 1563-1801* by Lionel Munby. A population estimate may be calculated by using a recommended multiplier of 4.75 which, when applied to 34 families in 1563, gives a population of about 162. In the first quarter of the eighteenth century, the number of families was about 60, giving a population of about 285.

Following the passing of the Population Act of 1800, the first census took place in 1801 and has continued at ten year intervals ever since. Initially, in 1801, the details obtained were used only for a summary of the population in the local area and then, unfortunately, all but a few were destroyed. In preparation for the 1841 census, the Population Act of 1840 was passed that enabled changes to be made. Each person had to give their name, age, sex, occupation and place of birth and a Registrar General was appointed to be responsible for the administration of the census.

The 1800 Act laid down that the 'answers are to be returned in writing by the rector or other officiating minister with the help of the overseers of the poor'. On 10 March 1801, the first census would have been carried out in Datchworth by the Reverend Charles Johnson with the help of William Field and John Rawley, the overseers.

The opening of Knebworth railway station in 1884 was accompanied by a rapid growth in the population of Datchworth, mainly in that area of the parish, increasing by nearly 57% in just over 25 years. However, just two days before the 1911 census, a boundary change removed part of Knebworth from the parish which had the effect of almost halving Datchworth's population from 981 to 550. It can be seen from the table below, that the parish suffered six changes to its boundary, the most recent being on 1 April 1990 when part of Burnham Green was placed in Tewin. This alteration reduced the population from approximately 1,655 to 1,494, about the same as it had been in 1965.

The number of houses in 1801 was 83, in 1911 this had risen to 127 and in 2011 the figure was 655. The population figures for these years were 410, 550 and 1610 respectively giving an average family size in Datchworth of 4.94 in 1801, 4.33 in 1911 and 2.46 in 2011.

The population figures for Datchworth are:

Year	Population
1801	410
1811	447
1821	494
Boundary change moving a large area of Knebworth to Datchworth	
1831	593
1841	581
1851	648
1861	635
1871	606
1881	626
Boundary change moving 'Knebworth detached' (Swangley's Farm and cottages) to Datchworth.*	
1891	672
1901	676
1911	981
Boundary change moving a large area from Datchworth to Knebworth including Swangley's Farm.	

Year	Population
1911	550
1921	577
1931	702
1941	War restrictions
1951	978
Boundary change moving large areas of Hooks Cross and Bragbury End to Aston and Stevenage	
1961	1220
Boundary change moving Burnham Green village hall area from Tewin to Datchworth	
1971	1605
1981	1655
Boundary change moving part of the south side of Burnham Green Road to Tewin	
1991	1494
2001	1626
2011	1610

* 'Knebworth detached' was an area within Knebworth parish surrounded by land in Datchworth parish as shown on the map on the back endpaper.

Employment

The 1841 census was the first of the detailed records collected and formed the basis of the method used today. This census and ones that followed have proved to be a valuable source of information which, in this chapter, has been applied to occupations and, in some cases, to the names of the parishioners shown therein.

Census data for any particular year is made public after 100 years and it is possible to view the returns on historical record websites.

The following table lists employment in Datchworth from the eight available censuses (1841 – 1911):

	1841	**1851**	**1861**	**1871**	**1881**	**1891**	**1901**	**1911**
AGRICULTURE								
Bailiff	-	-	-	-	-	1	1	2
Cowman	-	-	-	-	-	-	6	7
Chaff cutter	-	-	1	-	1	-	-	-
Dairy Worker	-	-	-	-	-	-	-	5
Farmer	13	13	11	6	7	5	7	7
Gamekeeper	2	2	3	2	3	3	2	2
Hay binder/Dealer	-	1	-	1	1	9	2	-
Horse keeper/Groom	-	-	2	-	-	3	14	9
Hurdle maker	-	1	1	1	2	-	2	-
Labourer	117	147	146	107	113	124	70	74
Pig Dealer	-	-	-	-	1	-	-	-
Poultry Dealer	-	-	-	1	1	-	-	2
Sausage skin worker	-	-	-	-	-	-	-	3
Shepherd	2	2	5	2	-	2	2	1
Traction Engine Driver	-	-	-	-	1	3	3	3
Wheelwright	1	1	2	1	-	1	-	2
Woodman	-	-	-	-	3	1	4	3
BUILDING TRADE								
Builder/Bricklayer	1	-	5	3	3	2	4	5
Carpenter	9	9	4	3	3	4	6	2
Gravel Pit worker	-	-	-	-	-	-	16	1
Labourer	-	3	-	6	4	4	9	6
Painter	1	-	-	-	-	-	1	-
Sawyer	-	1	3	2	4	4	5	1
Timber Merchant	-	-	-	1	1	1	5	-
Thatcher	-	3	1	2	4	4	2	-
SERVICE INDUSTRY								
Baker	-	1	2	1	-	-	1	-
Blacksmith	1	5	4	2	2	1	4	2
Butcher	-	2	2	2	2	1	6	4
Carrier/Carter/Carman	2	2	2	-	4	4	10	7
Coal Merchant	-	-	-	-	-	-	1	3
Draper	1	1	1	1	-	-	1	-
Higgler	-	-	2	2	1	-	-	-
General Dealer	-	-	-	1	2	1	2	2
Grocer/Costermonger	-	2	4	2	2	5	2	2
Land Agent	-	-	-	-	-	1	-	-
Laundress/Washerwoman	-	-	3	4	3	4	6	3
Lay Reader (C of E)	-	-	-	-	-	1	-	1
Messenger	-	-	-	-	-	2	-	-
Milkman	-	-	-	-	-	-	1	1
Nurse	-	-	2	3	1	1	1	1
Parish Clerk (Church)	1	-	1	1	1	1	1	1
Police Constable	-	1	1	1	1	1	1	2
Publican/bar worker	2	4	4	6	8	5	4	7
Railway worker	-	7	4	6	5	7	4	2
Rector/Clergymen	1	1	1	1	1	1	1	2

	1841	1851	1861	1871	1881	1891	1901	1911
Roadman	-	-	-	-	2	-	4	2
Schoolmaster	-	-	-	-	-	1	1	1
Schoolmistress	-	1	1	2	1	2	-	-
Shop Assistant	-	-	-	-	3	1	3	-
Teacher	-	-	-	2	3	1	1	-
Warehouseman	-	-	-	-	-	1	-	-
SERVANTS ETC.								
Butler	-	-	1	1	1	-	-	-
Charwoman	-	4	8	1	3	2	-	2
Coachman/Stable hand	-	2	-	-	1	-	3	4
Garage Keeper	-	-	1	-	-	-	-	-
Gardener	1	2	1	3	6	7	10	15
Housekeeper	1	5	2	1	1	1	2	1
Servants, Cooks etc.	9	15	24	22	19	26	15	17
OTHER INDUSTRIES								
Bookkeeper/Clerk	-	-	1	-	-	-	4	5
Barrister	-	-	-	-	-	1	-	-
Basket maker	-	-	-	1	1	-	-	-
Brick maker	-	-	-	-	-	-	3	1
Coach builder	-	-	-	-	-	-	5	1
Dressmaker/Seamstress	-	4	5	4	3	3	6	-
Electrical Engineer	-	-	-	-	-	-	1	1
Flower Manufacturer	-	-	-	-	-	-	1	-
Hatter/Milliner	-	-	1	-	-	1	-	1
Lace maker	-	1	-	-	-	-	-	-
Leatherman	-	-	-	-	-	-	1	-
Lime Burner	-	-	-	-	-	1	-	-
Outfitter	-	-	-	-	-	1	-	1
Rifle Butt Maker	-	-	-	-	1	-	-	-
Sieve maker	-	1	-	1	-	-	-	-
Shoe maker	1	1	1	1	1	-	1	1
Straw plaiter	-	9	1	2	-	-	-	-
OTHERS								
Aged	1	-	1	-	-	4	-	-
Idiots	-	-	2	-	-	-	-	1
Infirm	1	-	6	-	-	1	1	2
Independents	3	-	-	-	-	7	-	-
Land proprietor/ess	-	1	-	2	-	-	-	-
Pauper	7	11	-	18	-	-	-	-
Scholars	157	145	157	143	188	170	168	97
Soldier	-	-	-	-	1	-	7	1
Vagrant	6	-	-	-	-	-	-	-

When the 1911 census was taken, many women across the United Kingdom refused to be counted in response to the government's failure to grant the vote to women. The exact number who boycotted the census nationally is not known but it has been estimated at several thousand. However, looking at the Datchworth census it would seem that the women did not take part in this protest because in cases where a woman was apparently missing from the census, it was usually noted that the husband was widowed.

It can be seen from the data in the table that the main employment in Datchworth in the nineteenth century was related to the farming industry, which has been covered in Chapter 6 and it is noticeable in the censuses how many of the inhabitants were not Datchworth people. Prior to the introduction of the railway and motor vehicles, it was usual for workmen and servants to live on or near the farms where they worked. Most farmers gave lodgings to at least some of their workers, for example, in 1861 Henry Campkin of Datchworth Bury gave boarding to his shepherd boy, William Smith from Bramfield and one of his farm labourers, James Goodship from Welwyn. In 1871 he had two servants residing at the Bury, Emma Wright from Rushden, Northamptonshire and Emily Blandford from Potters Bar. In 1901, Samuel Wallace, from Scotland, owned Swangley's Farm where he lived with his wife and six children and gave lodgings to two domestic servants and five labourers. As well as Hertfordshire, these servants came from various parts of the country including Suffolk, Lincolnshire, Essex and London. In addition to board being provided in the main house, of course, many other labourers were given accommodation in farm cottages.

From 1891 onwards (since Knebworth railway station was built in 1884), it became more common for families from various parts of the country to settle in Datchworth. An example is that of the constable in 1891, Arthur Pumer, from Bedfordshire and his wife from Oxfordshire with their two children who were born in Wareside. Another example is that of the Reverend Andrew Amos from London who, in 1901, lived at the Rectory with his wife, Susan from Ireland, with their daughter who was born in London and son born in Datchworth.

Two of the gamekeepers, in 1881, Joseph Howe and George Turner, lived with their families in Keepers Cottage, Bragbury Lane. At that time the house was two dwellings and both were named Keepers House.

The ancient trade of hurdle-making was still in existence in Datchworth until the end of the nineteenth century. Wattle hurdles were usually woven out of hazel, ash or willow, and used as sheep enclosures. The hurdle maker listed in 1851 is William Wray who lived in a cottage at Govers Green. By 1871 his son, also William, was in the same trade and he was followed by his step-son, Harry Turner. Both men were still listed as hurdle-makers in 1901. But by 1911, William was listed as a 'finishing faller', an activity related to felling trees so probably working for Lawrance's timber merchants at Datchworth Green and Harry was no longer in the village.

The two higglers in 1861 were both female, Ann North, aged 42 who lived at Burnham Green with her two illegitimate sons and 79 year old Mary Brand at Painters Green. However, in 1871, the two higglers were men, father and son, both by the name of Daniel Shadbolt of Burnham Green. The higgler in 1881 was 58 year old Hannah Shadbolt. Higglers were licensed travelling dealers that sold small items, often dairy products, poultry and game, whereas a costermonger was a trader, usually selling fruit and vegetables, from a barrow.

There were six laundry workers listed in 1901. Four of these lived at 'Laundry Cottage', Bragbury Lane, where the head of the house was Abraham Bradley from Ireland, a retired army pensioner. His wife, Ellen from North Mimms, was a laundress and their two daughters, both born in Hampshire, were laundry maids. They also had a servant laundry maid living with them, Jane Newell from New Barnet.

The subject of police constables has been discussed in Chapter 5 but it is worth mentioning that the second constable recorded on the 1911 census, was a retired officer, Charles Simmons, who was residing at the Chequers public house, Bragbury End, where his mother was the landlord.

By present day standards, some houses were overcrowded and lodgers were still to be found in several cottages at the turn of the century, although in reduced numbers. In 1861, Daniel Shadbolt and his wife, Alice, who lived at Burnham Green, had eleven children, ranging from 1 to 20 years old. The 1911 census shows that the Hipgrave family who lived at Datchworth Green had 11 in the family, Harry Hipgrave, his wife, five daughters and four sons. Another family with William Tyler as head of the household, lived at Bulls Green, where there were 11 residents: himself, his wife, six sons, two daughters and a lodger. However, despite the odd few overcrowded houses, by 1911 many households were similar to those of today with two to four people per household.

The statistics in the table above for 'scholars' are children aged 5 to 13 years; they left school at 14. In the earlier years, some of these may not have attended school as it was not compulsory and a fee was charged. Many families would have sent their children out to work or kept them at home to help with household chores.

It wasn't until 1880 when an amendment to the Elementary Education Act 1870 (EEA) was passed, that 'compulsory' education was introduced for all children aged five to ten years (raised to 11 in 1893 then again in 1899 to 13 years), in order to stop child labour. The EEA 1880, passed the responsibility of attendance from parents and schools to the local authority, which included the provision for the making of byelaws to enforce attendance. The Act also penalised employers who employed a child aged under 13 who did not hold a certificate of achievement that ensured that a particular 'educational standard' had been reached.

In the EEA 1891 free education was provided for all children, which was funded by the government at the rate of 10s a year per child. The figures for scholars in the earlier years may be unreliable but, after the implementation of the Acts above, it can be assumed that the figures for the 1891, 1901 and 1911 census returns are more likely to be accurate. It should be remembered, however, that these children were split between three schools, Knebworth, Datchworth and Burnham Green. There is a noticeable drop in the number of scholars in 1911 after the boundary change that removed part of Knebworth out of Datchworth.

Local business

Alongside the information obtained in the census, another source where business and trade data can be obtained is in the collection of *Kelly's Directory of Hertfordshire,* which are available at the library. In the 1937 edition of *Kelly's Directory*, Datchworth has the following businesses listed:

Philip George Aris	-	Refreshment rooms, Club Cottage, Burnham Green Lane
Amy Buckridge	-	Refreshment rooms, Datchworth Green
S. Deards & Co	-	Haulage contractors, Hollybush Lane
Francis Deards	-	Market Gardener, Hollybush Lane
Ernest Farrin	-	Butcher, Datchworth Green
David Gaddie	-	Vermin destroyer, Datchworth Green
Herbert Drew	-	Poultry farmer, Inchkeith, Bulls Green
Lionel Richard Foreman	-	Nurseryman, Eyrefield, Bulls Green
Christopher Giddens	-	Builder, Hill View, Bulls Green
George Harradence	-	Joiner, Church Cottage, Datchworth
Mary Hornet	-	Confectioner
John Inns	-	Gamekeeper, Raffin Green
Mark Miller	-	Blacksmith, Datchworth Green
Peter Rudolph Mosdal	-	Skin merchant, Burnham Green
Tyler Bros.	-	Well sinkers, Burnham Green
Peter Burgess	-	Coal merchant
Sidney Good	-	Grocer and post office, Burnham Green
Leslie Howitt	-	Motor garage, Bulls Green
William Barringer	-	Grocer and post office, Datchworth Green

Philip Aris, who ran the refreshment rooms at Club Cottage, was obviously public spirited and generous. After his death he left in his will, dated 1974, a trust fund, which, at a later date, was to be distributed between the Oxfam charity and Datchworth Parish Council, specifically to be used for a children's playground at Burnham Green.

Lawrance's builders and timber merchants

One business that does not appear in *Kelly's Directory* for 1937 is that of Lawrance's building firm, though it is found in many previous editions. An early reference to the name 'Lawrance' occurred in 1638, when the family were first establishing themselves in Datchworth and they are found in the parish registers at Datchworth and Bramfield. *Kelly's Directory* for 1878 states that the Three Horseshoes (now the Tilbury) on Datchworth Green was kept by one of the William Lawrances, also listed as a builder and smith.

By the late nineteenth century, the Lawrance family had expanded their building company to include not only builders but carpenters, timber merchants and brick makers; the brick kiln was along Back Lane. In the early twentieth century, the family also became gravel merchants thus adding to their comprehensive list of businesses. The family's extensive timber and building business took up land on both sides of Datchworth Green. On the north side, this stretched from near the crossroads to Pettits, which was owned by the Lawrances at this time, where open-sided sheds were used for drying planks that had been made from freshly cut timber. Their saw-mill was on the south side of the green where cottages number 15 and 17 now stand. After the death of Frederick Lawrance in 1930, his widow, Margaret, sold the family's assets and this marked the end of the Lawrances' 300 years as tradesmen in Datchworth.

Figure 48: Frederick Lawrance's first steam wagon. Dobbie Nash was its driver. (c.1926) (Datchworth Museum)

Figure 49: East end of Datchworth Green showing one of the ponds – the supply of drinking water – and a pile of the Lawrance's logs. (c.1905) (Hertford Museum: HETFM 2831.779)

Farrin's butchers and slaughterhouse

Figure 50: Inside Farrin's barn showing the cool room and meat hooks where carcasses were hung.

Johnson Farrin was born in Datchworth in 1846 but from the age of five was brought up by his grandparents in the Red Lion, Welwyn, where his grandfather was listed as a 'victualler and farmer of 160 acres'. In 1877 Johnson married and returned to Datchworth to the house at the bottom of Rectory Lane, now known as 'Farrins', after the family name. Johnson and his wife, Amelia, had six children, all of whom at some point worked in the family business, the boys as butchers and the girls as bookkeepers. Their eldest son, Ernest, listed as a 'castrator' in the 1901 census, moved to Knebworth when he married but returned to Datchworth after the death of Johnson in 1917 to take over the family business.

The slaughterhouse was in a barn in the field next to the property. The barn adjacent to the road at Datchworth Green served as the butchers shop on the east side and a cool room for the storage of the meat on the west, where meat hooks still line the walls today.

In 1920 Ernest Farrin purchased the freehold of the 'dwelling house, shop, slaughterhouse and outbuildings' with 20½ acres of land from Abel Henry Smith for £1,374, with the help of a mortgage from Robert Wallace. In the early 1930s Ernest sold the property to Robert Wallace thus discharging the mortgage, however, Ernest and his family remained as tenants. At the end of the Second World War, in 1946, part of the land was sold for development, which is where Wheatcotes is now. Ernest continued running the butchery business until his death in 1953, which occurred less than two months after he had lost his wife, Susan, and, not having a son to continue the business, the butcher's and slaughterhouse came to an end.

Bulls Green garage

Bulls Green garage, or Alpha garage as it was first known, began to operate in 1925, long after the first motor car was registered in Datchworth on 12 September 1906. It was a dark green, two-seater, six-horse power Rover that belonged to Ronald Campkin, son of Thomas Campkin of Broomhall Farm at Watton-at-Stone.

Figure 51: Bulls Green garage (1932) with Leslie Howitt and 4 year old Claude Howitt. The bungalow in the rear was also built by Leslie Howitt and was called Notre Gite.

Figure 52: Bulls Green garage (late 1950s) with the new dome shaped extension added. Claude's Austin 7 on the left is still in his daughter's ownership today.

The garage was the inspiration of Harry Howitt and his son, Leslie. Harry left his gold, silver and jewellery workshop in London to live at Alpha Cottage in Coltsfoot Lane (now the White House). He also bought seven acres of land and took over the livery stables at the Horns public house. In 1910, having caught malaria, Harry's son, Leslie, returned to England from South Africa where he worked on a tobacco plantation. He moved to the village and purchased part of Bulls Green Farm and land elsewhere in the area.

In 1914, Harry bought his first car, a Ford Model 'T', which Leslie drove for hire and shortly afterwards Leslie acquired a Ford 'T' 4-tonner. Before long they both bought a second-hand Fordson tractor. Traditional local farmers were sceptical of this acquisition until the Howitts demonstrated the tractor's versatility. It could double plough as well as any two-shire team, and with the addition of headlamps it could plough after dark. Before long, other local farmers purchased tractors, which from time to time were in need of repair and Leslie, with his mechanical skills, offered a service for the repair and maintenance of tractors as well as cars. In 1923 the Howitts were selling cans of petrol at 10d per gallon and the garage became a full time concern in 1925 after the livery stables had been suitably adapted. The first petrol pumps were installed in 1927 sponsored by the Anglo Oil Company.

Harry and Leslie then decided to set up a taxi service that used Studebakers, Buicks and Hudsons, all large American limousines. Unfortunately Harry died in 1927 but Leslie continued to run and expand the business. Electricity was supplied to Bulls Green in 1930 and Leslie was quick to take advantage and immediately installed an electric petrol pump, a car washer and a hydraulic lift.

Later, Claude Howitt, Leslie's son, joined the family business and, having eventually taken it over, continued to run it until his retirement in 1989. Claude then sold the garage to the Knight brothers, Dave and Chris, who also owned Tewin garage. During their ownership, new fire safety regulations were introduced which meant that the garage could no longer sell petrol and this resulted in a serious loss of income, causing the garage to be no longer financially viable. The brothers decided to sell the site and in 1992 it was bought by a property developer who subsequently built the two houses that are there today, numbers 2 and 4 Coltsfoot Lane.

Post offices

There was one development in the nineteenth century which had a positive impact on the whole country. This was the re-formation of the postal system and introduction of the prepaid penny post by Rowland Hill in 1840, making postal communication more affordable. Before this development, post was paid by the recipient and the charge could be quite high, which many poor people could not afford and would be forced to refuse to accept their post.

Prior to 1840 Datchworth was served by the posting house at the White Swan public house, Stevenage, from where mail brought by carriers, like William Page of Datchworth Green, would be taken to other posting houses and transferred according to its ultimate destination.

The first 'local' letter box was erected in 1886 at Woolmer Green. Datchworth had its first letter box by 1908, which was located outside the old Rectory in Rectory Lane. By 1910 letter boxes had been installed at Hooks Cross, Bragbury End

Figure 53: Burnham Green post office (c.1935) (Datchworth Museum)

and Burnham Green; these had a Sunday collection but collections for the one at Datchworth remained on weekdays only.

The first government post office for our parish was also in Stevenage and the first mention of a sub-post office in Datchworth is in 1862, when William Shippin's grocery shop became a collecting office for letters only. The shop was in the Grade II listed seventeenth century building, next door to the Plough public house and has recently been converted into a separate cottage and tea rooms. Prior to the 1970s it had a dominant T-shaped chimney stack built of old 'thin' bricks which was removed when central heating was installed. Attached to this building, on the Bramfield Road side, was a very small lean-to type cottage which was demolished in 1937.

William Shippin was the son of farmer William Shippin at Hawkins Hall Farm and, from at least 1871, was listed as beer retailer in the Plough in addition to running the grocer's shop and post office. By 1899 he was authorised to issue postal orders but could not pay out against them. Before this, the nearest postal order and telegraph offices were in Watton and Knebworth. In 1902 William's widow, Mary Ann, succeeded him; she continued trading as a 'beer retailer, shop keeper and post mistress at Datchworth Green'. Mrs Shippin continued as sub-postmistress until 1910, when Henry Barringer, a draper, took over the premises.

Henry Barringer continued post office duties at Datchworth Green until 1929, but since 1917 his sub-office had been supplemented by two others in the parish. One was at the Three Horseshoes public house, Hooks Cross, where Charles Francis was sub-postmaster and the other was located at the White Horse public house at Burnham Green under William Francis.

A little later the post office at Burnham Green was moved to a wooden hut-like building that was located on the site of what is now number 1 Orchard Road. In 1933 Sidney George Wood was postmaster. It was demolished in April 1970 after the post office function transferred to George Tebbutt's shop in 1966. Tebbutt's ceased offering post office services in 2011.

At Datchworth Green, Henry Barringer was succeeded by William Barringer in 1929. In 1933 it is recorded that his shop was also a telephone call office.

During the Second World War, the sub-postmaster at Datchworth Green is listed as Henry Barringer; presumably William had enlisted for service. Henry's successors were:

1949 - 1965	Mr F. A. Seabrook
1965 - 1972	Mr H. W. Ashley
1972 - 1982	Mr F. L. Everatt
1982 - 2004	Mr Derek Scott
2004 - 2009	Ms Sharon Carter

Figure 54: Datchworth shop and post office (c.1936)

Figure 55: The Old Post Office Tea Rooms (2012)

Datchworth finally lost its post office in 2009 when Sharon Carter ceased trading in this capacity and the shop was converted into a tea room called 'The Old Post Office Tea Rooms'. This marks the return to Datchworth of a tea room to replace the one lost in the 1960s when the popular and widely known tea room that used to be located in the building across the road, now occupied by Datchworth Village Stores, closed down.

General stores

This building that now houses Datchworth Village Stores was built in 1929 by Frederick Lawrance, builder, who purchased the land on which it stands, formally a builder's yard, from Louisa Ewer for the sum of £10. Frederick Lawrance died the following year and in January 1931, Frederick's widow, Margaret, sold the shop, along with the bungalow and land to the west (now number 4 Datchworth Green and the Plough car park) to Reginald Steeds for £495.

After its construction the shop was occupied by Mr Charge, until the building and adjoining bungalow were again sold in 1932 for £500 to Gilbert Buckridge who added a café to the shop. It became a popular rendezvous for cycling clubs, with the distinctive CTC sign displayed over the front door and it was by no means unusual for the café, shop, bungalow and its garden to be full of cyclists at the weekend and on bank holidays.

Gilbert died in 1937, leaving the property to his wife, Amy. When she died in 1951, her son Joe continued to live in the bungalow and run the café and shop. During the Second World War, the shop was taken over by Nivea Cream where adhesive dressings were put onto reels. The building opened as a café again in 1947 and eventually, after a succession of proprietors, it turned back into a shop in the 1960s which has continued to be an essential part of village life ever since. Its current proprietors, Pinky and Pardy Kumar, first occupied the shop in 1989.

Joe Buckeridge died in 2001 and eventually, in 2004, the two properties were sold as separate lots by sealed auction, at which point Pinky and Pardy Kumar purchased the freehold of the lot which included the shop.

They sold the business and freehold in 2005 and the village was very sad to see them go. However, just eighteen months later, upon hearing that under its new owners the business was struggling, they bought the shop back again. The business has once again flourished under their popular ownership and they have recently started selling newspapers and magazines following the demise of the post office and newsagent business across the road.

The village store at Burnham Green originally started as a dairy and electrical repair business by George Tebbutt and his wife Daphne in 1948. It was initially established from a hut in their back garden but in 1964 the front room of their house was turned into a shop. The dairy business was sold off and the business was developed as a combination of electrical goods and repairs, general store, newsagent's and greengrocer's. In 1966 the post office business was also added.

In 1984 the premises were enlarged further so that the business occupied all three cottages, 102, 104 and 106 Burnham Green Road. The family

Figure 56: The Café & Tea Rooms, Datchworth Green. Gilbert & Amy Buckridge with Dollar the dog. (1933) (Datchworth Museum)

Figure 57: Datchworth Village Stores – Pardy Kumar (2012)

initially lived behind and above the shop but in 1966 they moved to properties at the newly built Burnham Close.

George retired just before the 40th anniversary of the business in 1988 and handed the business over to three of his six sons, Ian, Richard and Robert. Daphne and the wives of Richard and Robert continued to run the shop and post office, while the men concentrated on the electrical side of the business. Sadly George Tebbutt died the following year in 1989 after a long illness.

As the Tebbutt sons neared retirement age, they developed a plan to sell the shop. Number 102 Burnham Green Road was extended back and refurbished to make a deeper shop with a single frontage and flat above, whilst numbers 104 and 106 were converted back to cottages. It was in this form that the shop was eventually sold to the present owners, who retained the established trading name of Tebbutt's. The shop is now a newsagent and general store, the post office and electrical business having been discontinued.

Figure 58: Tebbutt's - when the shop occupied the ground floor of all three cottages. The water tower can be seen in the background that was demolished in 2004. (2000)

Sausage skin factory

In 1964 George Tebbutt bought the site to the rear of the above mentioned shop. The history behind this purchase is unusual. From the beginning of the century until 1964 the site was occupied by a sausage skin factory. The business was set up by a German man by the name of Fritz Jung. Fritz moved to Burnham Green with his wife, Edith, her sister (a milliner) and brother-in-law. In the 1911 census, Fritz had two employees that worked for him as 'sausage skin cleanser and dressers': Henry Groh from Bavaria and William Randall from Ramsgate who boarded in the Duck public house. Local residents explained that 'every Wednesday the process of boiling up animal guts to make the sausage skins took place. The nauseating odour could be smelt for about a quarter of a mile radius'.

George bought and closed down the factory saying that he 'bought it purely to ensure that it is never used for the same purpose again' and he applied for planning permission to build two houses on the land. East Herts Council refused his application on the grounds that it was green belt land and had 'existing rights' to have a factory there for the purposes of 'sausage skin making, glue making, maggot breeding, manure manufacturing and the boiling of blood for black pudding'. George, with the backing of many local residents, fought the council's decision and the story reached the national newspapers, where the headline in *The Guardian* was 'George's boiling blood puts wind up council'. The council quickly reversed its decision and George was given permission to build the two houses. Today, there are five houses on the plot known as Burnham Close.

Public houses

The Tilbury public house, previously named the Three Horseshoes, is a Grade II listed building and is mainly early eighteenth century but some of the interior appears to be older, such as the stud work on the ground floor and ceiling beams.

Originally the name the 'Tilbury' belonged to a sixteenth century alehouse which had a distinctive wooden chimney and was situated near the church. So close in fact, that members of the congregation who chose to sit in a well-hidden position could slip out through a door that used to be in the north aisle, have a drink and return to their seats unnoticed!

The old Tilbury was owned by the parish, to which the occupier paid rent, a matter that had to be clarified in preparation for the sale of parish properties in 1837. Henry Campkin of Datchworthbury Farm, who was also a churchwarden and overseer, stated that 'this [the paying of rent to the parish] had always been the practice as long as he could remember. William Smith [the occupant of the Tilbury at the time] had been paying rent to the overseers for many years'.

At the sale the Tilbury together with a cottage at Fownes (Pounds) Green were sold for £490 to William and Joseph Lucas, brewers of Hitchin. The cottage had been divided into two tenements, one for the parish clerk and the other for the poor. The Lucases sold these properties to Abel Smith, senior, in 1840 for £250 and, shortly after this, the Tilbury and its outbuildings were demolished and the land was absorbed into the churchyard. The cottage was restored to the parish to provide a house for the school mistress.

From 1823 to 1828 William Smith was landlord at both the old Tilbury and the Three Horseshoes at Datchworth Green. In 1829 the Three Horseshoes ceased trading as an alehouse and became a residential dwelling. At an auction on 23 June 1836, it was sold by William Taylor, surgeon of Watton, to John Allen for £340. The sale particulars read:

> A freehold estate situate on the east side of Datchworth Green, at the junction of the roads to Watton, Woolmer Green, Bragbury End and Hertford, consisting of a capital brick-built dwelling house, containing 2 attics, 2 bed rooms, parlor, kitchen, back kitchen with oven, dairy, a large cellar, barn, stable, wheelwright's shop, garden with a good pond of water, yard, orchard planted with capital fruit trees, garden in front, inclosed by a palisade fence. This desirable property is bounded by the roads on the southward and westward, an excellent situation for business, and capable of great improvement, containing 1a. 2r. in hand

By 1841 the Three Horseshoes was trading again and William Smith was once again the landlord. Following the demise of the old Tilbury, its licence and inn sign were transferred to the Three Horseshoes, so for a long time the sign showed 'Tilbury' on one side and 'Three Horseshoes' on the other. To add to the confusion over names, there is another 'Three Horseshoes' at Hooks Cross which the Lucas brothers, mentioned above, bought in 1825.

The pub still had its dual name 35 years later when the Datchworth Friendly Society was founded in 1876. Its regular meetings took place 'At the Sign of The Three Horse Shoes called Tilbury' as announced on the cover of the Articles of Agreement. Friendly societies probably originated from the need to help provide funds for burials in cases of poverty. This naturally

Figure 59: The Tilbury (1936) (Datchworth Museum)

Figure 60: The Tilbury (2012)

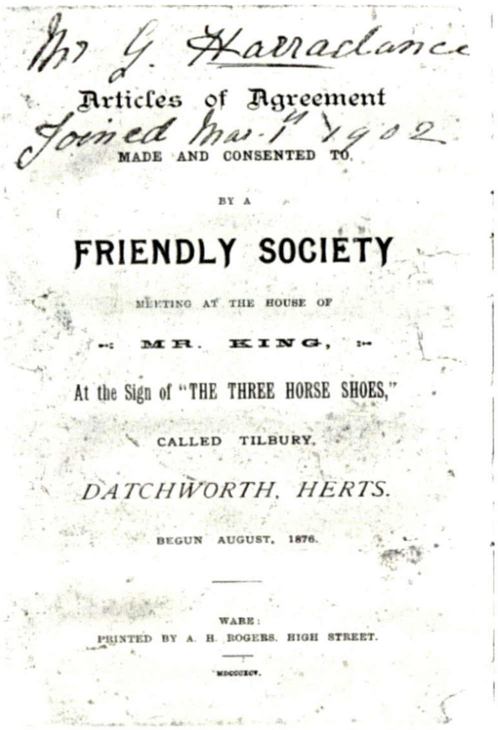
Mr G. Harradance
Articles of Agreement
Joined Mar 1st 1902
MADE AND CONSENTED TO,
BY A
FRIENDLY SOCIETY
MEETING AT THE HOUSE OF
MR. KING,
At the Sign of "THE THREE HORSE SHOES,"
CALLED TILBURY,
DATCHWORTH, HERTS.
BEGUN AUGUST, 1876.
WARE:
PRINTED BY A. H. ROGERS, HIGH STREET.

Figure 61: The front cover of The Three Horseshoes Friendly Society 1876 Articles of Agreement. (Five Hide Village)

progressed to the provision of mutual assistance in times of distress. The system became formalised by the Friendly Societies Act 1875, and so Datchworth residents had reacted promptly to the Act.

Joining the society meant a commitment to pay a certain amount on a regular basis to the society's funds and to attend meetings. In Datchworth's case, each member paid 1s 9d to the fund and 3d to the 'house' [i.e. the meeting place] where they met on the first Saturday of every month. These funds were available to help parishioners who were in distress resulting from sickness, bereavement, injury and a variety of other causes. In 1991 Ian Miller took over the pub and brewed his own beer 100 miles away in Burton-on-Trent. He named his two brews 'Five Hides' and 'Hop Pit'. During Miller's time at the pub it had the names of the 'Inn on the Green' and the 'Inn off the Green' and after he left in 2004, the name of the Tilbury was eventually restored. However, this was not without some controversy over the name. In 2006 a representative from Brakspear & Sons brewers put in a planning application for some internal alterations to the pub and to change its name to the 'Tin Cow'. This idea was vigorously opposed by the parish council, leading to the withdrawal of the request by the applicant.

Diagonally opposite the Tilbury is the Plough public house, built in the mid nineteenth century. Prior to the 1920s the building was divided into two with the alehouse on the left, the main entrance of which was along the passageway through the side door, and a small shop on the right. William Shippin, proprietor of the post office and grocer's shop next door, was also landlord of the alehouse from at least 1871 until his wife, Mary Ann, took over in 1902. In 1910 William Tyler took over the alehouse whilst the shop and post office was taken over by Henry Barringer.

The little shop on the right side of the Plough was occupied by Jane Lawrance, daughter of William Lawrance, carpenter, from at least 1861 until her death in 1898. The shop served as a general grocer and draper and in 1910, when William Tyler took over as landlord of the Plough, he also occupied the shop as a grocer and butcher. But sometime in the early 1920s the shop had disappeared and the pub absorbed the space, thus becoming the Plough as we know it today. In 2014 the Plough was sold by Greene King to Nick and Diana Collingridge, daughter of landowner John Wallace.

Figure 62: The Plough (c.1912-1920)

Figure 63: The Plough (2012)

Figure 64: The Horns public house – the thatched barn to the right burnt down in 2001 and is alleged to have housed the body of highwayman, Walter Clibbon. (c.1980)
(Datchworth Museum)

Along Bramfield Road is the Horns public house which dominates Bulls Green and some say that it has done so since 1543 or earlier. The small bar to the left of the entrance has part of the original structure of the wall exposed, showing 'trimmed close studs', and beside it hangs a framed letter from Hertford Museum, which suggests the wall could be fifteenth century.

In 1835 it was bought by the Lucas brothers when it was described as 'a dairy, stable, barn, cow house and two pigsties which were attached to the house, as well as three acres of pasture, fruit and timber', and above the main bar there was a hayloft until the 1920s.

In its time the Horns has acted as a farmhouse, livery stables and an auction room and served as a meeting place for traders.

The Horns has had several alterations and extensions from the seventeenth to the twentieth century. The thatched barn, which burnt down in 2001, was sixteenth century and is said to be where Walter Clibbon's body was stored before it was buried in its grizzly fashion at the spot where he was shot.

At Burnham Green was the Duck public house, renamed the Belmont Bar & Restaurant. Deeds for the building are in existence from 1834, but give no indication of use. However, in 1857, when it was conveyed to Richard Ginn, brewer of Hertford, the deeds state 'now used as a beerhouse called the Duck'. It was eventually taken over by McMullens Brewery and was extended in the early 1980s to add a small kitchen and eating area. It continued to run for many successful years until in 1995 McMullens sold the freehold to a property developer who closed the pub for further refurbishment. Unfortunately when the pub re-opened it was felt by locals that the traditional pub ambiance was lost, the new restaurant having replaced the darts and bar-billiards area.

Allegedly having run at a loss, the owner closed the pub in 1997, and in 1998 applied for permission to develop the premises into six apartments. The council received 82 letters of objection and a petition with 90 signatures. The parish council objected to the application which was eventually refused by East Herts Council and in 2000 the application failed again on appeal.

The Duck remained closed and in 2003 the owner applied for permission to change the property to a single residence. This too was rejected on the grounds of 'a loss of local service and amenity and detrimental to the vitality and quality of village life'. Eventually permission was approved to turn the Duck into a restaurant; the ground floor was extended to provide a larger kitchen and seating area to cater for 85 people. In 2010 a conservatory was added at the rear and extensive work carried out in the garden. It was after this

Figure 65: The Duck and local ladies visiting the mobile county library. (1959)
(HALS)

Figure 66: The Belmont Bar & Restaurant (2012)

phase of work that, after being known as the Duck for over 150 years, it became 'The Belmont Bar & Restaurant'.

Also at Burnham Green is the Grade II listed White Horse public house, allegedly named after a story concerning a local farmer and his white horse that were decapitated during the English Civil War and is described in Chapter 19.

The original building was of sixteenth century construction although much of it was destroyed in a serious fire in 2001. The rebuilding and refurbishment of the damage went on for over a year when tragedy struck again. In November 2002, only weeks before it was due to re-open, it caught fire again. Now that it has been restored to its former glory it is winning back its rightful position as one of Hertfordshire's leading 'country pub restaurants'.

Other public houses within the parish include the Three Horseshoes at Hooks Cross mentioned above when the Lucas brothers bought it in 1825. On Dury and Andrews' map of 1766 the building was shown as a house; whether or not an alehouse is unknown, but a victualler's licence, from at least 1806, was held by William Handley, who then sold it to the Lucases. Joseph Lucas sold it in 1876 when it was described as 'a messuage with yard, outbuildings, etc, being a public house called the Three Horseshoes and a cottage adjoining, formerly a blacksmiths shop'. Also, there is the Chequers at Bragbury End, a Grade II listed building dating back to 1727. It was originally used as a farmhouse on a 40 acre farm which included a slaughterhouse before it was taken over by a St Albans brewer in 1820, although it only received its full licence as a pub in 1919.

Residents' Memories

Reg Chalkley: The Plough public house used to be behind the present building, reached by side gate and alley. The present pub was a shop owned by Tyler, a butcher. Farrin's butcher's was at the bottom of the Green where the boys used to watch the animals being slaughtered. Pound House was owned by Burgess, coal merchant where Mrs King, a relative, ran a shop. Later Mrs Hornett started a shop from her cottage on the opposite side of the road. Down at the Green, in the grounds of Cherry Tree Farm, was where timber was sawn. One man would be in the pit and another at the top, to saw the trees.

Bill Nash: Half of the front room of the Plough was a general shop; the beer was sold down the passage at the side. My first job was as a milk round boy for Wallaces who farmed Mardleybury and Swangleys farms where there were dairy herds of Friesians. I would collect the milk in a large churn which was mounted on the front of a tradesman's bicycle. I hawked it around the village, dipping it out into customers' jugs. I later had a horse-drawn milk cart. Later, in 1927, I took on a job at the Waterford Gravel Pit where I worked 50 hours a week for £2 10s.

Louis Cubbage: The neighbour's sons worked with a knacker's cart, collecting dead horses.

Mr Tyler (Burnham Green): In general life was hard. The general employment position was very poor, till Welwyn Garden City came. However, apprenticeships were common but mainly in the building trade with Mr Lawrance on Datchworth Green. Mr Lawrance had a saw pit, five to six feet deep with one man inside at one end of the saw and one man on top at the other end to cut large trees into planks. Many women used to do stone picking from fields and were paid 1s per pile. The stones were used to make the roads; the large stones were broken manually by a stone breaker. They were spread onto the roads and water poured on to create mud (slurry), then a steamroller was used to level the surface.

George Shadbolt: When I was about ten years old, I loved helping to shoe the horses. Of course, I couldn't lift up a carthorse's foot at that age, so the blacksmith made a sort of tripod for the horse's hoof to rest on and I held it in position. He was a wonderfully clever blacksmith. I also used to help the chimney sweep. Once we were working at a house down Back Lane and after he'd got his brush pretty far up the chimney, he asked me to go outside and see if it had come through at the top. After a while I saw it come out at the top, and I gave him a shout, but when I'd got back inside he'd vanished. Presently he shouts again, and I couldn't tell where on earth his voice was coming from. Then I looked up the chimney, and there he was about halfway up the blessed chimney. They made the fireplace and the base of the chimney so broad in those old houses that a man could climb up quite easily.

Mrs Payne: We bought tea and sweets etc. from Mrs King at Pound Farm house, it saved us the long walk to Knebworth. Later when that went, Mrs Hornett began to sell things from School Green Cottage. I remember Holly Pits gravel pits still working and the gravel was taken by horse and cart to Knebworth.

Phyllis Smalley (Burnham Green): We had a small village shop but mainly we were served by local traders from old Welwyn and old Stevenage. There was 'Phil the Baker' who came from 'Coulsons' in old Welwyn in his horse and trap to deliver the bread and someone came round on a Saturday morning with the sausages for Saturday lunch. Mr Thody from Welwyn, the fishmonger, used to visit the village twice a week and shout 'Alivo, Alivo'. He would let my mum have a big bag of sprats for sixpence and us kids a bag of winkles for 1d. The two pubs were very popular; the White Horse had a skittle alley and the Duck was kept by old Mr Burrows, who looked like Buster Merryfield of 'Only Fools and Horses' fame, and his two sons, Ernie and Freddie. They sold sweets at the back door; vinegar flaps, sherbet fountains and packets of chocolate coconut tobacco, they could all be obtained for a halfpenny. There was also a sausage skin factory in the village and if the wind was blowing in the direction of your house, all doors and windows had to be shut. The stench was indescribable.

Jimmy Little: Work at the gravel pits at Waterford, Digswell and Hollybush, used to be a matter of very hard work: pick and shovel. The Waterford pit had two lorries, 12 men and horses and carts. George Currell, a carrier, ran a bus service of his own. He would take people to Hitchin and Hertford for special occasions.

Mrs Skeggs & Mrs Nash: Women were often employed in stone picking from the fields, potato picking and dung spreading. There was a saw-pit at the bungalow at entrance to Cherry Tree Farm, where they made coffins – you could choose wood for your coffin. There was also a brick factory (kiln) along Back Lane, about half a mile from which some cottages were built. The brick makers sat up all night to ensure no overheating.

10. The Church

Figure 67: All Saints' Church c.1835-40
Note the old Manor House in the background and the sundial on the tower
(HALS: DE/Bg/4/155)

All Saints' Church is located at the highest point of the parish which enables it to be seen from miles around. The site was part of land granted to Westminster Abbey by King Edgar, who reigned from 959 to 975, so it is probable that an Anglo-Saxon church existed in the same position.

Datchworth church has Norman origins and dates from the twelfth century. It was once surrounded by a moat, much of which has been filled in over the years. A survey conducted in 1829 shows the extent of the moat at that time (Figure 36). Some parts are still clearly visible after heavy periods of rainfall, particularly north of the school alongside the road and at the south side of the school adjacent to the church path.

The exterior

In common with a number of churches in Hertfordshire, the walls were built using flint rubble with stone dressings. In the case of All Saints' Church, it is thought that the stones were collected from the fields and the walls erected using local labour. A theory that is supported by the fact that the walls were not strengthened and supported using customary methods. Flints are still collected from the fields today to facilitate running repairs.

The Reverend Andrew Amos, rector from 1898 to 1907, wrote about Datchworth church in the *East Hertfordshire Archaeological Transactions* for 1902. He pointed out that the orientation of the church is slightly north of east, so the direction shown by the weathercock should be interpreted with care. This phenomenon is apparently not uncommon amongst English churches and it has been suggested that it was customary to orient churches by using the point of sunrise on their saint's day. Amos continues: 'it is clear that the saints day fell in the summer-time, ... [and] add to this that there is a local tradition that the church is St Mary's Church and not All Saints', it is a fair inference that the church was originally dedicated to St Mary Magdalene' whose saint's day falls on 22 July. The change of name came about at the Reformation when certain saints' days were written in the church calendar in black rather than red letters. These became known as 'black letter saints' and included St Mary Magdalene. This custom led to the dedication of churches so-named to be changed to All Saints'.

The earliest parts of the tower were built in about 1380 and Amos suggested that 'the tower was probably heightened after the Revolution, when the bells were either replaced or recast, as the date of them is 1673'. As the nineteenth century progressed, it was realised that the upper portion of the tower was becoming unsafe and so following discussions with the architect, Mr A Blomfield, work started in 1869 and completed in 1870.

These extensive renovations are perhaps best described in the following two extracts from the magazine *The Builder*.

16 April 1870:

> DATCHWORTH CHURCH
> It having become necessary, in consequence of the unsafe condition of the tower of Datchworth, to remove and reconstruct the upper portion, a lofty spire has been erected. In addition to this the old and somewhat inconvenient pewing has been removed, as well as the gallery, and the interior of the church has been reseated, repaved and restored, under the direction of the architect, Mr A Blomfield. The total expense is said to be over £1,000, of which sum nearly £950 have been raised. [Blomfield was one of the best known Victorian church architects]

30 April 1870:

> DATCHWORTH CHURCH
> The church here has been reopened. The architect, whose designs for the restoration have been carried out, is Mr A Blomfield, and the work has been executed by Messrs Lawrance & Son of Datchworth Green, builders. The floor of the edifice is paved with Staffordshire tiles, except that portion upon which the feet rest; this is boarded, while the seats are of stained wood. On the north side of the church a new window has been put in corresponding with one at the east end of the aisle. The other windows have been newly glazed and the stone framework put in repair. The original roof of the church has been retained, and a course or two of new colouring has given freshness to the appearance. A spire, with a 54 feet rise, has been added to the tower, the upper storey of which is new to the set-off; it has four new windows of 22 feet square, and the spire roof contains 16,000 oak shingles, and has four new dormer windows, which were contributed by three of the workmen engaged in the building. Much improvement has been made in the interior of the tower by the removal of two floors, as well as an old gallery in the front.

The re-opening of the church in 1870 during William Williamson's incumbency was the cause of great celebration. The Bishop of Colombo preached the sermon to a large congregation of Datchworth residents and visitors. There were so many people that extra seating had to be provided in the aisles.

The fabric of the spire has received regular maintenance over the years particularly in 1929, 1955 and again in 1971 when the shingle tiles had to be replaced. By 1980 the spire was in a disastrous condition and a professional survey showed that the work required was urgent and that the estimated cost would be £5,500. An appeal was launched and as a result of the splendid response from all parts of Datchworth, and further afield, the money was raised in five and a half weeks. However, as the repairs progressed, it was discovered that the deterioration was greater than first thought. An extra £7,500 was needed to complete the work and this was funded by the Department of the Environment. In 1995, the spire's 16,000 shingles had to be re-pegged and the lightning conductors were renewed and extended.

Figure 68: All Saints' Church 1995
Re-pegging of the spire's shingles and fitting of new lightening conductors.
(Datchworth Museum)

The interior

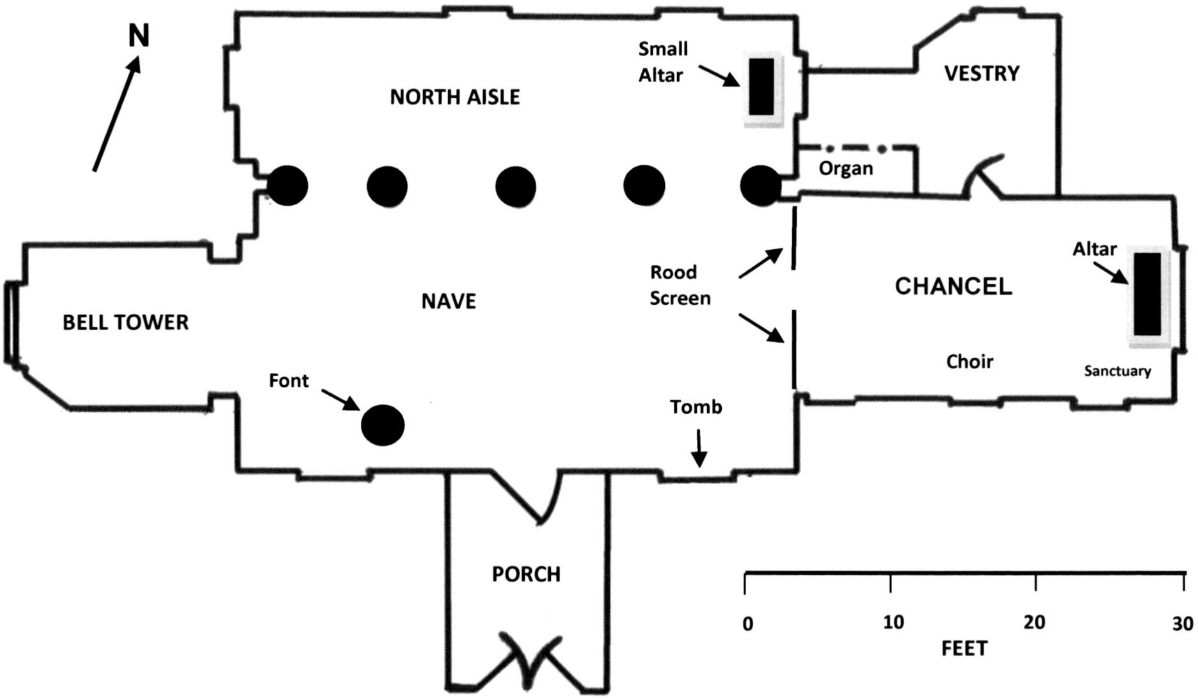

Figure 69: Plan of All Saints' Church 2012
(From a sketch by WB Emms)

The earliest part of All Saints' Church that survives is some of the south wall of the nave which dates from Norman times and is probably twelfth century. The church entrance is through the sixteenth century porch, with outer doors that were added in 1973 in memory of Harold Humphreys. The inner doorway was described by J E Cussans as 'a fine Norman doorway, with columns of Mansfield stone....the only Norman architectural feature in the building'. It was carefully restored by Mr Lawrance, the Datchworth builder, probably in 1870 when the rest of the renovations were done although some historians say it was in 1875.

On entering the nave, immediately visible on the left-hand side, is the octagonal font that dates from the year 1300 according to J E Cussans; although an entry in the *Inventory of Monuments in Hertfordshire* suggests that it is early fifteenth century. In the south wall of the nave, near the pulpit, is a tomb with a floriated cross under a fourteenth century arched recess. Its origins are not known but as the tomb is *c.*1350 it could be the resting place of Walter Maunsel, Datchworth rector from 1333 to 1349, who was probably a victim of the Black Death.

Until 1870 the nave had been furnished with pews that were numbered and allocated to named parishioners. *Five Hide Village* refers to the notebook of the Reverend C W Johnson that gives a contemporary list in 1825:

No		Present Occupier
1 & 2	Bragbury House	Wm. Manfield Esq.
3	Datchworth Green	Chas. Fuller Esq.
4	Raffin Green	Mr Thomas Green
5	Moat House	Mrs Campkin
6	Datchworth Bury	Mr Harry Campkin
7	Cherry Tree Farm	Charles Chappel
8	Bridge Foot	Chappel & V Page
9	Datchworth Green Ln	Wm Pallet & John Phipp
10	Colts Foot	Wm. Pennyfather
11	Hawkins Hall	Wm Shippin
12	*	
13	Bragger End Farm	Wm Pallet
14	Hoppers End Farm	Smith
15	Clerk's pew	The Clerk's family
16	Churching pew	Mrs Pennyfather & (?) Shore
17	Pounds Green Farm	Mr Webster & Mr Hays
18	Bulls Green and Burnham Green Farms	Joseph Shadbolt & Mr Warner
19	Hooks Cross and Ivy Cottage	Wm Handly, Jer. Smith Jn. Brinkly & Wm Lawrance.

A pew cannot be appropriated to Swangleys Farm, the house not being in the parish but so long as Mr John Wadsworth continues to occupy it he is accommodated with the pew No.12* which pew hereafter is allotted to the Farm at Bragger End, at present Mr Anderson's

Signed:
C.W.Johnson – Rector
George Price – Curate
Wm Manfield – Churchwarden
John Brinkley – Churchwarden

Note: Number 16 was the 'churching' pew that was reserved for a woman following childbirth. Having remained at home for 4-6 weeks following the birth, she went to church to thank God for the safe delivery of her child and be blessed by the minister.

The north aisle was added in the late thirteenth century, according to the *Victoria County History* (VCH), which necessitated removing the north wall of the nave and building an arcade in its place. The VCH went on to report that as a result of the arcade being badly out of the perpendicular, a truss had to be installed against it across the aisle supported by a buttress erected outside the aisle wall.

At the east end of the north aisle is a small altar, which is probably where St Dunstan's altar once stood. In 1512, Edmund Bardolf, of Hawkins Hall Manor, is said to have bequeathed four bushels of malt for a window at St Dunstan's altar. On the wall beside the small altar there are two brass plaques that were supplied by the Crouch family. The first of the two plaques was erected in memory of Jessie Jane Crouch who died in 1947 and in whose memory the altar was restored.

The chancel arch was built in the late fifteenth century but the chancel itself was re-modelled at the end of the sixteenth century and none of the original building is now traceable. It is not known when the vestry was added to the north side of the chancel, but it is considered by the VCH to be 'modern' and so is probably late nineteenth century.

The Reverend Williamson's notebook, written in the 1860s, gives historical details about the alterations that were made to the church in 1824-5. The chancel screen and the old oak seats were removed and the floor of the nave was raised. The church was 'pewed' with narrow form deal pews and a gallery was put up at the west end. The cost of these alterations, approximately £450, was mainly met by the Church Building Society. About £12 was raised from the sale of 'old timber' and 'old lead'; Williamson presumes that the latter came from the roof of the north aisle. His final remark relating to these changes was 'as far as possible everything done in 1824-5 was undone in 1870'.

Williamson also noted that he presented the church with a new pulpit and reading desk and 'a new warming apparatus' was introduced in 1861.

Other items in the church today that would have been there in Williamson's time include an oak chair in the chancel and in the nave a large oak chest with three locks, both of these are seventeenth century. The church plate includes a cup and cover paten dated 1569.

Recent repairs and alterations

In 2009 extensive work was done to the interior of the church. The plaster was removed from internal walls which were monitored for moisture reduction over many months before replastering could commence. The newly plastered walls required another period of time to dry and it was 2011 before decorating could begin. Also, during this period of repair work, the vestry had its roof re-tiled and its chimney removed. In addition the church brought in twenty-first century technology with the installation of a sound system that included a hearing loop.

Although the weekly running costs of the church are fully covered by the worshipping congregation, looking after its fabric has become increasingly difficult, particularly as it can run into many thousands of pounds. In September 2013, a scheme entitled 'Friends of All Saints' Church Datchworth' was launched, that invited parishioners to subscribe to a fabric fund on an annual basis thus ensuring that the church is there not only for the present residents but also for future generations.

The organ and the rood screen

An organ was eventually erected in the gallery but when this occurred is not known. Williamson refers to it in his notebook in 1860, when he reported that, 'at an expense of £25 10s raised by subscription', the 'barrel' organ was rebuilt and added to, so as to make it a 'finger' organ.

In 1870 the gallery was removed and the organ was dismantled and re-built in the south-west corner of the nave. Sometime before 1901 the organ was moved again to the north aisle alongside the small altar, then, in 1909, it was replaced by a larger organ that was erected in a specially built organ chamber in its present position on the north side of the chancel.

The current rood screen was erected in 1901 and the rood cross added in 1962. The screen was made and presented by the children of William and Martha Lawrance, in whose memory the screen was erected. The following letter was put in the parish magazine in December 1974, it was written by Miss E M Aberneithie, a descendant of William and Martha Lawrance:

> Sir,
>
> <u>All Saints' Screen</u>
>
> We visited your church on Harvest Festival Sunday, and purchased the Parish Magazine and were charmed with the cover photograph of the screen, and to find the sample Christmas card inside.

I must have some of these, as the church has a particular significance to our family. My Uncle, Mr Charles Lawrance, just celebrating his 86th birthday, and my Mother, Mabel nee Lawrance (sadly passed away last November 6th aged 92) were grandchildren of the William and Martha Lawrance in whose memory the screen was erected by their children.

It may be of interest to newcomers to your parish to know the peculiarly "family" achievement of the screen. William Lawrance was a local builder, timber merchant and farmer – at one time was licensee of the Tilbury. His sons took over the various trades. To make the screen William, the timber merchant, provided the wood (probably selecting the tree), sent it to Jack the youngest son, stone and wood carver and teacher at Leeds School of Art, who made and carved the screen which was sent back in sections from Yorkshire by rail, and erected in the church by Fred the builder. Probably the actual work of fitting it was done by Ben Hornett a very clever wood craftsman who worked for and was greatly esteemed by Fred Lawrance.

There may be a few older parishioners who remember the Lawrance family, indeed we met the lady and gentleman who live opposite the church and had an interesting chat. But it is sad that the generation is becoming fewer, and with their going such a lot of unwritten local history is lost too.

Yours faithfully,

E.M. Aberneithie

Bank View, Clavering, Nr Saffron Walden

Figure 70: Reverend Julian Tross (centre) supervising the overhaul of All Saints' Church bells in 1963. (Datchworth Museum)

The bells and the clock

In 1552, towards the end of Edward VI's reign, cash was needed once more in the royal coffers. Following the Dissolution of the Monasteries, church goods were reckoned to be another source of wealth, so royal commissioners were sent to all the counties to make lists of church vestments and other removable goods that were to be seized by the crown. This is the return that was made for Datchworth in 1552-3:

Assuming that this confiscation took place All Saints' was probably without bells for a time. However, of the six bells that are present today, five were hung in 1673 and were cast by Anthony Chandler, of Drayton Parslow Bell Foundry. The smallest bell became cracked and was recast in 1852 and a new bell was added in 1875 which was a gift from Daniel Pennyfather of Coltsfoot Farm. The bells were last overhauled in 1963 by John Taylor of Loughborough.

Figure 71: Alan Barsby & Peter Large renovating the All Saints' clock face in 2007

Original Entry	Interpretation
One chalice of silv' pcell gilte poz xiiij oz	One chalice of silver parcel gilt weighing 14 ounces
One cope of red vellat embrawdered with cloth of Tyssew	One cope of red velvet embroidered with cloth of tissue
One cope of blew saten silke	One cope of blue satin silk
One vestmente of rede silk with the albe	One vestment of red silk with the alb
One vestmente of blewe silke with the albe	One vestment of blue silk with the alb
One crosse of Cop and gilte	One cross of Copper and gilt
Four bells in the steple	Four bells in the steeple

Note: 'parcel gilt': partly gilded, usually on the inner surface of a vessel made of silver; 'tissue': a rich kind of cloth, often interwoven with gold or silver; 'alb': a long white vestment

The church clock was installed in memory of the rector, William Williamson, after his death in 1875. In 1899 Reverend John Wardale made a donation by deed which provided annual dividends of £1 2s 'to be paid to the parish clerk for winding up of the church clock'. Today this is absorbed into the general running costs of the church, as the clock is now electrically driven. In 2007 the clock face was removed and renovated after the minute hand had snapped off in a gale.

Windows

The stained glass windows of the church have, over the centuries, been altered, restored and replaced and the following section provides some background history.

There are two windows in the south wall of the nave, one on each side of the porch. The one to the east, dated about 1360, is the oldest remaining stained glass window in the church and shows Jesus with Mary Magdalene but the one to the west is now a plain leaded window.

The east window of the chancel was formerly in Watton-at-Stone church, from which it had been discarded but was salvaged and brought to Datchworth in 1861. Martin Harrison, author of *Victorian Stained Glass*, originally thought that the window was the work of Clutterbuck of Stratford, East London. Subsequently he revised his theory having studied several stained glass windows by William Jay Bolton, a talented artist in Victorian stained glass, the style of which bore a resemblance to Datchworth's east window. However, Bolton stopped manufacturing glass in about 1850, which in Harrison's view seemed rather a long time before 1861 when the window came to Datchworth.

Light was shed on the mystery following information found in some newspaper cuttings in the Gerish collection at HALS. It was reported in 1851 that Watton-at-Stone church had some extensive restoration that included the renewal of the east window.

An extract from Reverend Williamson's notebook helps explain why the date when it was erected in All Saints' Church was so much later:

> ... 1861, a stained glass window was inserted at the East end ... It was originally put up in Watton church in the Chancel opposite to where Mrs. Abel Smith sat. She did not like it. So it was taken down & after a time given to me.

Therefore it is quite possible that this window could have been amongst the last pieces of work manufactured by Bolton before he stopped work in 1850.

Figure 72: All Saints' altar window inserted in 1861, possibly made by Bolton.

The two windows on the south side of the chancel were replaced in 1864 in memory of the rector, William Williamson, and his wife, Jane. Of the two, the eastern window was given 'In memory of Jane Hutchison Williamson, from the parishioners of Datchworth, 1863'; there were 129 subscribers to the memorial. The western window was presented by the three sisters of William Williamson but the inscription was not inserted until 1876 following his death in 1875.

In the north aisle, the window in the west wall was replaced in 1876. It bears the inscription: 'This window was given by Mary, widow of Daniel Pennyfather in memory of the Pennyfather family long residents in this parish'.

Figure 73: 'The Light of the World' installed to mark the turn of the Millennium 2000.

Figure 74: Donated to All Saints' Church to mark the formation of the Team Ministry in 2005.

In the north wall of the aisle there are two windows and the western-most of the two has an unusual history. In its place there was once a door and the story behind this transformation is told by J E Cussans in *History of Hertfordshire*:

> This was closed about seventy years ago [about 1808] as it afforded too ready a means for the worshippers in the north aisle to slip out during the hours of divine service, unseen by the parson, to a public house [the original Tilbury] in the churchyard, within a few steps of the door. The doorway was then half built up, the upper part was enlarged and converted into a window and in the lower part, on the inner side, the font was inserted, the top of the bowl, which projected about a foot, being on a level with the window-sill.

By 1878, when Cussans' history was published, the font had been moved to 'its proper position by the south entrance'. The public house was sold and then demolished in the early 1840s.

In 2000, to mark the Millennium, this window was replaced by new stained glass in a design entitled 'The Light of the World'. It was made by a local artist and former resident of Datchworth, Maria Glenn, and funded by money raised by the 'Datchworth Millennium Fund' group.

On the eastern wall of the north aisle is another new stained glass window, which was donated by a member of the congregation to celebrate the formation of the Team Ministry in 2005. Once again, it was made by Maria Glenn and it depicts Jesus as the vine, linking the five churches in the team, that in turn are represented by the branches. It was blessed during the morning service on 20 February 2011 by the Bishop of Hertford.

The lower window in the west wall of the tower has two carved heads as terminals for the external drip-stone arch around the window opening. It is believed that these heads possibly represent those of the mason and his wife, Mr and Mrs Lawrance. This and the other windows in the tower – four in the upper tower and four dormer windows in the spire – were installed in 1870.

Figure 75: Sculptured heads either side of the west window in the tower of All Saints'.

Churchyard

In 1840, Abel Smith, senior, purchased the old Tilbury public house, along with one of the parish poor houses, for £250. Shortly afterwards, the Tilbury was demolished and the land donated to the diocese in order to extend the graveyard, the eastern boundary of which was marked by a wall that was erected in 1847. However, the ground was not consecrated for burial until 27 June 1905 at a cost of £3 3s.

In about 1954, 75 headstones were removed from their original positions and placed lying flat on the ground around the church building. Some of these have been replaced or added to in more recent years. Many of them are badly weathered and so are illegible but fortunately a list was made of them at the time they were moved. In addition to this, in 1982, the Hertfordshire Family and Population History Society visited Datchworth and noted down all monumental inscriptions at Datchworth church which have been recorded in *Hertfordshire Monumental Inscriptions: Datchworth The Parish Church of All Saints.*

Among the list of names on these gravestones are many well known Datchworth people, including several members of the Pennyfather and Lawrance families. Others listed in the table include:

Name	Year of Death	Age	Description
Henry Campkin	1898	66	Datchworthbury Farm (tenant)
John Wadsworth	1857	35	Raffin Green Farm (tenant)
James Talbot	1913	75	Datchworthbury Farm (tenant)
David Gaddie	1923	91	Hawkins Hall Farm (tenant)
Isaac Webster	1891	84	Hoppers End Farm (tenant)
Ernest Farrin	1953	76	Farrins butchers and slaughterhouse
Rev. Frederick Toller	1864	58	Father of school mistress Annie Toller in the 1860s
William Shippin	1844	54	Hawkins Hall Farm (tenant)
William Shippin	1898	62	Grocer, beer retailer and postmaster at Datchworth Green

Also on the list are the names of some people whose graves were marked by wooden constructions called 'grave-boards' that consisted of an inscribed plank supported by upright posts. Also called 'bed-head', 'dead-board' and 'leaping board', they are rarely used today because of their temporary nature. Examples of old grave-boards may be found throughout the Home Counties, usually in an area where stone was difficult to transport but wood was plentiful. The example

Figure 76: One of the few remaining 'grave-boards' in the churchyard. Leonard Cranwell died on the old A1 (B197) near the Red Lion public house. (Datchworth Museum)

shown (Figure 76) was photographed in Datchworth at least 30 years ago and is now almost completely illegible. It is one of five such boards that were in the churchyard at the time of the 1982 survey. Of the other four, two were in quite good condition, the earlier of these was dated 1890, but the other two were barely readable. Five boards are visible in the 1830s print of All Saints' Church (Figure 67).

By 2014 the churchyard had reached almost full capacity. To alleviate this situation Frank Pearman has offered land adjacent to the churchyard to the PCC. This extension will allow sufficient space for burial plots for another 50 years.

The new oak gates at the entrance of the churchyard from Bury Lane were installed in 1995. They were donated by Diana and Barry Norman in memory of Barry's father, Leslie, and their grandson Oliver (6 months old) both of whom had died within the previous year.

In 2008 three pedestal lamps were erected along the path leading to the church door to light up the way from Bury Lane during the winter months.

Figure 77: Garden of remembrance at All Saints' Church (2014)

Also the construction of a 'garden of remembrance' was begun with the erection of oak boards for the mounting of plaques to commemorate those who have been cremated. Following planning and groundwork preparations the memorial garden was finally completed in 2014.

The war memorial is of special significance in the churchyard as it is there that the names are recorded of Datchworth men who lost their lives in the two world wars. It was erected in 1919 and consecrated on 4 October of that year.

The Church Hall

There used to be a wooden hut in the southwest corner of the churchyard, which was built in 1983. Over time, this gradually fell into disrepair and so plans were made to replace it with a church hall. The hall was designed by Datchworth resident Brian Packman and was opened on 1 July 2004, with a service of blessing conducted by the Bishop of Hertford. It is available for hire and is suitable for a variety of activities and private functions. It is also used on a regular basis by several childrens' groups. The idea for these was introduced by the Reverend Coralie McCluskey and they include Mini Saints for toddlers and young children, Friday Funday for primary aged children, and Tweenagers for 11 to 14 year olds. There is also a Sunday morning group for children whilst their parents are taking part in the morning church service.

The 800th anniversary

In 1975 the church celebrated its 800th anniversary. A number of events were organised, including a walking pilgrimage to St Albans Abbey where a service was conducted by the rector of Datchworth, Reverend Julian Tross. There was a flower festival in Datchworth church but the highlight of the celebrations was a pageant which took place in the field to the west of the church on 8 July in the evening. The pageant was performed by school children and other young people of the village. It depicted scenes throughout the life of the church and particularly ways in which Datchworth residents have been involved in its development over the years. The pageant closed with the Reverend Tross ceremoniously writing an entry about the occasion in the church register. A full descriptive account of the pageant was prepared, a copy of which has been placed in HALS.

Figure 78: The old church hut (left) and new church hall (right) opened by the Bishop of Hertford on 1st July 2004.

Residents' Memories

Mrs Hurren: The social activities of the church were formerly held in the old Rectory.

Mrs Payne: When I was a girl we went to confirmation at Hatfield in a waggonette, all to be confirmed going together from the rectory. Also when a funeral took place at Datchworth church the coffin was carried from the village green, by friends or farm labourers, up the church footpaths, through fields from the village green, where there were two styles and there would be a change of hands and the bell would toll. Sometimes it was on a farm trailer or wagon pulled by a horse.

Norman Pearman: Dr Gardner's house [The Cottage on Datchworth Green] was a Baptist Manse.

Phyllis Smalley (Burnham Green): The Baptist chapel [now demolished] was one of the places the children went to Sunday school, also a small Church of England church [now Burnham Green village hall]. I went to both Sunday schools during my childhood. At the Baptist chapel we had lovely seaside outings. At the C of E church on Mothering Sunday we were given small bunches of flowers to take home to our mum. They would consist of violets, snowdrops and primroses. The little church had an organ and someone had to stand by the organist and pump a large handle up and down.

Mrs Skeggs & Mrs Nash: The rectors wore round hats and tail-coats. Mr Wardale had three maids and a cook. He frequently walked to Watton to visit his daughter then on his return would visit the public bath which was alongside the Homestead. Mr Wardale, with two other men, built the walls around the school and Pound House.

Reg Chalkley: My father helped Mr Wardale [rector] build the walls around the school and Pound House.

Arthur Arnold: In my teens [pre-1920] I began as a chorister and bell ringer for the church, which I continued to do for over seventy years. I taught the art of bell ringing to many others for All Saints' and other surrounding churches. At one time Datchworth church also had a team of hand bell ringers. I was once invited to a garden party at Buckingham Palace and also sang under Sir Adrian Boult in the choir at St Paul's Cathedral.

11. Nonconformity and the Baptist Chapels

Protestant dissenters

In Hertfordshire dissent from the Church of England became apparent in the early seventeenth century and associated activity spread across the county from the north-west especially during the Commonwealth (1649-1660). At the restoration of the monarchy in 1660, dissenting groups went into hiding but nevertheless by the 1670s secret gatherings were widespread in towns and villages. Several denominations evolved and groups of these tended to be concentrated at centres; Baptists at Hemel Hempstead, Presbyterians at St Albans, Independents in Hertford and later Quakers in Hitchin, Ware and Hertford. At this time, it had been reckoned that about 20 per cent of the population of Hertfordshire were dissenters, later called nonconformists.

In William Urwick's *Nonconformity in Hertfordshire* there are a few references to nonconformity in Datchworth but with no denominational distinction. One of the earliest being that of Thomas Rudd who was rector from 1569-1590, who, in 1576 was described as 'fit to catechise, not a graduate nor a Conformist', with no details about the nature of his nonconformity. In 1611 the Reverend William Paine presented Beatrice Truer at the court of the archdeaconry of Huntingdon, located at Hitchin, for not receiving communion, and later, in 1614, he reported that there were no 'recusants'. The term 'recusant' was often specifically applied to Roman Catholics but at this period usually referred to those refusing to attend Church of England services. Other court presentations included Francis Heaward, on 12 October 1662, and Robert Burr, in 1663, for not paying their church rate. There was also the case of John Uncle on 26 August 1666, who was presented 'for carrying himself disorderly in the church, sitting at the saying of the Beliefe when all the rest stand up, and using the same posture in all the prayers; for putting on his hat in time of divine service, for not receiving the sacrament at Easter, and for refusing to pay his Easter offerings'.

Attitudes towards the treatment of Protestant dissenters changed following the Toleration Act of 1689, which allowed them to worship in chosen premises provided that they were registered with the archdeaconry of Huntingdon at Hitchin. Datchworth was one of 76 parishes within this archdeaconry which itself was part of the diocese of Lincoln.

There was no immediate reaction to the Act in Datchworth as records of Bishop Wake's visitations reveal. In 1706, it was reported that there were no dissenters nor was there a meeting house. In 1712, there was one dissenter and in 1715, there was '1 Quaker lately come in' and no meeting house, so there was not much acknowledged dissenting activity in Datchworth before 1719 when the following registration was recorded with a list of witnesses:

> These are to certify that a congregation of Protestant Dissenters do intend to meet for religious worship at a new-erected place for that use in the parish of Datchworth, at a place called Petits, in the county of Hertford. We desire the same may be registered according to law. Witness our hands this 13th October 1719, Edw. Gray, Ed. Green, Tho. Smith, Moses Coventre, Benj. Chapman, John Farr, Thos. Coulson, Edw. Ives, John Bassett, Wm. Kimpton. Reg. 20th October 1719.

Thomas Coulson's name, mentioned above, first appeared in Watton as a witness in 1701. Also, his name appeared in Tewin in 1706 and 1707 and then, apart from Datchworth in 1719, he acted as witness at Aston in 1720. Benjamin Chapman played a similar supporting role, initially in 1698 in Watton and then in Datchworth and in Aston in 1720.

Both Thomas Coulson and Benjamin Chapman already had an interest in Datchworth as they, with Edward Green and Daniel Skingle, had purchased Pettits in 1718. Daniel Skingle had quite a reputation as a 'hedge-preacher', the name given to one who preached on the fringes or outside the established church. He had been appointed vicar of Essendon during the Commonwealth but was ejected in 1662. Much later he attached himself to Hertford Independent Church but before long became unpopular, especially with his peripatetic preaching activities in Braughing, Munden and Datchworth. He was eventually ejected from Hertford church and as Reginald Hine put it in *The History of Hitchin* 'he formed his own [church] at Datchworth' which is probably when he got involved with Pettits.

Pettits changed hands over the next few years and by 1729 was occupied by Benjamin Chapman, one of the original group of dissenters. His will of that year made particular mention of the meeting house as follows:

> If the trustees of the meeting house should have the desire to buy the said messuage or tenement for the conveniency of the meeting if they will allow you threescore pounds for the purchase ... that you should sell it to them only but not to any other person.

The last reference to the meeting house is recorded in a Datchworthbury Manor court roll dated 25 November 1768, when Philip Thicknesse was admitted tenant to 'a Cottage called or known by the Name of the Meeting house, now dilapidated together with a small piece or parcel of Ground thereunto adjoining called the Burying Ground'. The whereabouts of the said 'Burying Ground' is not known.

Other registrations in Datchworth were at 'the dwelling-house of Thos. Fletcher', where witnesses included John Lawrence, William Wrenn, Daniel Arnold and William Dawes as well as Thomas Fletcher himself. The date is not given for this but in 1809, the 'dwelling-house' of Elisha Mardell was used where William Button, John Farmer and Henry Asplen were witnesses.

Puritans

Puritanism was a movement arising in the sixteenth century that believed that the Church of England had adopted too many Catholic practices and there was a need to 'purify' its worship and ceremony, in particular, by condemning priestly vestments and church ornaments. On his way to his Coronation in 1604, James I (1603-1625) was presented with a petition signed by 1,000 Puritans begging for changes in church procedures that would satisfy their demands for, amongst other things, a reduction in ceremonial worship, but their wishes were refused.

Puritans remained under pressure to conform particularly during the reign of Charles I (1625-1649) with his archbishop, William Laud, causing those who were reluctant to compromise to emigrate to America. At Ware, in the 1630s, Reverend Charles Chauncy, great-uncle of the antiquarian Sir Henry Chauncy, incurred the wrath of Archbishop Laud and was eventually removed and, in 1637, emigrated to Massachusetts.

Animosity towards the monarchy grew amongst Puritans that stayed behind and became an element that eventually contributed towards the English Civil War (1642-1649); a period when Royalist sympathisers were sequestered and, where clergy were reclacitrant, Puritans often replaced the incumbent. This was the case in Datchworth, where the Puritan Simon Peck was appointed minister in 1644 to replace Richard Newman who had been sequestered.

Puritans enjoyed a powerful position throughout the period of the civil war and continued to do so under Cromwell during the Commonwealth (1649-1660). Close to Datchworth were the Thompsons, a Puritan family who lived at Watton-at-Stone, several of whom emigrated to Virginia. However, some returned and one in particular, Robert Thompson, was very friendly with Cromwell and was Navy Commissioner, a position he held from 1649 and throughout the Interregnum.

Puritanism was widespread in Hertfordshire, as reported by Reginald Hine in *The History of Hitchin*, where he quoted some typical names given to Puritans that were recorded in parish registers or muster rolls such as Lamentation Caudle of Braughing, and Mephibosheth Lamprey of Datchworth. At nearby Shephall John Rudd, 'an eminent Puritan', was appointed vicar in 1594. In 1596, he went to Cambridge and delivered a sermon in St Mary's Church that so offended the vice-chancellor that he reported Rudd's behaviour to Archbishop Whitgift. Under the threat of losing his living, Rudd 'recanted' his misdeeds and was allowed to return to Shephall where he remained until his death in 1640.

Burnham Green Baptist Chapel

The Baptist movement that evolved throughout Europe in the early seventeenth century had the view that baptism should not take place unless 'belief' was ensured, in contrast to baptism in infancy. Baptists also sought freedom of conscience and religious liberty and in England, similar to many Protestant dissenters, they followed the belief that Christ was head of the church rather than the reigning monarch and so they refused to be part of the Church of England. The first Baptist church to meet in England was in Spitalfields, London, in 1612. Following the Act of Toleration in 1689, Baptist churches sprang up all over England, mainly in towns.

In Hertfordshire, from 1810, Baptists and Independents (later called Congregationalists) belonged to 'The Hertfordshire Union'. Independents practised infant baptism, a philosophy that divided them from Baptists, but apart from this, the two groups had much in common. In 1878 they formed separate organisations, the Congregational Home Mission Society and the Hertfordshire Baptist Union. The latter aimed, amongst other things, 'to assist smaller churches and village preaching stations by grants'.

In the early 1880s the Baptist Union was apparently impressed by the evangelical work of A H King at Essendon and, after many meetings and appeals for funds over several years, the Essendon District Mission Hall was opened in 1885. Following its completion, the Union Committee decided that Mr King could assist in the initiation of other village missions and Burnham Green was chosen at this stage. By December 1886 the evangelist was preaching regularly in a converted farm building belonging to Earl Cowper. Although there were periods when attendances waned, they had improved sufficiently by 1908 to warrant building a chapel. In 1909 Burnham Green chapel was built on land provided by Countess Cowper and it occupied the

Figure 79: Burnham Green Baptist Chapel c.1950.

site where 129 Burnham Green Road now stands. After the death of Mr King in 1909, Stephen Sylvester took over its running in parallel with work at Datchworth.

After Mr Sylvester retired in 1920, the mission continued with reasonable attendance under Mr Savage, a minister from Hertford Baptist Church. In 1925 Vivien Sutton became its minister, once again jointly with Datchworth until 1929 when he resigned. At this point, Burnham Green was separated from Datchworth and linked with Hertford Baptist Church. The new lay pastor Mr J Barker, an engine driver, and the Reverend H R Cripps, from Hertford, ran Burnham Green so successfully that the congregation on a Sunday night rose from 20 to about 50, and the Sunday school prospered similarly. In 1930 a 'Missions Committee' was set up which restored the joint arrangement between Datchworth and Burnham Green; its main function was to oversee the working and the financial arrangements of the two churches and to provide some financial help. Burnham Green received £25 for alterations and repairs and later, in 1937, heating was installed using funds raised by the members.

The mission at Burnham Green continued to run under the leadership of Mr Barker, until 1951 when he resigned. During his time the chapel remained a popular venue until the onset of the Second World War. First the Sunday school closed and then attendance dropped so much that it was decided that the mission was no longer viable and in 1953 the building was closed. It was let to the Methodist church for a time but was finally sold in 1955 for £900; the proceeds went towards the building of Hydean Way Baptist Church in Stevenage. The building was demolished in 1957.

Datchworth Green Baptist Chapel

In 1888 the Baptist Union appointed Stephen Sylvester as a full-time evangelist, half of whose salary was met by Herbert Marnham, a local philanthropist and treasurer of the Baptist Union from 1900-1935. Initially Sylvester held meetings in four cottages at Datchworth as well as at venues at Woolmer Green and Bragbury End. A year later a cottage at Datchworth Green was acquired but this soon proved to be too small and plans were made to build a mission 'room' next to it. Generous funds were contributed by Marnham once again, and by 1893 the hall had been built by Messrs Lawrance. On 7 July 1896, 33 members were enrolled at Datchworth and in the following year there were 14 additional members. Once again there was not enough space, so the hall was enlarged in 1897 and by 1900 there were still 47 members and 40 children in its Sunday school.

By 1910 numbers had started to dwindle having dropped to 32 and in 1920 there were only 24 members. The First World War had a significant effect: not only were services disrupted but there were only five new members during this period and there were many losses. In addition, for a variety of reasons, members moved to other centres and were not replaced.

Sylvester, who had shared his time at Datchworth with Burnham Green Baptist Chapel, retired in

Figure 80: Datchworth Baptist Chapel Built by Messrs Lawrance of Datchworth.

1920. His departure was marked by a service of thanksgiving, presided over by the rector of Datchworth, the Reverend Benjamin Reed and addressed by Herbert Marnham. He was succeeded by the Reverend R E Mills who did not stay long. He left at the end of 1921 having apparently 'caused such difficulties that the Hertfordshire Baptist Union Committee was induced to seek his resignation'. The chapel closed for a time and after other abortive attempts to run the mission, Vivien Sutton was appointed in July 1925 and in November the church and the Sunday school re-opened, but after four years, Sutton resigned in August 1929.

The departure of Vivien Sutton resulted in Datchworth being separated from the Burnham Green mission and being linked with the Bunyan Baptist Church, Stevenage. Datchworth did not flourish and the building required £100-worth of repairs and so it was suggested that the chapel should close. However, Mr J F Keeble, a member of the Hertford Baptist Church, had a particular interest in Datchworth and was appointed lay pastor of Datchworth in September 1929. In 1930 he chose to use his honorarium of £20, for his services as a preacher, as a contribution towards repairs to the chapel. At the time Datchworth was once again linked with the Burnham Green mission.

During Keeble's leadership, a women's meeting was begun, a savings bank started and a magazine was produced and distributed around the village. In 1938, at a cost of £35 to the Hertfordshire Baptist Association, the chapel was refurbished and gas lighting was installed and later, other funds covered the cost of a new stove and an organ. During the Second World War a Sunday school was held for 20-30 evacuees and parties of East Enders visited, but in 1944 the women's meeting closed because women were employed at a munitions factory at Woolmer Green, however when peace was restored it was reinstated.

Quakers, or The Society of Friends, used the chapel for their meetings from May 1940, and stayed there until 1958, when the Datchworth meeting was amalgamated with the larger one at Stevenage.

Following the death of Mr Keeble, in March 1948, the leadership passed through several hands; first Mr Miller, then Mr Wood from Bunyan Baptist Chapel and in 1950 Mr Garner from Watford who was forced to resign through ill health. There was a new phase after this when the chapel became a branch of Christ Church, Welwyn Garden City, and a lay pastor, Mr R Sherry, was appointed. Attendances at Sunday school and at services were good at this time. However, from 1957 attendance numbers declined and in addition to this, by 1976, the building had deteriorated so much that it was decided that the chapel should be closed.

The chapel was auctioned in 1978 with planning permission to convert it to a private dwelling which did not materialise. However, the property was bought by the Lea Valley Railway Club following the destruction of their club house in Cheshunt and in January 1982 the club moved into their new venue. In 1996 it was named 'Stevenage & District Model Railway Club incorporated within the Lea Valley Railway Club', but this long title was simplified in 2009 to 'Stevenage & District Model Railway Club'. The club is still active today and the building has recently had refurbishments including new seating, toilets and kitchen area. Also the chimney has been rebuilt after it was knocked down by a falling tree and, following a bad flood during heavy rainfall in February 2014, a grant from the *Datchworth Parish Magazine* grants scheme was awarded for new flooring.

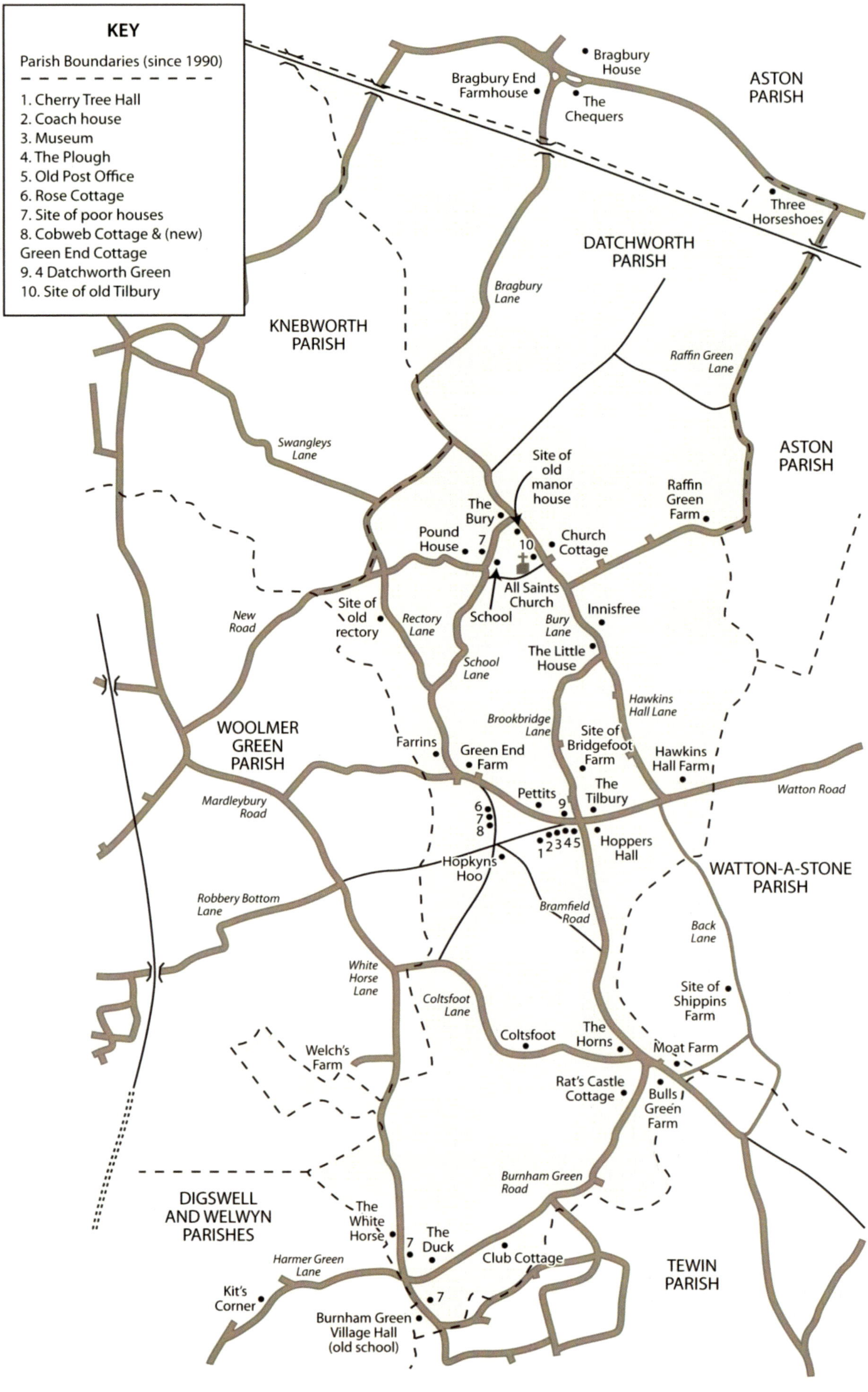

Figure 81: Datchworth parish boundary (2014) showing the location of the old houses (Designed by Charlotte Tebbutt)

12. The Old Houses

Under the feudal system all land was owned by the king who could grant land to his tenants-in-chief. According to Domesday Book, in order of seniority, these were bishops, abbots and barons. At the Dissolution land that had been granted to the monasteries was restored to Henry VIII, who then sold most of it to pay for wars with France and Scotland.

These ex-monastic lands and properties were overwhelmingly purchased by noblemen and gentry families, who, as landlords leased properties to 'tenants' who, in turn, might 'occupy' one of them and sublet others. However in some records, such as the 1829 survey of Datchworth (Figures 36 to 39), 'occupier' is loosely used for tenant or owner whether a particular property was lived in by the occupier or not, so these terms have been treated with some caution whenever found in documents relating to property.

There are several houses still standing in Datchworth today that were in existence a few hundred years ago, many of which are now protected by law as 'listed buildings' by the Town & Country Planning Act 1947. Most of these are mentioned in this chapter and others are in Chapter 9. Originally they were graded I, II and III, however, in 1970 Grade III was abolished and the buildings in this category were either moved to Grade II or de-listed.

By the time these old houses were built, Datchworth was divided into two manors – Datchworthbury Manor and Hawkins Hall Manor.

Datchworthbury Manor

Figure 82: Datchworthbury Manor House (c.1800) by HG Oldfield. (HALS: DE/Od/2 p497)

It is generally accepted that Datchworthbury Manor House and the church were surrounded by a moat, fragments of which remain. It would have enclosed the settlement of Daecca from which Datchworth derives its name. Henry III granted free warren to the Bury in 1253 and in 1719, in George I's reign, commoners were given free fishing in the moat which was famous locally for its plentiful perch.

The earliest record of the manor was in King Edgar's reign (959-975) when Datchworthbury was owned by St Peter's Church, Westminster. In 1554, by grant of Queen Mary, the manor passed to the Bishop of London who was still being paid an annual rent of £3 in 1693.

The first recorded sub-tenant was Hugh de Bocland. Some time before his death in 1176, the Abbot of Westminster made an agreement with Hugh that he could have the advowson of the church [the right to appoint a rector] provided he paid £1 at the time of each incumbent's institution.

At Hugh de Bocland's death, his daughter, Hawise, inherited the manor rather than his son William. As she was the wife of William de Lanvaley, the manor may have been part of a marriage agreement. After briefly losing the manor, the de Lanvaleys' lordship was restored and descended to William and Hawise's granddaughter, Hawise, who married John de Burgh. In 1240 the de Burghs conveyed the manor to Gilbert de Wanton for the rent of a pair of guilt spurs or the payment of 6d every Easter. It passed through the hands of the Melksops, then to Walter de la Lee, who held it in 1376 and bequeathed it to his two sisters, who left both shares to John Coke and subsequently to Thomas Coke, sometime between 1410 and 1428.

Sometime after this, the two halves went in different directions and the history becomes obscure. However in 1571 one half descended through the Appowells and was sold to Richard Foster. The other half had descended to the Shawardine family who, in turn, sold it to Richard Foster in 1572-3. So, after about 130 years, the manor of Datchworth was restored.

In 1614 Thomas Foster, possibly a descendant of Richard, made a will that left Datchworthbury Manor to his wife, Grizell. The arrangement was that for the first five years his son Thomas would be paid £5 annually and then would inherit the manor and if Grizell died before the five years were up, two trustees would be put in charge of all legacies. Grizell's will of 1617 suggests that this happened and it was probably from the younger Thomas Foster that John Gamon bought the estate in 1620.

Gamon, whose heirs Richard and Mary, founders of the Gamon Charity, sold it to William Wallis in

Figure 83: The Grade II listed Bury Farm barn (2012)

1693. Wallace was MP for Steyning (Sussex) for periods between 1705 and 1722. By 1719, when he sold Datchworthbury, he was having financial difficulties and eventually went bankrupt. He died in 1737, aged 80, 'within the rules of the Fleet prison', meaning that although he was technically an inmate, he lived close by, providing he paid a fee to the keeper.

The new owner of the manor was Edward Harrison, whose daughter, Audrey (or Ethelreda as she was also known), married Charles Townshend in 1723. Townshend was the son of the 2nd Viscount otherwise known as 'Turnip' Townshend who lived at Balls Park. At Harrison's death in 1732, Datchworthbury was inherited by Audrey Townshend where she remained until her death in 1788. Charles and Audrey Townshends' grand-daughter, Anne, married Richard Wilson who purchased the Bury from Lady Audrey Townshend's estate after her death. Only a few years later, in 1792, Richard sold the manor to Albany Wallis for £4,000.

In 1802, at Garroways Coffee House in London, the Bury was sold by Albany Wallis to Samuel Smith, who was a banker from Nottingham and came to the area in 1801 when he bought Woodhall Park. He began to acquire land in Datchworth, a trend that his son, Abel Smith, senior, continued until he had the ownership of about half of Datchworth land by 1838. The 1802 sale details described the manor house as 'Datchworth Lodge', and included Datchworthbury and Raffin Green Farms. Apart from 'three bedchambers, dining and breakfast parlours, kitchen, wash house and dairy', it had 'accommodation for servants, a yard with a coach house and a stable'. There was also 'a well of excellent water, a walled kitchen garden and some land attached'. The whole area adjacent to the 'lodge' amounted to about 5½ acres. Also in the sale was roughly 190 acres of land that surrounded the church and manor house and spread to Bragbury End.

In 1920, Abel Henry Smith began to sell the greater part of his Datchworth property. Datchworthbury and Raffin Green Farms were sold to Jeremiah Inns, a hay and gravel merchant of Stevenage.

The manor house itself had been rebuilt at least once and the final house, of 1728, was demolished in the early 1860s; remnants of the footings can still be seen today. All that remains of the original manor house and its farm buildings is the sixteenth century Grade II listed barn that lies parallel to Bury Lane. The present Bury Farmhouse is about 80 yards north of the manor house site and was built in 1854 by Henry Campkin; the farm was then 330 acres.

Charles Pearman took over the tenancy of the farm in 1913 and eventually, in 1947, secured the freehold from the estate of Jeremiah Inns, who had died in 1945. Charles's grandson, Frank, now owns the farm, which today covers 600 acres and is mainly arable. Charles Pearman became a parish councillor, followed by his son Norman and now his grandson Frank.

Norman Pearman was the chairman of the council from 1961 to 1973. During this time he released some land to the parish council for the purpose of building a village hall. In acknowledgement of this, the main room in the hall was named after him. Following Norman's tragic death in 1975, a public collection was made and a memorial garden with benches and flower beds was built in his memory on the Turkey Farm recreation ground.

Figure 84: Bury Farmhouse (2013)

Rectory

The old rectory, situated on the west side of Rectory Lane, was built sometime before 1800 and originally had about 14 acres of land adjoining. The upkeep of the old rectory eventually became a financial burden on the church and so, at a PCC meeting in February 1939, it was unanimously agreed to sell it. In the early 1950s it was

Figure 85: Datchworth Parsonage (Rectory) c.1800 by HG Oldfield. (HALS: DE/Od/2 p495)

purchased by Reginald Henry McCauley Abel Smith MC, late of Goldings, Waterford. He was the second cousin of Thomas Abel Smith at Woodhall Park and both men were great-grandsons of Abel Smith, senior. For many years there was no house for the rector in Datchworth as the current rectory, in Brookbridge Lane, was not built until 1954. The Reverend Francis Fraser lived in the Great North Road Hotel (now demolished) between Woolmer Green and Knebworth in the late 1940s.

Doubts have been expressed as to whether a rectory always existed on the site in Rectory Lane and it is likely that it has been rebuilt at least once. In the late thirteenth century Edward I wanted to raise money to join the Crusades in the Holy Land and was given permission by Pope Nicholas IV to tax the clergy at the rate of ten per cent of their income. To make an assessment, a list, called a terrier, had to be made of property and land belonging to the church. This was done in 1291 and Datchworth Rectory was valued at £6 13s 4d per annum as reported by J E Cussans in *History of Hertfordshire* but no indication of the site was mentioned. However, in a terrier dated 1607, its position was shown to be in Rectory Lane with 14 acres of land attached and the rectory was described as follows:

> .....the chiefest part of the building whereof is 62 ft. longe north and south and is 18 ft. broad east and west, which is devided into two stories conteyning 10 roomes, whereof 5 are upon the ground viz. one little lodgeing chamber, one seller, one hall, one parlor, one buttery. And 5 roomes overthese viz. one chamber over the seller and little chamber, one chamber over the hall with a closet or studye belongeing to it, and one chamber over the parlor, with a studye over it over ye buttery. One other part or parcell of the said dwelling house adjoyning unto the forenamed part and is 35 ft. longe east and west and 14 ft. broad, which containeth 4 rooms, viz. one kitchen and a brewhouse on the ground and 2 chambers and boarded over the kitchen.

There was also another 'parcell of buildinge' covered with thatch, 44 ft. by 15 ft, with 'three severall rooms upon the ground, and one roome at the west end hath a chamber boarded over it'. Another similar, but smaller structure contained three rooms and there was also a great barn, 94ft. long, with six bays, and a small barn 34 ft. long. These buildings were surrounded by a garden, an orchard and various yards.

In 1977 the rectory was burnt down in a serious fire in which Reginald's wife, Beatrice Abel Smith, died. Her 86-year-old guest managed to escape by climbing down a tree outside her bedroom window. The fire consumed many valuable antiques, paintings, and silverware. As reported in local newspapers, the cause of the fire was not established, but it was said by a member of Mrs Abel Smith's staff that she was a heavy smoker and was in the habit of throwing cigarette ends into her bedroom fireplace, although not all of them reached their target. Following the fire, the Rectory was demolished, the land sold and a new property named Cavewood was erected in its place.

Edward Young, who was rector of St Mary's Church, Welwyn, from 1730, wrote his poem entitled 'Night Thoughts' in 1742. It has often been said that the inspiration for this poem came to him while enjoying the shade of the yews in Datchworth Rectory garden. Reverend Andrew Amos, a former Datchworth rector, confirms this view in *The Transactions of the East Hertfordshire Archaeological Society (1902)* mentioning that the story had its origins in the early nineteenth century. Reverend Young was buried against the south wall

Figure 86: The old Rectory before being destroyed by fire in 1977. The tree on the right side of the door was used by Mrs Abel Smith's guest to escape the fire.

of St Mary's when he died in 1765, so Young was almost certainly in the area when he wrote the poem in 1742. About 130 years later St Nicholas chapel was built and so Edward's grave is now beneath the communion table.

Pound House

At the end of Hollybush Lane, opposite the school, is Pound House, formerly known as Old Pound House. It is Grade II listed as being early seventeenth century, with sixteenth century origins.

The immediate area has been known variously as Pond Green and Pound or Pounds Green and in old documents it appears as Founds or Fownes Green.

In front of the house there is a large pond, which is now part of the front garden but was, until it was purchased from the parish council in 1963, common land. In the nineteenth century it became known as Kings Pond, probably associated with 'Granny Kings Lane', and supplied Pound House and neighbouring cottages with drinking water. At the turn of the twentieth century a communal tap was installed in the grounds of Pound House which provided fresh water to local residents.

The wall surrounding the front garden of Pound House (Figure 139) was built by Reverend Wardale in the late nineteenth century, using concrete reinforced with scrap metal. In the early twentieth century concrete was also used for the extension to the south of the property, which joins the house to the octagonal structure, also built of concrete, which housed the hand pump and probably later the tap referred to above.

Figure 87: Pound House (2003)

Church Cottage

Figure 88: Church Cottage in the 1970s – George Harradence's son, Herbert, is tending the front garden.

The gothic-style, Grade II listed cottage opposite the church was built in the 1840s by Abel Smith, senior, to provide the parish clerk with accommodation after the sale of the parish properties in 1837. At this time the duties of the parish clerk, who was sometimes a junior cleric, were of a religious nature, rather than secular as they are today.

The first recorded mention of a parish clerk's house, is in records of a Court of Inquisition in 1628 when the clerk, Mr Arden, was given permission to erect a timber built tenement on a small piece of land belonging to the parish, where a church house had formerly stood. After the death of the Ardens, the house went on to be used 'for the benefit of the poor'. This timber tenement may have stood where School House is now.

In a legal declaration by Henry Campkin, associated with the sale of the parish properties in 1837, it states that 'for many years, the parish clerk resided in a cottage owned by the parish overseers at Fownes Green'. The cottage had been divided into two tenements, one for the parish clerk, the other was a poor house. The 1841 census shows that, after the sale of the cottage, Thomas Pallett was the parish clerk residing at the old Tilbury which was no longer an alehouse at this time but recorded as Tilbury House. By 1851 he was still the parish clerk but living in the newly built Church Cottage. In 1861 William Tyler was the parish clerk for a short time, before being succeeded by John Dennis in the late 1860s. John remained in Church Cottage as the clerk until the mid-1880s when George Harradence took on the position and the cottage.

George Harradence originally came from Litlington in Cambridgeshire. He decided to walk towards

London to look for work which he eventually found on the Woodhall Estate, initially living in Woolmer Green, before becoming the parish clerk for Datchworth and moving into Church Cottage. In 1920 George and his second wife, Jane, raised the money to buy the cottage from Abel Henry Smith. Their grand-daughter, Gladys, inherited Church Cottage on the death of her father Herbert in 1984. She stayed there until 2003 when she moved into residential care and the cottage was sold to the present owners.

Bragbury House

Figure 89: Bragbury House sketch by JP Neale 1780-1847 (HALS: D/EX886/19)

Bragbury End estate was a remote part of the manor of Standon Friars, part of which was situated within the parish of Datchworth until most of it was absorbed by Stevenage in the boundary change of 1953. Bragbury End has also been known as Bragborrows, Brackberrie, Blackbury, Bragger End and others. *The Place-names of Hertfordshire* gives the earliest version of 'Bragbury' as 'Brakeburue' in 1294.

At the end of the sixteenth century, the Bragbury estate was owned by Thomas Mitchell of Datchworth who held it of the manor of Standon Friars. The Rectory Manor, alias Standon Friars, originated in the twelfth century when it was granted to the Knights of St John of Jerusalem by Gilbert de Clare, lord of Standon Manor. The Knights of St John were a religious order that provided medical help during the Crusades in the eleventh century and formed the origin of St John Ambulance.

In 1540, at the Dissolution of the Monasteries, Sir Ralph Sadler, already in positions of power, was granted Standon manor. In the same year, he was granted Standon Friars following the suppression of the Order of St John by Henry VIII. The two manors, thus re-united, descended through the Sadler family until, in 1843, it was purchased by Arthur, 1st Duke of Wellington whose descendent, the 4th duke, was lord of the manor in 1900.

Bragbury House lies on the north side of the A602. It is Grade II listed as late sixteenth century, with about 45 acres of parkland which is watered by Stevenage Brook, a tributary of the River Beane. The house was substantially altered in the early nineteenth century with further extensions added in the twentieth century.

The Bragbury estate remained in the Mitchell family until 1701 when they sold the house and farm separately. The house was purchased by Sarah Rudd who, in 1709, married William Lucas of Hitchin. After William's death the house called 'Bragbury End Hall' with 120 acres of land was sold to Ambrose Proctor of Ware for £1,490. By 1818 William Lettsom was the owner when he sold the remodelled and enlarged property for £4,500 to William Mansfield who, in 1827, sold it by auction when it was described as:

> A very important freehold property called Bragbury End House. This very respectable freehold brick-built family residence is situate at an agreeable remove from the high road and screened by a belt of ornamental firs, shrubs, &c. and is approached by a carriage drive, presenting a good elevation, and contains a spacious entrance hall, dining, morning, and drawing rooms, handsomely fitted up, with good proportioned bedchambers with dressing rooms, water closets, &c.; the domestic offices are very conveniently arranged and well supplied with water. The grounds are disposed with great taste forming a park-like appearance, and ornamented with plantations, gravel walks, intersected by a fine piece of water. Garden inclosed with lofty brick walls clothed with choice fruit trees in the highest state of perfection; gardener's cottage, with several buildings &c. in excellent repair, and 30 acres of rich pasture land in handsome inclosures adjoining the house. The detached offices consist of a range of brick buildings, nearly new, with two coach-houses with men servants rooms over, good stabling, paved yard well supplied with water &c.

It was purchased by John Green who sold it to Abel Smith, senior, in 1840 but according to the census data, he was still living there in 1841 with his family and four servants. John died in 1848 but members of his family continued to live there until his wife's death in 1869. In the late nineteenth century Samuel Sharp Berger JP took on the tenancy of the house, eventually purchasing the house and farm from Abel Henry Smith in 1902.

During the First World War the house was taken over as a hospital for the duration; it was requisitioned again by the government during the Second World War. Later the building and its parkland were acquired by British Aerospace as its sports and social club until the mid-1990s when the house was converted into apartments and a small housing estate was built in the grounds.

Bragbury End Farm

On the south side of the A602 was Bragbury End Farm, a part of which was known as Miles Farm for a time. There were two homesteads in the eighteenth and nineteenth centuries but only the main Bragbury End farmstead still exists today and is Grade II listed as seventeenth century or earlier.

Bragbury End Farm was initially part of the estate which included Bragbury House, referred to above, each property being sold as a separate entity in 1701. At this time the farm was sold by the Mitchell family to Samuel and Elizabeth Parker, who, in 1717, sold the farm to Edward Harrison of Datchworthbury manor. Edward's daughter, Audrey, married into the Townshend family and so the farm remained part of Datchworthbury manor during their ownership, until 1801 when Lord John Townshend, of Tewin Water, sold the farm along with 53 acres of land to the sitting tenant, Robert Pallett. It would seem that Robert failed to repay a mortgage he secured on the farm, and in 1809 sold it for £1,300 to Edmund Darby.

On the death of Edmund Darby in 1833, Abel Smith, senior, gradually acquired the Bragbury End estate. He began by purchasing pieces of land and the farmhouse was obtained in 1834. This was added to when he bought Bragbury House in 1840, mentioned above. It was not until 1877 that he purchased the remaining four farm cottages. In 1889, Samuel Berger, already tenant of Bragbury House, took over the tenancy of the farm which by then consisted of 236 acres.

As already mentioned, in 1902, Samuel Berger purchased the two Bragbury End properties from Abel Henry Smith. Then, in 1912, he put the entire estate up for auction when it was described as 'a charming residence with delightful gardens, a farmhouse, homestead, 8 cottages and 247 acres in the parishes of Datchworth, Aston and Shephall', of which 235 acres were in Datchworth. It was bought by Major Arthur Bonfoy St Leger, a major in the service of the King's Royal Rifle Corps and a JP for Huntingdonshire.

The major immediately let the farm to farmer Samuel Wallace. The site remained as a farm until 1977, when it became a garden centre - initially trading as 'Roger Harvey Garden Centre'. In 1991 the listed farmhouse was converted into ground floor offices and a first floor flat, both ancillaries to the garden centre. The garden centre, by then run by Van Hage, closed in 2007 and the site was purchased by a property developer, who built 64 dwellings on three and a half acres of the land. The listed farmhouse and barns remained unoccupied and still are today, although, in 2011, permission was given to convert the sixteenth and eighteenth century barns into maisonettes and flats and to refurbish and modernise the farmhouse to form a five-bedroom dwelling house.

Raffin Green Farm

Figure 90: Raffin Green Farm. (2013)
The original cottage is at the far rear of the building

Raffin Green Farm has been recorded on an eighteenth century map as Ralfe Hanger Farm, and on nineteenth century maps as Raffinger Farm and Raughin Green. The original part of the house, to the rear of the building, is seventeenth or eighteenth century and was added to extensively in 1857 to become the more substantial property it is today.

The original 'two-up two-down' cottage is still in existence and has its original flagstone floor, fireplace, bread oven and copper (a vessel used for heating water or washing). Two of the original cast iron windows are still in place, but the other windows were removed to avoid window tax (sometime between 1697 and 1851) and not replaced again until the mid twentieth century.

Figure 91: The listed well at Raffin Green Farm (2014)

Figure 92: The bread oven, fireplace and copper at Raffin Green Farm (2013)

The barn attached to the cottage is seventeenth century and the other barns were added later. Other existing outbuildings include the outside earth closet [an early kind of lavatory] and a timber built bothy [hut] with a brick fireplace, which was possibly once used as a meat smoking room. There is also a beautifully maintained well, said to date from mid to late nineteenth century and is Grade II listed. Although other parts of the farm are older, the well is the only listed part within the grounds. It is a brick lined circular well with shaft supports and an iron and timber mechanism.

Raffin Green Farm was once part of Datchworthbury Manor and was included as part of its sale, mentioned earlier. In the 1802 sale, by Albany Wallis to Samuel Smith, Raffin Green Farm was described as '246 acres 1 rood and 34 perches of field pasture, arable and woodland, a farmhouse and yard with barn, stabling and outbuildings'.

In the 1820s the tenant of the farm was Thomas Green who, in 1824, married Mary Weathered Taylor, daughter of Thomas Taylor who was tenant of Mardleybury Farm. Thomas and Mary Green moved away from Datchworth in the early 1830s, when Alice Wadsworth took over the tenancy of Raffin Green Farm. Alice had other properties in the area that she either owned or leased and in about 1840 she moved to one of her farms in Knebworth leaving her children, John, Mary and Rebecca, to run Raffin Green. By 1851 John and his wife, Jane, were the occupants of the farm but, a few years later at the age of 34 John died, leaving Jane to run the farm and look after their two young children. In the 1861 census she is described as 'farmer of 252 acres employing 6 labourers and 3 boys'.

In the 1860s Jane purchased three newly built properties in Stevenage and presumably moved there, as, by 1871, Raffin Green was occupied by John Chapman who still held the tenancy in 1911. John Chapman was quite an important figure in the village; he was one of the school managers and was elected as one of the first councillors when the parish council was formed in 1894.

By 1914 John Inns, a parish councillor, was living at Raffin Green Farm. In 1920 Datchworthbury and Raffin Green Farms were sold by Abel Henry Smith to Jeremiah Inns, brother of John. John Inns died in 1944, followed by his brother Jeremiah a year later, without having had any children to inherit the estate.

Moving from Rats Castle Cottage, Jimmy and Jean Clarke took over the tenancy of Raffin Green in 1947. In the same year Charles Pearman, tenant of Datchworthbury, purchased both farms from Jeremiah's estate and then sold Raffin Green Farm to the Clarkes in 1951. Jimmy and Jean's daughter, Felicity Chambers, and her husband, James, still own the farm today, where they keep poultry and the land is used for summer grazing cattle and sheep.

Hawkins Hall Manor

The name 'Hawkin' may have derived from an entry in a court roll of 1365 that mentions William Haukyn. Nothing else is known until Hawkins Hall Manor was first mentioned in 1564, when it was in the possession of Edmund Bardolf (Bardolph) who was a younger member of the Bardolf family of Crowborough Manor at Watton-at-Stone.

However, it appears that the manor had been in the possession of the Bardolf family for some time before 1564, as in 1512 when Edmund Bardolf senior died, he left 3s 4d to Datchworth church, 20s to the parson, John Partrache with 6s 6d to buy a cope for the church and four bushels of malt

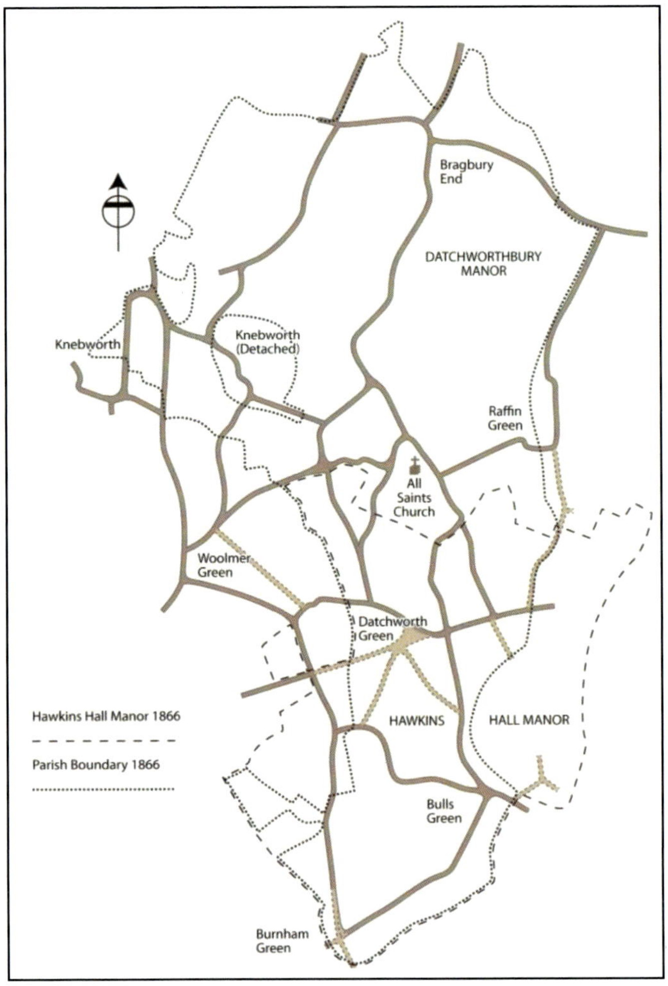

Figure 93: The parish boundary and Hawkins Hall Manor boundary in 1866. (Designed by Charlotte Tebbutt)

to provide a window at St Dunstan's altar. Unfortunately he left no details of his properties, but only states that all of his manors in Hertfordshire and Bedfordshire were left to his son, Edmund.

Edmund junior died in 1554 and in 1564 his wife, Elizabeth, had the manor of Hawkins Hall settled on her for life by their eldest son, Edmund. Edmund's mother died in 1586 and in 1591, he sold Hawkins Hall to Edward Fitzjohn and by 1657 it was in the hands of Ralph Pennyfather, who sold it in 1673 to Edmund Knight.

Hawkins Hall Manor consisted of land mainly in the southern part of Datchworth Parish but included land in Watton that may have joined the manor of Crowborough. Lands in Tewin and Welwyn were also part of the manor (Figure 93). Opposite the T-junction at the top of Brookbridge Lane the road name changes from Bury Lane to Hawkins Hall Lane. This is a significant spot because it marks the boundary between the two manors of Datchworthbury and Hawkins Hall.

Although Figure 93 shows a geographical boundary for the manor of Hawkins Hall, it is not unusual for a manor to contain pockets of land that are owned by another manor. An example of this is apparent in an extract from a court roll of Datchworthbury Manor (Figure 15a) that concerns property on Datchworth Green, which is within the boundary of Hawkins Hall Manor.

Innisfree

Innisfree, 14 Bury Lane, is a timber framed, sixteenth century Grade II listed house. It has exposed ceiling beams, with old wide fireplace openings. It was initially one of Painters Green Farm cottages which, from at least 1829, was occupied by the gamekeeper, John Shore and his family. After Shore's death in 1869 and subsequently his wife's death in 1871, the cottage was taken over by their daughter and son in-law, Benjamin Hornett.

There was possibly once quite a substantial property at Painters Green Farm called Painters Green House, which is mentioned in a 1701 mortgage agreement between Robert Kiddall, the Rt Hon Hildebrand Lord Allington, Baron of Killurd and George Allington, Haberdasher of London. The indenture included Hoppers Hall and land up to Mannards Lane, also called Manners Lane (Figure 1).

'Painters' Green may have originated from John le Peynter who appeared in a lay subsidy roll in 1294, according to *Place-names of Hertfordshire.* Records exist from 1657, when Ralph Pennyfather purchased the farm with Hawkins Hall and Hoppers End Farms. Pennyfather sold the farms in 1673 to Edmund Knight, who then sold Painters Green and Hoppers Hall as a separate concern from Hawkins Hall manor. In 1708, the Allingtons and Kiddall sold the two farms to John Hawkins and William Johnson of Grays Inn for £2,060. They subsequently sold both farms in 1717 for £2,394 to another brewer, of London, John Wellins. Both farms jointly passed through a few more owners until 1749, when Thomas Gripper bought Painters Green Farm on its own from William Blindell. Thomas was married to Elizabeth Williams, heir to Hawkins Hall, so eventually Painters Green once again became part of the Hawkins Hall estate, and both farms were still owned by the Grippers in 1810. By 1816 the farms were in the ownership of Michael Heathcote, who, in his will dated October 1816, left Hawkins Hall and Painters Green Farms to his son Samuel. In about 1880 Samuel Heathcote sold the estate to Abel Smith, junior, which by this time also included Hoppers End and Bridgefoot Farms.

The Little House

Figure 94: The stable block at the Little House with steps leading to the hayloft and the old entrance gates leading to Bury Lane (1997)

The Little House, 1 Bury Lane, was built in the seventeenth century and was also once part of Painters Green Farm. In 1749, when the farm was sold by William Blindell to Thomas Gripper, Thomas immediately sold the Little House with an acre of land to Edward Gew for £30. The sale of the Little House included a condition that the owner should allow the occupants of the cottages nearby 'passage into and out of the yard, garden or orchard to fetch water from the pond there'. There were eventually three ponds within the grounds of the Little House. In the early twentieth century the pond mentioned above was filled in after a fresh water supply was piped into the village. The second was filled in when the garage was built over it and the third remains as a feature in the field near to the current entrance.

The Little House was initially named 'The Cottage', until it was changed sometime in the early twentieth century. The original cottage, on the east side of the property, had two lower rooms with two bedrooms above. It is possible that two cottages had been amalgamated at one time, but no evidence to support this has been found in documents since 1749. Much of the original material is still evident in this part of the house, although the wooden floor in the lower rooms has been replaced by concrete within the past 15 years and the roof has been reconstructed sometime in the past 100 years. The first extension was added on the west side of the building in the late nineteenth century and more was added in the early twentieth century. Additional extensions and alterations were made in the late 1990s and are described below. In the garden there is an old stone that may have been part of the old manor house that was demolished in the 1860s.

The current owners, Will and Olek Topping, possess all the sales documents relating to the property since 1749. This collection has enabled a complete list of owners to be compiled since that year. At his death, Edward Gew, who purchased the cottage in 1749, left the property to his son Thomas who sold it in 1763 to John Brogrove for £20. The property stayed in the family until 1803, when John's grandson, James, sold it to William Harrington of Tewin, 'gent', for £25. In 1812 the owner was Andrew Harrington, who then sold it to Joseph Harrington for £45 in 1825. In 1831 Joseph purchased an additional piece of land behind the cottage from Samuel Smith. The area consisted of one rood and eight poles (roughly a quarter of an acre) and cost £15.

In 1868 Joseph Harrington wrote his will leaving his entire estate in Hertfordshire and Kent to a William Taynton of Kent. Joseph died in April 1872, but one month prior to his death he had signed an agreement to sell the Little House to Sydney Harrington of Datchworth, who in turn had agreed to transfer it to Henry Wild. As the will had not been revoked, William Taynton fought his right to the property, despite the agreement, and a lengthy and complicated legal battle ensued. Eventually, in 1882, Sydney Harrington lost the case and had to pay £300 to purchase it from Taynton, and Harrington transferred the property to Henry Wild as had been agreed ten years earlier. However, this was not the end of the story. In 1889 another legal battle took place when the London & Provincial Bank took the Harringtons and Henry Wild to court. The reasons for this court case are not clear but it would seem that a loan had been taken out by previous owners, using the property as security, and that the loan was not repaid to the bank. This time it was Wild who lost; he had to pay all costs and lost the property, which was then sold by the bank to Frederick Lawrance, Datchworth builder, in 1890 for £525.

Two years later Frederick sold the cottage, land and outbuildings for £740 to Thomas Bodey. This is the first mention of 'outbuildings' in the conveyances, therefore it is probable that the stable block was built at this time by Frederick Lawrance. Nellie Bodey inherited the property from her father when he died in December 1915 and in 1920 she bought a further four acres of land, adjacent to the property, from Abel Henry Smith for the sum of £300.

Figure 95: The Little House (2013). The section at the far right of the building is the original 17th century cottage.

Nellie sold the cottage and lands in 1938 to Enid Venebles for £1,625, who sold it in 1946 to George Pakenham for £4,750. In 1953 George donated half an acre of land to the Reverend Francis Fraser and Church Commissioners 'for the site of a parsonage house'. The new rectory was built the following year.

In 1957 the Little House was purchased by Lieutenant Alexander Houston and the Honourable Averil Houston, daughter of Odo Richard Vivian, 3rd Baron of Swansea. During their ownership, in 1969, the county council purchased a stretch of 765 square yards of the land to enable the straightening and widening of Brookbridge Lane. Around this time Mr and Mrs Houston moved the driveway entrance from Bury Lane to Brookbridge Lane and a few years later added a swimming pool and tennis court within the grounds. The Houstons lived in the property for 40 years before selling to William and Sheelagh Smith, who carried out extensive alterations to the house. Several extensions were added including a link building between the old stable block and main house making it, in effect, an extension to the property. Other alterations included the addition of a fitness gym, brick built double garage, porch and major interior changes.

Hawkins Hall Farm

Hawkins Hall manor house is situated at the end of Hawkins Hall Lane and bounded on the north of, what was once, the west to east Roman road from St. Albans to Colchester. Unfortunately not much is left of the fifteenth century Grade II listed house after a serious fire in 1927. Little of the original building survived but what remained was restored and used where possible in the rebuilding. This was not the first time that Hawkins Hall has been the victim of fire. In 1846, when the farm was occupied by Mrs Shippin, there was a fire that destroyed the stables, barn and cattle shed. The horses and cattle survived but a substantial amount of crops, faggots and some fowl, that were in the barns, were ruined. A newspaper at the time stated 'the labourers of the neighbourhood manifested the utmost alacrity in their efforts to quench the fire, under the direction of police constable Townshend, from the plentiful supply of water conveyed in buckets from a neighbouring pond'.

As mentioned at the beginning of this section, Ralph Pennyfather, who owned the manor in the mid-seventeenth century, sold it in 1673 to Edmund Knight. Edmund sold off other parts of the manor including Hoppers End and Painters Green Farms but Hawkins Hall itself remained in the Knight family, until 1730, when it was sold by his granddaughter, Susannah, to John Williams. John's daughter, who eventually inherited Hawkins Hall Farm from her father, married Thomas Gripper, owner of Painters Green Farm. Other nineteenth century owners include Michael and Samuel Heathcote then Abel Smith, junior. However, the 'tenants' of Hawkins Hall, since at least 1829, were the Shippin family who occupied the farm through much of the nineteenth century and whose name was probably given to Shippins Farm along Back Lane. Sometime in the 1890s farmer David Gaddie took on the tenancy and in 1920, his son, William, purchased the freehold along with 128 acres of land and two cottages at Datchworth Green (now Rose Cottage) from Abel Henry Smith for the sum of £3576.

Seven years later the hall was almost destroyed by fire. The Gaddies immediately built another house on land adjacent to Hawkins Hall, along Watton Road, allowing them to continue to live on the estate whilst the manor house was being re-built. The new house was, and still is, also named 'Hawkins Hall'.

Figure 96: Hawkins Hall Farm (2012)

Other more recent owners of Hawkins Hall include Mr Higgs who, in 1956, purchased Hoppers Hall purely for its land then immediately re-sold the hall with just seven acres of land. Later Hawkins Hall was purchased by Mr and Mrs Adorian and became the home of the Hays Hill Stud, which reared pedigree miniature Shetland ponies. These were shipped to Europe and also flown to the USA. In 1983, Anthony and Denise Georgiou (now Denise Gray) bought the property from Mrs Adorian, and re-instated the west wing of the property that was destroyed in the fire of 1927. A small and select team of craftsmen worked from 1989 for four years to complete the frame and two new staircases. The central oak frame was found to be on the point of collapse but with guidance from English Heritage it was dismantled, numbered and rebuilt successfully.

Shippins Farm

Opposite the junction of Hawkins Hall Lane is Back Lane that leads to Bulls Green. It is little more than a track now, but in former times was more heavily used and part way along was Shippins Farm. This consisted of a farmhouse and two cottages which were demolished in the 1950s. The farm itself is just outside the parish boundary, although it was within the manor of Hawkins Hall.

Hoppers Hall

Hoppers Hall is a grade II listed building that stands elegantly on the corner of Datchworth Green crossroads and was the homestead of Hoppers End Farm. Thomas Pennyfather's will of 1529 contains a bequest as follows: 'to Thomas my sone ... my house and lande ... called Hopps Ende'. Assuming that the 'house' referred to was not replaced, then Hoppers Hall may be older than originally thought. By the mid-seventeenth century Ralph Pennyfather, probably a descendent, held the property as part of Hawkins Hall Manor but it was eventually sold separately by Edmund Knight. Hoppers Hall passed through several hands in the seventeenth and eighteenth century, including Robert Kiddall, John Hawkins and William Blindell. Throughout this period Hoppers End and Painters Green Farms were sold together until 1749, when Blindell sold them as separate entities.

In 1832 Hoppers Hall was part of the sale by Richard and Rose Down, where Hoppers End Farm appears on the sale particulars as Lot II (Figure 100) and is described as 'a messuage [main house] containing 3 lower rooms, 2 bedrooms, barn, stable, cow house, yard, garden and about 2 acres of very superior meadow'. It was probably at this time that Hoppers Hall was purchased by Samuel Heathcote.

Inside the house, its rooms still contain the original oak beams, wide fireplaces and oak doors, together with the staircase with its ball-head newel posts, which are also probably original. It once contained a secret room, thought to have been a priest's hole, situated between the central chimney breast and the front porch. It was discovered by Mr and Mrs Thornton-Dewhurst in the 1960s during a course of electrical repairs – they resealed the entrance, which was accessed from the inglenook fireplace in the living room, but the main body of the priest's hole is now part of one of the first floor bathrooms. This discovery

Figure 97: Hoppers Hall (c.1920).

Figure 98: The original bake oven at Hoppers Hall.

suggests that the origin of the house may date from the late sixteenth century during the reign of Queen Elizabeth I but could be earlier according to Thomas Pennyfather's will of 1529 mentioned above. Further additions to the house date from the 1640s.

The kitchen still has a bake oven that was once well known to the villagers who used it to bake their own bread, for which they left a 'dole' [one of their loaves] for the owner. On the east side of the building is a single storey room thought to have been a tack room. This room has now been modernised to a certain extent to be used as a utility room, but the original beams, walls and ceiling are still evident. Still on the ground floor, there is now a snug lounge, which may have been a smoking room, probably for meat. Another interesting feature is the attic which in former times would have been servants' quarters. Access to and from the attic is provided by two discrete staircases, one leading to the kitchen and the other to the main staircase in the middle of the house.

Hoppers Hall ceased being a working farm in 1947 when Mr Tubbs, of Tewin, bought it and turned it into a private agricultural training college. Mr Tubbs sold Hoppers Hall in 1956 to Mr Higgs of Hawkins Hall Farm, who bought it principally for the land; he immediately sold the house with seven acres to Mr and Mrs Thornton-Dewhurst. In 1963 Mr Higgs then sold more land, adjacent to Hoppers Hall, to Howard White who built a bungalow named The Hawthornes (this has since been re-named Oaks Croft).

Prior to its use as an agricultural college, it is thought that the main entrance to Hoppers Hall was at, what is now, the rear of the property. It seems that this change was made when a single storey extension was built that replaced the original main entrance and housed a wash room, with toilets and wash basins for the college.

The house no longer holds the large amount of land it once had when it was a working farm – much of the land has been sold for the building of private dwellings, including Hoppers Lodge, Hoppers End, Hoppers Barn and more recently, Five Hide House. Hoppers Barn, to the north of Hoppers Hall, is seventeenth century. Following a fire in 1971, the barn was rebuilt then sold and is now a separate residence.

John and Jean Austin purchased Hoppers Hall in 1983 and set about improving the structure and fabric of the building, making it the attractive property that can be seen today. In 1990 some of the original land-holding was restored to Hoppers Hall, when John and Jean bought a plot adjacent to Hoppers Hall from Howard White of The Hawthornes. In 2002 they transferred this piece of land to their daughter, who, in 2004, built Five Hide House. An original 'cart shed' that was on the land is still in existence today and is part of the new dwelling.

Figure 99: Hoppers Hall (2007).

Bridgefoot Farm cottages

Bridgefoot Farm was located on the land to the east of Brookbridge Lane going eastwards to where Nutcroft is now and north to Hawkins Hall Lane. The homestead (now three cottages) was located at the north-west of the pond. The earliest mention of Bridgefoot Farm is in a will dated 10 July 1714 by Mary Randall, widow of John Randall who died in 1712. She left the homestead and lands to Margery Mardell, her great niece. It was in the hands of Rowland Mardell in 1715 according to the tithe records for that year.

PARTICULARS.

LOT I.

A ROOMY COTTAGE, FREEHOLD,

LAND TAX REDEEMED,

With 2 Bed Rooms, 2 lower Rooms, a Pantry, a Barn, Garden, and a Paddock or Orchard, containing together (more or less) 3 R. 7 P.;

In the Occupation of WILLIAM DARTON, *Tenant from Year to Year, at £ 5. per Annum.*

LOT II.

HOPPER'S END FARM, with a MESSUAGE,

Containing 3 lower Rooms, 2 Bed Rooms, Barn, Stable, Cow-house, Yard, Garden, and about 2 Acres of very superior Meadow Land,

In the Occupation of MR. PAGE, *Tenant from Year to Year, at an apportioned estimated Rental of £ 8. per Annum.*

LOT III.

A Piece of ARABLE LAND, in Datchworth Common,

Containing (more or less) 3 R. 10 P.;—and described in the Plan as No. 42.

LOT IV.

A DITTO, IN SLIDING DELL COMMON,

Containing 1 A. 1 R. 10 P.;—described as No. 41.

LOT V.

Datchworth Green FARM, with a Farm-House and Homestead,

Containing 2 lower Rooms, 2 Bed Rooms, Brew-house, Dairy, Pantry, 2 Barns, Stable, Cow-house, Shed, Yard, Garden, and several Pieces or Parcels of enclosed Arable and Pasture Land, containing together (more or less) 46 A. 3 R. 9 P.;

In the Occupation of MR. PAGE.

LOT VI.

THREE PIECES or PARCELS of ARABLE LAND,

CALLED THE MOTE FIELD, LONG FIELD, AND LOWER FIELD,

Containing (more or less)	6A.	3R.	26P.	
And THE SPRING,....	0	1	19	——— 7 A. 1 R. 5 P.

LOT VII.

COLT'S FOOT FARM, WITH A GOOD FARM HOUSE,

Containing a Kitchen, Hall, Parlour, Wash-house, and Brewhouse, Dairy, Pantry, 2 Cellars, 3 principal Bed Rooms, Men's Room, good Garden, Orchard, large Farm and Stack Yards, 4 Barns, 2 Stables, Cow-house, Granary, Hen-house, Piggeries, Wagon, Cart, and Cattle Sheds,

And several Pieces or Parcels of enclosed Arable and Pasture Land, and a Drift Way, containing (more or less) 164 1 38

In the Occupation of MR. PENNYFATHER, *a most responsible Tenant, at £ 160. per Annum.*

Also, William's Wood and White's Spring, in hand, containing (more or less) 7 3 16 ——— 172A. 1R. 14P.

Figure 100: Particulars of a sale in 1832 of the estate which included Hoppers End, Datchworth Green [Hopkyns Hoo] and Coltsfoot Farms. (HALS: DE/AS/1815)

It is not known how old the existing building is or whether it has been rebuilt at some point. In 1818 James and Rebecca Parish sold the farm to Charles Chappell, who also owned Cherry Tree Farm and the two cottages at the bottom of Brookbridge lane, which probably housed Bridgefoot Farm workers. By 1879 Bridgefoot Farm was in the ownership of Samuel Heathcote, when he sold it to Abel Smith, junior, along with Hawkins Hall, Hoppers End and Painters Green Farms. When the homestead was made into three separate cottages they were, for a time, addressed as 1, 2 and 3 Bridgefoot but are now known as 69, 71 and 73 Brookbridge Lane. This change was a direct result of the introduction of postcodes in England in the 1960s. The farm cottages were eventually sold as a private concern; the two at the bottom of the lane were sold to Louisa Ewer at the end of the nineteenth century and the properties near the pond in the 1970s by the owner of Hoppers Hall.

Cottages 7 to 17 Datchworth Green and the coach house

Adjoining the Plough public house on its west side are two mid-nineteenth century cottages, numbers 7 and 9. Number 7 no longer exists, the door having been bricked up to provide additional living space for number 9. The far west end of number 9 was the blacksmith's that ceased trading in 1953, and the forge now houses Datchworth Museum. These cottages, along with numbers 11 and 13, were once in the ownership of the Lawrance family. After the death of Frederick Lawrance his widow, Margaret, sold the four cottages to Robert Wallace in 1934 for £260.

Numbers 11 and 13 have been converted into a single unit. The building is seventeenth century and was originally weather boarded but in the 1950s a brickwork skin was built around it.

West of 11 and 13 is the coach house, built in the mid nineteenth century on the site of Cherry Tree Farm homestead which was still in existence in 1838. In 1931 the coach house was sold by Margaret Lawrance, widow, to Robert Wallace. At that time there was a lean-to construction on the west side of the building which, at one time, was occupied by a tin smith. During the Second World War the coach house was used as accommodation for the village 'fire engine', which in fact was a vehicle converted from a large car rather than a proper fire engine. To give sufficient depth to accommodate it, a wooden extension, now removed, was built on to the north side of the building. After the war, the fire engine became obsolete and the building reverted to its pre-war use as storage space for Cherry Tree Hall. A large house was built on the land behind the coach house in 1985 and the old building now serves as a general store for that property.

To the west of the coach house is a pair of single storey semi-detached cottages, numbers 15 and 17, that were built in the early 1930s also on the site where Cherry Tree Farm homestead once stood. After the demolition of the homestead, this

Figure 101: The east end of Datchworth Green: Girl Guide, Doreen Miller standing by the newly planted copper beech tree near to the weather-boarded cottages. The lean-to structure that formed part of the blacksmith's forge is attached to the side of No.9 (1935)
(Datchworth Museum)

site became a saw-mill that was owned and operated by the Lawrance family. In 1931 Robert Wallace purchased the site from Margaret Lawrance and erected the cottages.

Cherry Tree Hall

Cherry Tree Hall is Grade II listed as late sixteenth or early seventeenth century. It was originally two farm cottages belonging to Cherry Tree Farm. As mentioned above, the homestead of the farm stood where the coach house and cottage numbers 15 and 17 now stand, but was demolished in the mid nineteenth century. In 1930, Robert Wallace acquired the farm cottages, amalgamated them and carried out substantial alterations, including new wings to each side and adding two more chimney breasts. He then renamed the building 'Cherry Tree Hall'.

Cherry Tree Hall remained in the Wallace family until the mid-1970s when John Wallace, Robert's son, moved out and let the property for about five years to Jeff and Elizabeth Woodhouse who eventually bought the property from John in October 1980. Unfortunately, just two months later, Jeff died and Elizabeth had to sell the property and it was bought in 1981 by Clew and Jean Hughes, the present occupiers. The family lived in a caravan for several months whilst a team of builders carried out some necessary refurbishment which brought it to its current beautiful condition.

Since then Mr and Mrs Hughes have carried out further alterations. Between 1990 and 2003 three smaller extensions were added and considerable landscaping work was carried out in the gardens which included the addition of a tennis court, a swimming pool and a gymnasium. Later another wing and a fourth chimney breast were added to provide separate living accommodation above and a triple garage below.

Despite all the alterations that have been made to Cherry Tree Hall, the character of the old cottages has not been lost. The original tall red brick central chimney stack is still visible and the large inglenook fireplace with its lime mortar brickwork and seats by the fire continue to be a prominent feature. The internal lath and plaster walls have been maintained and also the internal doors, staircase and dark beams on the ceilings and walls are all original. Mr Hughes also pointed out that the large cedar tree in the front garden was planted on the day that John Wallace was born which makes it over eighty years old.

Hopkyns Hoo

Hopkyns Hoo is the charming thatched cottage that is situated at the far south-west corner of the green. It is Grade II listed and described as a seventeenth century timber framed house but Mr and Mrs John Mason, who lived there for forty years until they moved away in 1983, said that the house was built as a farmhouse in 1570. Much later, in 1822, it is marked on Bryant's map as 'Pages Farm' and it has also been known as Datchworth Green Farm. The last remnants of a moat remain as a pond within the property.

The property featured in a sale document dated 15 April 1779, described as a 'messuage at Datchworth Green abutting a moat' and it included 11½ acres of land that was bought by Richard and Rose Down from John Hart. This was part of a substantial purchase by the Downs that involved Coltsfoot Farm with associated land in Datchworth, Welwyn and Tewin, and also land in Stevenage and Ware. A list of fields was given amounting to an area of over 350 acres but did not include holdings in Welwyn and Tewin, so the total acreage was probably higher.

Figure 102: Cherry Tree Farm cottages (c.1920). Mrs Russell and Mrs Osborne stand in the doorway. (Datchworth Museum)

Figure 103: Cherry Tree Hall (2012)

Figure 104: Hopkyns Hoo (c.1950)
The Mason's are selling refreshments at the village fête.
(Five Hide Village)

Figure 105: Hopkyns Hoo (2012)
Extensions were added in 1986 and 1996

Another sale took place on 17 November 1832 (Figure 100) that included seven lots, of which Coltsfoot Farm with 172 acres was the largest, followed by Datchworth Green Farm (Lot V), which by this time, had about 47 acres of land and property that included a brew-house and a dairy.

In *Five Hide Village,* the story is told of how Hopkyns Hoo acquired its name. It begins in the First World War when the house was used as living accommodation for German prisoners working on the land. After the war was over, the house was empty and fell into disrepair. Eventually the leasehold of the house, owned by the Lytton family, was acquired by Robert Wallace who initially had the intention of demolishing it because it had deteriorated badly after tiles had been removed from the roof and sent to America. However, after demolition had reached a certain stage, the timbers that were revealed proved to be in excellent condition and the construction was strong, so it was decided to rebuild rather than continue with the demolition. The tiles were not replaced and the roof was thatched instead.

Sometime later the house was purchased by William Russell, a retired policeman, who named it The Nook. He lived there until 1934, when he sold it to Miss Edwards who made further alterations to the cottage, including installing a new fireplace in the original inglenook. In 1935 she purchased the freehold from the Lytton family and whilst perusing old deeds held by Lytton Estates, she discovered one of the farmers who had lived in the house during the nineteenth century was named Hopkyns and this inspired her to rename her cottage Hopkyns Hoo.

In 1944, during the Second World War, a German V2 flying bomb fell in the field behind Hopkyns Hoo, blowing the thatch off the rear of the property and breaking most of the windows in Cherry Tree Hall. The Masons (mentioned above) who lived at Hopkyns Hoo at the time were unhurt. When the Masons moved to the house, gypsies still came regularly to the village for seasonal work as reported in *Five Hide Village* and: 'One group always parked their caravan at Sedge Green and brought their ponies via the bridleway to graze on Datchworth Green ... They collected their water from a standpipe in the cottage garden by arrangement with the Masons'.

Green End, Cobweb and Rose Cottages

At the west end of the green just north of the sports pavilion is a group of cottages of interest consisting of Green End Cottage, Cobweb Cottage, Tudor Lodge and Rose Cottage.

Green End and Cobweb cottages were at one time a single dwelling and although the date of its construction is unknown, it was definitely in existence in 1829, when it was owned and occupied by William Lawrance, timber merchant and carpenter. The Lawrances, at this time, also owned Pettits and later purchased land and property stretching from Pettits to the crossroads, on both sides of the road. Eventually the cottage was divided into two dwellings and has remained that way ever since. Each side has been extended, the cottage to the south is called Green End and the one to the north is now named Cobweb Cottage.

However, this Green End Cottage should not be mistaken for the cottage of the same name that was part of Great Green End Farm, also called Green End Farm, and was located at the far end of the green, near Rectory Lane. There was a messuage called Green End and two farm cottages. Green End stood where numbers 60 and 62 Datchworth Green now stand, with one of the farm cottages adjacent to it and the other opposite, where 99 Datchworth Green is now.

Figure 106: Green End and Cobweb Cottages (2013). Looking at the roofline you can see the cottage in the centre when it was a single dwelling.

The farm's associated land ran from the rear of the cottages mentioned above, now named Green End and Cobweb Cottages, to the road and several more acres of fields on the east side of Rectory Lane going north to Church Field and east to Brookbridge Lane.

The earliest mention of Green End Cottage appears in 1584, when it was sold by Edmund Bardolf, lord of Hawkins Hall Manor, to Edward Gable, a Datchworth labourer. It was recorded as 'a cottage, orchard, garden, 3 crofts and a mead [meadow], 4 acres'. Four Acres was the name of the meadow behind the cottages at the west end of Datchworth Green.

In 1753 Charles Haynes inherited the farm from his uncle, Daniel Haynes, who came back from London to be buried in Datchworth as shown in an extract of his will dated 9 June 1753:

> I, Daniel Haynes, of St Stephen Coleman Street London, Gentleman, do make this my last will... I dispose of my estate as follows and first my Will is that my Body be carried down in a plain Hearse attended with one Coach by my Servant Elizabeth Raynor and buried very near the Monument of Robert King Esq without any Funeral Pomp in the Parish of Datchworth Hertfordshire. I give to my said Servant Elizabeth Raynor the Sum of five Guineas also all my Wearing Apparel whatsoever without exception...... I give devise and bequeath unto my Nephew Charles Haynes Eldest Son of Lovelace Haynes Esq all my Estate Real and Personal in the Parish of Datchworth aforesaid....

In the early 1760s Charles re-built Green End Cottage and in 1767 sold it along with the farm to Philip Thicknesse for £945.

Charles Fuller bought the farm from Thicknesse in 1777 and when Charles died, in 1825, he left Green End Cottage and farm, still described as 'orchard, garden, 3 crofts and meadow, [called] 4 acres', to Sarah Gregory. Sarah died in 1832 and left the farm to her brother, Jeremiah Gregory (see Figure 37).

Immediately to the north of Green End and Cobweb Cottages is Tudor Lodge, which was built on the site of one of the parish poor houses described in Chapter 16, and next door is Rose Cottage.

In the early nineteenth century the cottage was owned by William Taylor, surgeon of Watton, who put it up for sale by auction on 23 June 1836. At this time it was described as 'a cottage and carpenters shop situate on the west side of Datchworth Green, containing 4 rooms and a carpenters shop adjoining, yard and garden, in the occupation of Mr Field, carpenter...'. It was purchased by Abel Smith, senior, for £70, who divided the cottage into two dwellings and eventually, in 1920, sold them to William Gaddie of Hawkins Hall Farm. Gaddie, in 1933, sold them with nearly half an acre of land for £300 to Hender Delves Molesworth, the well known 'keeper of sculpture' for the Victoria & Albert Museum and author from Knightsbridge, London. Molesworth was also a Major in the Royal Artillery during the Second World War.

Molesworth amalgamated the two cottages and named the new dwelling 'White Cottage', selling it in 1935 for £500 to Christina Templeton, who lived there for 22 years. Having passed through another couple of owners, in 1971 White Cottage was purchased by Mr and Mrs Palmer-Lewis who, amusingly, renamed it 'Pussywillow Cottage'. However they sold it after only six months to Arturo and Laura Barone, for £18,500, who changed the name back to White Cottage and, in 1973, proceeded to carry out extensive work to the property including the addition of an extension, garage and wine cellar. In 1977, Ian and Janette Campbell purchased it for £42,500 and named it, as it is known today, 'Rose Cottage'. The first floor extensions with balconies to the rear and also the conservatory on the north side of the property were added at the beginning of the twenty-first century.

Pettits

About half way along the north side of the green is number 16, called Pettits. The property is Grade II listed as seventeenth century, but it has been suggested that the fireplace may be much earlier. The facade was added in the mid nineteenth century.

Figure 107: Pettits (2012)

There are two outbuildings, both Grade II listed as being seventeenth or eighteenth century and were built using old timbers. The one to the north-east of the house is now a garage. The other is to the west and the current owner, Julian Leach, thinks it is considerably earlier than the other outbuilding, the two buildings being very different in structure. It is said to have been used as stabling at one time but is now in effect an extension to the house having been joined to it by means of a link building in 1989.

It is possible that the name Pettits derived from one of its early owners. Parish baptism records list 'Thomas Pettit, sonne of Thomas and Elizabeth' who was baptised in Datchworth on 25 March 1638. Pettits has been mentioned in a number of documents, with dates ranging from the late seventeenth to the mid nineteenth century. One of the earliest of these is dated February 1684, concerning the sale of the property when Richard Wood bought it for £40 from Thomas Lucie. When Richard Wood died, his widow remarried and the property was bought by a group of people, amongst which were Thomas Coulson, Benjamin Chapman and Edward Green, all of whom were Protestant Dissenters. It was a year later, in 1719, that a 'meeting house' was said to have been erected nearby. Although Pettits passed through other hands, it passed back to Benjamin Chapman, subsequently to his widow, Bridget, and then, by 1766, to his nephew, William.

In 1769, when the property was purchased by Philip Thicknesse, the description mentions the 'messuage' and land amounting to about 23 acres. No more detail is given, except that it abutted Datchworth Green, 'upon the meeting house towards the south, up to the land belonging to Hawkins Hall towards the East and upon a way ... leading to the same land towards the north'. This is not the first time that Philip Thicknesse's name had been associated with Pettits. In 1768, in the Datchworthbury Court Baron proceedings, it was recorded that he had rented the meeting house, 'now dilapidated', for 5s (see Figure 15a).

From time to time parts of Pettits must have been separated from the original holding as there are several mentions in sales documents of 'an orchard thereunto adjoining, being part of a tenement heretofore called Pettits', also 'a freehold cottage with a curtilage [ground attached to the house] ... at the east end of a meadow called Pettits'. The latter is first mentioned in 1734 and finally in 1856, when William Lawrance was paying rent of 1s. William was probably the nephew of William Lawrance who, in 1838, occupied Pettits itself.

4 Datchworth Green

4 Datchworth Green was built in the late seventeenth century and is Grade II listed. *An Inventory of the Monuments of Hertfordshire,* published in 1911, states that it was two cottages made of plastered timber and brick and 'over three small gabled dormer windows are the initials B.W.D. and the date 1694, in raised plaster'. It is likely that the initials and date were removed when alterations were made to the property in 1929 by Frederick Lawrance.

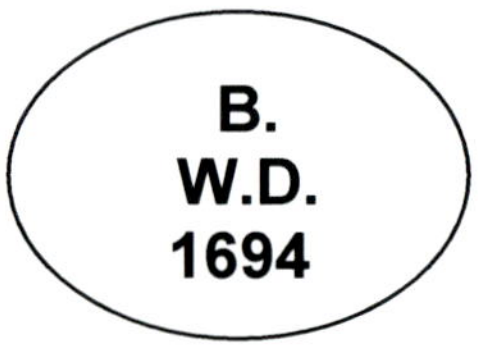

Figure 108: Initials over the three dormer windows of No.4 Datchworth Green

In 1772 William Pennyfather purchased the property from William Mardell when it consisted of two cottages that had formerly been a single dwelling. It remained in the Pennyfather family until 1865, when it was sold to William Lawrance, timber merchant, who, in 1866, took out a mortgage of £500 from Elizabeth Horn, using the cottages as security.

Upon his death in 1898, the £500 mortgage was still unpaid, so by order of William's will, the cottages were to be sold at public auction. They were bought by Louisa Ewer, widow of Woolmer Green, who also owned the two cottages at the bottom of Brookbridge Lane (now numbers 96 and 98), for £80. This payment was to be paid directly to the mortgagee, Elizabeth Horn, who in turn was to discharge William's heirs from owing the remainder of the mortgage and pass the deeds to Louisa Ewer.

Figure 109: 4 Datchworth Green (c.1936).

*Figure 110: 4 Datchworth Green (2012)
The first floor has been re-instated.*

In 1929 Louisa Ewer sold the cottages (now dilapidated and unoccupied) and land to the rear and west of the properties – which included what is now the Plough car park – to Frederick Lawrance for £5. In the same year Frederick also purchased the piece of land to the east, where the shop now stands, from Louisa for £10. It was at this time that the cottages were refurbished, converted back into a single dwelling and named 'Sulby'. The three dormer windows were removed when the ground floor had to be raised and with it the ceiling, which necessitated the removal of the upstairs rooms.

Frederick Lawrance died in 1930 and in 1931 his wife, Margaret, sold the bungalow, shop, a garage and the associated lands and outbuildings to Reginald Steeds of Crouch End, Middlesex, for £495. The following year Reginald sold the properties to Gilbert Buckridge for £500. Gilbert's son, Joe, used to tell the story that his mother made a substantial contribution towards this purchase having won the Irish Sweepstake.

Gilbert died in 1937, leaving the property to his wife, Amy. Amy died in 1951 and their son, Joe, continued to live in the bungalow initially with two brothers and a sister, but later on his own until he passed away in 2001. Eventually, in 2004, the trustees of Joe's will sold the bungalow, once again in a neglected state, together with shop, as two lots by sealed auction. A property developer won the bid for the cottage, who carried out extensive renovations that included re-instating the first floor with dormer windows, before selling it to the current owners.

Bulls Green Farm

Bulls Green is about half a mile along Bramfield Road and was possibly named after Geoffrey Bole whose name appears in the lay subsidy roll of 1294. Today Bulls Green is dominated by the Horns public house but was once the place where three farm properties met, Bulls Green Farm, Moat Farm and the considerably larger Coltsfoot Farm.

Bulls Green Farm is situated in the parishes of Datchworth and Tewin. The farmhouse itself (84 Bramfield Road) is in the parish of Datchworth and is a Grade II listed building. The exact date of the building of the house is not known, but English Heritage and British Listed Buildings put it as mid to late seventeenth century. However, recent re-rendering work exposed a small area of wattle and daub similar to that displayed in the Horns public house, which therefore suggests that it could be older. The re-rendering work also revealed a window that had been covered up, possibly to avoid the window tax (1697-1851).

The property was extended in the late eighteenth century and again in the 1970s. There is a mid nineteenth century former granary building, that was once listed but de-listed in 1986, and is now linked to the main house. At one time the farm had several barns but most of them were demolished in the twentieth century, although two remain and have been converted within the last 12 years into separate residential rooms.

Inside the original part of the house the living room is dominated by a large fireplace and, in the process of its restoration over 30 years ago, a Charles II coin was found. Some of the windows may be original and of particular interest is an upstairs bathroom window. It had been damaged

Figure 111: Bulls Green Farmhouse (2014)

Figure 112: Moat Farmhouse (2013)

by the bomb that fell on Bulls Green Nurseries during the Second World War and has been carefully restored to ensure that the buckling caused to the diamond leaded frame remains evident. Other original features include a fine brick well that has recently been unearthed by the current owners and also a large pond which is believed to be very old.

In 1839 Robert William Gaussen Esq of Brookmans Park sold the farm to Thomas Campkin, farmer of Sele Farm, Hertford. In 1903 Earl Cowper purchased it but it was sold by the heir of his estate, his adopted niece Lady Desborough, in 1919, as part of a large sale when she sold all 'the outlying portions of the Panshanger Estate', which included Coltsfoot and many farms at Digswell, Tewin, Bramfield, Hertford, Welwyn and Hatfield.

Moat Farm

On the opposite side of the road is Moat Farm (81 and 83 Bramfield Road), formerly known as Crouches Farm, which is another Grade II listed building. The house is mainly eighteenth century with extensions added in the nineteenth century. There is a much earlier sixteenth century barn, with a dairy and outbuildings added in the seventeenth century. The property takes its name from a moat that used to surround the farm buildings (Figure 38), parts of which are still visible in wet conditions.

In the eighteenth century Moat Farm was owned by the Townshend family, owners of Datchworthbury manor. At this time the farm consisted of 201 acres of land which were situated in the parishes of Datchworth, Watton and Tewin. In 1802 Lord Townshend sold the farm for £1,600 to Henry Campkin, whose son, William, still owned it in 1838. In 1866, by which time the farm was in the ownership of Earl Cowper, Abel Smith, junior, wrote to Earl Cowper suggesting an exchange of some land. This exchange eventually took place in May 1877, whereupon Moat Farm was given over to Abel Smith of Woodhall and Earl Cowper took over Coltsfoot Farm. Moat Farm is the only land in Datchworth still in the ownership of the Woodhall Estate today.

In 1894 George Little of Stevenage took the tenancy of the farm. The following year he joined the first parish council and was appointed highways surveyor. Later he moved to Hoppers Hall, where he died in 1936, and his son, James L Little, took over the position of farmer. The Little family went on to become a well-known and respected family in Datchworth.

Coltsfoot

About half way along Coltsfoot Lane, on the right, is Coltsfoot Farm (now Coltsfoot Country Retreat). The farmhouse, which was once a listed building, is not the original one, which is said to have been burned down in the mid nineteenth century. The barn to the east is seventeenth century and would have been part of the farm when it was also known as Colvers Farm. Over the years, several families have been associated with the farm: the Blindalls during the first half of the eighteenth century, the Pennyfathers, who were tenants in the nineteenth century and then the Franklins who started as tenants and then bought the farm in 1919.

It was during the tenancy of the Pennyfathers that the farm was part of the sale by Richard and Rose Down in 1832, as mentioned earlier. Coltsfoot Farm, with 172 acres, appears as Lot VII on the sale particulars (Figure 100) where it was quaintly explained that the property was 'In the occupation

Figure 113: Coltsfoot farmhouse (1919)
(HALS: DE/P/E66/7)

Figure 114: Coltsfoot Country Retreat (2014)

of Mr Pennyfather, a most responsible Tenant, at £160 per Annum'.

Coltsfoot Farm was part of Samuel Smith's gradual acquisition of land in the area and remained in the family until 1877, when Abel Smith, junior, exchanged Coltsfoot Farm with Moat Farm, as mentioned above, whereupon Earl Cowper became the landlord of Coltsfoot. It was then inherited by the Desboroughs of Panshanger, who in turn sold it along with 176 acres of land as part of a the large sale in 1919 as referred to earlier under Bulls Green Farm. It was bought by Thomas Tims Franklin for just over £28 per acre.

At the time Thomas's mother, Elizabeth Jane Franklin, was the sitting tenant and remained a resident until her death in 1940, aged 90. Thomas farmed in partnership with his brother, Philip Hugh, and in the 1950s the farm was known for its herd of Friesian cattle and its flock of 'Mammoth Bronze' turkeys. The farmstead was sold by Thomas William Franklin (Thomas Tims' grandson) in 1994 and was run as a commercial livery yard until 1998, when plans were submitted to convert the barns into a luxury holiday accommodation containing 15 rooms, which opened for business in 2000 and was renamed 'Coltsfoot Country Retreat'.

Rats Castle Cottage

Along Burnham Green Road, formerly called Hocuts Lane, on the right, is number 20, Rats Castle Cottage. It is Grade II listed as early seventeenth century and is contemporary with The Horns public house at Bulls Green, sharing many similar features.

Rats Castle was originally built as a row of farm workers cottages by the tenant of Coltsfoot Farm. The cottages, which once had internal ceilings providing an upper floor, have seen many changes, including being used as a cow shed at one time. It is now a single dwelling, with the internal ceilings removed to show the beamed and vaulted roof.

The current owners, Julian and Karen Carter, say that the thatched roof, beneath which much of the original thatch and fixings still exist, is built on a timber frame with brick, cobb stones, and wattle and daub. The heavily beamed interior is interesting, as many of the beams show evidence of having been re-cycled for the original construction, perhaps from earlier buildings or decommissioned sailing ships. The cottage also boasts flagged floors and three large open fireplaces with unique brick chimneys.

Jimmy and Jean Clarke owned the cottage from 1934 until 1947 when they moved to Raffin Green Farm. During their ownership the cottage was badly damaged when Bulls Green nurseries was bombed during the Second World War. The entire west wing was destroyed, forcing Mr and Mrs

Figure 115: Rats Castle Cottage (c.1940)
Jimmy and Jean Clarke are sitting outside with their daughter Nina on her tricycle

Clarke and their girls, Nina and Felicity, to be evacuated to their family in Wales whilst it was rebuilt.

Club Cottage

Club Cottage, 75 Burnham Green Road, is another Grade II building listed as early seventeenth century. It has a large inglenook fireplace with a seat. The stair tower with its wood panelling is original, as are the oak floorboards found on the first floor. Club Cottage was once a rendezvous for caravaners and cyclists, and in the 1937 *Kelly's Directory* is recorded as 'refreshment rooms', but the cottage ceased trading in this capacity in the 1970s.

Figure 116: Club Cottage (1999)

At Burnham Green itself, among the older buildings, are the White Horse and Duck public houses and also the village hall, which was originally built as a school. These are discussed in Chapters 9 and 13

There were many other cottages around the village that have since been demolished or converted into larger dwellings. One of the earliest estimates for the number of houses in Datchworth was made at a visitation in 1563 by an archdeacon from the Diocese of Lincoln. He was responsible for collecting information relating to the church and the parishioners. This would often include the number of families in the parish. In 1563, it was said that there were 34 families in Datchworth, so it is reasonable to suppose that there were 34 houses to accommodate them.

The Window Tax provides another source of information about houses, where names and payments are listed. However, exemptions are not usually given and there were evasions too, so the figures for Datchworth in 1715, given below, list only those properties that were taxable.

No of windows	Rates	No of houses in Datchworth
1 +	2s per house	18
10 +	6s per house	12
Robert King – Bragbury End House	£1 10s	1
William Blindall – Coltsfoot Farm	£1	1
Mr Miles - Datchworthbury	£1	1
TOTAL		33

David Hey states in *The Oxford Companion to Local and Family History,* that 'in 1709 the [tax] rates were increased for larger houses' but with no details given, so this could explain the three larger payments in the table above.

These results may be compared with a more reliable source provided by Bishop Wake's visitations of 1706, 1712 and 1715. Before a visitation took place, the incumbent was asked to answer some questions one of which inquired about the number of families that resided in the parish. As this was independent of matters relating to tax, it provided a more accurate idea of the number of houses at the time. In Datchworth's case, for these three years, there were 60 families and so, about 60 houses, compared with about 650 today. So, in about 300 years, the number of houses has increased by just under 600, and most of these, about 80%, were not built until the twentieth century and are described in Chapter 14.

13. The Schools

All Saints' School Datchworth

Figure 117: Datchworth School
Taken pre-1930s showing the bell turret that was added in 1859.
(Datchworth School)

The foundation

Datchworth was in the diocese of Lincoln until 1845 and there were regular visits from the diocese to check the state of affairs in the parish, which included questions about the presence or otherwise of a school in the village. Bishop Wake's four diocesan visitations between 1706 and 1715 reveal that there was no school in Datchworth. However, in 1715 there was a curate in charge of Datchworth parish who taught in the next parish, where several of the parishioners' children went 'to learn of him'. Unfortunately, there is no mention of the name of the 'next parish'.

The earliest mention of a school in Datchworth is recorded in *The Charity School Movement* by Miss M G Jones, originally published in 1938. It was one of 30 charity schools on a list that had been compiled in 1724 by the Society for Promoting Christian Knowledge (SPCK). Entries for Datchworth and a few neighbouring parishes are shown below [place-names are spelt as given on the list].

Charity School	Number of pupils
Aston	6
Datchworth	6
Shephall	20
Stevenage	25
Tewing	1
Wotton	20
Welwin	4

Nearly 100 years later, in 1818, there was a survey conducted in Hertfordshire about the education of the poor. In Datchworth there was no sign of a school although there was 'a Sunday school in which 35 children are taught'. Under the heading 'Observations', it was noted that 'the poor are desirous of having the means of education without expense'. Two years later, in 1820, as a result of the National Society movement, Datchworth School was founded, preceding the 1870 Elementary Education Act by 50 years.

The 'National Society for the Promoting of Religious Education' was founded in 1811 and was set up to raise funds to build schools and make provision for teachers. In the society's first ten years, 23 such schools were set up in Hertfordshire. The main objectives were to teach basic skills and to ensure the moral and spiritual welfare of the children, by establishing Christian ethics and principles. To this end, the children were provided with catechisms and Bibles for reading matter and slates on which to practise writing.

Another survey conducted in 1833, entitled 'House of Commons Education Enquiry', reported that the population of Datchworth was 593 and there was 'one day and one Sunday school attended by 19 males and 43 females daily and by 24 males and 50 females on Sundays. It is supported by subscription and payments from the children, altogether amounting to £35 per annum'.

The building

A rich source of information has proved to be the notebook of the Reverend William Williamson. Although he was inducted in 1849, it was not until the 1860s, after the death of his wife, that he began his notebook. The first entry related to the building of the school in 1820 is as follows:

> A School Erected on Pond [other spellings: Pound, Found, Fownes] Green by Subscription For the Purpose of instructing the Children of the Parish of Datchworth forever in the principles of the Christian Religion as Established in the Church of England.
>
> Expended in building and fitting up the School

Names of Subscribers

> Saml. Smith of Woodhall Esq. ground to build on and 17,500 bricks
> [Note: Samuel Smith had originally donated £39 7s 6d, then gave bricks instead of the cash]

	£	s	d
National School Society	40	0	0
Rev. C. Woolsey Johnson	22	6	6
W. Manfield of Datchworth, Esq.	23	19	3
Saml. Unwin Heathcote of Shephall Esq	20	0	0
Abel Smith of Woodhall, Esq.	20	0	0
Henry Smith of Woodhall, Esq.	10	0	0
Mrs Bulwer Lytton of Knebworth	10	0	0
Mr C. Chappel of Datchworth	10	0	0
	156	5	9

The Smith family, well known for their philanthropy, represented in this case by Samuel and his two sons, Abel and Henry, contributed a significant proportion of the subscription. Datchworth contributors included the rector at the time, Reverend C. Woolsey Johnson, William Manfield of Bragbury House and Charles Chappel of Cherry Tree Farm, who was churchwarden. The support of Mrs Bulwer Lytton reflects her interest in education, which is also recorded in *Knebworth, the Story of a Hertfordshire Village* by F A Richardson.

Reverend Williamson goes on to say that 'the school was extended in 1859 by the addition of a classroom 16ft 4in by 14ft, a porch 8ft square and a bell turret. The interior papered and suitably furnished. The Alteration and Additions cost £301 0s 11d.'

The school house then and now

Figure 118: School House in 1968, taken from the school playground. The outbuilding on the right consisted of an outside toilet, coal shed and wood shed.

The first mention of a home for the mistress was in 1859, when '£34 15s 7d was spent in furnishing Mistress' house'.

Williamson's only reference to the first mistresses was as follows: 'Miss Harrington was the first Mistress and was succeeded by Hannah Baulk'. Hannah Baulk was still schoolmistress in 1855, according to *Kelly's Directory for Hertfordshire* for that year.

The 'Mistress' house', now called School House, was built on a small area of land given back to the parish by Abel Smith, junior, in 1840, previously the site of one of the parish poor houses. The exact date when the school house was built is not known and it is possible that the building was the original poor house renovated for the mistress. When the 1851 census was carried out, Hannah Baulk, the school mistress, had moved away from her family into accommodation of her own, but it is not recorded whether this was the school house. The 1861 census states that the mistress, Anne Critchley, was living in the school house with two other school teachers, a trainee teacher and a servant.

The extension to the south side of the property was added in 1910. In 1968 Bob King became the headmaster and moved into the house. In 1971 he and his wife, Thora, purchased the school house from the diocese and added a second extension to the north side, demolishing the outbuilding that housed the outside toilet, coal shed and wood shed.

The teachers

On 10 January 1859 the notebook says that:

> Miss Critchley, student of Hockerill was appointed Mistress, Ellen Abraham from the orphan asylum pupil teacher. Miss Critchley, having left her situation as Schoolmistress on account of failing health, in December 1863, was succeeded by Annie Toller, daughter of the Rev. Frederick Toller. Aged 21 she was trained at Warrington Training College and until 16 at Lasterton School. Her salary as Mistress £35 ... as organist £10, making in all nearly £55 with nicely furnished cottage.

Miss Toller was mistress until the early 1870s and was succeeded by Miss J Stephenson. In about 1880 Miss E Booth took over the position of mistress, who was then succeeded by Miss C Clayton in the mid-1880s until 1890. At this point there was a change: the post of headmistress became that of headmaster and this remained the situation for 90 years until 1980, when Mrs A Stemp was appointed. Since 1981, the descriptions 'headmaster' and 'headmistress' have been replaced by the title of 'headteacher'.

The following table shows the list of 'heads' since 1890:

Name	From	To
Mr A Beswick	1890	1911
Mr C Thomas	1911	1915
Mr W Rushton Welch	1915	1932
Mr H J Figg Edgington	1932	1935
Mr F E Towler	1935	1951
Mr J H Norman	1951	1963
Mr L E A Howlett	1963	1967
Mr R King	1968	1980
Mrs A Stemp	1980	1983
Mr C Kitson	1983	1991
Miss J M Willatt	1991	2014

Mary Willatt retired in April 2014 and was replaced by Mr Stuart Whiteland in September of the same year.

Williamson also cared about adults and older children in the village and began a night school. This extract illustrates how the rector and his wife worked together as a team:

> We had an Evening School 2 nights in the week for about 5 months in Nov. 1859-1860, 1-2 [hours], which was well attended. My wife assisting and giving a pleasant tone to the whole. There was ½ hour writing ½ hour reading ½ hour arithmetic and then I read a tale on Pilgrims Progress for ½ hour. We gave coffee and a slice of bread and butter for ½ d., about half the cost. The attendance was about 30 of whom at least ½ were above 20.
>
> In consequence of my dear wife's death 8 Sept 1863 I had no Evening School for the winter months beg. Nov 1863.

However in 1865, the rector resumed the evening classes 'with the help of Miss Toller the Schoolmistress, John Dennis and Herbert and Elizabeth Dean (cook)' and these classes continued until at least 1867, when Williamson's notebook came to an end.

Education Acts, the managers' meetings and the school log book

Soon after Williamson's notebook ended, the 1870 Education Act was passed, which established 'school boards' for state schools that were funded from local rates. Voluntary and church schools, as in Datchworth's case, were to continue unchanged.

A House of Commons Education Enquiry was conducted in 1876 and by then Datchworth School was able to accommodate 104 pupils and the average attendance was 57. Government grants for 1875/76 were £42 15s 0d, voluntary contributions were £4 2s 0d. Weekly contributions from the children, known as 'school pence', amounted to £15 2s 2d.

In 1881 the school benefitted from a bequest which became known as the Bunting charity. Elizabeth Bunting bequeathed £500 in consols, the annual dividends amounting to £12 10s 'to be applied in supporting the Sunday school and day school held in the National Schoolroom'.

The 1902 Education Act brought voluntary and church schools into line with state schools, by allowing them to receive funding from local rates in addition to government grants. From then on Datchworth School would be closely monitored by Hertfordshire County Council. As a result, minutes of managers' meetings were required and a school log book had to be maintained by the head.

The first meeting of the managers was held at Datchworth School on Monday 5 October 1903, those present were: the Rev A. Amos, John Chapman, F.A. Lawrance, J. Smith, S. Wallace and H. Spooner. After electing the rector as chairman, John Smith as vice chairman and Mr H Spooner as correspondent, the meeting had to consider the problem of salaries. The headmaster, Mr Beswick, had applied for a rise. He was receiving '£80 per annum and House and Firing'.

> At the request of the Managers, Mr Beswick attended and stated his views on the matter, and intimated that if the salary was not raised he might tender his resignation... It was ultimately decided on the proposition of the Rector that the Master's salary be raised to £120 per annum and to pay his own House Rent and Firing.

The salary of Miss Hurrel, assistant teacher, was also raised from £30 to £35 per annum. The caretaker of the school was paid 2s per week and 3s during the holidays for 'scrubbing the school'.

This first meeting closed with a mention of the 'offices' [lavatories]:

> It was announced that the existing out-offices would have to be taken down and new ones erected away from the main building and the Rector suggested that Mr Abel [Henry] Smith be asked for a piece of land as a site for the same.

The logbook of the headmaster opens with a description of the school in 1904:

Length of main room	37 ½ feet
Breadth of main room	16 "
Recognised Accommodation	75 [children]
Length of classroom	16 feet
Breadth of classroom	13 ½ feet
Recognised Accommodation	27 [children]

It is clear from many entries that the state of the fabric of the school building and that of the headmaster's house caused constant worry, and the expense incurred was an annual anxiety to the trustees and the managers. On several occasions the pace was forced by the report of His Majesty's Inspectors, who complained about the state of the flooring, the lack of ventilation, particularly in the infants' classroom, the muddy and damp playground, the danger from the badly fenced moat and the poor condition of the 'offices'.

A further report relating to the 'offices' at the school is noted in the headmaster's log of 1905:

> Copy of H.M.I. report on the premises after visit 30th June 1905. Mixed School: The new Offices are very good but the Girls' offices should be entirely divided from the boys' playground. The dwarf wall between the yard and the moat should be raised or the yard should be protected by an effective fence or railing.

There are several references to sanitation in the managers' reports:

February 1914	paid J.W. Riggs Disinfecting school £1 5s 0d
December 1920	The emptying of the School pails is being undertaken by Wm. Furnell at an extra charge of 1/6 per week and this extra charge is being brought to the notice of the Education Authority with a view to its being paid permanently by them.
February 1921	Mr Welch reported that at times an offensive smell arose from School cesspool in meadow by side of road

Other entries about the fabric of the school include the bell turret needing repair, new concrete floors being laid, the gallery from the infants' room being removed and, in 1930, an agreement to bring electric light to the school, whereby the head's log reads: 'The Electric light is a great boon to the school during these dark afternoons.'

Inspectors and attendance

Though the fabric of the buildings was a cause for concern, the quality of the work done by the children was always praised by the inspectors. In 1906 the school received such praise that Hertfordshire County Council sent the school a special letter of commendation, based on the H.M.I report received:

> The discipline and tone are very good, the teaching is sound careful and intelligent, Drill, Singing, Drawing and Needlework are praiseworthy and though the work of the lower division is not without defects the general efficiency of the school is very creditable... the teaching [of the infants] is very pleasantly conversational and the children, who are very bright, happy and orderly, talk naturally and with confidence.

This high level of achievement was accomplished not only in a crowded classroom, but also with attendance problems. Attendance was a matter that was always an anxiety to the head of the school, whose concerns were twofold in that children who were absent could not learn and the government grant depended on the average rate of attendance.

In rural communities children were an important source of field labour but the lack of regulations relating to their employment had become a cause for concern. This was a national problem recognised in an Act of Parliament in 1876, where it was stated that no child under ten could be employed and no child between ten and thirteen unless they had attained a minimum required attendance and gained a certificate of educational proficiency.

Reference to this problem is made in school records in 1906:

> Received notice that the 'labour exam' will be held at the Boys School Welwyn at 2.15 on the 30th March. In accordance with the County Council Scheme allowing boys to be absent from school during the period between June 15 and October 15 provided that 250 attendances had been made between the months of October and June ... [3 boys] have fulfilled the required conditions and ... may be employed in Agriculture.

In 1903 Datchworth had one of the worst average attendances in the Hertford district and in 1904 the managers said that between £30 and £40 per annum was lost to the school funds by non-attendance. They hoped that absenteeism would drop 'now that the deficit was to be made up from the local rates and not the subscribers. Parents were reminded that the school was open 10 times a week and not 8 as seemed to be all that was expected'.

The condition of the roads and the state of the children's boots also caused attendance to drop. An entry in February 1919 reads:

> Another low attendance this week owing to the roads being deep in slush caused by the thawing of the snow. The boots of the children are very bad, the leather seems to absorb the water instead of keeping it out. Children are allowed to sit without their boots.

Childhood illnesses

Attendance figures were also affected by childhood diseases. The school was regularly swept by epidemics of scarlet fever, chicken pox, whooping cough, measles and, occasionally, diphtheria. An Act of 1907 provided a school medical service and gave the authority the power to shut schools on health grounds. In January 1914 the school was shut for two weeks owing to scarlet fever. The headmaster reports: 'I reopened the school this morning after consulting the chairman of the Managers about the low attendance, 30%' and continued his entries as follows:

February 19th	School closed until March 9th owing to Scarlet fever and Diptheria.
March 23rd	The children assembled at 8.55 am but were dismissed as the Managers did not think it advisable to open school before they had consulted the Medical Officer as a fresh case of Scarlet Fever had occurred near the school. School closed until April 1st.
April 1st	I opened the school this morning the attendance is very low, 25 present out of 75.
April 9th	School closed for Easter holidays.
April 24th (after Easter)	Notified one case of Scarlet Fever to Dr Dunn.
April 29th	Received letter from Dr Dunn advising closure of school until May 25th. Notified H.M.I. by telegram.
June 9th	The school was opened on June 2nd but I was advised by the Medical Officer not to resume work until today as my son had contracted Scarlet Fever.
June 15th	Owing to Mumps and Scarlet Fever 22 children are absent this morning.

The school was not closed again and two interrupted terms finished without further mishap. However, following this exceptional period of illness, concerns were being raised about the state of the moat that surrounded three sides of the school. It had been condemned by the medical officer and as well as being smelly and a hazard to the children's health, it was also regularly overflowing causing damage to the road. In March 1915 the issue was discussed by the parish council, who resolved to contact the district council with the view that the moat should be drained and filled in. The district council agreed to drain the moat and fill the north end but the school mangers were to fill the portion at the back and south end of the school.

Attendance awards and holidays

In an effort to improve attendance, prizes and holidays were given regularly. The presentation of prizes for attendance was an annual event but Margaret Pearman had the distinction of being the only pupil to receive a watch, which was awarded 'for five years perfect attendance'. Margaret Pearman became Margaret Shepherd, who went on to serve the school for many years, first as a 'pupil teacher' and then teacher.

Figure 119: Mrs Shepherd's class at Datchworth school (1933)
(Datchworth Museum)

Other attendance award entries include:

October 28th 1904	Holiday given by the order of the Managers as the average [attendance] for the last month has been over 90 per cent.
December 23rd 1908	The following won County Council prizes for regular attendance. Prizes at 3s: Frederick Culvert, William Burgess, Mabel Savage, Elsie Maud Taylor, Percy Allenby, Herbert Taylor, Alfred Thomas Wilmott, Margaret Pearman, Arthur Penn, Maud E Arnold and Stanley Arnold. Prizes at 2s: Alice Brown and Edith Hornett. The following received certificates: Dorothy Scott, Maggie Wilmott, David Gaddie, Elsie May Scott, Elsie Chalkley and Henry Taylor. Infants: Reginald Chalkley and Ralph Collins.

There were other holidays and treats. In 1907 the sister of the Reverend A. Amos was married. 'The school was opened Tuesday afternoon instead of Tuesday morning owing to the wedding of the rector's sister. Mrs Amos sent up oranges and sweets and buns for the children in the afternoon. The attendance was good.'

The school was often closed early on the day of Stevenage fair so that the children could go. An entry on 21 September 1928 combines holidays, attendance and contact with other schools.

> All children making a perfect attendance for the week were allowed to go home at ¼ to 4pm and as a reward for same the football team were permitted to accept a challenge to play Knebworth School boys at Knebworth. For this purpose, those boys who wished to play left school at 3pm instead of taking part in organised games on their own premises. The game at Knebworth commenced between 3.30 and 3.45pm. John Arnold's ankle was broken at the end of this match about 4.45pm.

The increasing population began to put pressure on the school's capacity. In December 1908 the county council proposed to erect a school for 150 pupils near the railway station at Knebworth to accommodate children from the rapidly growing parts of Welwyn, Knebworth and Datchworth. However, the parish council considered that the new school should house 250 children. The county council modified their plans accordingly for a school to be built in Swangleys Lane. However, three years later, in 1911, this part of the parish was annexed by Knebworth in one of Datchworth's many boundary changes, just as the new school was completed.

The impact of the First World War

The first mention of the First World War appeared in the headmaster's logbook on 7 September 1914. The entry age of five years old was waived to allow a little girl, whose father had enlisted, to attend school so that her mother could go to work. In May 1916, it was reported: 'There are now 7 children on the school registers who are at work for the period of the war. This reduces the percentage of attendance by 7.5 each week.' By September 1916, there were ten children absent for the period of the war but some children were not 'legally' absent for agricultural work. In December 1916, the headmaster, Mr Welch, says; 'Mr Wallace (farmer) who was harrowing and ploughing his potato field allowed the villagers to pick up those potatoes that had been missed by the pickers. Some picked up as many as 4 or 5 bushels a day and this led naturally enough to further absences from school.'

The farmers were obviously working hard to help feed the nation with little help and the children and the school had to rally round, as shown in this entry on 10 October 1917:

> Mr Franklin, farmer, called at the school and asked if he could have some of the school children to assist in potato picking owing to the scarcity of labour. The headmaster visited all the local farmers to ascertain their respective needs and the general feeling was that the children would be very useful for a fortnight. The school closed for 2 weeks for potato picking.

Not only did the school help the local farmers with potatoes, but the school garden was taken over for food production. On 27 February 1917 the log book reads; 'Commenced work on the Rectory plot today. All the children in Class 1 employed in this food producing work. The plot consisting of about 25 sq. poles of ground was mainly to be used for the production of potatoes and beet.' 1918 proved to be a disastrous year for the potato crop. A wet spring meant that the potatoes had to be re-sown and on 6 September:

> The potatoes in the school emergency plot were torn up and eaten by Mr Little's bullocks. The animals, in order to get at the potatoes, have broken down tough thick stakes and trampled down the barbed wire and netting. To save the rest of the crop they had to be dug up hurriedly by the children. It was decided that this plot could not be used again as the potatoes had been partly destroyed last year in the same way.

Apart from potato picking, the children spent time gathering blackberries and were paid 3d per lb. These were then sold, and in 1918, it was recorded that about 300 lbs were picked.

Mr Welch continued to worry about attendance figures. Even an air raid seemed to him a poor excuse for missing school. On 5 October 1917 he reports that: 'The attendance this week has been very disappointing owing chiefly to colds and the Air Raid on Monday. Percentage of Attendance 74.6. It is impossible to get all the children well on with their new work with such an attendance.'

The effects of the long war and the need for new recruits had an impact on staffing levels at the school. An entry on 14 June 1918 read: 'William Lawrance, Pupil Teacher, was 18 years of age on May 28th, was medically examined on June 1st and is called up for the army on June 29th.' Mr Welch was exempted, as were all school teachers over 32 years of age. Pupil teachers were difficult to come by and Mr Welch notes that: 'In this neighbourhood, any girl or boy over 15 years of age can earn from 25s to 35s per week at Henlow Aerodrome, together with a free pass on the railway from Knebworth station.'

There is no mention of the armistice or of any school celebrations to welcome peace in 1918. This may have been because the end of the war coincided with an influenza epidemic. By 15 November 1918, the school was badly affected by 'flu' and it was closed on 20 November to 16 December. At this time the rector wrote in the church magazine that Mrs Scales, an assistant teacher, had lost a son and daughter-in-law, as well as a daughter and grandson, as a result of influenza, 'which has been a terrible scourge in these parts.'

Between the wars

It was not until July 1919 that the managers sanctioned an extra week's holiday in connection with the Peace Celebration 'and in accordance with the expressed wishes of His Majesty King George.'

In the period after the First World War events moved fairly smoothly at the school apart from the ever present problem of the 'offices'. After several unsuccessful attempts to deal with matter, it was decided in 1937 to build new lavatories at a cost of £190 and a second water closet at the school house for an extra £7. Attempts to raise money by borrowing from the landowner were thwarted because no-one knew who owned the land on which the school stood. The new lavatories were nevertheless installed. The headmaster wrote on 4 February 1938: 'Today a new [water] system of sanitation has been completed for both the school and school house, a much needed and greatly appreciated improvement.'

However, the managers were now in debt for £350. Robert Wallace offered to lend this sum on security of the school property. Thus it became even more necessary to solve the question of the land ownership. The matter was not resolved until 1953, when a further extension to the school was being planned. In response to a query about the ownership of the land, Thomas Abel Smith wrote to Miss Esdaile, one of the school managers:

> Dear Miss Esdaile,
>
> Thank you for your letter of July 11th. I am afraid I have no record of the past history of the School Playground at Datchworth and I am not aware that it is still my property. If this should prove the case I shall be very glad to convey it free of charge to the school.
>
> Yours sincerely
>
> T. Abel Smith.

The problem of ownership was settled, but the new lavatories were not free from problems. The pipes were prone to freeze in winter and a reference in the headmaster's log is typical of many: 'The very severe frost during the Christmas holiday caused extensive damage to the pipes and cisterns in lavatories outside which has now been made good.'

It was reported that two managers, both appointed in 1903, ceased to serve the school in this period between the wars, Frederick Lawrence died in 1930 and Mr H Spooner resigned in 1934.

Second World War

The routine running of the school ended in 1938 as the first indications of the likelihood of war appeared in the school logbook:

September 28th	Received stretcher and first aid equipment under A.R.P. Children fitted with gas masks in Village Hall.
September 29th	A squad of labourers from Mr R. Wallace of Woolmer Green worked at trench digging in the school playground... About 30 feet of trenches were completed and 45 feet more commenced.

The next day, 30 September, Neville Chamberlain returned from Munich with his famous piece of paper bearing Hitler's signature agreeing to 'peace for our time'. Nevertheless, the local ARP group continued to make several visits to the school, testing and supervising the trenches during the year.

The headmaster's entries for September 1939 are as follows:

September 4th	Owing to the outbreak of war on September 3rd School did not open this morning.
September 8th	On Thursday and Friday 7th and 8th inst. the school was used as a place of assembly for all children of school age resident in the village who enjoyed games on the meadow, country walks and gardening in the school garden in charge of the three schoolteachers, Miss Walker, Mrs Shepherd and the Headmaster.
September 11th	School opened at 9am this morning. Nurse called. 4 permanently resident pupils admitted. 4 L.C.C. evacuated children (with parents) admitted. 15 children from self-evacuated families admitted.
September 12th	2 more children from self-evacuated families admitted. Nurse inspected the heads of all children present (72). The Headmaster and boys commenced making dugouts for the refuge of children in case of air raids during school hours. Expert craftsmen will assist later I hope.

The school staff immediately had to cope with numbers of evacuated children. The associated problems were social as well as administrative. Children far from home had to be fitted into a new way of life and throughout the war, the numbers were constantly fluctuating. By February 1940 the early batch of evacuees had drifted back to London and then later in 1940 a group of children from the Mount Pleasant junior school in Hastings was sent to Datchworth. These children were initially taught as a separate group in the village hall until October 1941, when: 'The Hastings, L.C.C. and other children attending the Village Hall were then formally merged into Datchworth School.' The joint school was arranged thus: 'The Headmaster and Mrs Shepherd to take 64 children between the ages of 10 and 13 years in main schoolroom. Miss Graham (from Hastings) to teach 32 children between ages of 6 and 9 in the Village Hall. Miss Walker to take the remaining 24 children of 5 and 6 years of age in the school.' This arrangement lasted until January 1943 when the village hall classroom was closed.

As in the First World War, children were recruited for potato picking and to help at harvest time which caused the headmaster to worry about the interrupted education, as recorded on 8 October 1943:

> Attendance in the upper class was very low indeed this week, 107 out of a possible 290 [total attendances, not children] owing to the children potato picking for Mr J L Little and Mr F H Temperly.

Children helped in other activities such as knitting socks, scarves and balaclava helmets for the Soldiers' Comforts Fund and aiding the efforts of the Women's Institute in gathering rosehips.

The introduction of school meals for the children during wartime was a change that was to become permanent. Initially these were provided at the village hall in the summer of 1942 until the new school kitchen was completed in 1944. On 30 August the log reads: 'the first meal was served from the school kitchen to 35 children who ate the meal in the classroom. The desks were covered with small tablecloths made by the senior pupils.' Then, on 20 December: 'Christmas dinner of Roast beef, 2 vegetables, plum pudding and custard and mince pies served to the 47 children who stayed.'

The headmaster, Mr Towler, records two bombs that fell locally: 'During the holiday, on Wed. 23rd August 1944, an enemy 'flying bomb' fell in Datchworth Parish in Eyrefield Nurseries, Bull's Green rendering three families homeless – Facey, Harris, Collins.' On 8 January 1945, the day that school reopened after the Christmas holidays; 'a rocket fell and exploded near Fir Grove (Baines Wood) about 4.19pm soon after school had closed for the day. There were no casualties but some material damage was caused to buildings at Jubilee Corner and along Baines Lane. A few windows were broken at Bury Farm, Old Pound House and in the Church.'

In the spring of 1945 Mr Towler made this brief entry in the logbook, written in red ink; 'May 9th: School closed on Tuesday and Wednesday, V.E. days' holiday'.

After the Second World War

Towards the end of the war, R A Butler's Education Act was introduced in 1944 which was designed to provide free secondary education. The leaving age was to be increased from 14 to 15 years in 1947; the initial proposal of 16 years was not effected until 1972. Secondary education was to begin at the age of 11 in one of three types of school: grammar, technical and secondary modern. In the case of Datchworth School, it was decided that all children aged 11 and over should be sent to a larger school. The result was that in January 1946, ten pupils were transferred to Knebworth School. After this change, Datchworth became a 'Junior and Infant' school with an initial roll of 48.

The bad winter of 1947 is reflected in the head's log:

February 7th	Influenza and Influenza Colds, added to the difficulty of movement on severe frost and ice, have been responsible for the large drop in attendance... 57
February 11th	After the children had left school on Tuesday afternoon the Headmaster discovered a small fire burning under the fireplace at south end of large classroom and along the joists leading thereto. With help the fire was extinguished in about 1½ hours but not until the fireplace had been broken through and several floor boards removed.
February 12th	The children attended school as usual in the morning but on the advice of the Education Department, school was closed at dinner time and no alternative means of heating could be devised. There was an electricity cut and no oil.

The school was reopened on 17 February 1947.

School managers continued to deal with school administration until the early 1970s when they became known as 'governors' rather than 'managers', otherwise, their duties remained the same. Examples of those who went through this transition were Norman Pearman and Bill Nash. The longest serving member of the Board of Managers was James L Little who resigned in 1960, after having given a remarkable 48 years to the school.

School developments

In the post war recovery the population of the village increased as new houses were built. This meant that the school became too small to accommodate the growing number of children. There were many discussions about building a new school on the area of land where Nutcroft now stands. Finally it was decided that the proper course of action would be to expand the old school and eventually there were to be five further extensions to the school between 1954 and 2003. Being a Church of England school most of the funding for such projects comes from the Diocese of St Albans who in turn receives grants from the government.

The first of these extensions was for a new classroom which began in April 1954, at cost of £1,382. This room was built on the eastern side of the original building, and was visited by a school inspector in 1955, who reported as follows:

> In Sept. 1954 a new and very pleasant room came into use; money collected locally made the building of this room possible without any call on diocesan funds. Managers are to be congratulated on this achievement and also in re-roofing and substantial improvement to the lighting in the larger of two original rooms which have recently been carried out.

However, there was still room for improvement, as the inspector continues:

> There is no staff room and no storage space. The cloakrooms are cramped... The sanitary accommodation is some way from the main building, the urinal that is unroofed and has not an automatic flush, is in need of resurfacing... There is no hot water supply.

Following the inspector's report, in 1961 a classroom of 700 square feet, internal lavatories and a boiler were added to the school, at a cost of £8,359. This extension was opened and dedicated on 18 September by the Bishop of Bedford.

The population of Datchworth continued to increase and once again the school was faced with the problem of overcrowding. When the last extension had been built in 1961, the school had 71 children, but by September 1968 there were 107 pupils. Whilst plans were put in place for a further extension, temporary accommodation was provided for the growing number of children. The staff room was used as a classroom and a

Figure 120: All Saints' School, Datchworth after having five additions to the original building (far right) (2013)

caravan was purchased to provide additional space. On 7 January 1969 the managers accepted a bid of £10,590 to build two new classrooms, one open plan for infants, the other for juniors, plus additional lavatories, an internal corridor and an office for the headmaster. This large extension, which almost doubled the size of the school, was opened and dedicated by the Bishop of Hertford in October 1969.

In 1970 there were national celebrations for the 100th anniversary of state supported primary education in Great Britain. For Datchworth it represented the 150th anniversary of its school, which was marked by the first visit of the newly appointed Bishop of St Albans to a school in his diocese; the Bishop went on to become the Archbishop of Canterbury. He wrote in the following message in the school logbook:

> On the occasion of the 150th anniversary of the school I was happy to spend an afternoon here. This is my first visit to any school in my diocese. I hope that all future school engagements will be as enjoyable as this. A lively place with the atmosphere of a happy and purposeful family.
>
> Robert St Albans
> June 10th 1970

The school had hardly recovered from the previous building work, when plans for yet another extension began in December 1971. The new plans included a dual-purpose assembly hall and gymnasium, an additional classroom and a new kitchen on the south of the original structure at a cost of £34,050. This extension took some time to complete, and the headmaster wrote on 5 September 1972: 'School reassembled at 8.55am in an incomplete school. Electricians, painters, carpenters etc. still working. Many items of equipment still overdue. Once again the sheer professionalism of the staff conquered most difficulties.'

From 1971, pupil numbers fluctuated, starting from a peak of 144, they fell to just 63 in 1980 and then rose to 105 in 1995. Subsequently, the numbers continued to rise steadily until, by 2012, they had reached 165. In 2003 another new classroom was added at a cost of about £100,000. Various fundraising events enabled the Parent Teacher Association (PTA) and parents to raise £21,500 towards the cost, the remainder being funded by government grants. Initially this classroom was a standalone building but has since been connected to the main building by a corridor.

Further internal alterations have been made in the last few years, including a new cloakroom and storage area, improved facilities for people with disabilities, a larger school office and a music room. Externally, a section of the field adjoining the playground was purchased and other additions included a gazebo, an open outdoor classroom and an award-winning wild life garden.

In contrast to the early years, the school has benefitted from a larger teaching staff including 14 full and part-time teachers. The expansion of the school has been due to many factors. As well as new housing, a government policy was introduced that encouraged parents to seek schools of their choice that brought children in from further afield.

The school has continued to receive complimentary reports from both Ofsted and R.E. Inspectors. Of particular note is the 'outstanding curriculum' shown by the wide range of studies including music lessons, French and Latin as well

Figure 121: Datchworth school football team 1933:

Ernie Ewington
Muffy Nesbit, Ken Webb, Charlie Penn, Basil Miller, Len Draper
Bernie Reynolds, Ernie Ingram, Herbie Nash, Bernie Skeggs, Bob Croft
Eric Austin, Eric Ewington
(Datchworth Museum)

Figure 122: Datchworth School football team 2003 after winning the Stevenage league cup, with their coach, Nick Webb (former Hitchin Town goal keeper).

Boys names Left to right:
Andrew Williams, Martin Peacock, Alex Game, Steven Lee, Ben Jay, David Hulman, Matthew Bristow, Alex Nee, Max Difford, George Wallace.

as ICT reflecting current advances in technology. The variety of sporting activities has increased considerably since that early football match reported in the school log book in 1928, enabling participation in a variety of competitive events. The school also continues to keep its close connection with the church and with the parish priest, who is a frequent visitor to the school.

Links with the local community and other schools are maintained through activities such as dancing at the village fête, entertaining members of the Elderberries club at Christmas, attending the Citizenship Awards in Hatfield and competing in the inter-village sports day and other sporting festivals and tournaments.

The large thriving school represents a monument to the courage, faith and generosity of the nine subscribers who began in 1820. Its development owes much to the PTA and the school governors, the former through fundraising and social events, and the latter by assisting the head teacher in the areas of finance, curriculum, health and safety, the building and personnel management.

Burnham Green School

In 1843, a school was erected at Burnham Green for the children of the outlying parts of Welwyn, Datchworth, Digswell and Tewin parishes. This, like Datchworth School, was funded by public subscription; 'Lord Cowper and the Rectors of these four parishes being the trustees and forming a Board of Management'.

The first mistress was Mrs Campkin, who died in 1851 and was succeeded by Mrs Turner. The school then went through a bad patch, with several rapid changes in teachers. One mistress, Miss Bairstow, left after seven weeks because it was 'too dull'. However, in 1863, improvement came when Mary Ann Wade took on the post. She was an experienced teacher: 'who refuses to be in a Government school from indignation at the treatment of mistresses under the revised code and has come here for, house furnished, coals and £20 a year'. The Reverend Williamson records that: 'this woman of firm character reduced the school into excellent order'. In 1865, her salary was raised to £25 a year. The last mistress was Mrs Spooner who was appointed in 1879.

At that time the main hall was the classroom and the mistress lived in the remainder of the building. There was a separate front door to the living accommodation where there was a staircase leading to two upper bedrooms. The lounge of the mistress's house was where the kitchen is now. A fireplace was situated below where there is now a

Figure 123: A plaque mounted on the building.

Figure 124: (Now) Burnham Green Village Hall (2013)

serving hatch. There was another fireplace in the main hall but this too has been removed. The original kitchen has been replaced by toilets for the disabled.

The building was licensed as a church at the beginning of the twentieth century and became a Sunday school that was well attended during the First World War. The registers for the time show that the old parish surnames were still in evidence – Shadbolt, Burgess, Whittenbury. Mrs Spooner was the Sunday school teacher, assisted by Mrs Rose. The infant school continued to operate there until 1929, after which the building was used by All Saints' Church for Holy Communion and as a chapel and mission hall for Burnham Green. The Sunday school continued until the 1960s.

During the Second World War the use of the hall for a private infant school was revived for a few years with Mrs Olive Smith as teacher. According to ex-pupils Felicity Clarke (now Fizzy Chambers) and Barbara Franklin (now Barbara Edwards), Mrs Smith was very strict and the children were quite frightened of her. Fizzy also recalls that the children had to pay 1d per week to use the mistress's outside 'lavvy' which was round the back of the building. The private school ceased business in about 1949.

In the early 1950s a meeting was held to decide the future of the hall. Out of the 40 parishioners that attended, only 13 were in favour of keeping it as a place of worship. The second, and preferred, option was for it to be used as a village hall

In 1953 the 110-year-old building was purchased from the St Albans Diocesan Board of Finance by the villagers, through the Social and Welfare Committee, for £850. The church furniture and accoutrements were transferred to All Saints' Church, Datchworth. The inventory included preacher's robes, four brass candlesticks, one chalice, one paten, and one alms-plate. The pulpit, which was of carved oak, was sold for £10 to the South Durham Mission to the Deaf & Dumb.

The church's little library is of some interest. There was an 1848 illustrated Bible valued in 1950 at £30 and 1676 'Quarles Emblems'. This was a book of religious or moral poetry, each poem illustrated by an allegorical picture based on a biblical quotation; a book of enormous popularity in its day.

The village hall is now a registered charity administered by a village hall committee, acting as management trustees. It is a venue for meetings, antique markets, lectures and social functions and also currently houses a twice-weekly outreach post office service, thus continuing to be an important amenity for the people of Burnham Green.

Datchworth Pre-school

The nursery school was first set up by Mrs Hone in May 1962 in the old village hall (or 'hut'), until it moved in to the new village hall that opened in 1972. It is said that the idea for a nursery in Datchworth came about in the late 1950s, when many middle class families began to move into the village. Not being satisfied with starting their children's schooling at the obligatory age of five years, they were sending their young children to private nurseries outside Datchworth, until some of the parents argued that the village should have its own nursery.

The nursery was a privately run business until January 1991, when it was decided to change it to a formal nursery administered by a committee with the aim of becoming a charitable institution. To do this, they had to apply for affiliation to the Pre-school Playgroup Association (PPA) and in the spring of the same year its membership to the PPA was confirmed.

In 1993, when the nursery became a registered charity, it was already being up-graded to conform to the requirements of the 1989 Children Act. This legislation laid down numerous standards to which the nursery had to conform, not least of which was the requirement that a minimum of 50% of the staff should be qualified. In 2007, with the implementation of the government's Early Years Foundation, it became necessary for 'all' staff within the setting to be NVQ level 3 qualified, with the leader having a Degree in Education. Christine Hills decided to step down as leader following these new regulations; however, she continued to work as a general assistant until she eventually retired, after 29 years, in 2013. The previous voluntary help from interested and involved mothers was forced to change to staff with a high degree of professional status.

Figure 125: Pre-school Nativity play in the old village hall. Helena Nettell (Tom Beachcroft's granddaughter) sits at the front, second in from the right. (1963)

By the middle of 1993 the limitations of the room used in the village hall were becoming apparent. The committee agreed that an extension to the village hall would meet the nursery's requirements for the foreseeable future and be the most cost-effective scheme.

The planning and the necessary public relations work fell mainly on the shoulders of Lesley Chambers and Claire Bennett, both of whom were founders of the re-organised nursery. In December 1993 the pre-school committee embarked upon the ambitious appeal programme to raise the £30,000 required to build the extension.

Many parishioners as well as mothers of children in the nursery became involved with various fundraising projects. One of the most vigorous and enthusiastic of these was Diana Norman, a well-known writer and Datchworth resident, who became Patron of the Nursery Building Fund. As a result of a miscellany of well-supported activities, grants from a variety of local organisations and authorities, and many generous donations, the necessary money was quickly raised, enabling the building to go ahead.

Thus it was in October 1995 that the nursery school, renamed Datchworth Pre-school, moved into its new room. The opening ceremony was performed by Diana and her husband Barry of T.V. fame, attended by well over a hundred people who were variously involved in the project. In recognition of Diana and Barry's valuable support, the new room is dedicated to their late grandson, Oliver.

By 2007 it was decided that the new pre-school room was in need of a re-vamp. Therefore with money raised from the committee's continuing fundraising efforts, a complete refurbishment of the room took place during the summer of that year, which included redecoration, new furnishings and kitchen area. In addition, a grant of £2,500 was awarded by the county council which enabled the replacement of many of the old worn toys and indoor play equipment.

The committee and staff then decided to venture into the installation of an all weather outdoor play area which included an overhead canopy. In 2009, upon a successful application to the county council for a grant of £25,000, the canopy was ordered and fitted at a total cost of £27,300. The garden area was resurfaced, raised flowerbeds installed and new outdoor play equipment purchased. The new garden area was officially opened by the former chairperson, Helen Otero, who instigated the project.

The Pre-school is now very successful and popular, with a full capacity of 26 children per session, running five mornings per week as well as some afternoon sessions and lunch club every day.

Figure 126: The opening ceremony of the new pre-school room in 1995 – Diana Norman, Claire Bennett & Barry Norman.

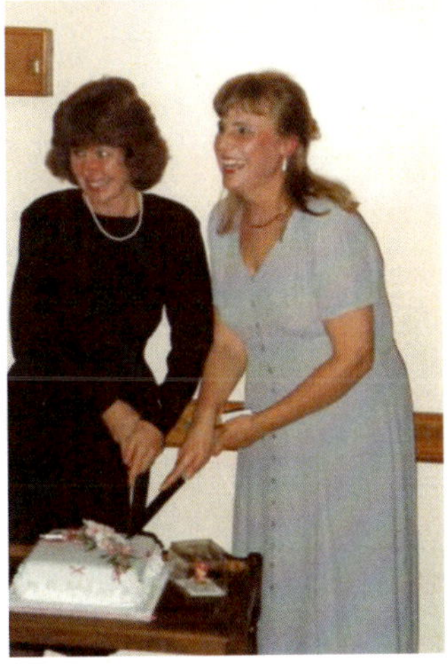

Figure 127: Claire Bennett and Lesley Chambers at the opening of the new pre-school room.

Tiddlywinks

The Mother & Toddler group originated in 1986 and was set up by Jackie Nash and Julie Appleby. For many years it was held weekly on an afternoon in Datchworth Sports Club. Each week Joe Buckridge, along with his trusty dog, would walk down from his cottage at the crossroads to retrieve the toys that were stored in the loft, then at the end of the session he would return to put the various toys, bikes etc. away again. For many mothers and carers this afternoon was an important part of their week, meeting others with young children and babies.

In 1992 Datchworth Pre-school, who were based in the village hall, were looking for ways to attract more children. After much discussion, the parent committee suggested setting up a new Mother & Toddler group in the village hall, in the hope that most of these children would, as they grew older, go on to attend the pre-school.

At the beginning of 1993, Claire Bennett, Sarah Hulman and Sue Game took over the running of the toddler group and set up the new organisation, renamed Tiddlywinks, in the village hall for one morning a week. A lot of time was spent cleaning and sorting the old toys and going to car boot sales to buy newer ones. Very soon, with popularity, the group opened its doors twice a week and happily, many of these children went on to attend the Pre-school, gradually boosting its numbers.

Residents' Memories

Phyllis Smalley (Burnham Green): Our family went to Tewin Cowper Endowed School and had to walk – no school buses in those days. In cold weather we would carry a hot baked potato to school to keep our hands warm, and eat it when we got there. No hot school dinners, generally it was jam sandwiches for lunch. The boys did gardening and looked after the bees. The rainfall was taken every day. On our way home from school, Mr Hopkyns would be standing at his orchard gate and would give us apples which were ate before we got home. Sometimes he gave us dropped cookers to take home. Whilst at Tewin School we went on a trip to Panshanger House [now demolished] by invitation of Lord and Lady Desborough. We walked from Tewin across the fields to Panshanger. Big white sheets were laid all over the floors and carpets. We were given a lovely tea party and then a magic lantern show, then shown around the vast kitchen. I remember the huge number of pots and pans, all gleaming, round the wall and on the shelves, but above all the huge bells all round the top of the wall with room numbers under them. Races were held in the park and then we were given an apple and orange on leaving.

Bernard Reynolds: I finished my education at Datchworth School in 1934 where I learned to write on slates encouraged by the cane and ruler on the knuckles.

Mr Tyler (Burnham Green): I attended school at Burnham Green first before transferring to Datchworth. The former only had one classroom and one teacher.

Louie Cubbage: On my way to school, in all weathers, I used to have to take father his hot breakfast to him at work at Raffin Green Farm.

Mrs Skeggs & Mrs Nash: The school boys used to skate on the moat at the school. Once they found a man's body embedded in the ice, the head looked like a bundle of rags. The man was a stranger. The body was held by the rector in the church, a grave was dug and he was about to be buried when the body was claimed by his brother.

Reg Chalkley: I remember a body of a man being found frozen in the moat at the school.

Mrs Skeggs: The school had two classrooms, a bell tower and about 100 children in 1890/1900 period. When we broke up for holidays we had a tea party at the rectory.

14. 20th Century Building and Planning Disputes

The period between 1920 and 1980 was marked by the building of approximately 550 additional dwellings, some of which were constructed soon after each of the two world wars by the district council. Later, private enterprise was responsible for building several houses, some in groups and others as 'infill'. Few of these developments came with the blessing of the parish council or residents.

Social Housing

In September 1917 the parish council was asked to inform the district council of details regarding 'houses for the working classes in the parish'. It was reported that there were 101 cottages of not more than £8 rateable value. Three of these had one bedroom, 63 had two bedrooms, 32 had three bedrooms and 3 had four bedrooms. Six of these were unoccupied and the parish council made the comment that there was no need for more housing.

However, by 1921, six council houses had been built by the Lawrances in Bury Lane near the church and these were the first of their kind in the village. There were no bathrooms, so usually a tub was used for bathing and was filled with water that had been heated on a solid fuel kitchen range or stove. Clothes were washed in a large container called a 'copper', which, again, was filled with heated water. Cess pits were provided for sewage and oil lamps were the standard form of lighting until electricity was installed in 1929. These council houses were followed by more in Bury Lane in 1928 and others along the east side of Hawkins Hall Lane and along Burnham Green Road in the 1930s.

More social housing followed after the Second World War. In 1946 Wheatcotes was built on land that was once part of Farrins. Then came Nutcroft, that was built in several phases; the first batch of houses were built in the 1950s with the completion of the final batch in the early 1970s. In 1970 Datchworth had the distinction of being the recipient of the Hertford Rural District Council's 1000th council house. The final phase of 'council' house building in Datchworth was in 1980 when twenty-two bungalows and four maisonettes were added in Hawkins Hall Lane.

Shortly after the completion of this last phase of house building, pressure to provide housing eased. This came as a direct result of a low growth policy adopted by the county council according to its County Structure Plan. This new policy came into force in 1981 and was fulfilled by the district council by granting permission for infill development only, thus protecting Datchworth from undue expansion.

However, exceptions were made and resulted in a collection of houses being built to form Pennyfather Close and Nash Close. In 1996 planning permission was approved for two housing associations to build four houses along Hawkins Hall Lane and another six on land off Hawkins Hall Lane. Land was purchased from East Herts Council for £1 and permission was given for this development, in response to a survey which had highlighted a need for affordable housing for local residents. A few of these were shared equity properties, enabling local first time buyers to get on the property ladder, the rest were for social rent. The naming of the road off Hawkins Hall Lane coincided with the death of Bill Sharman, a former member and chairman of Datchworth Parish Council. The council requested that it should be called Sharman Close in Bill's honour, but this was turned down by the district council because in the interim a '25 years after death' rule had been introduced and so the name chosen for the road was Pennyfather Close.

In 2000 planning permission was granted to build ten more properties on an area of land adjacent to Pennyfather Close. This was named Nash Close at the suggestion of a previous parish clerk, Betty Clark, after one of the oldest family names still associated with the village. As with Pennyfather Close, these houses were partly shared equity properties and partly assigned for social rent. A condition was placed on both developments that the dwellings must be occupied by local residents or previous residents of the parish. If nominations from the parish could not be met, then applicants from outside the parish would be considered. In 2002 the district council passed the responsibility for all administration and maintenance of social housing in the parish to the housing associations.

Private Development

After the Second World War housing development accelerated. In 1946 the New Towns Act established a plan for building new towns and Stevenage was the first of these to be built. Shortly after, in 1947, the Town and Country Planning Act laid down conditions designed to control 'urban sprawl' into the countryside that might threaten villages like Datchworth. In particular, all towns and villages were to have a 'development plan' indicating clearly how areas should be built on or preserved.

Council housing continued in Datchworth until 1980, as already mentioned, but this was alongside private enterprise schemes, many of which were vigorously opposed by the parish council and residents. Those that were acceptable included 24 houses in Raffin Park built in the late 1950s and early 1960s. In the mid-1960s these were followed by developments such as Foldingshott with 15 houses, Raffin Close with 17 houses and a few houses along Raffin Green Lane.

At the same time as the large scale developments, there were a considerable number of individual housing projects, particularly within the wooded areas of Burnham Green Road and the lanes around the church. Until 1960 the north side of Datchworth Green was sparsely populated with large gaps between the houses but now every space is occupied.

Brookbridge Lane

At the beginning of the twentieth century there were only a handful of properties along Brookbridge Lane, of which Bridgefoot Farm cottages still remain. Two old bungalows were demolished to allow Meadow Close to be built and another bungalow, built in about 1838, was demolished in 2001 and replaced by number 82 Brookbridge Lane. Other bungalows were added along the east side of Brookbridge Lane between the wars, some of which have been extended in recent years. The new rectory at the top of the lane was built in 1954 to accommodate the Reverend Julian Tross after the decision had been made to sell the old rectory in 1939.

Green belt regulations contained planning requirements suggesting that there should be no building on the west side of Brookbridge Lane. This interpretation was used by the parish council when, in 1967, a plan was proposed for building on a site that is now Abbots Close. The parish was joined in its opposition for the plan by the district council and a number of Datchworth residents. A Public Inquiry was held at which, despite the green belt regulations, the Inspector decided that the development could proceed on the grounds that the proposed site was well within the village boundary and was not being used to any particular advantage. The four houses on either side of Abbots Close followed in 1969.

Another proposal that was eventually granted permission was that of Beechcroft, formerly the site of a derelict builders' yard. The initial application that was submitted and approved was for three houses, but the developers had allowed the planning approval to lapse. They re-submitted their application in 1986 but in the interim a new District Plan had been adopted with more stringent conditions and so their subsequent application was unsuccessful. However, the parish council realised the need for compact, affordable accommodation for elderly residents and suggested that plans should be drawn up for the consultation and approval of the parish. The developers agreed to this and in 1988 a public meeting was held. It gave its support to the application, which was able to use a clause in the District Plan permitting certain 'needed' developments. The application was approved to built seven bungalows. Prospective buyers were subject to restrictions on age and the 'local residential qualification'.

The completion of these 'retirement' bungalows coincided with Tom Beachcroft (author of *Five Hide Village*) moving from the village. It was suggested to the builders that the development might be named after him, therefore the name 'Beechcroft' was chosen.

In 1978 Meadow Close was built on the west side of Brookbridge Lane, a development that was closely linked with the demise of the old turkey farm and is mentioned later in the chapter.

Until the late 1960s the east side of Brookbridge Lane only consisted of three Bridgefoot Farm cottages and a handful of small bungalows that were built between the two wars, as mentioned earlier. Most of the of the housing on this side began in 1968 following a chain of events that started in 1920, when Abel Henry Smith sold the greater part of his property in Datchworth. This included nearly 2½ acres of land on the east side of Brookbridge Lane which was subsequently purchased by the county council for £100 and then leased to the parish council for allotments. In 1968 this land was sold by the county council with planning permission for houses to be built for private ownership. The development was for eight houses in Brookbridge Lane and another twenty-three, in what is now Great Lawne. Also at this time five houses were built at the bottom of Brookbridge Lane, south of Bridgefoot Cottages. As the years passed gaps were gradually built on and by the end of the twentieth century every space had been filled.

Residential developments 2014

Plans for two large scale development proposals have been put forward in recent months. The first is a proposal to build 20 properties on the industrial and paddock areas at the Pound Farm site. This scheme has been unanimously disapproved of by the local residents, who in turn have the backing of the parish council. The second proposal is for nine houses to be built on the White Horse Farm site at Burnham Green, in place of the existing farm buildings.

Unsuccessful Planning Applications

In 1970 three controversial development schemes were submitted that met with powerful resistance from Datchworth residents. The first was for houses to be built on the mobile home site off Burnham Green Road behind Club Cottage and the other two related to building in fields north of Watton Road; between them these schemes would have added a significant number of houses to the village.

The parish council shared the anxieties of parishioners and the chairman, Norman Pearman, called a public meeting to discuss the matter and how best to present objections. The main outcome was the formation of the Datchworth Preservation Society, which was able to co-ordinate public opinion and represent the views of its members if and when it was necessary. According to the 'objects and constitution' of the Datchworth Rural Preservation Society, the aims were 'to preserve as many of the amenities of rural life as were compatible with a growing population' and also 'to foster good and well-spaced housing and to oppose housing that seemed unsuitable and overcrowded for village life'.

A Public Inquiry was held on 21 May 1970 in relation to the proposed scheme near Club Cottage, at which the recently formed Datchworth Preservation Society gave evidence and presented a petition signed by 220 people. The Inquiry was attended by 79 Datchworth residents and letters had been written by 48 people. The weight and quality of the opposition impressed the Inspector sufficiently for him to turn down the application. However, two years later, a second application was made to build on this site resulting in a similar local reaction which led to another Public Inquiry in 1974. The scheme was opposed by Datchworth Preservation Society with the support of Tewin Society, a group that was formed in 1969, and once again, the application was rejected.

Plans for the Watton site were presented in two stages. In the first place, 40 houses were to be built, somewhat densely, on land to the west of the Hawkins Hall Lane junction. Later, on a much larger field, on the east side of Hawkins Hall Lane, there was to be another development consisting of several hundred properties. These proposals led to another Public Inquiry at which the first of these schemes was discussed. Once again, there was fierce opposition from the parish and district councils, supported by the preservation society which by then had over 400 members, this rose to about 600 in 1982. Again the development plan was rejected and the second application was withdrawn.

However, all three of the above sites still remain on the district council's list for possible future development. Recently they were put forward as potential sites for consideration within the new District Plan which is expected to be 'in place' in 2015. Nevertheless, none of them has so far been included in the new plan and in the case of the Hawkins Hall Lane sites, which consist of 50 acres in total, they were rejected by the district council on the grounds that the possible size of a development would be 'totally out of scale for the area' and would completely alter the character of the village.

The Turkey Farm

In the early twentieth century this area of land to the west of Brookbridge Lane was cultivated to provide turf for customers including Wembley Stadium and Tottenham Hotspurs Football Club. In 1956 it was purchased by Hall Mark Turkeys Limited for use as a turkey farm where turkeys were raised, slaughtered and prepared for sale. In 1972 the farm closed and plans were put forward for the site to be developed. In view of the likely number of dwellings that could be built, an original plan to sell the site for building was rejected. The plan was modified to sell only a small part of the area for building, reserve part as a recreation ground and the remaining 11 acres was to be kept for agricultural use. As a result, Meadow Close was built, which contains 15 houses and eight acres was given to the parish to be used for recreational activities such as football, bowls and basketball. Leisure plots [allotments] were also made available and play equipment was provided for the youngsters. There was also a tree-planting scheme, which has enhanced the appearance of the surroundings and a special garden in memory of Norman Pearman who died in 1975.

In 1988 the play equipment installed in 1981 had rotted and so had to be removed, apart from the embankment slide that is still there today. New play equipment was installed which was designed by Year 6 children at the school. Apart from this, the Turkey Farm recreation ground remained much the same for over twenty years, until 2007, when a succession of additions were made over the next five years. In the summer of 2007 the play equipment that was installed in 1988 was declared dangerous in the annual safety inspection and had to be removed. Again Year 6 school children contributed ideas and the parish council provided a zip-wire and multi-use climbing bridge in the winter of 2008 at a total cost of £17,383.

The installation of the new play equipment intensified ongoing concerns regarding the ever increasing number of cars driving through the ground to gain access to the bowls club and leisure plots. This traffic was not only damaging the grass but was a potential danger to children playing there and so the parish council initiated discussions with the bowls club and the plot

Figure 128: The turkey farm 1963 – On the far left are the two old cottages where Meadow Close is now. In the bottom left corner are the old allotments, where numbers 45 to 55 Brookbridge Lane and Great Lawne now stand.

holders to find ways of minimising vehicular access. It was eventually decided to extend the car park by adding the lower level, providing more convenient access for those with walking difficulties. In January 2009, once the new play area was complete, the extended car park was then enclosed by installing wooden bollards and a lockable gate. A specified number of bowls club members and leisure plot holders have been entrusted with a key to the gate, provided that they adhere to strict conditions as instructed in a written agreement with the parish council. To further assist the leisure plot holders, a storage container was purchased to provide a secure place where big or heavy items or tools could be stored.

Also in 2009 the planting of an orchard and wild flower meadow took place. The project was instigated, arranged and overseen by Councillor Vivien Marshall, who organised funds for the project having secured a grant of £2,500, awarded by the Big Lottery Fund. The planting took place one day in the spring, with the help of local volunteers and the guides and Diana Norman provided refreshments for everyone from the boot of her car. The trees in the orchard bear apples, pears and plums and, in the meadow, a wide variety of wild flowers and grasses have been planted.

In 2010 an issue was raised by the leisure plot holders that their crops were being ruined by rabbits and muntjac. The parish council

Figure 129: The first Turkey Farm play area 1981. (Datchworth Museum)

Figure 130: The Turkey Farm orchard with the wild flower meadow in the background (2012).

encouraged the plot holders to obtain quotations for suitable fencing and apply for a grant from the district council to fund the work. Roy Cook took on this task and his application was successful: a grant of £2,400 was awarded and the rabbit-proof fence and gates were erected in the spring of 2011.

The parish council had several failed attempts at securing grants for the refurbishment of the old basketball area. However, in 2012 their attempts came to fruition and they successfully obtained grants from three different sources, which together with many years of savings, was enough to enable the old basketball area to be re-surfaced and made into a multi-use play area. At the Annual Parish Meeting that was held on the 1 May 2012, parishioners, young and old, were invited to put forward ideas of how they would like the area to be used. It was eventually agreed that there should be a basketball, netball and five-a-side football court, a small area for young children to ride bikes and a hump for scooters and skateboards. Grants amounting to £15,000 were awarded, the parish council paid the additional £11,000 that was required and the project was completed in the spring of 2013.

The planning conditions for the turkey farm area stipulated that the remaining eleven acres should always be kept for agricultural use. It has been mentioned earlier that existing green belt policy has, in principle, ruled out new building on the west side of Brookbridge Lane. Therefore when a property developer purchased this land with the intention of building on it, his applications to build were unsuccessful. The land was neglected and so it deteriorated but was occasionally used for grazing and was eventually sold to David and Gill Lines in 1988.

The existing barns and land were in poor condition. It took the Lines family nearly ten years to clear the site and to restore the land to a satisfactory condition. More years were spent refurbishing the buildings and constructing a horse exerciser and arena. The area became a well-established livery, rehabilitation centre for ex-racehorses and a polo centre.

Figure 131: Dean & Jade Lines with some of their polo ponies (2011).

Dean Lines, David and Gill's son, was, until recently, a professional polo player with a history of glittering achievement. He was repeatedly chosen to play for England and won the 'Best U21 Player of the Year' on three occasions and many 'Most Valuable Player' awards. He became an internationally renowned player in countries including Argentina, Spain, New Zealand and Uruguay. Dean retired from professional polo due to injury in 2014, but continues to play and coach polo. He also re-homes and trains ex-racehorses for polo and breeds polo horses.

Behind the Turkey Farm recreation ground, to the west, is a field that belongs to Frank Pearman of Bury Farm. In the past Frank's father, Norman, allowed this field to be used as a training ground for the tug-of-war and football teams and then, in 1970, when the first rugby team in Datchworth was formed, it too was given permission to use this field for its training and matches. The first pitch was laid in 1970 and then, due to a rapidly increasing rugby section of the sports club, a second pitch was laid in 1972. In 1978 planning permission was approved for eight metre high floodlights on half of the second pitch, which was then extended in 1991 to cover the whole pitch. However, in 1997, sixteen metre high floodlights were erected illegally and action was taken by the district council, whereby an enforcement notice was served for the removal of the floodlights. This was not carried out but in 1999 planning permission was eventually granted providing that the lights were lowered to ten metres and strict time constraints were adhered to. In 2013 the sports club was given permission to erect lighting on one of its new pitches behind the club house, on condition that the old floodlights on Frank Pearman's land behind the village hall were removed.

Green End Barn

Around the village green unoccupied spaces were gradually filled during the 1960s, 70s and 80s. One such building was Green End Barn, on the south side of Datchworth Green near the sports club, which was not a new construction but one that made use of an ancient barn as the basic framework. The large barn had been built in 1680, originally at Olives Farm at Hunsdon, some 15 miles away and had been purchased by a developer who had to find a suitable site on which to re-erect it. Having failed to obtain planning permission elsewhere, he submitted an application to re-erect the barn on some land that belonged to Cherry Tree Hall. Despite opposition from residents, 150 of whom signed a petition

Figure 132: Green End barn (1985).

Figure 133: Green End Barn (2006)

against the scheme, planning permission was eventually granted.

In 1985 it was dismantled, timber by timber, and rebuilt on the site and by the end of 1986, the building was completed as a luxurious five bedroom house. It was purchased in 1987 by a supposed Middle Eastern prince. He turned out to be a confidence trickster living in a council house in Stevenage who defrauded his bank, which then repossessed Green End Barn. He was eventually tried and sent to prison in 1990 amidst much publicity in the national press. In 1989 the property was purchased from the bank and the new owners made some major internal alterations. It has subsequently changed hands several times.

Hawkins Grange Farm

Hawkins Grange Farm was another development that caused some controversy among the residents of the parish. Following the sale of Hawkins Hall Farm in 1983, Mrs Adorian applied for planning permission to build a four bedroom property on land adjacent to Hawkins Hall Farm, in Hawkins Hall Lane. Although the proposal was heavily objected to by residents and the parish council, permission was granted by the district council and Hawkins Grange was built. The property remained unoccupied for many years but was eventually bought, together with a few acres of pastureland, in 2003, by the current owners, Roger and Jane Dodson. They modernised the house and until 2012 ran a successful bed and breakfast business. The site now includes stabling and an agricultural barn.

Despite opposition from the parish council, in 2010, Mr and Mrs Dodson were given permission by the district council to build another luxury four bedroom property on the land adjacent to Hawkins Grange. Known as 'The Grange', it is a timber-framed construction and has many 'eco-friendly' features recognised as such in *Real Homes* magazine. Mrs Dodson was also featured on the Lloyds Bank website, having been filmed with the new building as an ambassador for rural business diversification.

After the sale of Hawkins Hall Farm and Hawkins Grange, Mrs Adorian moved away from Datchworth but remains the owner of nearly fifty acres of land off Hawkins Hall Lane which is currently used for pasture and agricultural purposes. It is this land that has been registered with the district council for possible development, as mentioned earlier in this chapter.

Figure 134: Hawkins Grange with The Grange in the background (2012)

Harwood Park Crematorium

In early 1992 an application was submitted to the district council for a crematorium on the Datchworth side of the Knebworth to Watton Road. W. Austin & Sons, funeral directors of Stevenage and Welwyn, supported by the parish council, argued that the area was badly in need of such a facility to accommodate the ever-

Figure 135: Harwood Park Crematorium (2012)

increasing number of requests for cremation rather than burial. Residents of Datchworth, Knebworth, Aston and Bragbury End joined forces to oppose the scheme.

Following several local public meetings, a planning meeting at County Hall and the presentation of a thousand-signature petition, the council's officers recommended that the application be granted. However, as the district council had limited powers under green belt regulations, the planning committee had no option but to overturn this recommendation. The decision was appealed against and subsequently, in July 1993, the application was granted. The Inspector, in allowing the appeal, said that 'there was pressing need for a crematorium which would relieve the distress of local mourners and for this reason he would allow the development on green belt land'.

Harwood Park Crematorium eventually opened in 1997. The name 'Harwood' derived from its founder, John Harwood Austin of Hoppers Hall, who sadly died on 1 April 2012. It is now well established and is recognized as a valuable facility for the local community. It has the added feature of a fine view of All Saints' Church spire through the window in the main seating area.

In 2001, upon the retirement of John, his daughter Claire took over the role of Managing Director of the 300-year-old Austin family business. W Austin & Sons Ltd was originally established in 1700 in Graveley, a small village between Stevenage and Hitchin, as a builders and undertakers. In the early nineteenth century the company moved to Old Stevenage, where they continued the business for over 150 years, and were responsible for constructing many of the residential streets. Upon the death of his father, Arthur 'Bill' Austin, in 1965, John took over the business and in 1978 closed the building side of the firm deciding that there was a greater future in the funeral business.

The head office for Austin's Funeral Service still remains at its site in Old Stevenage, although the business now operates from many Funeral Arrangement Offices throughout Hertfordshire. Austin's acquired ownership of other local companies such as Geo W Blow Funeral Directors

Figure 136: John Austin – Founder of Harwood Park Crematorium.

in 1987, and in 1997 they bought Alfred Scales Funeral Directors and Francis Mander Stonemasons. Since John took over the business in 1965, the number of funerals carried out by Austin's has increased from 150 to approximately 1,200 per year. The crematorium too has had similar success, having carried out 1,366 cremations in its first year to over 2,200 today, confirming the Inspector's view that there was a pressing need for a crematorium in the area. To add to its success, in 2014 Harwood Park Crematorium won the 'Anglia in Bloom Best Crematorium Award' in the Eastern Counties which cover Cambridgeshire, Bedfordshire, Hertfordshire, Essex, Norfolk and Suffolk.

Thrift Cottage

Far from being controversial, but an example of imaginative innovation, was the building of an 'eco-house' at 52a Burnham Green Road. In 2001 Lydia Howitt, the daughter of Claude Howitt, a previous owner of the Bulls Green garage, took on this enormous challenge.

Lydia is a primary school teacher and also works part-time for the Green Party. She purchased the three-quarter-acre plot and proceeded to design and build the timber-framed one-bedroom house with a turf roof, compost toilet and solar hot water panels. Nearly all the materials used in the building of the house are natural, locally sourced and fossil fuel free, in order to reduce the carbon footprint and the use of chemicals. The compost toilet uses natural processes to turn the sewage into compost for the organic orchard and allotment and all the domestic waste water is used in the garden. A wood burning range provides heat for cooking, hot water and domestic heating.

Lydia married architect and builder Robert Somerville in 2003 and they put their skills together to complete the house in 2006. They have since acquired adjacent land to plant an orchard and intend to create an organic small-holding. They are also in the process of adding a second bedroom to the property. They hold regular open days for anyone interested in viewing their low energy project.

The house is named 'Thrift Cottage' after Anne Thrift, who lived on the site in a caravan for nearly fifty years. Anne was born with albanism, she was partially blind and deaf but was an intelligent, friendly and well-liked lady. At the age of 14, Anne went into service for a well-to-do family in St John's Wood, London. Their house was bombed during the Second World War, at which point the family and Anne moved to Datchworth. Anne soon began to work for many families in the Bulls Green and Burnham Green area by doing housekeeping, dog-walking and looking after children. Shortly after the war ended, Anne was left a legacy by one of the families who employed her, with which she bought her caravan. She approached Mr Franklin of Coltsfoot Farm, for whom she also worked, and asked if he would allow her to pitch her caravan on a piece of his land, to which he readily agreed. For the first twenty or so years her water supply came from the pond or rain filled water butts, until the late 1960s when her new neighbours, Chris and Liz Woodd-Walker, ran a hose pipe from their property to fill her water butts. Around the same time one of her employers arranged for an electric supply to the caravan, so that Anne could have electric lighting, a fridge and eventually radio and television.

Figure 137: The eco-house, Thrift Cottage (2012).

Anne always had a dachshund dog for company and she loved to work in her beautiful garden, which she had developed from the surrounding plot and which was featured in a 1974 edition of *Homes & Gardens* magazine. Her wheelbarrow has been recycled and is now installed as a cooker hood in Thrift Cottage. In the mid 1990s Anne moved from her caravan to a bungalow in Hawkins Hall Lane where she died in 2005, just after her 100th birthday.

Figure 138: Anne Thrift with her dog, Honey (1970s)

1 Hawkins Hall Lane

One planning application that has been under dispute in recent years is that of a development at 1 Hawkins Hall Lane. The site has been the subject of a number of applications and appeals since a private developer purchased the land, including a quaint old bungalow. In 2007 permission was approved to demolish the bungalow and erect a single replacement dwelling. Although the bungalow was pulled down, no subsequent building of the new house took place and the timescale of three years lapsed. Further applications were submitted in 2008 for six one-bedroom apartments and three two-storey dwellings, but both these applications were objected to by many residents and the parish council. Planning consent was refused by the district council and an appeal to the Secretary of State was unsuccessful. At the time of this book going to print permission had been given for two semi-detached properties named Jasmine and Rose Cottages.

The state of the housing market and the future

The depression in the housing market through the late 1980s up to the late 1990s brought an end to the rapid turnover of housing. House prices fell and properties remained unsold. Negative equity affected Datchworth as it did throughout the country. For instance, in 1985 a detached house in Brookbridge Lane was advertised for sale at £179,950. It was extended to include an extra bedroom and other amenities but in 1995 was on the market for just £129,750. Another example is that of the newly built Beechcroft where the properties were initially for sale at £95,950 in 1989. Just five years later, in 1994, the asking price was £69,950. This situation led house owners to invest money in their properties by adding extensions and updating facilities rather than moving.

These years of depression were followed by a boom in the housing market, which saw The Homestead in Raffin Green Lane advertised for sale in 2000 as the first £1 million property in Datchworth, followed a few years later by 1 Bury Lane, The Little House. The Little House is a prime example of the vast increase in prices from the slump in the 1990s, to profits attained by extending and updating along with the rising housing prices. In 1997 it was sold for £600,000; when it was sold again, just eight years later in 2005, the price had almost trebled.

Until recently the East of England Strategic Plan proposed the building of 83,500 new houses in Hertfordshire, of which 12,000 were intended for east Hertfordshire. However, the new government that was elected in 2010 is in the process of making changes to planning requirements. The original strategic plan is still technically in operation until the new District Plan, for development up to 2031, has been finalised, which it is hoped will be in 2015. It is expected that the new plan will show a housing requirement for east Hertfordshire of 15,000 properties; however, current proposals indicate that Datchworth is not expected to accommodate any large developments.

As part of the new planning provisions, local communities are being encouraged by the government to produce a Neighbourhood Plan. This would have to adhere to the requirements of the District Plan but will enable local residents to react to any building proposal within their area, including design, size and style of any new builds. Although early indications show that Datchworth parish has been relieved of the need to provide any significant housing, as directed by the District Plan, there will inevitably be applications put forward by private developers, and the existence of a Neighbourhood Plan would be a useful tool to fight for or against new proposals.

15. All Saints' Rectors

The diocese

Datchworth church was founded during the twelfth century, when the modern county of Hertfordshire lay partly in the diocese of Lincoln and partly in the diocese of London. In 1845 the whole of Hertfordshire became part of the diocese of Rochester. It was in 1877, as a result of the Bishopric of St Albans Act of 1875, that the diocese of St Albans was founded and was formed from parishes in Hertfordshire and Essex that had previously been part of Rochester diocese.

The patrons

Hugh de Bocland, the earliest recorded sub-tenant of Datchworthbury manor, was granted the patronage, also called the advowson [the right to appoint a rector], some time before 1176 when he died. Unfortunately there is no known record of All Saints' incumbents in the 1170s or for the next 70 years.

However, by 1240 John de Burgh, who had married Hugh de Bocland's great grand-daughter, Hawise, was lord of Datchworthbury and Walkern manors. He granted Datchworthbury to Gilbert de Wanton but kept the advowson of Datchworth with his manor of Walkern. So it was de Burgh, and not de Wanton, who had the right to appoint the rector of Datchworth. The first to be recorded was Nicholas de St Alban in 1249.

The descendants of John de Burgh held Walkern with the patronage of Datchworth parish for the next 200 years. In 1506 Walkern manor was sold to Sir William Capell, Lord Mayor of London. This included the Datchworth patronage which changed hands several times until 1725, when William Capell, 3rd Earl of Essex, the grandson of Elizabeth, Countess of Essex, sold the patronage to William Hawtayne, the incumbent at the time. A few months later Hawtayne sold it to William Greaves, Fellow of Clare Hall, Cambridge, who, in turn, conveyed it to his college in 1747. Clare Hall retained the patronage of All Saints' for over 200 years, changing its name to Clare College in 1856.

Historically the living associated with a parish could be held by a resident rector or an institution such as a monastery. In the latter case a vicar would be appointed to care for the parishioners. A resident rector, which was the case in Datchworth, would have benefited from the full range of tithes, unlike a vicar who was not eligible for the valuable tithes of timber and arable crops, which went to the institutional rector. Tithes are explained more fully in a later section.

Patrons and rectors in the Middle Ages

The patrons had family links descending from John de Burgh either directly or by marriage, apart from royal intervention in 1477, when Edward IV appointed John Furneys. This may have occurred following the death in 1476 of William, Lord Morley, whose son Henry was a minor, so was too young to become the patron. Henry was not formally patron in his own right until 1486.

RECTORS with date of institution where known	DATE	PATRONS	MONARCHS
Nicholas de St Alban	1249	John de Burgh	Henry III
Ernald de Berkele			"
Walter de Guise	1271	John de Burgh	"
Thomas de Ayet	1292	Robert Fitz-Water, Knt.	Edward I
Ralph de Hesham	1294	"	"
John de Northwold	1322	Robert de Morley, Knt.	Edward II
Richard de Ely	1323	"	"
John de Wynferthing	1332	"	Edward III
Walter Maunsel	1333	"	"
John Cagon	1349	"	"
John Brunygge	1349	"	"
John Day	1368	William de Morley	"
John Byllingham			
John Andrew	1388	Thomas de Morley	Richard II
John Hogge			
Peter de Alcobasse	1423	Anne, Lady Morley	Henry VI
John Whitchurch	1424	"	"
Thomas Pattishall	1433	Thomas, Lord Morley	"
John Perneys	1433	"	"
Thomas Clerk	1460	William, Lord Morley	"
John Furneys	1477	the King	Edward IV
Lawrence Drobbill	1481	John, Duke of Suffolk, and Henry, Lord Morley	"
John Kyrton	1482	Sir William Parker, Knt.	"
William Panke	1486	Henry, Lord Morley	Henry VII
William Baxter	1488	"	"
William Harrison			

Although little is known about the medieval incumbents of All Saints, some of the early names give an indication of where they originated, such as St Albans, Ely and Ayot, also Northwold and Winfarthing, both in Norfolk, whereas 'de Guise' probably refers to a district in northern France.

Walter Maunsel (1333) died of the Black Death in 1349, and his successor, John Cagon, resigned after only one month and may also have been a victim. Thomas Pattishall (1433) was another rector who was in office for only two months for reasons unknown.

Religion in the sixteenth century

Until the early sixteenth century, England was part of the Roman church and so conformed to Catholicism, although in Europe there were rumblings of Protestant Reformation. Henry VIII (1509-1547) was determined to divorce his first wife against the ruling of the church but succeeded in 1533 having sought permission from Thomas Cranmer, Archbishop of Canterbury. This forced him to break his allegiance with the Pope and subsequently he was declared Supreme Head of the Church of England in 1534. Although there were many Protestant influences throughout Henry's reign, he remained a devout Catholic and it was only when Edward VI (1547-1553) succeeded to the throne, that England became a Protestant country and church services were conducted in English.

Under Mary I (1553-1558), Catholicism was restored and the English church was reunited with Rome. She was succeeded by the Protestant queen, Elizabeth I (1558–1603) who broke the connection with Rome, became the Supreme Governor of the English church and attempted to steer a careful path between the two faiths but was intolerant of extreme views.

Wills are a useful source of information for investigating how religious variations in the sixteenth century influenced ordinary parishioners. Lionel Munby examined a set of Datchworth wills with this in mind and his findings are revealing. The style of a traditional Catholic will includes in the preamble references to 'our lady St Mary and to all saints, bequests such as leaving 4d to the mother church of Lincoln and 20s to the priest to sing thirty masses for the dead. These would have been normal practice before Henry VIII's reign.

The earliest Datchworth will that showed signs of a modified Catholic preamble was that of John Goodman, made on 8 April 1532, when he omitted the saints from his dedication. Later, in 1539, Thomas Fynch, on 26 September, and his mother, Cecilie, on 6 November, also made wills that lacked the full Catholic formula, having left no bequest to the church. These showed hints of early reformist sympathies.

However, on 10 June 1550, in the middle of the Protestant rule of Edward VI, Richard Saundere made a will containing most of the Catholic elements but avoided a request for masses to be sung and instead he asked the overseer of his will, his son-in-law, John Tyler, 'to see all things paid and discharged for the health of my soul, my father's and my mother's soul, and all Christian souls'. This particular will was witnessed by William Downham, Datchworth rector from 1548-1554, who had Catholic leanings, so the significance of its style may be more associated with the rector than the testator. Details of William Downham's background are included in the next section.

Patrons and rectors in the sixteenth and seventeenth centuries

RECTORS with date of institution where known	DATE	PATRONS	MONARCHS
John Lichfield	1543	Sir Giles Capel, Knt.	Henry VIII
William Downham	1548	John Core, clk.	Edward VI
Robert Manners	1554	Sir Henry Capel, Knt.	Mary I
Thomas Rudd	1569	Sir Edward Capel, Knt.	Elizabeth I
Clement Rudd	1591	Thomas Rudd of Preston	"
Edward Topsell	1598	the Queen	"
William Payne	1600	Thomas Rudd of Preston	"
Edmund Stubbing	1622	William Drury of Weston, Norfolk for Mary Payne	James I
Richard Newman	1623	Edward Rudd of Kings Walden	Charles I
Simon Peck	(1644)	the Parliament	"
Thomas Stacey	(1650)	"	Interregnum
Thomas Hackett	(1655)	Arthur, Lord Capel	"
Richard Newman	(1660)	Arthur Capel, Earl of Essex	Charles II
Thomas Hackett	1663	"	"
Charles Baggaley	1672	the King	"
John Gaile	1694	Elizabeth Capel, Dowager Countess of Essex	William III & Mary II

Note: Dates in brackets indicate doubt about their accuracy

Henry, Lord Morley, the last of the medieval patrons, married and died without issue in 1489, and Walkern manor, with the Datchworth patronage, passed to his sister who sold it to Sir William Capel. It remained in the Capel family, on and off, for over 200 years, although occasionally it was leased. As an example, in 1603 Arthur Capel and his son Henry leased it to Thomas Rudd of Kings Walden for 25 years. Royal intervention occurred again in 1598 by Queen Elizabeth. This time it related to the buying or selling of a religious post, known as 'simony', a practice that had been made illegal in 1588 and probably involved the Rudd family who featured both as rectors and patrons during that period.

Arthur Capel, Ist Earl of Essex, died in 1683 and after the intervention by Charles II for unknown reasons, Capel's widow Elizabeth, Dowager Countess of Essex, was patron by the time John Gaile was appointed in 1694.

The earliest sixteenth century rector was probably John Partrache who was mentioned in Edmund Bardolf's will dated 1512, but this is the only known reference to him. William Downham (1548) was born in *c.*1510 and became a brother at Ashridge Priory. He received a pension of £6 13s 4d at the priory's dissolution in 1539. In the same year he entered Exeter College, Oxford and by the time he reached Datchworth, he had acquired several theological qualifications and was chaplain to Princess Elizabeth. When queen, Elizabeth was instrumental in advancing his career until he was designated bishop of Chester in 1560. He was, however, a well known papist and was lax in the discipline of Catholics who refused to attend Church of England services, particularly amongst the gentry with whom he consorted. This inaction caused the queen to write a severe letter in February 1568 that said 'we find great lack on you, being sorry to have former expectation in this sort, deceived'.

He did not change his ways and was in similar trouble in 1574 and again in 1577. C S Knighton in the *Dictionary of National Biography* makes a final comment: 'His wife, much stronger-willed than her husband, bore two sons, George Downham and John Downham, a bishop and a puritan: Downham sat so long on the fence that his seed fell either side of it'.

During the Civil War, Richard Newman was banished because of his Royalist sympathies and replaced by Simon Peck, Thomas Stacey and Thomas Hackett. Hackett was educated at Trinity College Dublin and, according to William Urwick in *Nonconformity in Hertfordshire*, was presented to 'Thachworth, alias Datchworth' on 15 June 1655. He remained there until 1660, when Newman was eventually re-instated soon after the restoration of the monarchy. He returned for another spell until he was promoted to Bishop of Down and Connor in 1672. Historical accounts provide conflicting views regarding the dates of these events. It has been decided to use those given by Urwick but, where there is doubt about their accuracy, brackets have been used.

It was Elizabeth, Dowager Countess of Essex, who gave a Frenchman, John Gaile, the position of rector at Datchworth in 1694. At that time he was already employed as tutor for her son, Algernon, Earl of Essex with whom he travelled to Italy. There are intermittent entries in the parish register reflecting his occasional attendance, for example, he noted the destinations of monetary collections that were made for a variety of causes. In January 1699 the sum of 'five shillings fourpence farthing' was collected 'for loss by fire in Minehead in Somersetshire', and later, in April, the sum of 'four pounds sixteen shillings and ninepence' was collected for 'the Vaudois and French refugees'.

In 1702 an entry at the beginning of the first parish register, but out of chronological order, records the following event:

> Christopher Rapper a Trouper and Elizabeth Yong were married on 20th April 1702, with the Consent of the Hon. Major-General Lumby and Major Croaker his captain in the camp before Maestricht, by me Chaplain to Major Lumby.
>
> [signed] John Gaile
> 20 September 1702

He died in 1709 at Brussels in Flanders.

Patrons and rectors 1709-1954

RECTORS with date of institution where known	DATE	PATRONS	MONARCHS
William Hawtayne	1709	Elizabeth Capel, Dowager Countess of Essex	Anne
Edward Smith	1747	Clare Hall, Cambridge	George II
Charles Woolsey Johnson	1785	"	George III
Edward S Bunting	1829	"	George IV
William Williamson	1849	"	Victoria
John Wardale	1876	Clare College, Cambridge	"
Andrew Amos	1898	"	"
Henry William Fulford	1907	"	Edward VII
Joseph Perry Dyer	1912	"	George V
Benjamin Reed	1917	"	"
Alec Percy Daniels	1929	"	"
Stephen Francis Shairp	1932	"	"
Jesse Colbeck	1942	"	George VI
Francis Fraser	1947	"	"

When William Hawtayne was inducted as rector in 1709, he was already rector of Elstree and continued to run both parishes in parallel until 1718. During that period he lived at Elstree and appointed a succession of curates to care for Datchworth souls, for an annual stipend of £30.

Having started his professional life as a 'pluralist', he continued to justify the label by becoming vicar of Shephall after leaving Elstree until 1733, and then, mysteriously, becoming vicar of All Saints', Leighton Buzzard, Bedfordshire. He held this position alongside his Datchworth commitment until he died in 1747. A memorial tablet, inscribed in Latin, is mounted on the north wall of All Saints' chancel.

In addition to his parochial responsibilities, he was engaged as chaplain to Caroline of Ansbach, George I's daughter-in-law, probably soon after George I's accession to the throne in 1714. Hawtayne kept this position until, as the wife of George II, she became queen in 1727.

Hawtayne must have been well thought of, as he was asked to preach several significant sermons that were published soon after their delivery. Three of these survive. The first was preached on 20 January 1715 at Elstree, on the day of thanksgiving for George I's accession to the throne. The new king's Coronation had occurred a few months earlier on 20 October 1714, an event somewhat marred by street rioting, started by Jacobites who had been 'waiting in the wings' during Queen Anne's reign. It was in this atmosphere that Hawtayne preached this long sermon outlining George's lineage and attempting to reassure the congregation of his suitability to be king.

Charles Woolsey Johnson was our longest serving parson, having been rector for 43 years. He was one of the subscribers who contributed towards the building of the school in 1820. After his death on 30 November 1828, an entry was written in the vestry minute book (14.3.1829):

> At the present time there is No Incumbent of this Parish Although the last Rector Charles Wolsey Johnson has been dead upwards of three months. He was Rector of this Parish 43 years. Since his death there has been three Batchelors from Clare Hall Cambridge but they will not except [*sic*] the living; in consequent of that the Churchwarden as [*sic*] taken out a Sequestration which Impowers him to put a person in the Parsonage House and to appoint a Curate to do duty in the Church and to pay him.

Eventually the position was taken by Edward Swanton Bunting (1829), who was rector at the time of change in the management of tithes, that represented an important part of the rector's income. In 1838, following the Tithe Commutation Act of 1836, all tithes were commuted to cash in Datchworth, a procedure that must have made life much easier for the incumbent. Bunting died in 1849 and for a brief spell, a curate, Mr Murrell officiated until the installation of William Williamson later in the year.

William Williamson was educated at Westminster School and Clare College, Cambridge, became a fellow of Clare and started his career as a barrister from 1830-1839. He was ordained deacon in 1841 and priest in 1842. Williamson was rector of Datchworth from 1849-1874 and during his incumbency, he kept a notebook packed with information about the church and the school. He died in 1875 and the clock on the tower was given as his memorial.

John Wardale, another fellow of Clare College, was his successor. He came to Datchworth in 1876 and is remembered for having built the wall round Pound House and the school. In 1899, at his own expense, he made financial arrangements to pay the parish clerk an annual fee of £1 2s for winding up the church clock.

Figure 139: Reverend Wardale's concrete wall in front of Pound House pond. (Five Hide Village)

Andrew Amos was educated at Charterhouse School and became an enthusiastic and successful footballer. Yet another product of Clare College, he earned his 'blue' and subsequently played for several football clubs and for England in 1885-6. He was ordained in 1887 and after spending some years in Rotherhithe, he moved to Datchworth in 1898 where he stayed until his death in 1907. While he was in Hertfordshire, he played for Hitchin Town Football Club and represented Hertfordshire Football Association.

In the twentieth century a few of our rectors had travelled widely before they came to Datchworth. Joseph Dyer (1912) spent his early career in Burma and India from 1885 to 1907, becoming Archdeacon of Rangoon in 1899. He returned to England in 1907 and after five years came to Datchworth as rector.

His successor, Benjamin Reed (1917), was ordained and employed in Australia before coming to England in 1878. He ministered in several places in the north of England before coming to Datchworth in 1917. It was in his time that the first village fête was held in the rectory gardens in 1928. A brass memorial plaque was mounted on the north wall of the chancel in All Saints' Church soon after his death in 1929. It states that: 'Through his efforts the steeple of this church was restored'.

Alec Percy Daniels came to Datchworth in 1929, having just spent three years as rector of Carnarvon in Western Australia. In former years he had been awarded the Military Cross in 1916 and was appointed 'Temporary Chaplain of the Forces' 1915-1919.

He was closely followed in 1932 by Stephen Francis Shairp who had recently returned from Cape Town where he had been for four years. According to parish magazines in the 1930s, he was a great supporter of the annual fête which continued to be held in the rectory garden and nearby paddock.

Jesse Colbeck, who took over in 1942, could not live in the rectory because by then the decision had been made by the church PCC to sell it, so he lived at Arboga, Raffin Green Lane. Having graduated at Durham University in 1914, he moved to a diocese in northern China and remained there until 1942 when he moved to Datchworth. In 1947 he returned to China to the Cathedral in Peking and died there in 1949.

When Francis Fraser was inducted into All Saints' in 1947, there was still no rectory - so he lived in the Great North Road Hotel in Knebworth that has since been demolished. During the Second World War he held the position of Chaplain of the

Figure 140: A rectory garden party (c.1920)

<u>Back left to right</u>
'Lucky' Croft, Arthur Arnold, Albert Steer, George Furnell

<u>Centre Left to right</u>
Mrs Furnell, Mrs Barringer, 'Nishy' Nash, Alf Skeggs, Herbert Harradence, Mr Rushden Welch, Frederick Lawrance, George Little, Jane Pearman, Hannah Chalkley.

<u>Front left to right</u>
Elizabeth Phipps, Marion Bland, Charlotte Gaddie, Mrs Welch, ***Rev Benjamin Reed,*** *Mrs Reed, Margaret Lawrance Helen Little, Amelia Farrin, Annie King*
(Identification by Ken Webb)
(Datchworth Museum)

Forces, Emergency Commission 1939-45. He left All Saints' for Braughing in 1954, was a rural dean from 1961-65, retired in 1973, and died in Worthing in 1977.

Changes to the ministry

INCUMBENT	YEAR	THE MINISTRY	MONARCH
Julian Chamings Tross	1955	United with Tewin 1976	Elizabeth II
Paul Robert Betts	1979	United with Tewin	"
Richard Syms	1995	Union with Tewin dissolved 1999	"
Coralie McCluskey	2004	Welwyn team ministry formed 2005	"
Susannah Underwood	2011	Welwyn team ministry	"

Figure 141: Reverend Richard Syms in Datchworth church.

Julian Tross took office in 1955 and was the first rector to live in the newly-built rectory in Brookbridge Lane. During his incumbency he was appointed Rural Dean of Stevenage in 1971 and Honorary Canon of St Albans in 1972. It was four years later that the parishes of Datchworth and Tewin united and so Julian Tross became joint rector of All Saints' and St Peter's Church, Tewin, until his retirement in 1979.

A ditty composed by Tom Beachcroft in 1979 is a tribute to his popularity. It was published in the October issue of All Saints' parish magazine:

J Just a moment then while I
U Utter words of great good will
L Long may Julian live and flourish
I In his home and fear no ill
A After years of splendid giving
N Now he's earned a peaceful rest
T There we wish him joy and gladness
R Reaping everything that's best
O Oh! We feel both joy and sadness
S So our hearts towards him flow
S So with love we let him go

Paul Betts followed Julian Tross in 1979 who had came to us from the St Columba Centre, Cambridge, before which he was vicar of St Paul's, Finchley, for 13 years. In his early days he worked in the ministry in Exeter, Plymouth and Cheltenham.

After the retirement of Paul Betts in 1995, Richard Syms, a worker-priest working in theatre, film and television, who lived locally, cared for the parish of Datchworth on a part-time basis. Initially this was a local, informal, but very welcome arrangement, but later he was appointed priest-in-charge, though still part-time. It was during his time that the link with Tewin ceased in 1999.

Over the years he appeared in some well-known TV series and films, including *Nowhere Boy*, *Gangs of New York* and the award-winning *The Iron Lady*, and has of course played a vicar on many occasions.

In 2003 Richard resigned as it became clear that such an informal arrangement could not last forever, and that the logical future for Datchworth was as part of a team ministry. Since leaving Datchworth Richard has been appointed as associate priest at the Actors' Church in Covent Garden.

After Richard left, a number of retired ministers helped maintain the ministry. Then, in August 2004, Datchworth welcomed its first female priest, Coralie McCluskey. She and her family moved into the Rectory in Brookbridge Lane. On 26 September 2004 there was a thank-you service in church for Reverends Mike Shaw and Mervyn Terrett who had been so helpful during the vacancy. The Harvest Festival Service on the 3 October 2004 was the first service taken by Coralie at Datchworth as Priest-in-Charge.

At the beginning of 2004, a series of meetings took place, chaired by the Venerable Trevor Jones, Archdeacon of St Albans. These were attended by the rector of St Mary's Church, Welwyn, Canon Dr Alan Winton, his churchwardens and the churchwardens of St Peter's Church, Tewin, All Saints' Church, Datchworth, St Peter's Church, Ayot St Peter and St Michael's Church, Woolmer Green. From these meetings, the five parishes started working together informally in August 2004. The legal entity was confirmed by the Privy Council in 2005

Figure 142: Reverend Coralie McCluskey, the first Team Vicar of Datchworth and Tewin

Figure 143: Reverend Susannah Underwood

and so the 'Welwyn Team Ministry' was formed, and Coralie became the first 'Team Vicar' for Datchworth and Tewin.

As a village church, All Saints' has greatly benefitted from being part of the team ministry by joining in worship with the other churches during major celebrations of the Christian Year and for the popular 'summer evensongs' that take place in a different team church on summer evenings from July to September. Each parish within the team ministry retains its seperate identitiy and is managed by its own Parochial Church Council.

Alan Winton, team rector of the Welwyn Team Ministry, was appointed Suffragan Bishop of Thetford in the Diocese of Norwich in June 2009. In September of that year he was succeeded as team rector by Dr David Munchin who, for eight years immediately before his appointment, had been vicar of Hatfield Hyde in Welwyn Garden City.

On 23 January 2011 the last service was taken by Coralie before she and her family left Datchworth to move to her next appointment. The whole parish bade farewell to a very popular vicar. For a short period, once again, several retired ministers helped out, including Tom Gladwin. The church then welcomed Susannah Underwood and her family into the village. She was licensed as team vicar of Datchworth and Tewin on 7 September 2011.

Income of the Clergy

Tithes

Originally a rector's or a vicar's income, otherwise called the 'stipend', came from several sources. Tithes were an important element that represented one tenth of all produce, whether it was grown on the land or was the product of animal husbandry. They were collected on an annual basis by the church incumbent and until the early eighteenth century, most tithes were collected in kind but this was an arduous business and led to endless disputes. One can only imagine the difficulties associated with collecting milk, dealing with a swarm of bees, and sorting out a tenth of that year's number of lambs or calves for example. Clergy developed their own ways of dealing with these problems and in the case of milk or bees, a monetary substitute was often used.

William Hawtayne, who was rector at Datchworth from 1709-1747, kept a remarkable record of his tithe collecting from 1711 until his death in 1747. Some examples of his entries regarding cash payments are as follows and include a 'cottager' and his garden:

> In lieu of Tythe milk and Calfe for each cow, yearlie 5s.
> For ewes in lieu of lambs, and wool per score, 10s. For each pigge 2s;

Cottagers, if they have an orcharde which is goode 1s 6d or 2s;
Other cottagers 1s and some but six or seven pense.

Farmers who grew crops each year had the problem of laying out the sheaves of corn so that, in theory, the parson could arrive and select every tenth sheaf, although he often had a team of 'tithing' men who assisted with this task.

It was during this period that a gradual change took place between collecting tithes in kind and being paid an agreed amount of money in lieu of tithes. These were called 'composition agreements' and were carefully reviewed every three years or so to guard against fluctuating corn prices getting stuck in favour of either the farmer or the tithe collector. In 1712 Hawtayne had organised 28 such agreements ranging from £2 to £16 per annum.

If the parson was a rector, he was eligible for all the tithes, 'great' (eg crops, timber), and small (eg calves, wool, eggs), whereas a vicar would only benefit from the small tithes. Historically, in cases where the rector was an institution such as a monastery, the vicar was a 'stand-in' to care for the souls.

All tithes were commuted to a 'tithe rent-charge', following the Tithe Commutation Act of 1836. The amounts paid varied year by year according to the price of corn. Datchworth's tithe award was in 1838 and all the agreed amounts were recorded in a book which was accompanied by a map the following year, with numbered fields. This is depicted on the endpaper at the back of this book. As an example of an entry, Mrs Wadsworth, tenant of Raffin Green Farm, paid a tithe rent-charge of £33 18s 6d on just over 138 acres. This amounted to about 5s per acre.

The Glebe

The 'glebe' was land provided for the resident priest by the lord of the manor and its origins date back to the late seventh century. In this way the priest had a means of subsistence and, maybe, a source of income. It was often situated near the church or the parsonage and sometimes incorporated strips in the open fields. Datchworth's glebe consisted of about 15 acres near the rectory and another 9 acres of strips distributed over the open fields. Once allocated, the land belonged to the church unchanged until a legal procedure, such as parliamentary enclosure, changed the status of the land and the parson was duly compensated. Sometimes the rector would let glebe land and this was the case for most of William Hawtayne's incumbency (1709-1747). Roughly 100 years later, Edward Bunting was letting the glebe in the open fields but dealt with the land around the rectory himself.

Hawtayne's combined average income from tithes and glebe from 1711-1720 was £117 2s; whereas in 1838 Bunting was in receipt of £481 10s.

Other sources

There were other sources of income that included fees for parochial duties, such as baptisms, marriages and burials. In former times, they were called 'surplice fees'.

Examples of these were listed in a Datchworth parish register dated 1785. Fees for strangers' burials were more expensive because a 'stranger' was someone who had died within Datchworth parish but formerly had lived in a different parish. The executors of a deceased stranger were usually charged double the parish fee for burial.

Surplice Fees in the Parish of Datchworth 1785	£	s	d
A marriage by Banns	0	5	0
A certificate of Marriage	0	3	0
Churching a woman[1]	0	0	6
A certificate of Baptism	0	2	6
A burial in the Chancel	3	3	0
Ditto of a Stranger	6	6	0
A burial in the Churchyard	0	1	0
Ditto of a Stranger	0	10	6
Leave to set up a Rail[2] or Stone in the Churchyard	0	10	6
Ditto for a Stranger	1	1	0
Leave to lay down a flat stone in the churchyard	1	1	0
Ditto for a Stranger	2	2	0

Notes
1. 'Churching a woman' was a ceremonial blessing to a mother soon after her recovery from childbirth.
2. A 'rail' was made of wood and was placed alongside a grave parallel to its axis. It acted as a marker.

In 1884 John Wardale is recorded in *Crockford's Clerical Directory* as having received a tithe rent-charge of £481, fees worth £4 and £37 rent from letting his 21 acres of glebe. This gave a gross income of £522. Near the end of his incumbency in 1898, this had dwindled to £381, mainly because of the reduction in the value of the tithe rent-charge, which was the main component of his stipend.

It was acknowledged before long that Datchworth clergy were suffering financially and so could be eligible for 'Queen Anne's Bounty', a fund set up in 1704 by Queen Anne 'for the Augmentation of the Maintenance of Poor Clergy'. In essence, it was a contribution to the rector's stipend according to need. Joseph Dyer was the first to benefit from this in 1914. Over the next few years continued reduction in the tithe rent-charge resulted in an increase in the 'Queen Anne's Bounty' element of the rector's income.

This practice continued until the Tithe Act of 1936, when all tithe rent-charges came to an end and were replaced by redemption annuities payable to the State by landowners for 60 years ending on 1 October 1996. Former tithe owners were compensated out of Government Stock. The last mention of the glebe in *Crockford's Directory* was in 1938 and after that seems to have disappeared as a parochial asset. In 1948 the Ecclesiastical Commissioners and Queen Anne's Bounty merged to form the Church Commissioners. Initially their focus was to oversee the income of clergy.

An illustration of how these early ecclesiastical bodies could provide help where needed was found in a parish magazine dated September 1932. Stephen Shairp was instituted in July 1932 and needed some repairs and improvements done to the rectory. In his 'Letter from the Rector' in the parish magazine, he wrote; 'due to the decline in the income of the benefice the Governors of Queen Anne's Bounty have authorised a loan of £313 to enable me to put the electric light and a new hot-water system into the Rectory and to carry out an improvement to the roof gutters. Towards this the Patrons [Clare College, Cambridge] have made a benefaction of £100 and we are hoping that in the Spring this will be met with a grant of £100 from the Ecclesiastical Commissioners'.

The Parish Share

Payment of clergy income became centralised in 1973, when parish assets were transferred to their respective dioceses. Clergy were then paid from this fund. Hitherto a parson's stipend had depended on the wealth or otherwise of his parish, so the arrangement of pooling resources was regarded as being fairer.

In order to maintain the fund, parishes are required to make an annual contribution, formerly called the 'diocesan quota' but now known as the 'parish share'. It is so-called because it represents the parish's share of the cost of running the diocese, some of which goes towards paying the clergy. In 1984 Datchworth's share was £3,800, and in 2013 it had risen to £32,244.

Raising the money for this annual payment is one of the many financial responsibilities of the Parochial Church Council. PCC income arises from several sources, including fees from baptisms, weddings and burials, hire of the church hall and gift aid rebates. However, it is from the congregation that the most significant contribution is made. There are cash collections at church services but in addition, since the mid-1960s, through periodic 'stewardship campaigns', worshippers have been encouraged to pledge a regular, financial commitment so that the church's finances can be better planned and managed.

A possible forerunner of the stewardship campaign is described in a parish magazine of November 1932 but did not materialise. Stephen Shairp wrote in his monthly letter that it was absurd to depend on the annual fête and collections 'for ordinary expenditure such as music, heating, lighting, cleaning, salaries, insurance etc' and he announced that he had a scheme in mind. In essence, he suggested that each member of the congregation should give a certain amount each week, according to their means, and 'stick to it'. This was to be called the 'Church Membership Fund'.

However, when this was discussed by the church council, it was reported that it approved the scheme in principle 'but in view of previous disappointments no practical proposals were brought forward and the matter has been tacitly allowed to drop for the present'. It appears that this scheme did not come to fruition, as in subsequent magazines it is not mentioned again.

There is heavy reliance on donations and fundraising. Annual flower festivals, music festivals and quiz nights are organised by a band of volunteers. Much appreciated income is also received each year from the proceeds of the village fête, parish magazine and from fundraising efforts from individual residents, such as the late Margaret Kirk, who spent many years making and selling items such as coasters, tea towels and trays, donating all of the proceeds to the church fund.

Gifts to Missions and Charities

Over the years some of the parochial income has been set aside for contributions to worthy causes such as Christian Aid, The Bible Society, British Red Cross, The Children's Society and the Helen Keller Centre in Jerusalem. One memorable benefactor was a charity called 'Linking Lives', that was set up by Annette and Barrie Glenn to provide help for the people of a settlement called 'Ha Simone' in Lesotho in southern Africa.

In 1996, a link with an African village was started, spearheaded by Annette Glenn who went to live in Lesotho, with her husband Barrie, whose family came from Datchworth. Lesotho is an independent kingdom landlocked by South Africa and, in this small mountain village, it was the first time a white lady had been involved in their lives. Annette and Barrie lived on a mountain construction site, while Barrie was employed as part of a team of engineers constructing a dam in the Maluti Mountains. The Highland Water Scheme was a thirty year scheme which was designed to build three huge dams in Lesotho to transport water into South Africa through tunnels built into the rock. It was one of the largest water projects in Africa. In Lesotho water is known as 'white gold'.

After witnessing the poverty in the mountain villages, Annette made a vigorous appeal to Richard Syms. It was subsequently agreed with Datchworth PCC that communications would be initiated by Annette from Lesotho. A Datchworth support group was set up, headed by Richard Syms, Anne Charles, Rosemary Airey, Lynda Dent and Mary Willatt, who was head teacher of Datchworth school at the time. Letters were written to Basotho families and gifts of clothes were sent to the children of Ha Simone.

Very soon money was sent to build a well for fresh water in their village, to install an electricity link and make a start on a block of toilets, as there was only one pit latrine for the whole village. Most families exist by planting and harvesting their own crops of maize and cabbages, but some years the crops would be ruined by drought or floods.

As well as the many contributions from Datchworth school and Datchworth PCC, another generous supporter from Datchworth is Ruby Jackson, who lives in Nutcroft. Ruby has sponsored a girl from Ha Simone, called Amelia Mohobelo, for over ten years by providing financial help towards her education and has sent countless parcels of clothes, books and other gifts. Amelia has recently given birth to her first child, a baby boy, who has been named Jackson in honour of Ruby.

Annette and Barrie returned to England in 2006 and set up a registered charity called 'Linking Lives' and have continued to work tirelessly to improve the lives for the people of Lesotho. The provision of an education for the children of Ha Simone whose parents could not afford to send them to school has been among the charity's many achievements. The charity has also provided a pre-school building with one teacher and a cook, as well as a container full of pre-school equipment, bicycles and computers.

Figure 144: New water pump at Ha Simone 2001

16. The Poor Law

The Elizabethan Poor Law Acts

The Poor Law Act, passed in 1563, was the first of several Acts in the reign of Elizabeth I that were devoted to the control and relief of poverty. Part of the Act stated that churchwardens were to collect alms on a weekly basis from members of the congregation for eventual distribution amongst the poor. If anyone refused to pay, they were liable for punishment. This was a formalisation of a voluntary arrangement that had been enacted in 1536 at the time of the Dissolution of the Monasteries, when responsibility for maintenance of the deserving poor was passed from the monasteries to the parishes.

Prior to this, most legislation was designed to deal with beggars. From 1494, if they were disabled, they could beg in their own parishes. From 1531, after being assessed, magistrates could give them a licence to beg, a concession that remained until 1572. Able-bodied beggars, however, were subjected to ever increasing draconian measures. From 1494 they were liable to 'be set in the stocks for three days and three nights and have none other sustenance but bread and water'. Whipping was added as another punishment in 1531, which was re-affirmed in the Elizabethan Act of 1563, in which more rules stated that persistent offenders could have an ear burned, be imprisoned or be executed.

The 1563 Act put the poor into three categories. First were the able-bodied for whom work would be found and then secondly the 'idle poor' who were able-bodied, but were unwilling to work. This group, which often included vagrants, could be punished as already described and, from 1576, could be committed to a 'house of correction'. The third group were the impotent poor (elderly, children, handicapped, sick, lunatics) who could not look after themselves but would be cared for in almshouses or hospitals.

The 1598 Relief Act enabled parishes to levy a poor rate, calculated at an agreed amount in the pound, based on property values. In some cases the funds raised were used to build premises to provide shelter for paupers. These structures are regarded as being the first 'poor houses' and were often built on waste land with the agreement of the lord of the manor. Materials such as hemp, wool and flax were provided to set the able-bodied poor to work and poor children from the age of seven could be apprenticed, which had the beneficial effect of reducing pressure on poor relief funds.

The Poor Law Act 1601 laid down procedures for churchwardens and prominent local landowners in each parish to be appointed as 'overseers of the poor'. They were to be responsible for setting the poor rates and supervising their collection from property owners. They also dispensed money or food to the deserving poor and were responsible for the poor houses, the provision of which had been made compulsory by this Act.

'The Old Poor Law', as the 1598 and 1601 Acts were subsequently called, consolidated and replaced all previous legislation and was to provide the essential pattern for the treatment of the poor until it was superseded 233 years later by the Poor Law Amendment Act in 1834. This Act remained unchanged until after the Second World War, when the National Assistance Act 1948 was implemented.

Provision for the poor in Datchworth

It is not known when Datchworth had its first poor house but, according to a reference in *Five Hide Village,* at least one was in existence at the beginning of the seventeenth century, as the following extract from a Court of Inquisition, held at Ware on 3 June 1628, shows:

> .... by the oaths of 15 people, who say that there was formerly a Church House at Datchworth, belonging to the inhabitants with a little pightle [small enclosed piece of land] pertaining to it, which house was sold by the said inhabitants and then the said pightle lay open to the street.
>
> One Arden, the Clerk of the Parish, requested of the inhabitants to erect a little tenement on part of the pightle, to this the inhabitants agreed and gave him the timber for it to be built and suffered Arden and his wife to dwell there during their lives.

This extract probably relates to the area where School House now stands. The Inquisition went on to record that after the death of the Ardens, the 'inhabitants admitted John Lucye as their tenant at 12 shillings a year, this was paid to the Churchwardens'. For reasons unknown, Lucye was 'put out' and the house was let to Thomas Tyler at the request of William Payne, who was rector from 1600 until his death in 1622. After the Reverend Payne died, Tyler refused to pay rent as he said it was a church house. It was proved that the house 'belonged to the inhabitants and that the premises shall forever remain at the disposal of the inhabitants for the benefit of the poor of Datchworth ... Tyler to give up possession and pay all (ten years) arrears of rent'.

This particular dwelling started as a residence for the Clerk of the Parish and appears to have been built at the expense of the parishioners rather than using church funds. It was then let for rent; this rent was used 'for the benefit of the poor'. Later the house was lived in by poor families.

There are several examples in Datchworth vestry minutes of lists of 'poor rate' payers and the one for 28 December 1731 is typical. In this case, the rate was 8d in the pound and the amounts paid were based on the valuation of property either owned or rented. About half the rate payers had properties valued at £5 or less and, of these, there were eight parishioners whose dwellings were valued at £1, the lowest valuation on which poor rate was paid at this time. The total amount collected on this occasion was £25 7s 8d. The following table shows a few extracts from that record:

A Rate made by the Church Warden and the overseer of the poore and other Inhabeters of the Parish of Datchworth in the County of Hartford at a Vestre Hld the 28 day of December in the year 1731 for the Relefe of the poore of the Parish at 8d in the pound. [Val = valuation of property]				
Poor rate payer [spelling as found]	Poor rate payment			Val
	£	s	d	£
Mr Hawtayne Rector for Glibe Land & Tythes and other land	1	18	0	57
James Whithall for the Bury	1	13	4	50
Esqr Harison for Woods Landlord at the Bury	0	6	8	10
the Widow Crawley for Bragerend farm and other land	1	10	0	45
Richard Blindell for Coltsfoot and other land	1	4	8	37
William Butterfield	0	11	4	17
William Blindall for Panters Green farme and other land	0	10	0	15
John Pearcese the Butcher	0	4	8	7
Mr Daniel Haynes	0	4	0	6

Out of the 59 names on the list, the highest rate payer was the Reverend William Hawtayne who was rated mainly on his 'glebe land' and the tithes that he had collected from his parishioners. Another high rate payer was James Whitehall, tenant of Datchworthbury. Landlord Edward Harrison paid rates on the woods belonging to the 'Bury' that he had chosen not to let. Widow Crawley of Bragbury End and Richard Blindell of Coltsfoot Farm were also among the top five rate payers. William Blindell sold Painters Green Farm to Thomas Gripper in 1749 and Daniel Haynes was at Green End Farm which he bequeathed to his nephew Charles in 1753.

James Whitehall and William Butterfield are mentioned as churchwarden and overseer respectively in the following indenture, dated 1732, concerning the apprenticeship of a girl to a butcher called John Pierce of Ware. Bearing in mind the unconventional spelling shown in the 1731 poor rate list, this could be the butcher named as John 'Pearcese'. He possibly had property in Datchworth but ran a business in Ware.

> This indenture made the twentieth day of January ...1732. Witnesseth that James Whitehall Churchwarden of the Parish of Datchworth... and William Butterfield... Overseer of the Poor of the said Parish by and with the consent of his Majesty's Justices of the Peace ... have out and placed, ... Catherine Reith, a poor child of the said Parish, Apprentice to John Pierce Butcher of Ware with him to dwell and serve from the Day of the Date of these Presents until the said Apprentice shall accomplish his [*sic*] full age of twenty one years or Day of Marriage during which term the said Apprentice shall faithfully serve in all lawful business according to her Power Wit and Ability; and honestly orderly and obediently in all things demean and behave herself towards her said Master ... during the said term. And the said John Pierce for himself, ... shall ... during all the term aforesaid find provide and allow unto the said Apprentice, ... sufficient Meat Drink and Apparel, Lodging, Washing and all other things necessary and fit for an apprentice.
>
> And shall also and will so provide for the said Apprentice that she [is] not in any way a charge to the said Parish or Parishioners of the same ... And at the end of the said term shall and will make, provide allow and deliver unto the said Apprentice double Apparel of all sorts, good and new (that is to say) a good new Suit for the Holy-Days and another for the Working-Days. In Witness thereof these present Indentures interchangeably have put their Hands and Seals...

The indenture was signed by several people including the rector, William Hawtayne.

Settlement Acts and Gilbert's Act

The 1601 Act was further adapted in 1662 with the Settlement Act and in 1782 with Gilbert's Act, before the passing of the Poor Law Amendment Act in 1834.

The Settlement Act of 1662 introduced new legislation to control vagrancy, which was still a problem despite the poor laws that had been enacted so far. Prior to this, people were free to move from parish to parish in search of work. Each parish had the responsibility of caring for the poor, financed by the poor rate, so strangers attempting to move into a parish without employment were likely to become a burden if they sought poor relief. The new Act stated that vagrants would be returned to their home parish within 40 days of arrival if they had not found any work or if they were unable to rent property worth at least £10 per year.

After 40 days a stranger could claim 'settlement' in his adopted parish thus having the right to claim poor relief, which, if it occurred, was an unpopular eventuality. The Settlement Act of 1697 had a clause that alleviated this problem by ruling that anyone seeking settlement in another parish should go there with a certificate stating that, if poor relief was sought, the home parish would take him back. All paupers were expected to wear the letter 'P' sewn on their clothing as well as the initials of their parish, which led to them being called 'badgers', but many parishes did not comply with this. It was just over 100 years later that badging was abolished, when Gilbert's Act was passed in 1782.

An example of a settlement certificate, dated 18 May 1700, relates to a family entering Datchworth parish from Welwyn. It was signed by three churchwardens and an overseer of the poor, all from Welwyn, and two JPs.

> Wee the Churchwardens and overseer of the poore of the parish of Wellwin in the County of Hertford Do Certifye the Churchwardens and overseers of the poor of the parish of Datchworth in the County of Hertford aforesaid: that we own and acknowledge John Crawley his wife Elizabeth and three children to be inhabitants legally settled in our said parish of Wellwin and hereby oblige our said parish to receive and provide for them whenever they shall happen to become chargeable to the parish of Datchworth they not having otherwise acquired a legal settlement therein in testimony whereof wee have hereunto sett our hands and seales this eighteenth day of May Anno Domini 1700

Under 'Gilbert's Act' (mentioned above), also known as 'The Relief of the Poor Act', parishes were enabled to provide a workhouse or poor house for the elderly, sick and orphaned where some work would be provided. Able-bodied paupers were to be given employment near their homes and if they refused such work, they would be sent to a house of correction. Parishes could carry out these duties on an individual basis or could combine with other parishes nearby to form a 'union' that would then be served by a single poor house. In either case, there was to be 'a visitor', who had a role similar to a chairman, and a board of guardians, all appointed by the parish or parishes. This effectively removed the responsibility of managing the poor from the overseers to the committee in charge of the poor house, but overseers still had the duty of collecting the poor rate.

A document, dated 4 December 1793, suggests that at that time Datchworth was not conforming to the legislation of Gilbert's Act but was nevertheless setting up a system of supervision over one of its poor houses. The document is a contract agreement between 'the Churchwardens and the Overseers of the Parish of Datchworth and Mr Wm. Bowley', a practice often adopted by parishes as a compromise. The first of five 'Articles' listed in the document states that 'Mr William Bowley is to maintain the Poor in the parish and Workhouse of Datchworth, finding them necessary Clothing Bedding etc. from the first Day of December 1793 until Easter Day 1794 for the sum of Eight Guineas Per Month Viz counting 4 weeks to the month'. The period of the contract was exactly five months for which William Bowley was paid £8 8s.

According to the other four articles, Bowley was expected to ensure that clothing and bedding were in good order and to be responsible for the maintenance of furniture and fixtures. The parish would cover any costs incurred if the necessity arose. In case of sickness or broken bones, doctor's charges would be met 'extra by the Parishioners of the Parish of Datchworth'. He was also responsible for ensuring that fathers of bastard children of the poor were taken to account and made to pay for their children and any extra expense that this might involve would be covered by the overseers of the poor.

Although the word 'workhouse' is used in the document, there is no mention of the provision of work in the 'Articles'. Part of the arrangement would have allowed Bowley to earn money by putting the poor to work by any means he liked, but usually it was in a local trade or 'profitable' employment.

The agreement was signed by churchwarden William Field, overseers George Bassett and Richard Bowley, and also William Bowley. Finally it was 'agreed' by James Hall, Henry Campkin and William Allinson.

Gamon Charity

The Settlement Acts of 1662 and 1697 must have increased the awareness of national concerns regarding the poor. It was during this period, on 28 October 1685, that Richard and Mary Gamon, owners of Datchworthbury manor, set up the Gamon Charity. An annuity of 40s charged upon their estate was granted to the churchwardens who were to use it 'only for the poor of the parish of Datchworth... and to be yearly distributed for and amongst the poor of the said parish forever for their better relief...'. Until 1825 the money was used by the churchwardens to buy bread which was given away each Christmas. Money was then given instead of bread until 1832, when it was noticed that 'recipients immediately on receipt of their portions retire to the public house', so it was decided that the distribution of bread should be resumed.

The administration of the charity was taken over by the parish council when it was formed in 1894. Parishioners were still benefitting from it in the early twentieth century – there were 99 people in 1910, however numbers had dwindled to 22 by 1940. In 1946 the charity was managed once again by the church and in 1961 an agreement was made that allowed the owner of Bury Farm, Norman Pearman, to be relieved of the annual commitment with a one-off payment of £80.

The churchwardens decided that the remaining funds should be confined to deserving cases only. In 1965 £4 was donated to Mr and Mrs Newman for spectacles and a year later Mr and Mrs Turner 'had the misfortune to have their house burned', so they were given £6. There were no subsequent awards and the Gamon Charity ceased operating, officially being removed from the charity register in 2000.

The sale of Datchworth's poor houses

By the middle of the nineteenth century the support of the poor had become an increasing burden to the parish, particularly financially. The Poor Law Act of 1601 was no longer adequate for the relief of the poor and so it was replaced by the 1834 Poor Law Amendment Act, which relieved the vestry of one of its most onerous duties. The poor were no longer the responsibility of the parish, the parish poor houses were closed and sold off and paupers were to be sent to central workhouses.

The sale of Datchworth's poor houses, along with the old Tilbury and a piece of garden land where, it is said, another poor house had previously stood, was authorised at a meeting in the church on 31 May 1837. On 15 November 1837 an auction of five Lots was held at the old Tilbury, by order of the Poor Law Commissioners (Figure 145). Receipts from the sale were credited to the 'board of guardians' and used for such purposes as directed by the Poor Law Commissioners.

As part of the bill of sale it was stated that: 'The vendors possess no title deeds to any of the Lots, it is therefore... stipulated, that no objection shall be made to the title ... but proof of possession by declaration ... or by the occupation of paupers shall be conclusive evidence of the title of the vendors'.

One such declaration made by Thomas Mardle, aged 65 years old, associated with the sale of the poor houses in 1837, stated that:

> .....a piece of Garden Ground situated at Burnham Green in the said Parish now in the tenure of John Ewington. That I recollect it about fifty years ago when a Bank was thrown up around it..... That I recollect some Bricks standing on it which were like a foundation. That I have heard a Poorhouse stood on it and I have heard that three persons were starved to Death in it but that was before my time.

This piece of garden ground was situated where 1 Orchard Road is now and the declaration indicates that the poor house in which persons had starved to death had been demolished sometime in the early 1770s. This could be the poor house where the Eaves family perished in 1769; the story is recounted later in this chapter.

Another Burnham Green poor house was situated on the opposite side of the road from the one mentioned above, close to where 2 White Horse Lane now stands. It is described in a deed of 1701, when Edward Lawrance leased the cottage to the overseers, John Randall and Daniel Nash, for the sum of £2 10s 'for the use and benefit of the poor.' It was stated that this was for a period of 2½ years but a survey conducted in 1829 shows that, by then, the cottage, described as a poor house, was in the ownership of the overseers of the poor. In 1837 it was sold by the Poor Law Commissioners to George Lawrance for £70. The cottage was demolished almost immediately, as, by the time of the 1838 tithe award, there is no evidence of the building and the site is recorded as 'garden land' in the ownership of S. Sutton.

Datchworth Green poor house was situated at the western end of the green (where Tudor Lodge now stands). It was sold to John Hankin Bentley for £30 in 1837, when the occupier was Spencer Shadbolt. A year later it was sold to George Jeffries for £50, an amount that he had borrowed from James Hawkins, a miller from Surrey.

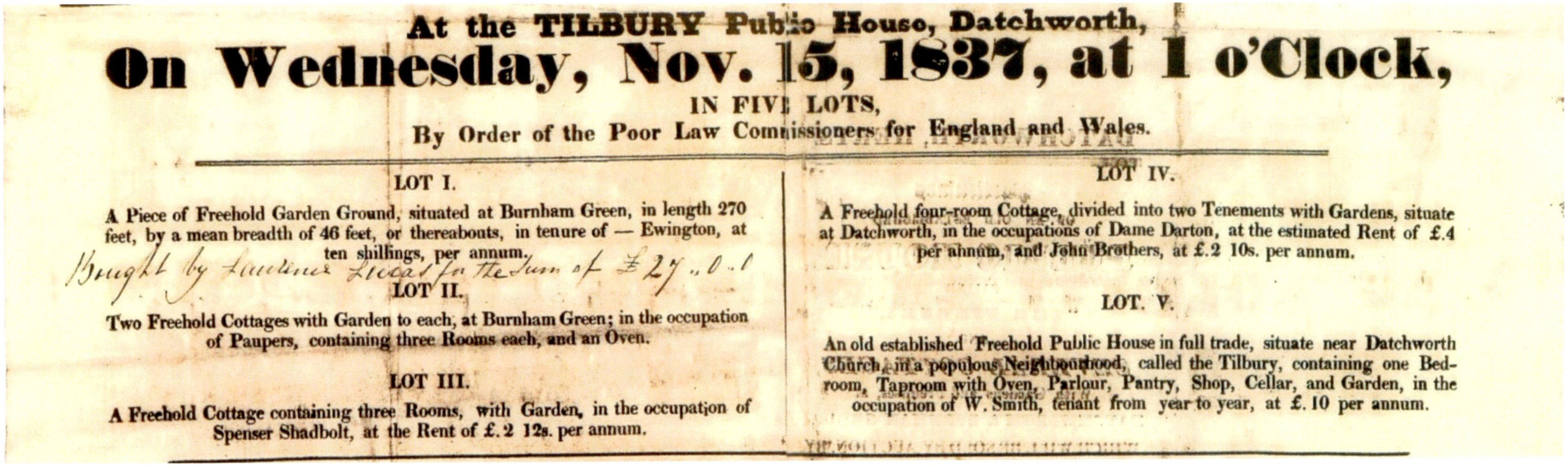

At the TILBURY Public House, Datchworth,

On Wednesday, Nov. 15, 1837, at 1 o'Clock,

IN FIVE LOTS,

By Order of the Poor Law Commissioners for England and Wales.

LOT I.

A Piece of Freehold Garden Ground, situated at Burnham Green, in length 270 feet, by a mean breadth of 46 feet, or thereabouts, in tenure of — Ewington, at ten shillings, per annum.

Bought by Laurence Lucas for the Sum of £27..0..0

LOT II.

Two Freehold Cottages with Garden to each, at Burnham Green; in the occupation of Paupers, containing three Rooms each, and an Oven.

LOT III.

A Freehold Cottage containing three Rooms, with Garden, in the occupation of Spenser Shadbolt, at the Rent of £.2 12s. per annum.

LOT IV.

A Freehold four-room Cottage, divided into two Tenements with Gardens, situate at Datchworth, in the occupations of Dame Darton, at the estimated Rent of £.4 per annum, and John Brothers, at £.2 10s. per annum.

LOT. V.

An old established Freehold Public House in full trade, situate near Datchworth Church, in a populous Neighbourhood, called the Tilbury, containing one Bed-room, Taproom with Oven, Parlour, Pantry, Shop, Cellar, and Garden, in the occupation of W. Smith, tenant from year to year, at £.10 per annum.

LOT I.	Area of land at Burnham Green where a poor house stood, until *c.*1770, where 1 Orchard Road now stands.
LOT II.	Burnham Green poor house – now demolished and was close to where 2 White Horse Lane is now.
LOT III.	Datchworth Green poor house – now demolished and was where Tudor Lodge now stands.
LOT IV.	Poor house near Datchworth church where School House now stands.
LOT V.	The old Tilbury public house and outbuildings – now demolished and the land incorporated into the churchyard.

****

Sale details reported in the Hertford Union Guardian minutes, 16 Dec 1837:

The Clerk reported that the Datchworth parish property was sold by Kimpton & Son, on 15th November last, in 5 lots to the following persons and at the following prices:

LOT 1	Lawrance Lucas on behalf of Thomas Prior	£27.0.0
LOT 2	George Lawrance	£70.0.0
LOT 3	John Hankin Bentley of Hertingfordbury	£30.0.0
LOT 4	William Lucas junior of Hitchin	£85.0.0
LOT 5	William Lucas junior of Hitchin	£405.0.0
	Total	£617.0.0

Figure 145: Handbill of sale dated 1837, showing particulars of the parish poor houses, land and the old Tilbury (HALS: D/EPT 2963)

George failed to repay the debt, so in 1842 the cottage, by then in a decrepit state, was transferred to James Hawkins who then demolished it and in its place built two timber cottages. In 1852 James applied for a mortgage of £250 on security of 'the two cottages now built on the site of the cottage [poor house] on Datchworth Green formally occupied by Spencer Shadbolt the cottage having been demolished'. However, James died just four years later without repaying the mortgage and his widow had to sell the cottages. She sold them to Abel Smith, senior, who paid £150 directly to James Hawkins' mortgage lender. The two cottages were eventually demolished and replaced with a single dwelling, Tudor Lodge, in 1957, which was extended in the mid-1980s.

The church poor house was situated opposite the school, where School House is now. In 1837 it was sold to William and Joseph Lucas, brewers of Hitchin, along with the old Tilbury public house, for a total cost of £490 (£405 for the Tilbury and £85 for the cottage). A legal declaration made by Henry Campkin, churchwarden and overseer, associated with the sale of the poor houses in 1837, confirms that:

> A four roomed cottage divided into two tenements with gardens, sited at Fownes Green, Datchworth in the occupation of Dame Darton and John Brothers, that James Titmass, church clerk, living in part of the last mentioned cottage, more than 20 years ago for which he paid rent to the parish. The other part always was and is occupied by paupers put in there by the parish officers. But John Brothers is not a pauper but holds his part of the cottage for one shilling per week.

In 1840, the Lucases sold the Tilbury and cottage to Abel Smith, senior, for £250, who handed the properties back to the parish. The Tilbury was demolished and its land became part of the churchyard and the cottage site was eventually used to provide a house for the school mistress.

Hertford Union Workhouse

Under the new regime of the Poor Law Amendment Act 1834, parishes were grouped together into unions, collectively known as 'poor law districts', governed by a 'board of guardians', reminiscent of Gilbert's Act about half a century earlier. These unions became jointly responsible for the administration of poor relief. Village paupers were moved to a central workhouse, usually based in an urban area, and each parish elected a guardian or guardians, depending on its size. Paupers were housed, clothed and fed and children were educated. However, in return for this care, inmates had to work for several hours per day.

The Hertford Union was formed on 18 June 1835 and served Datchworth as well as 17 other parishes. Henry Campkin was Datchworth's first guardian. Initially, the Hertford Union used an

Figure 146: Hertford Union Workhouse (c.1905)
(Hertford Museum: HETFM 2833.331)

existing parish workhouse, spending £350 to have it adapted. In 1867 the building of a new workhouse commenced. The land was purchased from Lord Townshend and it was built at a cost of £12,000 and was designed to house 250 inmates. The workhouse was situated on the Ware Road at the foot of Gallows Hill and opened in 1869.

Records show, that between 1847 and 1916, at least 96 Datchworth paupers were sent to Hertford Union Workhouse, of whom some were admitted several times. For example, James Gregory was admitted and discharged at least eight times in a two year period. His final stay lasted fourteen years, and his death was recorded in the discharge register on 10 April 1889, aged 69. Henry Ilott was admitted and discharged at least seven times over a 20 year period, the final occasion being on 3 September 1908 when he was 'discharged by the order of Datchworth and taken to Hill End Asylum'.

Some women who were expecting an illegitimate child were sent to the workhouse and the register of births lists ten such Datchworth women between 1850 and 1909. One of these, Caroline Hipgrave, gave birth to two of her children in the workhouse, Henry on 3 December 1858 and the following year, George on 25 November 1859. Another woman is Martha Webb, who gave birth to a daughter, Emily, in 1868 and was released shortly afterwards. However, six years later Martha and Emily were both re-admitted. It is not known what happened to Emily, but Martha eventually died there in 1896 aged 52.

Of the 96 recorded Datchworth admissions to the workhouse, 42 of these were parishioners over the age of 65, and 32 of these are recorded as having died there. A total of 50 Datchworth residents died whilst in the workhouse, the youngest being two year old James Darton, an illegitimate child who was born there on 26 November 1850.

On occasions a whole family would be sent to the workhouse. In Datchworth's case, this included Eliza Smith and her five children, aged fourteen, ten, eight, four and one, who were admitted in 1875, and in 1902 John and Alice Jackson with their four children, aged between two and thirteen years old, became inmates.

Another Datchworth resident who was admitted to the workhouse was Rebecca Wilmott. In 1856, at the age of 19, Rebecca had been living in a cottage which she and two other girls were renting from a person in Hertford. It was reported that 'they had been living in a state of almost indescribable filth and misery and disgusting immorality. There was no furniture in the cottage, the beds were merely straw littered down and the occupants had been in the habit of receiving male visitors of the lowest class'. An order was made by the Hertford Board of Guardians to admit Rebecca to the workhouse and it was suggested that the parochial committee should 'interfere to prevent such a state of things as that described happening elsewhere in the parish'.

Workhouses were officially closed in 1930 following the Local Government Act 1929 which passed the responsibility of the poor to the county councils. The Hertford Union Workhouse closed in 1919. The building was taken over by the county council, who converted it into a residential school for the mentally handicapped. The school eventually closed in 1968 and the building was demolished in the 1970s. When the workhouse closed, inmates were dispersed to St Albans and Ware workhouses and the Hertford Poor Law Union itself was dissolved in 1924.

The clock tower on the workhouse building came from Ware church in the 1880s. Upon the demolition of the workhouse, the clock tower was transferred to All Saints' Church, Hertford.

The tragic story of the Eaves family

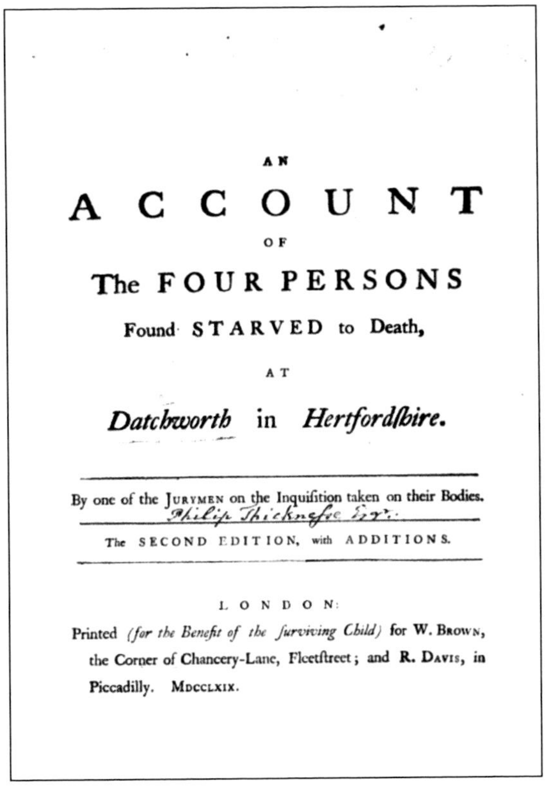
AN

ACCOUNT

OF

The FOUR PERSONS

Found STARVED to Death,

AT

Datchworth in *Hertfordshire.*

By one of the JURYMEN on the Inquisition taken on their Bodies.

Philip Thicknesse Esqr.

The SECOND EDITION, with ADDITIONS.

LONDON:

Printed *(for the Benefit of the surviving Child)* for W. BROWN, the Corner of Chancery-Lane, Fleetstreet; and R. DAVIS, in Piccadilly. MDCCLXIX.

Figure 147: Title page to Thicknesse's starvation story. (HALS)

Datchworth has on record one of the worst cases of a whole family perishing from neglect, allegedly having been left to starve to death in one of the parish poor houses. The full story was told in a pamphlet written on 18 February 1769, by Philip

Thicknesse, entitled *An Account of the Four Persons Found Starved to Death at Datchworth, in Hertfordshire* and is available at the British Library.

Thicknesse begins his account by attacking with vigour the members of the vestry whom he held responsible for the severe neglect and death of the Eaves family:

> The following narrative of an affair so shocking to humanity, and so alarming in this country, (famed throughout the world for charity and benevolence) however simply told, cannot but make a deep impression on the mind of every reader ... I have neither abilities nor inclination to work upon the passions of the reader; nor any other motive to publish this account, but the hopes that it may not only prove to have a good effect with those *'in this parish who may have neglected their duty'*; but that in every parish throughout the kingdom, those, whose more immediate care it is to provide for the poor, may be roused to a sense of their duty.
>
> To succour and relieve the distressed, is a great and God-like act; and it is undoubtedly the duty, and in the power of every individual to do it: And yet in no kingdom are the Poor more hardly dealt with than in this; especially in extensive, but obscure parishes, where scarcely any gentlemen reside. In these it is usual for three or four '*upstart*' necessitous freeholders to combine to form a vestry, and engross the whole power of every kind in their hands. I need not go *'far from my own house to see such a parish'*...

The account goes on to explain that, on 23 January 1769, he was told by a 'day-labourer' that 'four or five persons were found dead in a poor house on the green and that they had perished from want of food, attendance and a habitable dwelling'.

Thicknesse responded to the day-labourer's report and went to see the facts for himself and found:

> .....a small hut, consisting of one room, without floor or ceiling, 14 feet long and 12 feet broad, un-thatched in some places, a window frame without glass at one end and on the opposite side a large hole in the plastering through which I could have got. There I beheld the four dead bodies, emaciated beyond any conception, lying on a very small quantity of dirty peas straw, spread on the bare earth. The man had on a piece of shirt, the woman was quite naked, as were the children..... they must have perished with cold in such a house and in such naked conditions.
>
> .....the third child, a boy of eleven years of age, was found crawling on the floor amidst the dead bodies of his father mother brother and sister, cramp'd and emaciated; and tho' sensible, unable to tell how long the other part of the family had been dead.

The account does not specify on which 'green' the poor house was situated but when *Five Hide Village* was written and published in 1984, it was thought that 'the green' referred to Datchworth Green. However, the *Hertfordshire Archaeological Note and Queries* newspaper, dated 4 April 1903, states '...that the tragedy which took place in January 1769, happened at the hamlet of Burnham Green, a mile and a half distant...' Other material has also come to light that would suggest that the tragedy took place at Burnham Green.

As previously mentioned in this chapter, in relation to the sale of the poor houses in 1837, Thomas Mardle declared in a legal document that a poor house had existed until about 1770 at Burnham Green, in which people had starved to death. It has also been mentioned earlier that in 1701 a property nearby was leased by Edward Lawrance to the church overseers for the use of the poor, a function that continued until its sale in 1837. Therefore, at the time of the Eaves tragedy there were two poor houses at Burnham Green. Indeed Thicknesse states at the end of his account that:

> I cannot finish this account without expressing my surprise and concern that this disaster does not seem to make any impression on those whose more immediate duty it is to see that other poor do not perish likewise: for nine women and children are now in a hut within 100 yards of that in which the family perished. (Figure 38)

Thicknesse's account also mentions that another pauper had died in the same house in 1763; his wife, Susanna Statton, claiming that he too starved to death, but the parish officers claimed that Mr Statton and the Eaves family died of 'the gaol distemper'. 'Why then', asked Thicknesse, 'was this family put into an infectious house.' This statement itself could explain why this poor house at Burnham Green was demolished about 1770.

Also, Thicknesse had several properties on Datchworth Green which were so close to the poor house that he would surely have been aware of such events if they had occurred in that particular dwelling.

A View of the Poor House of D——— in Herts address'd to the Overseers of England.

Figure 148: The horrific illustration which accompanied Philip Thicknesse's pamphlet. (HALS)

Returning to his account, Thicknesse had discovered that, three weeks previously, the Eaves family had been found to be ill. The overseers of the poor visited and left half a crown with a neighbour to buy the Eaves some food, which she did. Since then, no one had been near them. A report had been spread that they were suffering from 'gaol fever', so-named because it was commonly found in gaols. It was an infectious disease called flea typhus which at that time could be fatal. It is not surprising, therefore, that the villagers were avoiding close contact with the family. When the dead bodies were first discovered by a local shepherd boy, the food and change were still lying where the neighbour had left them.

Thicknesse wrote to John and Samuel Bassett, churchwarden and overseer of the poor respectively:

> Mr Bassett,
>
> I desire, nay, I require that you do not cause the four dead persons, namely, *James Eaves*, his wife and two children, to be buried till the coroner has held an inquest on their bodies, and the cause, and authors of their death, are properly enquired into.

Having received no reply, Thicknesse started to investigate what had happened to the bodies. On his way to the place where the family had died, he met a cart driven by a man who was accompanied by the constable. The cart appeared to be loaded with boxes but upon enquiry, he discovered that the cart contained two coffins, partly concealed by straw and litter. The constable then confessed that he was taking them to be buried by order of the parish officers.

Thicknesse then returned home and wrote to Dr Smith the rector, to ask him to give his assistance to 'bring this seeming dark transaction to light'.

The rector said he understood that, at a meeting of the justices of the peace and the coroner, Thicknesse's papers were seen, but the justices had gone ahead and ordered the bodies to be buried. But, so far, he had only received the order verbally which was not sufficient. Therefore he had directed that the bodies be placed in the church and he had also put a stop to the burial.

Thicknesse then appealed to Mr Searancke, of Hatfield. On 25 January 1769 he received a letter from Searancke containing the following:

> ..... As the law vests the officers of a parish with a power to raise money for the relief of the impotent poor; if they, with a deliberate intension, suffer them to perish, it is a crime little short of murder; but I am afraid not punishable as such.

> A gaoler is guilty of wilful murder, that suffers a prisoner to die through duress: Can an officer of a parish be guilty of a less crime, that with-holds necessary relief from a pauper, whom it is his duty to provide with all necessaries proper for his case.
>
> I never did hear of a similar instance to that under your consideration; and by making a public example, the like may be prevented.

At this point the coroner was contacted and ordered to direct the parish officers to summon a jury to assemble the next morning. Upon speaking to the constable, who had been directed to summon seven parishioners for a jury, Thicknesse said that he was ready and willing to serve upon it, but the constable replied that he had orders from the churchwarden that he should not be upon the jury. However, despite the efforts to exclude him, Thicknesse became the foreman, but complained that the rest of the jury 'composed of the most illiterate part of the parish, while many substantial farmers were within reach, and I think they all were, or all who spoke were, of a different opinion with myself'.

According to the evidence given by the members of the jury who spoke, the Eaves family did not die through lack of care, attendance, provisions or of a habitable house. But the coroner assured Thicknesse that there had been great negligence somewhere and that the only alternative was to find it 'wilful murder, or that they died a natural death, but the latter verdict did not in the least obstruct other legal proceedings against any persons, who might, upon further enquiry, appear culpable'.

It appeared that no surgeon had ever been sent to examine the bodies and therefore, upon Thicknesse's direction, the hearing was adjourned until the next day. Accordingly, Mr Frost, a surgeon from Hertford attended the next hearing where he agreed that 'he never saw bodies more emaciated, and that certainly there had been great neglect somewhere; and particularly that no person of the faculty [medical profession] had been called in to visit them'.

Further details were also brought to light by witnesses. A neighbour said that:

> The surviving boy was the only one, for a long time, that was able to crawl out. He had once or twice borrowed the lid of my oven. When he came, he was almost naked, having only a kind of sack over his shoulder. When I asked him why he did not go into service, he replied, because the parish would not clothe him, and no one would take him naked. However, he had not been for the oven lid within the last fortnight, nor had he appeared. But I did see the poor mother crawl out about ten days ago, with a kettle to get a little water from a kind of pond, at a small distance from the house, that in endeavouring to carry it, she fell down, left the kettle, and crept on her hands and knees into her hovel again, and this was the last time any of the deceased persons were seen alive.

An older son who was 'in service' had visited the family about Christmas time and had found them 'ill and in a starving and helpless condition'. He went to the overseer's house to ask for relief but the overseer was not at home and the woman there was abusive and sent him away. On his way back, he met the overseer who refused to give them any assistance. He accordingly informed his parents who replied: 'Then we must perish'. He planned to visit his parents again, but living at some distance, his 'dame' [mistress] would not give him leave, and he saw them no more.

The parish officers continued their defence that the family had died of gaol distemper and, despite Thinknesse's perseverance, the Eaves were found to have died from natural causes.

Having failed at the inquest, Thicknesse was so convinced that the parish officers were guilty of neglect that he took them to the Court of the King's Bench in London. However, according to the following report, he was unsuccessful and the case was quashed.

> Cause was shown in Kings Bench, by Parish Officers of Datchworth, why an information should not go against them, when, upon a full hearing, the court was unanimously of opinion that there was not the least ground for such an information and ordered the rule to be discharged.

Thicknesse took the surviving child, William Eaves, into his own house. He records that 'the boy is recovering his health but he can give no account of the horrid scene which passed before his eyes; it is therefore natural to conclude, his mind was at that time froze up with his body'.

Shortly after the failed hearing at the King's Bench, Thicknesse continued to pursue his belief that conditions for the poor had to be improved. He made a public appeal for donations that would go towards the relief of the poor in that parish, where 'besides the surviving child of that family, many poor in the same parish are in almost as starving and wretched a condition'.

Thicknesse's pamphlet sold well and the scandal, having been reported widely, must have brought unwelcome publicity to the village. It is noticeable that, at a vestry meeting on 28 March 1769, new overseers, William Wallis and William Allinson, were appointed instead of the Bassetts and in the following month, at another meeting, a rate towards the relief of the poor was agreed at 12d in the pound. The poor house at Burnham Green was demolished and the site eventually became used as garden ground [allotment], possibly to grow food for the poor of the parish.

The story of the Eaves, who had been married at Datchworth church fifteen years before they died, was brought to light again recently when, in 2009, the story again hit the national and international headlines when Thicknesse's pamphlet was unearthed at the British Library. Following this, the Reverend Coralie McCluskey decided to have a plaque made in tribute to the family. The plaque is mounted on a wooden display board in the churchyard.

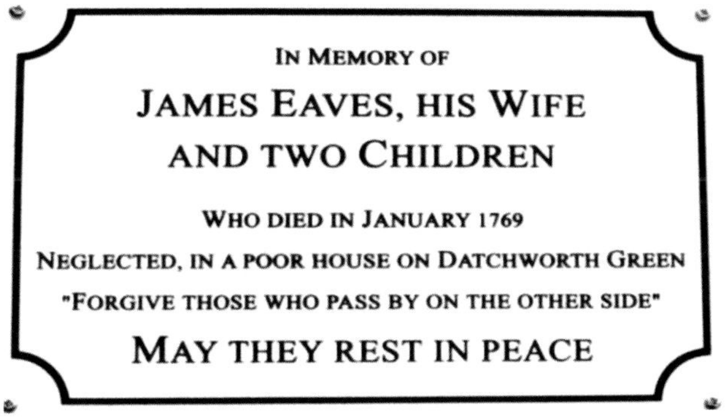

Figure 149: The plaque erected in memory of the Eaves family in All Saints churchyard.

Unfortunately this plaque has been inscribed with 'in a poor house on Datchworth Green' not Burnham Green. This is because at the time it was made it was commonly believed that the incident took place on Datchworth Green following the entry in *Five Hide Village.*

Philip Thicknesse

Philip Thicknesse did not personally sign the account of the Eaves story which was described as being 'by one of the Jurymen on the Inquisition taken on their Bodies'. However, his name was added to a copy then at the British Museum. It is commonly assumed that this Philip Thicknesse was 'Captain' Philip Thicknesse (1719 – 1792). He was a well known author, eccentric and troublemaker and the lengths taken with the Eaves tragedy were certainly in keeping with the Captain's style. But, surprisingly, there is no mention of Captain Thicknesse having been in Datchworth or any reference to the Eaves story in either his *Memoires and Anecdotes of Philip Thicknesse* written in 1788, or in the *Oxford Dictionary of National Biography*. Although in the latter, it is stated that he moved to Welwyn in 1766 for a short time, before moving to Bath in 1768. Any reference to his movements between then and 1775 is not recorded. Perhaps the failed court action, mentioned above, contributed towards these omissions.

In 1767 Philip Thicknesse purchased Green End Farm at Datchworth Green for £945 from Daniel Haynes. At the time the farm consisted of a messuage, two cottages and 16 acres of land. The cottages were at the west end of Datchworth Green, near Rectory Lane, and the land included the meadow behind the poor house and several fields to the north of Datchworth Green. In November 1768 he also took on the tenancy of a cottage 'by the name of the Meeting House now dilapidated together with a small piece or parcell of Ground thereunto adjoining called the Burying Ground...' (Figure 15a). Then, in April 1769, he purchased Pettits and 23 acres at a cost of £70 from Randall Lawrance. However, in October 1769 he was summoned to Hawkins Hall Court Baron for arrears of rent to the lord of the manor on both Green End and Pettits, whereby the 'bailiffe' was ordered to seize goods in lieu of the debt for both charges.

In 1775 Thicknesse gave Green End Farm to his wife 'for and in consideration of the love and affection which the said Philip Thicknesse hath for Ann his Wife and for and towards making a proper provision for her...'. By this time, the farm consisted of 18 acres along with the messuage and two cottages. On the 10 May 1777 the Thicknesses sold their Datchworth properties to Charles Fuller. Upon the sale of Green End Farm, they nearly lost £45 on the deal as they asked for £900 when they meant to say 900 guineas!

Thicknesse had the reputation for being a quarrelsome person, a characteristic that inspired Philip Gosse to choose the title '*Dr Viper*' when he wrote Thicknesse's biography. However, there were other aspects to his character and John Nichols, in *Literary Anecdotes of the Eighteenth Century*, described him as 'a man of probity and honour whose heart and purse were always open to the unfortunate'.

Residents' Memories

Louie Cubbage: Father told me about Miss Farrin catching smallpox. A tin hut was built in field between Farrins and the Rectory. It became called Hospital Meadow.

Bill Nash: Times were hard but by careful housekeeping and good gardening our family never went hungry. But there was no money for extras, clothes were home-made and old clothes were cut down for the children. For medical attention we had to walk to Watton. The only children's care was done through the school by the nurse, who was mainly concerned with the head.

Phyllis Smalley (Burnham Green): When the QVM hospital opened in Welwyn on 24th July 1934, the school children lined the drive to the hospital, it was opened by The Duchess of York [later to become Queen Elizabeth – the mother of Queen Elizabeth II]. We all had little union jack flags to wave. My dad helped to build the hospital and my parents paid 3d a week for our medical needs – a sort of hospital club.

Bernard Reynolds: I lost many friends to TB in my teenage years.

Reg Chalkley: When I was at school there was a diphtheria outbreak in the village. Five of my family were together in hospital at Hertford. Some village children died. The field next to the old rectory was called Hospital Meadow. It was given this name when Miss Farrin had smallpox and she was put in isolation in a sort of hut in the field.

Mr Tyler (Burnham Green): Poaching was common, not so much as a sport but more a way of getting a decent meal.

17. Troublemakers

Over the years Datchworth has had its share of miscreants whose misdemeanours have been reported in various ways. John Carrington of Bramfield and Tewin, farmer, overseer, tax collector and local constable, kept a diary from 1798 until his death in 1810. He was close enough to Datchworth to be aware of such events and there are a several entries relating to them. In addition to his diary, reports from old newspapers and Quarter Sessions records have been useful sources for the stories that follow.

Sarah Pelham

In 1807 Mrs Sarah Pelham of the Chequers public house, Woolmer Green, was charged with 'being in possession of two silver spoons, 'knowing them to have been stolen'. She was sentenced to 14 years transportation. She won the sympathy of John Carrington who went to Datchworth, as well as the other neighbouring villages, collecting signatures for a petition for her release. On 18 May 1807 he wrote in his diary:

> To Datchworth to Esqr Fullers at the Bottom of Thatcher (Datchworth) Green, had a Good Glass of old Rum, from thence to the Revd. Mr Johnsons at the parsonage to see if they would sighn Mrs. Pelloms Pittition to save her being transported, but they would not ....

On 2 June he went 'To Diggswell and Wellwin to see Waller to sighn Mrs Pelloms Pittetion, Saw Waller & more Sighend it ...'. Two days later he went to London 'on Dunn poney to present a Pittition for Mrs Pellom' who by this time was in Hertford Gaol. He delivered his petition to the clerk of the office at the Treasury on 6 June, who promised to give it to the Secretary of State 'for the home Department', Lord Hawkesbury, who in turn would deliver it to the king.

He was still working on Mrs Pelham's behalf five months later when instead of going to church on 6 November, he called on and requested 'Esqr Brands at Kimpton Hooe to Speek for Mrs Pellom' who was still in Hertford Gaol. Mr Brand promised to help her. However, despite Carrington's endeavours, Sarah was transported to Australia, arriving there in December 1808.

Walter Clibbon

The killing of a well-known highwayman is another story that John Carrington vividly recorded in a notebook called 'The Arithmetic Book' that predates his formal diary. The individual concerned was Walter Clibbon or Clibborn as it was also spelt. He was a seller of cakes and pies and, with his sons, had formed a gang of footpads [robbers on foot] who roamed Hertford market observing the trading and noting those who had done well financially. Local public houses were also frequented, where those who had profited particularly well were apt to boast about their successes. Having identified their quarries, they would dress in farm labourers' smocks, and with blackened faces, would lie in wait for their victims to return home. On 28 December 1782 they had targeted a Datchworth man but, unknowingly, had met their match. Carrington tells the story as follows:

> On Saterday 28th of December 1782 about 6 clock in the evening was Shott Dead Old Walter Clibbon, And one of his sons Taken, about 30 pole [160 yards] from O[a]kenvaley Bottom toward Bulls Green in the Parish of Tewin [now part of Datchworth]. This said Clibbon was a labouring man and when this happened lived at Babbs Green ... Wareside and used to go a rob[b]ing with his sons as they grew upp as footpads every winter season, for he kept them at home for that purpose And had done maney great and abusive Robreys ...
>
> [On this occasion] they came to a wood nere Bools [Bulls] Green erley this Satuday morning and there Stayd till Evening with intent to robb homewords, they robed in smock frocks with there faces blacked, the first they stoped was Whittenburys son, of Datchworth, in a Little Cart and Instead of his going on to Datchworth after being robbed turns on the left on the first opening and came to Quino Hall [Queen Hoo Hall] to tell his uncle Benjm Whittenbury wt had happened.
>
> The Uncle told him he had just parted from his Father and his other Uncle as they came home together. Therefore he calld his man Geog North and bid North take the Gunn and calld his son Thos and he took his stick and Dogg and these 3 went to the bottom but before they came their they [Clibbon and sons] had stoppd the 2 Brothers, one they robbed the other run away, when they Come to the Bottom, Mr Ben Whittenbury told his man and son theyd walk up the hill and go home, but they [Clibbon and sons] came out of the wood and Attacked them thinking they was others coming from market, they atacted without speaking and knocked Mr Whittenbury down and Mr Whittenbury knocked the old Clibbon

> Down and a great Batle for some time till they overpowered Mr Whittenbury and he calld for his man to shoot, which he Did and killd the old Roogue on the Spott.
>
> He shoot him in the Brest for his gun allmost touched him, after this one son run away, the other was taken and Hanged at the Lent following Assize, and a coroner came on the Monday following also Jury met and they found he met his death as he deserved and they buried him by the roadside where he was dead.

Having bravely dealt with this group of scoundrels at great personal risk, Benjamin must have been a local hero and, as a reward, The Lord Lieutenant presented him with a 28 oz silver cup engraved with the following inscription as quoted in the *East Hertfordshire Archaeological Society Transactions* 1902:

> This cup, the gift of James, Earl of Salisbury, Lord Lieutenant, to Mr Benjamin Whittenbury of Queen Hoo Hall, presented this 31st day of January 1783, in consideration of his spirited behaviour on Saturday December 28th 1782 in risking his life and securing Joseph Clibborn, the son, after having been instrumental in shooting Walter Clibborn, the father, a most notorious and inhuman offender, by which means the County of Hertford was delivered from the depredations of a most desperate set of villains.

Figure 150: The gun that was used to shoot Walter Clibbon together with a fragment of the original Clibbon's post in the box on the left.
(Michael Clark of Tewin Society History Association)

Whittenbury's 'man', George North, who delivered the fatal shot, was tried for murder but acquitted. The gun he used was a half inch bore flintlock 'fowling piece' [a light shotgun used for shooting wildfowl], five feet eight inches long. The gun and silver cup were sold at an auction in 1856; both were bought by Mr B Page, the cup for £10 and the gun for 21s. The latter is now on display in a glass cabinet at Hertford Museum.

Following the shooting on the Saturday night, Clibbon's body was placed in a barn adjacent to the Horns public house. On the following Monday it was buried, with a stake through it, at the spot by the side of the road where the shooting had taken place. A post was erected there, and when it deteriorated, was replaced first by the East Herts Archaeological Society, after the First World War, and again at a later date by the Hertfordshire Society. A fragment of the original post is on display beside the gun at Hertford Museum.

Incidences such as the Clibbon case set tongues wagging and many stories were spread among locals in the following years. One such tale came from a member of the Lawrance family which stated that:

> Mr Lawrance's great grandfather saw Jimmy Wilson of Hoppers Hall, being drunk, mixed blood from the corpse with his ginger ale and marked the face of another and a fight broke out. The next night, the body, which was laid out in the barn adjacent to the Horns public house, was dragged by the heels out of the barn, the feet struck the threshold and the stiffened corpse rose up. This scared the people present and they thought it better to bury the body, near the spot where Clibbon was shot, with a stake through it to prevent its ghost rising out of the grave.

Figure 151: Clibbon's post in Bramfield Road.

The Shadbolts

The Shadbolts had a reputation for being troublemakers for much of the nineteenth century, some of whose offences appear in the tabulated list at the end of this chapter. Most of their misdemeanours were associated with petty crime but some were more serious, including an incident that involved Daniel Shadbolt, who had the responsible position of parish constable. In May 1864 a report appeared in a local newspaper about a court case that concerned a disturbance in The White Horse public house at Burnham Green.

Daniel Shadbolt had been charged with assaulting John Nash, 'a respectable looking labouring man, whose head was enveloped in bandages'. Nash's account of the event was as follows:

> I was playing at Four Corners with others at the public house [The White Horse] kept by Ezekiel Croft at Burnham Green. Shadbolt came and said 'stop the game!' I asked the landlord if he wished us to stop and he said no. Shadbolt then kicked the pins down then said he was going to throw the ball away, but when he made a grab for the ball I put my hand down and stopped him. He shoved up against me and asked me to hit him, he then walked away, we thought he had gone home. He came back five minutes later with his staff and handcuffs and said 'I mean to stop this game'. He then struck me on the side of the head with his staff, without receiving any provocation. I had not spoken to him on his return and I was quite sober. I have been laid up and kept my bed for eight days as a consequence of the injuries.

Following cross examination and several witness accounts, the bench censured Constable Shadbolt for his excessive zeal, cautioned him to be more discrete in the use of his staff in future and fined him 1s with 19s costs.

However, one of the miscreant Shadbolts went on to become a highly respected citizen. At the age of 16, Benjamin Shadbolt, who lived in a cottage (now demolished) opposite Club Cottage in Burnham Green Road, was committed to three weeks hard labour in 1841 for stealing a pole from Samuel Sutton. Four years later, Benjamin, along with his brother Jonathan, uncle Soloman and cousin George, was charged with burglary 'of a roll of material from Mrs Brindle's shop', On 10 July 1845 they were tried and found guilty. The judge commented that they 'were a bad lot who had evaded the authorities for a very long time!' All four were sentenced to transportation: Soloman for 20 years and Benjamin, Jonathan and George for 15 years each. They were all married and had nine children between them.

In 1858, after serving his sentence in Australia, Benjamin moved to New Zealand, re-married and had sixteen more children, having left one daughter behind in Datchworth. He began a career as a timber merchant and eventually had a timber mill and later acquired a 405 acre farm which he named 'Hertford Farm', where he acted as a farmer, stock-keeper and butcher. There must have been many working horses on the farm which necessitated the need for a blacksmith, yet another skill that Shadbolt acquired. His interest in horses developed and he became a race-horse owner and breeder.

At different times he was a publican, mail contractor and operated the first public transport on Banks Peninsula that consisted of an open buggy drawn by two horses. He was a founder member and president for many years of the Banks Peninsula Agricultural and Pastoral Association. In 1875 he gave land to build an Anglican church, which still stands today. His success as a business man and as a philanthropist caused him to be regarded as 'the local squire'.

Despite the reputation of Benjamin's ancestors, his own reformation may well have had a positive effect on at least two of his descendants. His great-grandson, Maurice Shadbolt (1932 – 2004), became a well-known New Zealand author and playwright. He wrote many novels including *One of Bens* and in 1989 he was awarded a CBE for services to literature. Another descendent was Tim Shadbolt, a New Zealand politician, Mayor of Invercargill and popular TV personality. Tim's successful election as mayor in 2010 was his eighth mayoral term, making him the longest serving mayor in New Zealand, during which time he had the doubtful distinction of having lost the mayoral chains twice. In 2012 he set the Guinness World Record for the longest television interview which lasted 26 consecutive hours.

Figure 152: Benjamin Shadbolt. (1825 – 1882) (Pauline Conolly, NZ)

Of the other Shadbolts who were transported with Benjamin, Jonathan eventually disappeared to the Western Australian gold-fields and was never heard of again. George married a fellow convict and went on to become a successful farmer, blacksmith and carpenter in Northern Tasmania. He helped build his local church and was the first superintendent of the Sunday school to be appointed. The oldest of the four, aged 46 when he was exiled, was uncle Soloman, who was treated for dysentery for the final six weeks of the journey to Australia. However, on arrival at Norfolk Island he was discharged as being medically fit and transferred to Van Diemen's Land in May 1847, then to the Tasman Peninsular to carry out his sentence with the other convicts. However, Soloman died less than a year later, in January 1848.

Soloman's involvement in petty crime earned him the reputation of being one of the more notorious Shadbolts. However long before he was sentenced to transportation a serious accusation had been made against him. In 1826 he was arrested on suspicion of killing a man. It was reported in the *Hertford Mercury* dated 7 January that the body of a man had been found in a moat full of water quite near to the Horns public house at Bull's Green. The body, that of Thomas Chalkley, was removed from the moat and taken to the pub to await the coroner's inquest. It was said that Solomon Shadbolt and his brother Joseph were the last people to have been seen with Chalkley and that Chalkley was sober when he left the pub. The Shadbolt brothers were therefore detained and questioned. However, the coroner returned a verdict of accidental death, concluding that 'the poor fellow had missed his footing in the dark and fallen into the freezing pond' whereupon Soloman and Joseph were discharged.

George Hill

In January 1865 George Hill, bricklayer of Datchworth, was charged with stealing a dark bay mare, a bay mare and a pair of trousers, all the property of Thomas Raw, Hertford. Hill pleaded guilty and was sentenced to 12 months imprisonment with hard labour. Hill asked if Mr Lawrance, builder of Datchworth, could be called to speak in his favour. Mr Lawrance was in the gallery, but declined do so.

Benjamin Whittenbury

In 1866 Benjamin Whittenbury, labourer, was charged with assaulting William Chapman of Burnham Green. A rather different character from his name-sake who was the hero of the Clibbon case. The *Hertford Mercury* dated 1 September 1866 reported: 'Whittenbury [was] an ill-looking, powerful man and Chapman, a handsome man with a well-formed head, refined countenance and a very bright but rather wild looking eye and feeble intellect'. Chapman stated 'I was in the White Horse public house at Burnham Green and was induced to sell my jacket worth 18s for 3s 6d which I spent on treating the men in the house. When my money had all gone, Whittenbury began punching me and threw me across the room and dragged me through a pond'. Police Constable Day reported to the court that 'Whittenbury was always ill-treating Chapman, he had known him thrown in a pond and stamped on'. Whittenbury was fined 2s plus 7s 6d costs.

William Chapman

In February 1867 William Chapman of Datchworth, 'who is said to wander about like a vagrant and give much trouble to the county police', pleaded guilty to stealing a coat valued at 1s and a rule valued 1s belonging to Arthur Peck, stonemason. The rule was in the pocket of the coat that he took from Mr Peck's work-shed. Chapman sold the coat the following day for 8d to John Wells, who worked for Alfred McMullen and who found Chapman asleep in McMullen's chaise. Chapman pleaded 'I'm sorry I done it, I never did such a thing in my life before, I never did, I should not have done it only I was drunk and silly'. Mr Smithson, chairman of bench at Borough Magistrates, told him 'you are liable to go to gaol for three months, but the bench wish to deal leniently with you and as you seem to be a poor half-witted creature, they give you 14 days of it'.

Illegitimacy

Throughout history illegitimacy has had certain legal, as well as social, consequences. A bastard lacked the right to inherit the family estate and could not bear the father's name. Failure to find the father meant that the mother and child had little means of support. The Poor Law Act of 1576 contained a clause that attempted to meet this problem by stating that once the 'putative' father was found he had to take responsibility for maintaining the child.

In 1732-3, another Act was passed summarising amendments that had been made in the intervening years. A woman expecting a baby out of wedlock was supposed to declare the fact and name the father, who was then obliged to maintain the child according to a 'bastardy order' or 'bond' instructed by the court of Quarter Sessions. If he refused, he was liable for a gaol sentence whereupon the parish would support the mother and child until the father agreed to pay maintenance and also to reimburse the parish. An example is that of Benjamin Squire who, in 1750, had a maintenance order made against him in respect of the bastard daughter of Elizabeth Allen of Datchworth. He failed to pay the 1s per week and in 1760 was served with a Bastardy Order shown in Figure 153 with its transcription.

In the early sixteenth century illegitimacy accounted for about 1 or 2% of baptisms. This rate had risen to only 3% by the 1750s which, according to W.E.Tate in *The Parish Chest,* marked a turning point, when there was a sudden rise in illegitimacy rates. These reached a high point of 7% in the middle of the nineteenth century. Increased social mobility, which allowed young people to move away from home, is regarded as one of the causes. Being released from the constraints of their family, peers and the church, they were perhaps more likely to indulge in irresponsible relationships.

It is possible that some illegitimate children were born to women in a stable, but illegal, relationship with one man, however, illegitimacy was still frowned upon and occasionally the fear of discovery led to infanticide. Datchworth had its fair share of cases involving bastard children, illustrated by the following examples.

Rebecca Brownsell

In 1851, 13 year old Rebecca Brownsell was living with her grandmother and brother, John, at Rats Castle Cottage. She was listed in the census as a servant; probably to Edward Pennyfather of Harmer Green Farm. At the age of 14, she gave birth to her first illegitimate child, Mary Pennyfather Brownsell. By the time Rebecca was 23, her grandmother had died and Rebecca had become the head of the household having given birth to three more illegitimate children, one of whom died shortly after birth. By 1871 Rebecca and her brother had moved to the White Horse public house in Burnham Green with seven listed illegitimate children. John eventually took over as the landlord of the White Horse, married, had three children of his own and took on three of Rebecca's children. Meanwhile, Rebecca moved into a cottage, given as 1 Burnham Green Road, remained unmarried and went on to bear another four illegitimate children, bringing the total number of offspring born out of wedlock to 12. According to family descendants, Edward Pennyfather fathered all Rebecca's children, and this seems likely as, according to Pennyfather's will, that was granted probate in 1900 following his death, he left a substantial sum of £100 to Rebecca. The larger part of his estate was left to his brother, John, and it was stated that at John's death Rebecca and her children would inherit the residue.

John Gregory and Mary Anne Adams

At the magistrates' court in March 1860, John Gregory of Datchworth was charged with being the father of the illegitimate child of Mary Anne Adams of Bengeo. Gregory admitted to being the father but was not forthcoming with his payments and therefore Mary Anne Adams wished for an order. An order was made for John Gregory to pay 1s 6d per week and 10s arrears to the plaintiff.

Robert Kiddall

Robert Kiddall was a gentleman and yeoman of Datchworth, once owner of Hoppers Hall and Painters Green farms. In 1719 Robert was committed for want of sureties in respect of the bastard child of Mary Allan, spinster. However, in 1730 Robert, claiming to be old and unable to work, turned the tables and took his own five children to court to order each of them to pay 1s per week towards his maintenance. His daughter attempted to appeal the order but was unsuccessful. In 1741 Robert's son, Thomas, was up before the court and ordered to pay the 1s per week in accordance with the previous order of the court. Thomas continued to default on the order and the following year was taken to court again and this time ordered to pay 2s per week maintenance to his father.

Mary Smith

On 4 July 1829 the *Hertford Mercury* reported the sad case of Mary Smith, a 37-year-old married woman with seven children. She was in court following an investigation instigated by neighbours who were suspicious about her activities in the preceding months. It was known that her husband, Jeremiah, was a lunatic and had been in an asylum for at least 15 months so that when she was obviously pregnant, it was clear that the baby would be illegitimate. Charges were made against her that she denied initially, but after witnesses' testimonies she confessed to having given birth to a baby, but that it was still-born. She had disposed of it by wrapping it up in a bundle with some stones to add weight and thrown it in a pond. The body was examined by a surgeon from Watton, William Taylor, whose doubts about the cause of the baby's death were sufficient to commit Mary to gaol for one month for 'concealing the birth of her infant child' as reported in the *Mercury* on 11 July.

Mary Page

Mary Wiltshire married Joseph Page on 26 October 1839. A year later she gave birth to their daughter, Eliza. At this time Mary and the baby were living with her parents in Tewin whilst Joseph continued to live with his parents in Hunsdon.

A few years later Joseph was sentenced to 14 years transportation and eventually Mary acquired a cottage in Burnham Green and went on to have many children in his absence. The parish baptism registers for Tewin and Datchworth show the following:

23 August 1846	Emily, illegitimate daughter of Mary Page
20 May 1849	Alfred, illegitimate son of Mary Page
7 December 1851	George, illegitimate son of Mary Page
21 March 1855	Sarah Ann, illegitimate daughter of Mary Page 'whose husband is under sentence of transportation'
27 August 1859	Alice, illegitimate daughter of Mary Page, 'the husband has not returned from transportation'
10 February 1861	William, son of Mary Page, 'the husband has not returned from transportation'
10 June 1867	Maria, daughter of Mary Page, 'Husband in Australia'

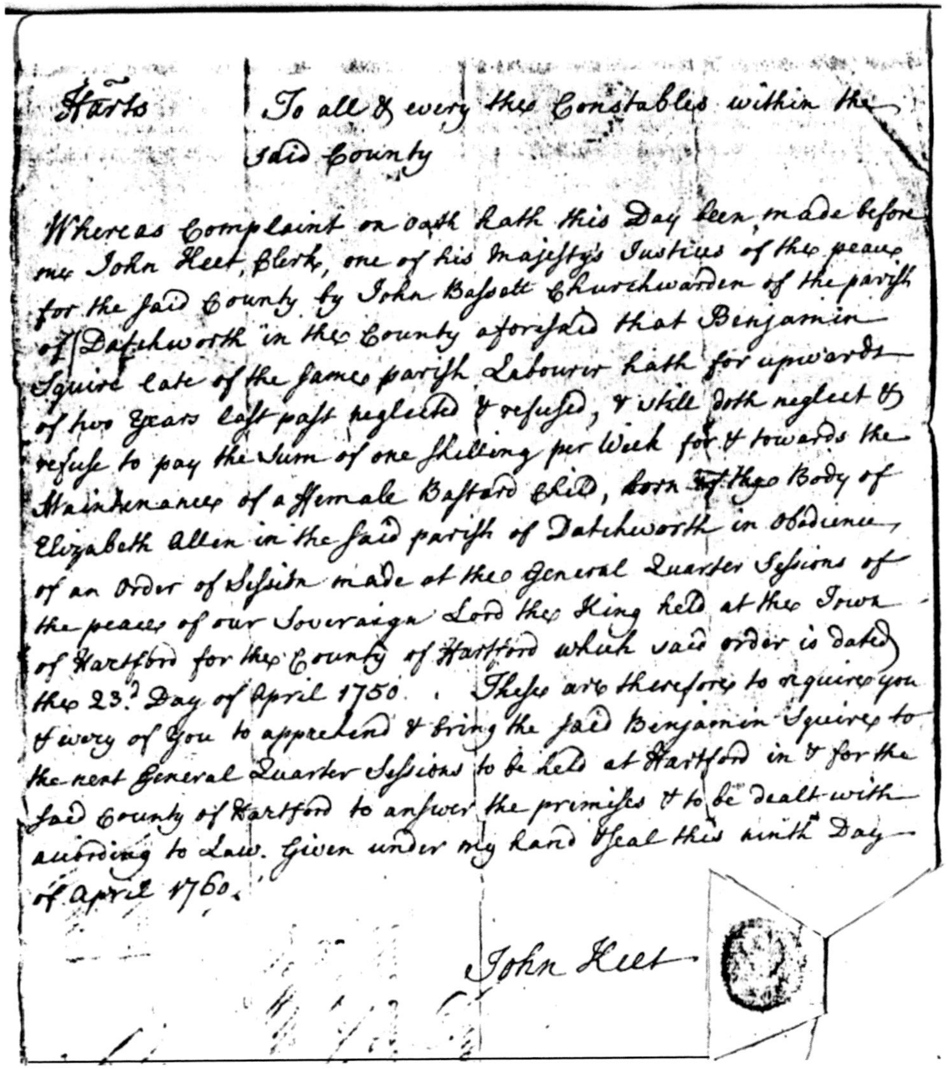

Harts

To all & every the Constables within the said County

Whereas Complaint on oath hath this Day been made before one John Keet, Clerk, one of his Majesty's Justices of the peace for the said County by John Bassett Churchwarden of the parish of Datchworth in the County aforesaid that Benjamin Squire late of the same parish Labourer hath for upwards of two Years last past neglected & refused & still doth neglect & refuse to pay the sum of one shilling per Week for & towards the Maintenance of a Female Bastard Child, born of the Body of Elizabeth Allen in the said parish of Datchworth in obedience of an Order of Session made at the General Quarter Sessions of the peace of our Sovereign Lord the King held at the Town of Hartford for the County of Hartford which said order is dated the 23rd Day of April 1750. These are therefore to require you & every of you to apprehend & bring the said Benjamin Squire to the next General Quarter Sessions to be held at Hartford in & for the said County of Hartford to answer the premises & to be dealt with according to Law. Given under my hand & seal this ninth Day of April 1760.

John Keet

Figure 153: A Bastardy Order and transcript, dated 9th April 1760: a warrant against Benjamin Squire who had defaulted on his payment of 1s per week to Elizabeth Allen. (Image: Five Hide Village)

More examples of Datchworth miscreants found in Quarter Sessions Books, Herts Assize records and newspaper reports:

Date	Name	Offence	Punishment
1587	George Cowper	Sheep stealing – 8 valued 26s 8d from John Turner and 3 valued 17s from John Sebrough	Death
1621	Thomas Jones	Burglary – stealing 40 pieces of tin worth £5, a cloak 10s and a hat 4s from William Payne	Death
1780	William Bozier (29)	Housebreaking – Clothing and shoes value 13s from Thomas Arnold. Shirts stockings and handkerchiefs value 5s 6d and 2 guineas from Daniel Young	5 years hard labour on the River Thames
1781	William Clexley (21)	Burglary – stealing 5lbs of wheaten bread value 1s from William Knairsbrook	Death – repealed to 1 year hard labour on the River Thames
1785	Charles Knight	Stole in a field a purse and 2 guineas from George Wigman	1 month gaol and publicly whipped for 100 yards
1826	Thomas Draper (27) & Joseph Flint (29)	Stole a ewe sheep value 20s from Henry Campkin	Death – repealed to 2 years in the House of Correction, Hertford.
1827	Spencer Shadbolt (28)	Stole a lamb value 5s from William Shippin	Death – repealed to 12 months in the House of Correction, Hertford
1828	George Bailey (23) Joseph Godfrey (20) & George Garner (23)	Stabbing of Thomas Field, village constable. Took place in the Horns PH	Acquitted
1829	Soloman Shadbolt (32)	Stole 112lbs of clover hay value 3s from George Wilson	12 months gaol
1829	George Darnell (30) & Spencer Shadbolt (30)	Stole three trusses of straw, value 1s 6d and one hundred pounds of straw, value 1s 6d from William Pennyfather	George Darnell - Not guilty Spencer Shadbolt - 2 months imprisonment with hard labour and twice whipped
1832	James Wootten (22)	Burglary – stealing ½ lb pork value 4d, ¼ lb cheese value 2d and 1lb bread value 2d	Death – repealed to life transportation
1833	Henry Chalkley	Stole two bells, value 4d, from William Sheffield	10 days imprisonment with hard labour
1835	George Darnell (36)	Stole a truss of straw value 3s 3d from William Watson	6 months in the House of Correction, Hertford
1835	William Tyler (40)	Stole 2 bushels of barley value 9s and a sack value 2s from Beaumont Cole	Acquitted
1836	James Barton	Assaulting Benjamin Bowley, constable and rescuing William Ewington from his custody	Acquitted
1837	Joseph Darnell (21)	Violently assaulting Thomas Muncey and robbing from him 1s in silver, 4d in copper pieces, a knife, comb and nail piercer	7 years transportation
1838	Spencer Shadbolt (38)	Stole 5 pecks of wheat in the chaff value 7s and a sack value 1s from William Campkin	7 years transportation
1838	John Smith	Burgling the house of Joseph Holdstock with intent	Acquitted
1838	George North (42)	Receiving stolen goods – a bushel and a half of oats and beans mixed value 6s from Joseph Jackson	6 months gaol at Hertford
1840	James Smith (18)	Breaking into the dwelling of Benjamin Fitzjohn and stealing a gown, shawl and cake of bread	10 years transportation (died on the outbound journey)
1841	Joshua Page (26)	Stealing from his employer	14 years transportation

Date	Name	Offence	Punishment
1842	James Skeggs, William Ewington, William Ancient, Thomas Gray & William Laurence	Assaulting Charles Thresher, constable of Hertford	6 months imprisonment with hard labour each
1842	James Nash (alias 'Plum' of Tewin)	Stole a spade and pick from John Fletcher of Datchworth.	Acquitted
1842	James Nash (alias 'Plum' of Tewin)	Stole various articles to the value of £1 0s 6d from Thomas Hunt of Tewin	14 years transportation 'because of previous convictions' (died on the outbound journey)
1842	John Butterfield	Stealing one hen from Mr Campkin	3 weeks imprisonment, one week to be solitary confinement and the remainder with hard labour
1843	Soloman Shadbolt (45) Daniel Shadbolt (20)	Lurking on the premises of Mr Sutton, with intent to commit a felony	Committed for 2 months to Hertford House of Correction as rogues and vagabonds
1844	Richard Smith (19)	Stealing a knife, bread and cheese from James Hornett	7 years transportation 'because of previous convictions'
1844	Joseph Shadbolt	Stealing a smock-frock value 4s from his employer, William Edwards	2 months imprisonment with hard labour
1848	Charles Watson (22)	Receiving 7 pigs knowing them to have been stolen from Robert and Alice Wadsworth	7 years transportation (died before transportation at the Millbank Penitentiary, London)
1848	George Darnell (21)	Stealing a pair of trousers from Thomas Hills	1 month imprisonment, one week to be solitary confinement and the remainder with hard labour
1851	William Lawrance	Default of payment of fine for setting snares for game on land belonging to Mr Heathcote	3 months imprisonment
1851	Joseph Brand	Stealing a pair of stockings from the shop of Alfred Tarrant, Hertford	1 month imprisonment, one week to be solitary confinement
1851	Jarvis Phillips	Assault on Eleanor Miles 'having knocked her down and occasioned the disfigurement usually termed a black eye'	Fined 4s 6d plus costs
1851	John Nash	Using snares for the purpose of taking game	In his absence was fined £5 plus 14s 6d costs and a warrant of commitment for 3 months was issued
1852	Charles Farr	Riding and sleeping in his wagon	Fined 1s plus 8s costs
1853	Elisha Mardell	Using a gun with the purpose of taking game	Fined 40s plus costs
1854	David Nash	Stealing a faggot from Henry Campkin	1 week imprisonment, to be kept in solitary confinement
1856	Anne Ephgrave	Stealing four handkerchiefs from her previous employer, Mr Quelch	1 month imprisonment with hard labour
1857	David Gibson (20)	Rape of 15-year-old step-daughter, Mary Revell, whilst the girl's mother was in the infirmary.	20 years transportation
1859	Richard Smith (16)	Stealing a gun from Tyrwhitt Drake	6 months imprisonment with hard labour
1859	John Brown	Stealing 7 faggots from Richard Fensom	1 month imprisonment
1863	William Izzard (21)	Arson attack of a stack of hay at Great Amwell, property of William Shambrook, and embezzling £3 from his master John Watson of Datchworth	10 years transportation (found drowned in Toodyay in 1866)

Date	Name	Offence	Punishment
1866	Richard Fensom (farmer & cattle dealer)	Moving a cow and calf in contravention of the Cattle Disease Act	Fined £5 plus £3 4s 5d costs
1867	John Brooks	Charged by the Rev W Williamson of obtaining money under false pretences	3 months imprisonment with hard labour
1867	David Shadbolt	Cruelty to a sheep by shooting in the leg	Fined £1 and £2 6s 6d costs
1890	James Britnall	Stealing a faggot value 3d	Fined 10s 6d plus costs
1890	George Redshaw	Stealing a horse value 70 or 80 guineas	12 months imprisonment with hard labour
1890	Harry Page	Non-compliance with school byelaws	Fined 1s 6d
1890	James Croft, Alfred Penn, Joseph Hipgrave, Frederick Burgess & Walter Deards	Riotous and indecent behaviour in Datchworth church	Each fined 5s costs plus – Croft, Hipgrave & Burgess 10s each, Deards 12s 6d, Penn 15s.
1891	George Tyler & Elisha Mardell	Trespassing in search of game	Fined 10s each plus costs
1891	Noah Phipps, Thomas Hipgrave & George Tyler	Trespassing in search of game	Phipps fined £1 plus costs, Hipgrave fined 10s, Tyler fined 12s 6d
1891	Noah Phipps	Attempted burglary at Jane Lawrance's shop	12 months imprisonment

18. Colourful Characters

Several village 'characters' have already been mentioned, including the villainous Walter Clibbon, the eccentric troublemaker, Philip Thicknesse, the petty criminal turned philanthropist, Benjamin Shadbolt and the charmingly unconventional caravan dweller, Anne Thrift. There are other characters worth mentioning that lived on the brink of normal society, and Kit Nash, still talked about today, is no exception.

Kit Nash

Kit Nash was a notorious poacher and was the illegitimate daughter of Sarah Nash. She lived with her two children, Eleanor and Valentine, and her mother, in a small cottage with about an acre of land between Burnham Green and Harmer Green, where she had 'squatter's rights'. At her baptism she was named Caroline Nash, but she was always known as Kit or Kitty Nash. In 1879 Kit married Henry Darnell, known to locals as Jack, who was recorded as a wood dealer and poacher. Jack was rarely seen by the locals and later on disappeared completely. It was rumoured that he was deported to Australia but as deportation to Australia ended in 1853, this is unlikely.

Kit was renowned for her wild appearance and habit of carrying a gun around with her. She frightened some people but many others befriended her, including members of the local aristocracy on whose land she poached. She would hide her catch of pheasants under her plentiful skirts, and as it was not 'proper' to search a 'lady' in those days, Kit often got away with her misdemeanours. Consorting with people in high places was also to her advantage: both Lady Cowper at Panshanger and Lady Salisbury of Hatfield were fascinated by her. They would visit her regularly bringing her presents, including hampers of food. Kit was also occasionally taken to Panshanger and Hatfield Houses, possibly to be shown off to high society friends as something of a curiosity. However, Kit's association with nobility gave her some immunity from the attentions of police and farmers who as a consequence gave her a wide berth. Once, when she was in hospital, it is said that she asked a visiting friend to 'go and see Lady Cowper and tell her that Kit would like a pheasant'. The friend smuggled a pheasant in, which Kit kept in her bed for several days until it was so 'high' the matron insisted on cooking it for her.

Despite help given by Lady Cowper and Lady Salisbury, Kit was often to be found in court. At the age of 16, she was convicted of her first offence for stealing and from then on was convicted of various offences including assault, damage and drunkenness but her favourite pursuit appeared to be poaching. By the age of 44, Kit had a list of 22 convictions and had been to prison on at least four occasions. The more serious offences were recorded in national newspapers and the Home Office prison registers.

On 17 February 1873 Kit was arrested for shooting PC George Summerling. The *Grantham Journal* dated 8 March 1873 reported that a Mrs Darnell, the owner of a cottage in Harmer Green, returned home after two years away, to discover that, in her absence, Kit had taken possession of her property. Mrs Darnell called the police, at which point Kit locked herself in her mother's cottage next door. She knocked a few bricks out of the dividing wall, loaded her gun and pointed the muzzle through the aperture into Mrs Darnell's house. When PC Summerling arrived and entered the house, Kit 'fired the gun and lodged a quantity of shot in the hindermost part of the policeman's body'. During the summing up, it was reported that 'there were no less than twelve previous convictions against the prisoner for various offences'. Kit was found guilty of 'shooting at the policeman with intent to do him grievous bodily harm' and was sentenced to five years 'penal servitude'. PC Summerling continued to work for the Hertfordshire Constabulary and was

Figure 154: Kit Nash on the left with her two children and her mother outside their cottage at Harmer Green. (c.1895)
(Tewin Society History Association)

eventually promoted to sergeant in Watford where he remained until his retirement in 1894.

On 27 July 1885 Kit was charged with 'maliciously wounding a dog, the property of Thomas Parkins'. She was tried on 18 October, found guilty and was given a sentence of two months hard labour. Two years later, on 31 October 1887, she was arrested for stealing 'a quantity of grain, the property of Edward Pennyfather'. The constable in this case said that 'the prisoner had been convicted of different offences and was the most notorious poacher in the neighbourhood'. She was found guilty and sentenced to nine months imprisonment with hard labour. Whilst carrying out this sentence, Kit gave birth to a son. He was born on Valentine's Day 1888 and therefore was called Valentine.

On 24 October 1891 Kit was charged with 'feloniously wounding Isaac Darnell with intent to do him grievous bodily harm'. She was held in custody until the trial on 4 December, where she was found not guilty and discharged. Another incident occurred less than two years later, when Kit was charged with 'trespassing in search of game and killing partridges without having a licence'. The *Blackburn Standard,* dated 14 January 1893, reported that 'the defendant, wearing a mans hat and coat, was seen leaving her garden at Harmer Green, carrying a double-barrelled gun...and firing at a covey of partridges...caught a wounded bird, which, with two dead ones, she put into her coat pocket'. During the summing up, it was reported that the defendant had 21 previous convictions against her, the last being under the Poaching Act 1890. Kit was found guilty and fined £1 for trespass and £2 10s for poaching.

Residents' memories, recalled in the late 1960s, provide some vivid details about Kit. Mrs Bygrave of Nutcroft recollected: 'She married a man called Darnell, or something like that, but he never seemed to be around. She lived for many years at a spot still called Kit's Corner, near Barnes Wood, Burnham Green. Her one room wooden hut had an earthen floor, covered with straw. Stone jars stood around the walls – some of them held sweets. When Kit offered us sweets, we accepted but never ate them because they were so dirty'. Mrs Bygrave added that as a child she enjoyed the company of Kit who was described as being usually dressed like a man, wearing trousers and a flat cap and smoking a white clay pipe.

Another Datchworth resident, Mrs Joys, also recalled Kit Nash. She said: 'We used to live opposite her. She was very mean and loved her apples, and when they were ripe she would sit on a box at her garden gate, with her gun resting by her leg, until it got dark, to stop people from scrumping her apples. When it got dark she would go into bed, which was just a pile of dirty rags. She kept pigs and was very cruel to them, they were half starved and she would beat them with sticks and shout at them. She would keep us awake some nights with her shouting. When she was very old and not looking after herself, I was asked to cook meals for her; I did for a little while but she was so filthy I had to stop. She used to take a whip to bed with her because, she says, that a man called 'Old Saggins' haunted her at night, so she used the whip to keep him off.'

The name 'old Saggins' is significant when related to an entry in the 1881 census. Kit's mother's name was recorded as Sarah Spriggins implying that at some time Sarah had been married to a Mr Spriggins. He was probably 'old Saggins' who may have treated Kit badly in some way, giving her cause to be frightened of him and to keep the whip by her bed.

Another resident's memory comes from Mr Willie Ward, a wheelwright from Tewin. He recalled: 'As a boy I rode by Kit's Corner on a new wooden bicycle. Kit came rushing out, carrying her gun as always and demanded to see the 'new contraption'. In terror, I got off the bike and let her study it, and then she asked to see how it worked. This I willingly showed her and rode away.'

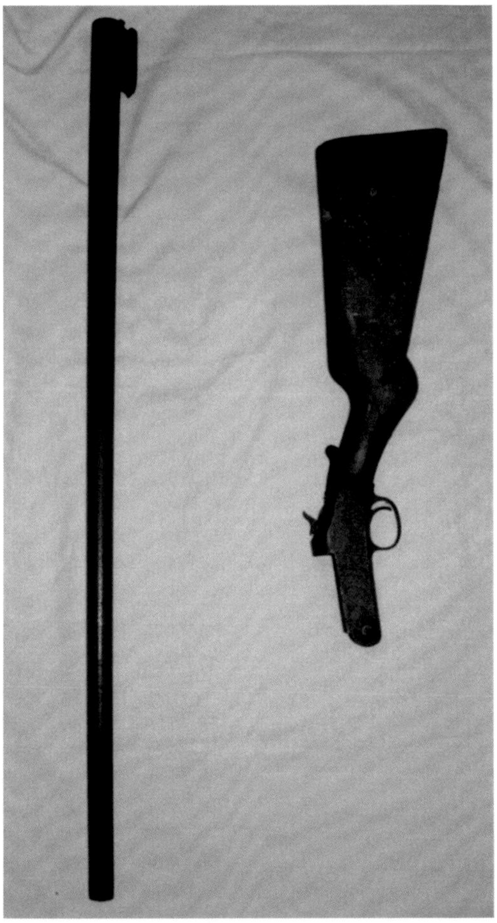

Figure 155: Kit Nash's gun split into two parts. She would strap a section to each leg under her skirt. (2013)

Both Mrs Joys and George Shadbolt, another local resident, told a strange tale of her alleged powers:

> One day a man was bringing a load of wet malt from Watton. It makes a very heavy load, and the carter was using a wagon and four horses. They were struggling hard to bring the wagon up the steepest part of the hill. The carter was urging them on. They had just about reached level ground when Kit Nash stepped out of the bushes and said 'You give those horses a rest now. They deserve it. You're on the level here'.
>
> 'I can't wait to rest them', the carter said. 'I'm in too much of a hurry to get this load delivered.'
>
> Kit stepped into the road, and simply looked at those four horses, and they just wouldn't budge, not an inch. The carter couldn't do a thing. He was a bit scared of old Kit anyhow. After about five minutes she said 'You can go on now but don't you go over-doing them.' At once the horses took up the strain and moved on.

Kit enjoyed the power she had over horses. People, at the time, thought she was a witch, but information has recently come to light explaining the 'trickery' she used that gave her these powers. Mrs Joys had heard that she 'whispered in horses' ears', but her technique was more involved than that and remains a secret. However, some members of her family inherited the secret and continued to use her methods successfully when working with horses. Incidentally, the descendants who provided some of the information about Kit, still feel that there is a stigma associated with being related to her and so have asked to remain anonymous.

Kit Nash, with her eccentric lifestyle, inevitably had many stories told about her, no doubt 'adjusted' or 'elaborated' as time has gone on. Nevertheless, although she lived at Harmer Green just over the parish boundary, she was well-known in Datchworth and has earned a place in the parish's local history.

Finally, when Kit's health began to fail and cataracts caused periodic blindness, she was taken to Hatfield Workhouse where she died of pneumonia in 1930, aged 81, and was buried in Digswell churchyard (now known as St John's Church in Digswell Park). Her dilapidated little cottage was pulled down in 1934, the land sold and an elegant house built in its place. This house was and still is called 'Kit's Corner'.

Figure 156: A memorial stone in Digswell churchyard erected in memory of Kit Nash.

In Memory of
Caroline Darnell
("Kitty Nash")
Who died October 9th 1930
Aged 81 Years
"Not the righteous not the righteous
Sinners Jesus came to call"

Sally Rainbow

Sally Rainbow was an eighteenth century woman, alleged to be a witch and so was ostracised by the people in her village. She lived in a cave that was part of a chalk pit in Bramfield woods, which subsequently became known as 'Sally Rainbow's Dell'. Sally was feared by the locals and the dell

Figure 157: Sally Rainbow's Dell in Bramfield Woods. Although a deep chalk pit is still evident, there is no longer any sign of the cave. (2014)

was avoided by everyone in the area. It is said that she would terrorise local farmers, casting spells on their cattle to give them diseases that would ultimately destroy them and their calves. In an effort to dissuade her from these supposed activities, farmers would leave food at the edge of her dell.

It was generally believed that her dell was used as a hideout for highwaymen and robbers, such as Walter Clibbon, after robbing people travelling from Hertford market. The dell has since gained the reputation of being haunted and as such has attracted paranormal investigators.

Harry 'the one-eyed tramp'

A more recent colourful character is Harry 'the one-eyed tramp' (real name Aaron Parker). Harry came from a large Romany gypsy family to whom he remained close to throughout his life – apart from his identical twin brother whom he never got on with. His family travelled around the country in Romany caravans and would settle for short periods of time, earning money by making and selling pegs to the locals. Harry, however, preferred to live in the woods calling himself 'a gentleman of the road'.

He first came to Datchworth in 1982 wearing an old Etonian tie and settled in the woods at Raffin Green Farm. In 1988, after having a major cancer operation, the gypsy section of the county council supplied him with a caravan in which he lived in a field behind the farm. He subsequently underwent a second operation for a rodent cancer on his face, whereby an eye and some of his nose were removed and replaced by a skin graft.

Eventually, after sixty years without a roof over his head, Harry was given a bungalow in Benington. However, he was not happy there; he much preferred the outdoor life and also said that people ridiculed him because of his one eye. Therefore, after two years, he handed the keys in and moved back to his 'bent' [self-built structure made from branches, covered with tarpaulin] in Datchworth, because, he said 'that people had been very kind to him in the village'.

He lived at Raffin Green Farm for the next twelve years. Initially in his 'bent' in Bury Wood, and then in a caravan in an open barn behind the farm buildings. He did all his cooking on a tripod over an open wood fire. In 2002 he moved in to a bungalow in Hawkins Hall Lane where he remained for the last eighteen months of his life, when in the spring of 2004, he died at the age of 84 years old. His ashes were buried in the wood at Raffin Green Farm.

Harry loved animals and enjoyed working on farms, and, at one point, worked in a family circus with animals. He would also earn money by sharpening knives and garden tools on a grinder driven from the front wheel of his bicycle, which he called 'The Old Lady'. He was also a Second World War veteran and claimed that on one occasion, he saved a plane when the pilot had been killed.

On occasions, he would pack up his belongings and put them in his self-made trailer that fitted to the back of 'The Old Lady' and travel around the country. Once he went to Wales for a 'holiday' for a month.

Apart from the short period in Benington, Harry lived in Datchworth for twenty-four years and became very well liked by many people but none more so than Mr & Mrs Chambers of Raffin Green Farm who said that 'he was always very well turned out and polite, he was trustworthy, loyal and we enjoyed his company. He couldn't read or write but was an avid listener to his wireless and was, consequently, very well 'read'. He was a very wise man on country matters and folklore.'

Pardy Kumar from Datchworth Stores said that he misses Harry, he was his best customer and came to the shop every day. However, although those that knew Harry well had a great deal of respect for him, the children of the village were not so kind. They would taunt him about his disfigurement or were scared of him because of it, but Harry was a tease and would soon frighten them off.

Figure 158: Harry in his camp in the woods at Raffin Green Farm sitting by his open wood fire cooking tripod and his 'bent' in the background. (c.1992)

19. The Most Haunted Village In Hertfordshire

Datchworth is reported to be the most haunted village in Hertfordshire. A statement that is echoed by author Ruth Stratton who says that she knows of at least twenty ghosts in the village which is a significant number in such a small area. Ruth is the author of *Haunted Hertford* and co-author with Nicholas Connell of *Haunted Hertfordshire: A Ghostly Gazetteer*. She goes on to say that 'Datchworth has got spooks galore. It's a very strange village; the sort of place where you go and feel that time has stood still. Although it is a lovely village, there is an unquiet, brooding atmosphere; you feel as though something's waiting to happen'.

Of all the research that Ruth has carried out in Hertfordshire, her favourite ghost story involves Datchworth.

Rectory Lane

In Chapter 16 the tragic story of the Eaves family is related, who were left to die of starvation and cold in a poor house at Burnham Green. The bodies were then taken in a cart to Datchworth church for burial, probably travelling down White Horse Lane and then up Rectory Lane. It is this journey along Rectory Lane where hauntings are reported to take place.

Ruth explains that one evening she visited Rectory Lane with a friend. It was after dark and they were walking along the lane and chatting and all of a sudden they felt a rush of air as though a car had sped past them, but that was not the case. It came with such force that it pushed them into the hedge. They were astounded and confused, as there was nothing there, but they knew that they had experienced it. Ruth went on to recount that several years later, whilst researching her book, she came across another lady who had had a similar experience, where she had felt something like a large vehicle with horses passing her and she too was pushed into the hedge.

A similar report involved two women who were walking up the lane when they heard a rushing sound of a vehicle behind them. One of them pushed the other into the hedge for her safety, but nothing passed them and the noise suddenly died away. Other accounts vary. Several agree that they are aware of a definite noise, whereas others say that whatever it is, glides silently by with a rush of wind. Of those that have seen the apparition, some say they saw the cart alone, without its horse, and others say that feet were observed dangling from the end of the cart.

In 1998 Ruth did some work with Carlton Television, when their *London Tonight* programme featured Datchworth. The TV crew concluded Rectory Lane to be 'one of the most unsettling places they had ever visited'.

Datchworth Green

A nocturnal event concerning another horse-drawn vehicle was witnessed by a resident walking towards Datchworth Green, in which direction, history does not relate. She heard a sound that appeared to herald the approach of a horse and cart. Peering into the darkness she could see nothing. However, the increase in the noise, of what now seemed to be a coach and four horses, was making her feel very frightened. Fearing that she would be run over, she jumped into the hedge, facing away from the road, and definitely felt the sensation of the animals and the coach passing by. The noise vanished as quickly as it had approached, but nothing was seen.

A couple from Datchworth reported seeing an unusually dressed woman standing near the swings on Datchworth Green. They were astonished to realise that the figure was dressed in 'old fashioned' clothes and that its feet were not touching the ground. They said that they were not frightened and walked towards the lady, but she suddenly vanished.

Allegedly the Plough public house also had a ghost. A previous landlady said that she had often been troubled by a middle aged man appearing behind her whenever she looked into a mirror. Eventually she visited a clairvoyant who said that the lady apparently had a spectral admirer by the name of Jacques who had lived in the eighteenth century. Parish records have revealed that there was, indeed, a family in Datchworth by the name of Jaques (also spelt Jeaques). Thomas and Mary Jaques had two sons, both named John and both of whom were buried in Datchworth; one in 1765 at the age of 38 and the other in 1791 listed as a 48 year old 'gent'.

There are accounts of unexplained 'happenings' in a couple of the old houses on Datchworth Green. A previous owner of Pettits, Mrs Walters, told of hearing footsteps of 'somebody' ascending the stairs and then often walking from room to room overhead. These noises had been witnessed by her family and friends but thorough investigation proved negative, and nothing was ever seen. Also, in Hoppers Hall at the crossroads, the owner says that her grandchildren refuse to play upstairs, particularly in the attic, or sleep in any of the bedrooms alone. The owner also said that they had a visitor once who was involved with the supernatural. She explained that the 'house is full of ghosts but they are very happy spirits'.

Hawkins Hall Lane and Bury Lane

Along Hawkins Hall Lane a lady dressed in black has been seen shuffling along at night. She has been described as 'seeming to be heading somewhere with purpose and looks to be bent over with old age'. It is not until she is seen from the front that it is realised that she is not bent with age, but is headless. It is said that she may be the ghost of a woman who hanged herself in the nineteenth century after the sudden death of her husband.

Members of a family living in Bury Lane have claimed that they have often seen a dark shape hurry past the back window. The husband once saw an old man peering in through the same window, but when he rushed outside the man was nowhere to be seen.

People living in another house in Bury Lane have seen the ghostly white figure of a lady both in the back garden and inside the house as well. The family has also reported inexplicable shouting and the sound of footsteps in the house.

Bramfield Road

In Chapter 17 the story of Walter Clibbon is told. He was the notorious robber who was eventually killed in Bramfield Road where his body was buried, and to mark the spot a post was erected. It is in this area that strange happenings have occurred.

Members of the Luton Paranormal Society have visited this location on a couple of occasions, equipped with cameras and devices to measure temperature and record sound. In 2004 seven of the members went to the site where, at a specific point by a tree very close to Clibbon's post, they noticed that their equipment was behaving oddly. The temperature reading was fluctuating from plus five to minus seven degrees Celsius. Although the night was cool, it definitely was not freezing. The cold spot covered an area of about 1.5 square metres and the phenomenon was witnessed by several of the members. The camera also acted strangely when it began to take pictures of its own accord. It was dark and no-one was aware of the flash going off but when the pictures were developed it appeared that it had been used. They also heard noises in the vicinity that sounded like a table being dragged along a wooden floor.

In 2010 five of the members re-visited the site and, as they walked, two of them witnessed a white misty figure floating diagonally across the road and one saw what he thought was a man standing by a tree. Another member also reported seeing a spectre of a grey dappled horse. Again, on this visit, the heavy scraping noise near Clibbon's post was heard.

Local residents have also reported such things as groaning noises, horses' hooves and seeing strange shadows. In the 1980s one man reported that he was driving down Bramfield Road when a woman in white Victorian clothing walked in front of his car. He braked and stopped his car further down the road and turned round to see a man pick up the woman and carry her to the side of the road, into the trees. The driver returned to the spot where the man and woman were but could see no sign of them.

Other sightings have taken place in Bramfield Road near Moat Farm. A young girl, dressed in old fashioned riding attire, on a pony has been seen in the area at dusk. On one occasion, a witness questioned where the girl was going as she thought it odd that the girl was out riding at such a late hour as it would soon be dark. The girl replied 'I have far to go' and then disappeared into the woods.

White Horse Lane

There have been varying reports of haunting in White Horse Lane and all have involved horses. Sometimes both horse and rider have been seen and other witnesses have reported a headless white horse. One lady said that in the 1960s she saw a white horse, about fifteen hands high, that appeared to be grazing in the field behind her cottage. But all of a sudden it vanished when there was nowhere that it could have gone.

In 1990 another local was driving along White Horse Lane and was approaching the public house when he noticed a horse and rider galloping up behind him. He pulled over to let them pass but just as they had gone by the horse and rider vanished.

There are two theories as to the origins of the haunting in White Horse Lane. The first goes back to the St Brice's Day massacre on 13 November 1002 which was a battle between the Saxons and Danes and it is said that many Danes were slaughtered. Some say it started at Welwyn but its origins are cloaked in mystery and no evidence has been found to support this idea. The white horse was the emblem of the Saxons and they may have left their symbol at Burnham Green as a mark of their victory. A famous example of the Saxon emblem is the huge white horse that is visible on a hillside above Salisbury plain and is reported to be the oldest of many that were carved throughout the country.

The second theory relating to this particular haunting dates from the English Civil War [1642-1651] when a farmer by the name of Pennyfather, who lived at Welch's Farm and was a staunch Royalist, was attacked by the Parliamentarians and decapitated. It is said that the farmer's head was put on a spike and placed in the stable yard as a warning to all. Furthermore, Pennyfather's white horse would not be led away quietly and so they decapitated the horse too. It is believed that it is this horse that haunts White Horse Lane. Many locals have reported seeing the headless horse and it is said that it is impossible to make any animal walk along the lane at night. The White Horse public house and the lane are named after its legend.

Church Area

The churchyard and the surrounding area is probably the most haunted part of Datchworth. The late Diana Norman, author of *The Stately Ghosts of England*, once brought an experienced medium to the village to see if any phenomena might be present. She concluded that there was a presence of many spirits in the air, especially in the churchyard.

The earliest anecdote comes from a poem written by Reverend Francis Fraser and published in the parish magazine dated December 1949, entitled 'Who Rang This Christmas Peal?'. The poem relates to Christmas 1660 following the Restoration of the monarchy. The returning rector, Richard Newman, was determined that a Christmas service would take place in that year, but had no-one to ring the bells. Over the preceding 11 years during the Commonwealth, the practice of bell-ringing had declined severely and it was too late to teach a new team for that particular Christmas. Nevertheless, the rector was determined that the service would go ahead and a new team of bell-ringers would be sought in time for the following Christmas.

Christmas day dawned and the rector awoke to the sound of bells. The rector and some of his flock approached the church, but as soon as they entered through the church door, the bells stopped and there was no sign of anyone in the tower. When the service finished and everyone had gone home, the rector closed the door and turned to walk away from the church, when once again, the bells began to toll.

Another more recent episode occurred in September 2011 in the church. At about 1am two police officers were doing a routine night patrol through the village, when they noticed that a light was on in the church and stopped to investigate. On entering the church they heard noises, unnerved they left the building and decided to call for back-up. A van load of police officers and a low flying helicopter soon arrived. On searching the church building, again the officers could hear noises in the bell tower, but on completion of the search nothing was found. Eventually Peter Tobitt, the churchwarden, was called out to lock up the building. It was never discovered who had turned on the light and the police put the mysterious noises down to a church ghost.

The next incident occurred in the churchyard. A lady reported that one evening, whilst walking the dog, she took a short cut through the graveyard. She said that the atmosphere became oppressive and then she heard loud noises all around her, like the chattering of a troop of monkeys. Her dog reacted to the noise, his heckles rose and growling he fled from the churchyard. It is said that many shadowy figures have been seen there at night.

Just outside the churchyard there have been other unexplained experiences. A previous resident of 33 Hollybush Lane reported that on several occasions she had seen the figure of a lady with long red hair and wearing bright clothing. Her appearance was usually preceded by the sound of tinkling bells. At other times she only heard the bells and the footsteps of the spirit walking round the house. It is not known who this colourful lady was and the house itself is not very old, however, it is possible that a farm cottage existed on the site many years previously.

Church Field, opposite the church, has also been the location of a number of sightings. As recently as 2011 two ladies saw a figure of a woman going through the field and into the church. They explained that she was wearing a long sepia-coloured coat and was bent over as if she was very old, although she moved surprisingly fast. Her head seemed to be buried in the coat, obscuring her face. Curious to see who this unusual looking lady was, the two witnesses went into the church to find her, but there was no-one there. They then returned to the churchyard and continued their search but again there was no sign of the old lady, who seemed to have vanished into thin air.

An apparently old man, wearing a floppy hat, has also been seen in Church Field, according to a witness, who was surprised to see him walking rapidly towards the edge of the field. One minute he was there and then suddenly he had gone.

A little further south in Brookbridge Lane where some stables are situated, another strange occurrence took place. In 1988 the owner was in the yard chatting with a friend when a lady with an old black 'pushbike' suddenly appeared. The lady was described as being about sixty years of age, wearing a headscarf and loose slacks. Being private land, the owner asked the lady if she could help, to which the lady replied that she was on her way to Knebworth. The owner explained to the lady that it was impossible for her to get to Knebworth via the stables, but the lady said 'yes I can, I follow that road there'. She pointed across the field but there was no road or track. The owner was puzzled but nevertheless directed the lady out of the yard onto Brookbridge Lane and gave her instructions explaining how to get from there to Knebworth. The owner and her friend then turned round to walk back to the stables, but out of curiosity, and to ensure that the lady was indeed leaving the yard, they both looked back, but she had completely disappeared. The two women could not understand where she had gone as there was no way she could have reached the gate at that speed and there was no other exit from the area without climbing over a fence.

Mardleybury

Although it is just outside the boundary of Datchworth, mysterious sightings at Mardleybury are worth mentioning. The first of these events occured at Mardleybury near to the pond where a 'grey lady' has been seen several times. She is described as having long, fair hair and wearing a flowing grey gown or cloak. The legend that surrounds this phenomenon concerns a young lady who lived at Mardleybury Manor in the eighteenth century. One night on her way home from a party, her coach took the bend at speed and ended up in the pond where she drowned. Many drivers have reported spotting her 'sudden' appearance causing them to brake violently which has occasionally led to accidents. One night, in 1984, The British Psychic and Occult Society held a vigil at the pond. At 4.15am a definite whitish mist in the shape of a woman hovered about the water at the far end of the pond. Photographs were taken of the apparition but when the prints were developed there was nothing there.

The second ghost at Mardleybury is in Mardleybury Manor house. A previous owner explained that there is one particular room where many strange things happen. Objects get thrown around or moved. There is the sudden and inexplicable smell of incense and sounds of heavy breathing, crunching and a variety of bangs and thuds. A cleaner of the house also said that she had witnessed an object being moved around and pictures falling off the walls for no apparent reason.

Figure159: Mardleybury pond and manor house (c.1936)

20. Village Organisations and Entertainment

Datchworth parish stretches from Bragbury End to Burnham Green, a distance of about four miles. Despite the spread-out nature of the village, it is a close-knit community with many social ties and is characterised by the variety of organised activities that abound today. Bands of volunteers are involved with the successful running of the church, parish council, school and Pre-school which have been discussed in earlier chapters. In addition to these, there are many other organisations in the village that continue to flourish and provide entertainment to its people thanks to the hard work of local volunteers.

The Church and Rectory

In the early days the majority of competitive sporting pastimes were organised by the regulars at the public houses, such as cricket, football, tug-of-war, skittles and quoits. Bowls and croquet were both played at the rectory. Apart from these, most other forms of entertainment, such as dances, whist drives and outings, were organised by the church.

Figure 160 shows a group of Sunday school children, near the Baptist chapel at Datchworth Green, leaving for a trip to Southend in 1934. Some children attended more than one Sunday school and provided they attended regularly, they qualified for the equivalent number of outings.

A former Burnham Green resident, Phyllis Smalley, recollected going to Sunday schools at both the small Church of England church [now Burnham Green Village Hall] and the Baptist chapel [now demolished]. She particularly enjoyed 'the lovely seaside outings' arranged by the chapel.

Figure 160: Sunday school outing to Southend in George Currell's charabanc. Outside 54 Datchworth Green (1934) (Datchworth Museum)

After the end of the First World War there were changes. In the 1920s Datchworth's first football team was formed, the cricket team was revived and there was even a ladies cricket team. Other developments included the first village hall, which was erected in 1925, the establishment of Datchworth Women's Institute in 1927 and in 1928 the first village fête was held in the Rectory gardens. In the mid 1930s increased leisure facilities were offered to villagers as a result of the 'village green improvement scheme'. It was described as 'the conversion of a green into a national fitness and recreational centre' and as part of this scheme a children's playground, tennis courts and a cricket pavilion was erected.

Women's Institute

Datchworth's Women's Institute was formed in 1927. In the 1980s, when *Five Hide Village* was written, the secretary of the W.I., Tina Hews, was interviewed. She gave the following account of the early days of the organisation:

> The meetings were held on Wednesday afternoons to start with and the children came along too and sat on rugs on the floor. Three of today's members were founder members, Mrs B Hurran, Mrs E Dunsdon and Mrs G Taylor. Mrs Hurran was on the first committee formed. The President was then Mrs Todd and the secretary Mrs Sharman. The membership at the outset was about 30 and gradually increased until, in 1970, there were 83 members. Members paid 2s 6d to join in 1927 and 4d for visitors. In 1949, the fee was 3s 6d and 5d for visitors. In 1928, a big fête was held in the Rectory gardens and the W.I. ran competitions and sideshows. There was dancing on the floodlit lawns.
>
> In 1965, Mrs Hurran was chosen to go to Buckingham Palace to an afternoon party to mark the Golden Jubilee of the National Federation of Women's Institutes. In the same year the W.I. choir, with only thirteen singers, won two cups and a gold star at the County Singing Festival at Hatfield; yet another cup was won at St. Albans. The Drama group also took part in the Golden Jubilee Revue at Harpenden.
>
> Members of the W.I. have benefitted greatly by going to the W.I. college (Denman) in Oxford for a variety of courses, other courses are held at High Leigh in Hoddesdon every two years. There are many courses held now for sport, including competitions for tennis, badminton, bowls, golf and chess. The W.I. craft exhibitions have a very high standard and Datchworth has had notable successes in 1982 and 1983.

Figure 161: Datchworth Women's Institute 1954

Back left to right:
Mrs Asplin, Mrs Cracknel, Lil Draper, Mrs Catlin, ?, Mrs Savage, Mrs Mason, ?, Miss Myers, ?

Centre left to right:
Mrs Giddens, ?, Mrs Hurren, Doris Bunyan, Mrs Cherney, Mrs Templey, Mrs Laurance, Isabel Cowan, Mrs Gaddie, ?.

Front left to right:
Maisie Kellier, Elsie Austin, Joan Smith, Mrs Payne, Mrs Collins, Jessie Little, Mrs Birch, Mrs Norman.
(Datchworth Museum)

The National Federation of Women's Institutes performed 'The Brilliant & The Dark' in the Albert Hall on 3 June 1969. It was an operatic sequence for women's voices. The dramatic presentation in the arena, which accompanied the singing included 32 dancers chosen from various Women's Institutes in Hertfordshire, only a few with ballet experience, one of which was Doreen Hodson-Smith from Datchworth. The county also invited the 32 dancers to produce a special version for a performance in the St. Albans Civic Centre on 11 June of that year. The Datchworth choir led by Jessie Little were invited to combine with other local W.I. choirs to form the choral part of the production.

Elderberries

In the hard winter of 1962-63 the rector, Julian Tross, formed a small committee in aid of the older inhabitants of the village with a view to improving their social life and welfare. This was officially established as 'The Datchworth Old People's Welfare Association', and was affiliated to the 'Hertfordshire Old People's Welfare Council'. The committee decided that an 'old people's club' should be formed and this was established in 1963. It was named the 'Elderberries' and still flourishes today.

The Elderberries meet in the village hall one afternoon every week for a social gathering which includes tea, games and entertainment. They also have regular outings and are invited to many social functions, including the Christmas concerts at the school followed by a seasonal dinner served by the children. The success of the organisation has continued thanks to dedicated volunteers who organise teas, entertainment and provide transport for its members to enable them to attend meetings and functions.

Sports Club

Figure 162: The cricket pavilion 1965 (Datchworth Museum)

Figure 163: The sports club 2012

The clubhouse and grounds

The old cricket pavilion, mentioned above, was built in the 1930s on the south side of Datchworth Green (Figure 42). A replacement was constructed largely by volunteers, including some of the cricketers themselves. The new pavilion included facilities such as a bar, toilets and showers and was opened on 25 July 1965. At that time, apart from being a base for cricketers, it became the headquarters for the tennis club and in recognition of this development, its name was changed from Datchworth Cricket Club to 'Datchworth Cricket and Sports Club'. Then, in the early 1970s, when the rugby section joined, the club was renamed again to Datchworth Sports Club as it is known today.

In recent years improvements and some additions have been made to the clubhouse thanks to income received from regular fundraising activities. A lounge bar now complements the original main games and T.V. bar, a new car park extension has been built and toilets and showers have been modernised.

Although for many years cricket and tennis were played on the village green, rugby took place on two pitches in the field behind the village hall. The sports club's eventual aim was to consolidate all sporting activity onto one site, around the pavilion. By 1988 more than £10,000 had been raised to create new rugby pitches adjacent to the clubhouse on land leased from local farmer, John Wallace. In 2005 the club acquired planning permission to lay a new full sized rugby pitch, two mini pitches and a second cricket ground on the field to the west of the pavilion. Approval of this application included the condition that one of the pitches behind the village hall was to be returned to agricultural use. So, in 2011, the rugby club relinquished their first pitch which had been played on for over forty years.

James Norman Little was, over the years, instrumental in running the club and improving sporting facilities in the village, especially those relating to cricket. In November 1982 he wrote an article for the parish magazine where the following extracts give some insight into the club:

> ...Visitors to our club are always impressed by the picturesque venue and I sometimes think that people who have recently moved to the village may have been a little influenced in living here by our village green and cricket.
>
> We run two cricket teams, three Rugby 15's and tennis is played in a local league. Table Tennis is also represented by two teams ... Apart from Table Tennis indoor activities have not yet been mentioned; during the long winter evenings we have a very keen set of people who play Dominoes in a local league, with some success, also a Ladies' Darts Team ...
>
> A Club Dinner Dance and presentation awards is held annually in late October or November... Perhaps one of the social high spots has been our Palace of Varieties, which has run in the Village Hall on four nights for the past thirteen years. Members and friends of the club have had a lot of fun in presenting these shows ... (which) have enabled us to make several donations to Multiple Sclerosis.

The Little family is still involved with the sports club. Jimmy's widow, Jessie, continues to be club president and her son, Ian, is actively involved in the administration of the club. His role includes overseeing the management and development of the ground-works for what is now a much larger organisation and a registered Community Amateur Sports Club.

Cricket

Cricket was well established locally by the end of the eighteenth century, as recorded by John Carrington in his diaries (1798-1810). He lived at Bacon's Farm in Bramfield and had a wide circle of friends and many interests that included watching the occasional cricket match, about once a year, often in September. However, one that was played on 22 July 1799 concerns Datchworth. His entry describes not only his interest in cricket but his appreciation of good food and drink. His somewhat erratic spelling is as found.

> Went to Earl Burfords at St Pauls Walden Bury ... was treated very kindly by his Ld Shipp with Good Rost Beef and Bear. Went from thence to gustard wood to Cricket Match between Datchwarth Lads and Kimpton, Datchworth was winners by Great odds'

There was no score recorded but in a match in 1807, between Tewin and Lord Cowper's builders working at Panshangar, 'the Tewiners beat them Shamefully, 143 notches in both innings'. At the time runs were called 'notches' because each run was recorded by making a notch in a piece of wood, every tenth notch being deeper to facilitate the final calculations.

The next reference to cricket in Datchworth occurs in the Reverend Williamson's notebook. Williamson records that a cricket club was started up in Datchworth in 1862, by Dan Wilshere, and a score book showed that a team was still in existence in 1872. Unfortunately, there is no continuous record of nineteenth century cricket in Datchworth.

The formation of the current club is said to have taken place in the living room of Mr Barringer, the postmaster, in the early 1920s and the subscription was 6d per week. Initially matches were played in a meadow behind Cherry Tree Hall. Eventually the venue for matches was transferred to Datchworth Green after a reasonable surface had been prepared. This involved a considerable amount of work as the ground was still used for grazing at the time.

The club has grown considerably over the years. It has introduced a colts section, offering coaching and matches to children aged seven to fifteen, and a significant number of those go on to play for the senior teams. The seniors run three teams on a Saturday in The Saracens Hertfordshire League and one Sunday team in The North Herts League. The club has over ten qualified cricket coaches and has recently been recognised by the English Cricket Board with its Clubmark Accreditation.

Figure 164: Steve Nash's 60th Birthday celebration match (2011)

Back left to right:
Andy Draper, Steve Nash, Will Nash, Steve Groves, Laurie Shaw, Steve Stroomer, James Scott.

Front left to right:
Ian Little, John Wells, Jeff Davies, Stuart Warrington, Phil Nightingale

The Little family was mentioned earlier as being instrumental in the running of the club but there are other members whose families have also been involved for generations, predominantly the Nash family that continues to be the backbone of the cricket section. Steve Nash, now in his 60s, is still playing cricket and is the sports club treasurer. He also prepares the wickets, helps his wife Jackie with the cricket teas (a mantle Jackie took over from Steve's mother, Lil). Steve was also a key figure in starting the rugby club in the late 1960s. He has been playing cricket for the village since a teenager, and to date has scored nearly 20,000 runs for the club, taken over 2,000 wickets and over 500 catches. This, alongside everything else he has done for the sports club over the years, is a remarkable contribution. Steve's two sons, Will and Rob, seem to be following in their father's footsteps, so the family tradition continues.

Rugby

Datchworth Rugby Club was formed in 1969. Nick King, the prime instigator, became the first captain and Tottenham Old Grammarians the first opponents. With no pitch or headquarters, all matches in that inaugural season were played away. Then, in 1970, Norman Pearman generously allowed his field behind the village hall to act as the home pitch, an area previously used by the football team that had been disbanded a few years earlier. Two showers in the old village hall became the changing facility.

Figure 165: Earliest known rugby team photo 1975.

Back left to right:
John Lewis, Dave Thompson, Nick Page, Dick Stabler, Phil Newton, Colin Tomson, Andrew Little, John Hume.

Front left to right:
Steve Nash, Gerry Gimblett, Paul Warsop (Capt.), Simon Ellis, Trevor Johnson, Steve Lawrence, Dave Gristwood.

The new rugby club then attached itself to the long standing cricket club and the summer cricket pavilion doubled up as a winter rugby clubhouse. With more teams quickly emerging, another pitch was needed and Norman again came to the rescue. In 1972 the sloping ground behind the village hall was levelled to create a second pitch.

In 1977 Charles Morris, an ex 1st team skipper, launched mini rugby for seven to eleven year olds and from it sprung 'junior and colts rugby', which in turn provided a major contribution to the senior club. Charles, having moved to Cheshire, died in November 1990 just after leaving the pitch at the end of a match at Rochdale at the age of 51. A large number of people travelled from Datchworth to be part of over 300 mourners at his funeral, marking the respect felt for him in the world of rugby.

Junior rugby continues to flourish. In a recent tournament held for all local junior schools, sponsored and run by Saracens Rugby Club, the day closed with Datchworth school as winners.

Tennis

The third main sector of the sports club is the tennis club. The first tennis courts were laid in 1935, to commemorate the Silver Jubilee of King George V and Queen Mary's reign and also as part of the village green improvement scheme. The courts were initially grass but in 1948 a hard surface was constructed. Up until the mid 1960s the tennis courts were owned by the parish council, until it decided to hand them to the well established sports club, with the stipulation that they must be made available to all Datchworth residents. This meant that unlike the rugby and cricket clubs, the tennis courts could be used by anyone in the village without becoming a member of the club, providing that the courts were not being used for coaching or matches.

The tennis club's popularity has fluctuated. The 1990s was a slow period until Fran Attrill became involved with the club, actively encouraging youngsters to take up the sport and eventually taking the positions of chairman and secretary in 2004. With Fran's leadership and determination, the tennis section is thriving once again. There are now five qualified tennis coaches, adding to the success of the club. Weekly coaching sessions are held year-round and competitive tennis is played throughout the summer and winter in various local leagues.

Figure 166: Winners of the Ladies Doubles in the Club Championships 2012. Jenny Larke and Viv Poultney.

Other Sports

The Bowls Club

As already mentioned, in the early twentieth century bowls used to be played in the gardens of the old Rectory. In 1976, when part of the turkey farm land was given to the parish as a recreation area, it was decided that a potential amenity could be provided here for a bowls club.

In 1978 a meeting was held in the village hall where an agreement was reached to form a bowls club, open to men and women. A committee was formed consisting of a chairman (Les Walker),

Figure 167: The members of the Datchworth Bowls Club at the opening on 9th May 1982

Back left to right:
B. Cook, K. Godfrey, J. Roffe, E. Upfold, V. Blay, G. Price, J Nash, J. Harwood, G. Taylor, B. Gilbert, M. Willcox, J. Smith, M. Chinnock, M. Murfin, W. Smith, G. Mardon, A. Mardon.

Centre left to right:
J. Russell, H. Cook, S. Parker, P. Tatham, E. Tatham, L. Dunnington, E. Dunnington, G. Walker, L. Walker, E. Murfin, N. Smith, N. Warwick, H. Arnold, A. Warwick, J. Arnold, G. Briars.

Front left to right:
H. Godfrey, G. Willcox, D. Wright, B. Briars, L. Roffe, M. Warwick, J Wright, A. Upfold, D. Gilbert, J. Arnold, J. Russell, W. Price.

secretary (Harry Cook), treasurer (Les Roffe) and three members Janet Roffe, Gladys Walker and Arthur Warwick. This committee took on the huge task of raising the funds to provide the village with a six-rink green and club house. The newly formed club had 22 members and by the end of the first year this had risen to 43. By the end of 1979 there were 63 members and today's membership is roughly the same. However, whereas the annual fee in 1978 was £1, today this has risen to £50.

Not yet having a green of their own, Datchworth was offered the use of the Knebworth Bowls Club facilities until the Datchworth green was ready. Eleven matches were played in 1979, none of which were won by Datchworth.

An area of land was leased from the parish council for the purpose of building a new green at a peppercorn rent of £1 per year. The initial lease was for 28 years, but in 1987 this was extended to 50 years. The estimated cost of having the green built professionally was in excess of £20,000, so members of the club decided that they would undertake as much of the preparatory work as possible before calling in Ernest Doe & Sons to lay the green at a cost of £12,000. The funds for the project were soon raised with grants, fundraising schemes and loans from the bank and individual members.

The work for the green was able to go ahead, but unfortunately no money was left for a clubhouse, but Arthur and Gladys Marden, members of the club, donated a second-hand builders hut to serve as the clubhouse. Throughout 1981 a band of members spent much of their time painting the hut, lining the inside walls, installing windows, toilets and digging trenches in preparation for water and sewage pipes.

The bowls green was officially opened on 9 May 1982 by the President of the Hertfordshire Bowling Association and the Hertfordshire County Women's Bowling Association.

By the late 1980s the original clubhouse was beginning to fall into disrepair. The cost of erecting a new one was £38,000, and with more grants and loans, a new building was erected and opened on 31 March 1990. Also a shed to store

Figure 168: Members of the bowls club at work on the builders' hut, which served as a clubroom from 1981 to 1990.

Left to right:
Steve Arnold, Basil Briars, Arthur Mardon, Gladys Mardon and Les Roffe.

equipment was purchased and an automatic watering system was installed in 1994.

Today the club is justly proud of its playing facilities. The green has matured greatly since 1982 and is now considered one of the best in Hertfordshire; a fact recognised by the County Association and the East Herts Bowls League who select Datchworth as one of the venues for playing the final rounds of its competitions when a 'neutral' green is required.

In 2001 the club purchased two short mat carpets that enabled them to run a Short Mat League in the village hall during the winter season. It is named after George Willcox, one of the club's past hard-working members. The club's first indoor fixture was the 2000-2001 season against Riverain Indoor Bowls Club.

The club deserves praise for the playing standards it has reached since its formation in 1979 and, of the many successes achieved, a few are worth a mention. Since joining the Stevenage & District Mixed Bowls Association in 1983, the Datchworth team has won the league six times and knock-out competitions three times. The team also joined the Welwyn & Hatfield Bowls league in 1998 where it has won a number of league titles as well as twelve individual and team knock-out competitions. Datchworth was also the winner of the Inter-Village league in 1987 and runner-up in 1989, 1990 and 1995. In 1994 the team joined the Jubilee league (run by Stevenage Town) in which Datchworth has won four times.

Individuals too have acquitted themselves with honours. In 1989 Janet Roffe was runner-up in the County Singles and as such represented Hertfordshire in the All England National Competition Finals at Royal Leamington Spa. In 1996 she won the Scarborough Open Ladies Singles title. Over the years, several Datchworth men and women have represented the county. In 2011 the men won the Letchworth and District Bowls Association's Cairns Cup.

Figure 169: Datchworth Bowls Club 1982.
(Datchworth Museum)

Figure 170: Datchworth Bowls Club pavilion which replaced the original hut in 1990.

Doreen Hodson-Smith was President of the Hertfordshire County Women's Bowling Association in 1997. Jim Wright was President of Letchworth and District Bowling Association in 2000, followed by his son David in 2003 and 2007. In 2006 Jim James was President of East Herts Bowling Association.

Tug of War

Tug-of-war was a significant part of the sporting scene in the village during the 1960s, when a Datchworth team competed at a number of shows and events throughout East Anglia and the South East, with a reasonable degree of success.

It all started just after the Second World War, when teams from nearby villages would compete in friendly rivalry at local fêtes, and the challenge at the time was to beat the Burnham Green team. The sport declined during the 1950s until, in 1959, Bob Swan of Mardleybury Manor generously provided a trophy to be presented at the annual Datchworth fête competition. This was the trigger that inspired regulars at the Tilbury to form a team that was enthusiastically led by Roger Higgs of Hawkins Hall Farm. Arthur Arnold was enlisted as coach and trainer, and later he was succeeded by Dougal McHardy. This new team won the inaugural event and repeated their success the next year.

Following these triumphs, the lads began to compete at events further afield and joined the Tug of War Association, which eventually became part of the Amateur Athletics Association (AAA). Serious training took place two evenings a week in the field behind the village hall. In the middle of the field there was once a large oak tree which acted as a training aid whereby the team would haul a barrel of concrete up to a large bough via a rope and pulley. Having become part of the national tug-of-war scene, the Datchworth team was faced with competing against teams of a higher standard and lost the trophy for the next two years. However, after continuous hard training, the trophy came back to Datchworth in 1963, 1964 and 1965. The team was at its best in the mid-1960s and the highlight was probably competing at the national AAA championships at the White City Stadium in July 1966. Joe Buckridge was secretary and treasurer and his accounts records show that 12 teams were now competing at the fête and in the four years following 1965 the trophy went to other teams.

The team began to disintegrate during the late 1960s and finally disappeared after the 1970 season. However, at the Silver Jubilee celebrations, in 1977, a tug-of-war between local teams was revived for the day and the trophy went to the Nutcroft team.

Figure 171: Datchworth tug-of-war team outside the Tilbury (c.1960)

<u>Back left to right:</u>
Dougal McHardy, Fred Wright, Pete Nash, Roger Higgs, Dave Nash

<u>Front left to right:</u>
George Newman, Denny Wright, Arthur Arnold, Gordon Izzard, Alan Woodlock

Football

Football teams were formed in Datchworth on and off from the early 1920s until the late 1960s. In 1934 Charles Pearman offered the use of the field behind the village hall to members of the Datchworth Rovers Football Club, who, at that time, shared the field with a herd of grazing cows. It was in the late 1960s that rugby had taken preference over football and so the football team was disbanded. Many villagers still partake in football today but unfortunately are required to join teams outside the village.

Figure 172: One of the last football teams in Datchworth – Datchworth United 1966 after winning the Herts Jubilee Cup, beating Much Hadham 1-0.

Back left to right:
Joe Creighton, Derek Croucher, Mick Brownsell, Owen Durston, Ken Lusty, Al Ephgrave and Michael Chalkley (mascot)

Front left to right:
Brian Carrick, Terry Hewitt, Brian Manning, Robin Gale, Vic Meech
(Datchworth Museum)

Village Hall

Apart from the sports clubhouse as a venue, much of the village entertainment now takes place in the village hall. The original building (Figure 45) was a crude wooden hut situated inside the entrance to the present car park on the left, alongside the high hedge, at right angles to the existing village hall. A fund for a parish room was set up in 1911 using some surplus cash that had been left from the village's celebrations of King George V's Coronation. The amount was £2 8s and was to be 'donated towards a fund for a parish room'.

The land where the hall was to be erected was sold by Abel Henry Smith to John and Jeremiah Inns, as part of the Datchworthbury estate, in 1921 and the hut, which was to be used as a village hall, was subsequently built on the site in 1925. In 1948 Robert Wallace purchased some land from the Inns brothers' estate following their deaths in the mid 1940s, part of which included the land where the hut was situated, which he immediately donated to the parish council.

It was at this time that the first official committee was formed to manage the village hall with the parish council as custodian trustees. The committee was eventually made official under the Charities Act 1960 by the Secretary of State on 21 January 1965. The scheme for the management committee stipulated that:

> .....the committee shall consist of twenty members, that is to say, seven elected members, eleven representative members to be appointed from various village organisations and users of the hall, and two co-opted members.

The hall was very popular and provided a regular meeting place for the football, tennis and cricket clubs, Boys' Club, Girls' Club, Women's Institute, Young Wives' Club, Youth Club and PCC. In addition to these, regular entertainment was organised by the Village Hall Entertainment Committee. Its whist drives and dances raised much needed funds for the hall and continued to run for many years. It was also used as a base for servicemen during the Second World War. In 1957 Norman Pearman donated an additional piece of land to the hall to provide a small car park.

The village hall itself required a tremendous amount of upkeep and the committee tirelessly raised funds for many years to cover costs of regular redecoration and repairs. In 1960 renovations included a new front porch, a gas water heater to 'replace the troublesome copper', and gas heating. However, condensation on the walls inside the building soon became a serious problem and it was said that the new gas radiators exacerbated the problem and eventually the walls and floors deteriorated badly. A sub-committee was formed to deal with the condensation issues. Ventilation bricks were installed beneath the floors, the inside walls were panelled and polystyrene tiles were fitted to the walls of the ladies cloakroom to prevent damp damage to their clothes. However, these steps were unsuccessful, so in 1966 an expert was called in to examine the situation. It was concluded that 'the fault lies within the structure of the hall and elimination of condensation would be virtually impossible'. It was at this time that the proposal of a new village hall was first mentioned.

At a village hall meeting in 1967, Mr Hoy, the chairman of the sub-committee, made the following announcement:

> The present hall is too small for its present needs and condensation problems are as great as ever. Furthermore, with a new hall, the needs of various organisations could be far better met. The question of siting has been discussed, and although more convenient sites have been considered, the present site is favoured, if only for the fact that there would be little money needed for the purchase of land. The proposal is to obtain land at the rear of the present building on which the new

Figure 173: Datchworth Village Hall (2014)

> hall would be built. The land occupied by the present hall would be allocated to a car park. A rough estimate of the cost was determined at £10,000. A hall of dimensions of 60ft by 20ft is envisaged.

This proposal, which was put to the vote, was unanimously agreed by the village hall committee. One of the 'more convenient sites' mentioned above, that had been considered by the sub-committee, was at Nutcroft. The committee approached the parish council and asked if it could purchase or lease some of the Nutcroft land from the district council, but these options proved too expensive. The Datchworth Preservation Society recommended that an alternative area should be sought anyway, as Nutcroft was likely to become highly populated as a result of the district council's housing plans for the 'working classes'. Subsequently, Norman Pearman, who was chairman of the parish council at that time, offered a half acre of land to the rear of the existing building for the new hall. In addition to this, the parish council purchased another piece of land from the district council to enable the provision of a larger car park. As with the 1948 conveyance of the old hall, the parish council were to be custodian trustees and a management committee was to be responsible for the day to day running of the hall. The land exchanges were formally agreed in April 1972 and a schedule within these conveyances reads:

> The object of the foundation shall be the provision and maintenance of a village hall for the use of the inhabitants of the parish of Datchworth without distinction of sex or political, religious or other opinions, and in particular for use for meetings, lectures and classes, and for other forms of recreation and leisure-time occupation, with the object of improving the conditions of life for the said inhabitants.

The proposed new building was to be of mainly timber construction and consist of a large hall with seating for 240 people and a stage. It was planned to have a small hall, kitchen, bar, committee room and cloakrooms. In addition, there was to be another multipurpose room that could be available for a variety of activities such as a youth club but unfortunately plans for this room had to be discarded due to the extra cost. Building of the hall began in early 1972, at a cost of £23,375, £10,000 of which had been raised by donations and fundraising schemes. Lack of funds meant that volunteers were called upon to demolish the old hall and construct the car park. The new hall with garden areas and car park was opened on 14 October 1972.

The management committee has continued to administer the running of the hall successfully. The hall provides a regular meeting place for small groups such as the parish council and the fête committee and is ideal for a variety of activities. Groups and clubs such as the Women's Institute, Elderberries, Lace makers, Guides, Brownies and Rainbows meet regularly as well as the Pre-school and Tiddlywinks. The large hall is also used for dog training, zumba dancing and sports such as badminton, winter indoor bowls and junior tennis. Fees from hiring out the hall for parties, wedding receptions and other functions help the hall to earn its keep.

Museum

Datchworth Museum was instigated by local resident, Doreen Hodson-Smith. For many years Doreen had been collecting artefacts and other historical items relating to Datchworth and in 1984

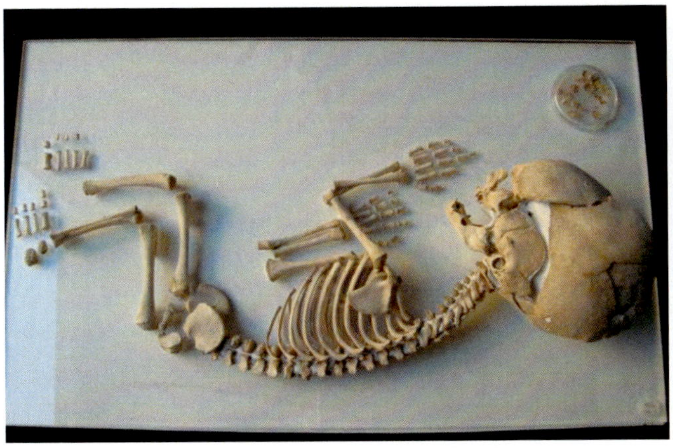

Figure 174: One of hundreds of exhibits to be seen in the museum – a skeleton of an infant that was found in the early 1980s, during the excavation of an Iron Age ditch at Raffin Green. The skeleton was one of about eighteen, all believed to be Roman.

Figure 175: Stephen McPartland MP signing the visitor's book in 2011. The original blacksmith's bellows can be seen on the left.

the parish council officially appointed her 'Village Recorder and Archivist'. Initially the material was stored at her house but eventually the collection was so vast that this became impractical. An added complication was that the items were not readily available for the public to view.

A suggestion was made that the disused blacksmith's forge at Datchworth Green might provide an ideal location for a museum. The blacksmith's had ceased trading in 1953 and the building had remained unused ever since. Doreen approached John Wallace, of Broomhall Farm, and asked him if he would be willing to rent it for the use of a museum. John agreed provided that the old forge and its bellows were kept undisturbed, to which Doreen readily agreed, as she recognised that together these would be a focal point in the museum.

In 1990 Doreen's husband Clive, took on the challenge of converting the building into suitable premises to house Doreen's collection. With help from Howard Carrick and Frank Pearman, the old clay floor was removed. It was then paved with bricks donated by Frank from the old eighteenth century barn in School Lane that had blown down in the same year. Donations of money, fixtures and fittings and glass display cabinets were forthcoming from local residents and traders.

The museum was officially opened in January 1991 by John Wallace and was dedicated to the memory of his late wife, Hetty. A committee was formed to become trustees of the museum. Having applied for charitable status, it was formally granted in January 1992. The museum subsists on the proceeds of a donation box at the museum and regular contributions from 'Friends of Datchworth Museum'.

When the museum first opened there were about 200 artefacts on display, now there are over 900. The museum spans Datchworth's history, from locally found fossils, including a 10,000 year old Stone Age axe, to files of old newspaper cuttings and photographs. One recent addition to the museum, which is already an historical item, is the telephone kiosk that is situated outside 1 Datchworth Green. This was sold by British Telecom to the parish council for the sum of £1 in 2009, who subsequently gave it to the museum. It is now used for the display of the local Parish Footpaths Map and other local information notices.

The Parish Magazine

There are many references to the parish magazine throughout the book and therefore it might be appropriate to add something about its background and how it functions today. The parish magazine was initially simply named *Parish Magazine* and was published by the St Albans Diocese, consisting mainly of a diocesan contribution. One page was allocated to each of five villages: Datchworth, Little Munden, Great Munden, Sacombe and Watton. The resident parson of each parish supplied an article to the magazine.

At a Parochial Church Committee (PCC) meeting in December 1934 the decision was made by Reverend Stephen Shairp that Datchworth should have its own magazine. It was to be named *Datchworth Parish Magazine* and was launched in January 1935. To start with, much of the bulk of

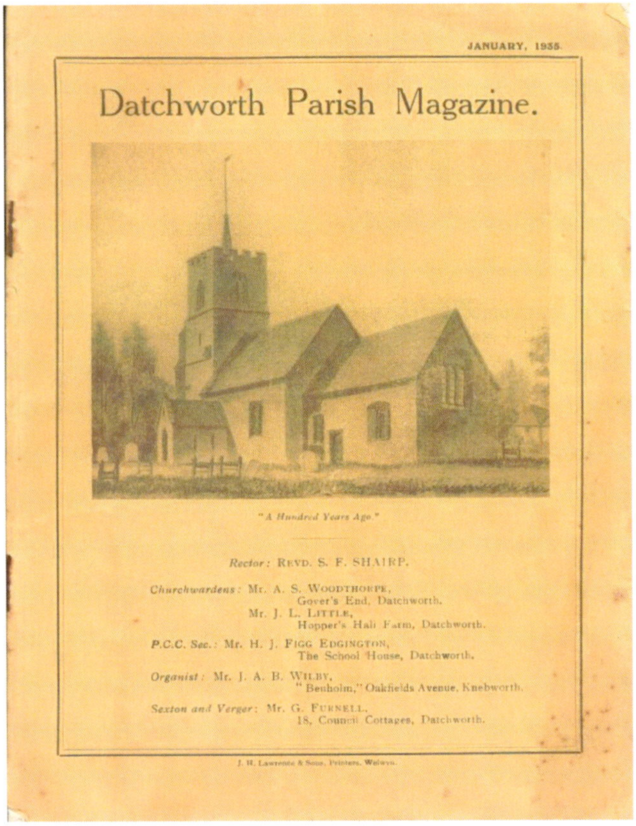

Figure 176: The first Datchworth Parish Magazine January 1935.
(Datchworth Museum)

the magazine was still taken up by the St Albans Diocese section, but Datchworth now had six pages of its own material, although much of this space was occupied by local business advertising to help cover the printing costs.

As time went on, the magazine issues became somewhat sporadic and the irregular nature of their publication was causing a financial loss to the church. In 1969, in an attempt to overcome this problem, Reverend Julian Tross approached Wally Emms and asked if he would become editor of the magazine and also if he would consider ways to make it profitable. The church gave Wally £400 to help towards printing costs and he set up a committee which consisted of both PCC and other village members. The magazine was then renamed *All Saints Church Parish Magazine*. As well as bringing in more funds by increasing the paid-for advertising, the committee also charged residents for the magazine at a cost of about 10d per copy. In the first year of publication the magazine made a profit for the first time of £750, which was handed over to the Church Restoration Fund. Wally and Barbara Emms kept the magazine going for a remarkable 28 years, until they finally handed over to a fresh committee in 1997.

Today the magazine is still published by a sub-committee of the church that consists of volunteers, most of whom are not regular members of the church. In 2011, upon the resignation of the editor, Ralph McCluskey, husband of Reverend Coralie McCluskey, the new editor, Ron Hulman introduced colour printing to the magazine for the first time. Magazine profits continued to rise and over recent years the annual profits have been around £3,000 which had, up until 2012, continued to be been given to the church. At a meeting held between the Parish Magazine Committee and the PCC in March 2012, an agreement was reached that in future, 50% of the profits would be forwarded to the church and remaining funds could be applied for by other organisations within the village. At the same time, it was agreed to change the name of the magazine again by reverting back to its original name of *Datchworth Parish Magazine*.

The Village Website

With the ever increasing demands of technology, one step taken to bring Datchworth in to the twenty-first century was undoubtedly the introduction of the village website. This was on the suggestion of the current chairman of the parish council, Chris Wilkins. On joining the parish council in 2003, Chris formed a group, independent of the parish council, to set up and run a website that would be used for anything in Datchworth, in particular, its organisations and activities. Chris led the group and was joined by John Gordon as the technical expert who did most of the groundwork. The team includes Tony Charles, who contributes on technical matters as well as looking after the church section of the website and, Sara Miller who acts as secretary. A more recent addition to the group is the parish clerk, Wendy Prowle, who assists John Gordon, having learnt the HTML syntax and so is able to apply changes to the site. All members of the group are involved with other organisations in the village, which enables the site to be kept up-to-date with what is going on and provide contact details for information.

Initially it was hoped that the website address would be 'Datchworth.com', but unfortunately this had already been purchased, therefore it was decided to use the name 'Datchworth.info'. Nowadays most organisations in the village have their own web pages on the site or links from 'Datchworth.info' to their own websites and, although it has been a slow progression, more and more villagers are beginning to use the site on a regular basis.

Datchworth Village Fête

In the parish magazine of August 1928 it was reported that a big fête was held in the Rectory gardens to raise money towards the restoration of the church tower and steeple. It appears that this was the first Datchworth fête. The article reads:

> PARISH FETE – The most successful united effort for many years was made towards reducing the cost of the restoration of our Tower and Steeple on Saturday 7th July, in the Rectory Garden. From 3.00 p.m. until 10.30 hundreds of visitors and friends kept coming, taking part in all the shows and amusements so liberally provided. Tea and Refreshments were largely diffused, every stall was stripped by purchasers, and when at last a day of golden sunshine was over, we felt that Datchworth had 'done itself proud.' As far as we can ascertain £94 has been the result financially, of the effort, and we face the future with not much over £100 to clear our dear old church from debt.
>
> This effort, so hearty, so enjoyable, so sociably useful in which our friends came from far and near – all over Herts and further, must become an annual feature in Datchworth…

and so it appears to have become!

Mr & Mrs Abel Henry Smith opened the fête. There was a jumble stall, ice cream, produce, sweets, refreshments and a school stall, as well as pony cart rides. There were competitions and guessing games including; 'cocoa-nut, baby show, cake weight, coal weight, pig weight, skittle bowling, rifle shooting, fish pond, hidden treasures and quoits'. The article also says that: 'At 5.00 p.m. a concert directed by Miss King and her friends was a great attraction. Large numbers took part in the dance on the lawn from 8.30 to 10.30 p.m., the band was most efficiently in the hands of Mr Foster'.

In 1931 the fête was opened by Lady Lytton and raised £40 for 'laying on water to church and churchyard, and the painting of the clock'. In 1933 Sir Arnold Wilson MP opened the fête which raised £60 towards a new heating system in the church.

During the Reverend Stephen Shairp's term of office (1932-1942), he was greatly involved in village life, particularly the annual fêtes. In an extract from his 'Letter from the Rector' in the August 1933 parish magazine, it can be seen that he was most enthusiastic in his praise:

> My dear People, the great event of the past month has been the Fête which was an unqualified success. Firstly, the Clerk of the Weather, after giving us some anxious moments, dealt very kindly with us.
>
> Secondly, everything went off so smoothly and pleasantly, and there was an entire absence of those disagreeables, which can easily mar such an occasion.
>
> Thirdly, we were well supported by our friends and the attendance was quite good.
>
> Fourthly, it was a financial success, and although we are not yet in a position to publish exact figures we expect to be able to announce a balance of about £60. Sir Arnold Wilson, our new Member of Parliament, most kindly took the place of Lady Lytton and declared the Fête open in a capital speech. The stalls, which made a most delightful appearances with the gay awnings against the background of evergreens, were furnished with a wonderful variety of attractive things. Perhaps the most delightful feature of the afternoon was the Children's Dancing.

He went on to say 'the tea which is always so important a feature deserves special mention. On all sides I heard the comments that it was quite the best tea I've met at a Fête and the pretty caps and aprons of the waitresses, which were very cleverly made, added much to its attractiveness'.

In 1959 the fête was combined with the flower show which, in the 1920s and 1930s, was a

Figure 177: Datchworth Village Fête 2013

separate event held on Bulls Green. The rector, Julian Tross, announced that 'the summer event, on behalf of the church and hall funds, will be changing to "Summer Fête and Sports with Flower Show"'. The flower show eventually died out but the fête remained.

Earlier in this chapter there was mention of the successes of the Datchworth tug-of-war team. The tug-of-war was a regular event at the fête throughout the 1960s but sadly it is no longer held due to the lack of teams willing to take part. However, amateur teams were put together on occasions specifically for the fête, the last one taking place in 1999.

Datchworth fête is traditionally held on the second Saturday in June and continues to be an annual village activity and, through the combined efforts of many contributors, it succeeds in raising money for the village hall, church and other village causes. The profits distributed have risen year on year and in comparison with the early days when £40 was raised in 1931, 80 years later, in 2012, the profits amounted to a highly commendable £11,800.

The fête is organised and run by a dedicated group of local people and stalls are provided by many of the other village organisations. The Woman's Institute, for example, has provided a stall every year since that first fête in 1928 and must have made thousands of cakes and tons of jam to sell to help boost the fête's takings. Whilst the aim is partly to raise money, it is also valued as a traditional family entertainment for the village and also for visitors from far and wide.

Figure 178: Tug of War team at the village fête 1967

Left to right:
Dave Nash, Roy Edwards, Robin Gale, Bernie Furnell, Colin Bygraves, Aubrey Reynolds, Mick Brownsell & Pete Nash

Burnham Green Festival

Figure 179: The spitfire at Burnham Green Festival (2013)

At the beginning of the Second World War a group of Burnham Green residents formed the Burnham Green Social & Welfare Society. Its aim was to raise funds to support the families of men called up for active service. The Society's work was invaluable and greatly appreciated. It was from these early fundraising activities that the Produce Show and Festival originated which became an annual event. The society was so successful that it had sufficient funds left over after the war to buy the old mission church (formally the school) in 1953, which is now the Burnham Green Village Hall.

Les Davis, the chairman of the society, recalls memories of the early festivals, including the large marquee that housed the produce show which was very popular. There were darts, a tombola, a coconut shy, a bran tub, 'guess the number of beans in a jar' competition and skittling for a pig, where the winning prize was a live piglet! There was also a large table with coloured segments, around which people sat. At the centre of the table was mounted a full sized aircraft propeller which spun to indicate the winner. There was a tug-of-war and many other sporting events including 100, 200 and 400 yard races and the Burnham Green Mile which Les himself won in the 1960s.

Unfortunately by the mid 1960s support had diminished and so the festival and produce show was discontinued.

However, in 1995 during a successful party held on the green to celebrate the 50th anniversary of VE Day, the present Burnham Green committee decided to re-establish the festival. On August bank holiday of that year the first of the present day festivals was held. The modern day festival includes many stalls, sporting events and a funfair. There is also a display by a spitfire that comes from Duxford Airfield and for many years has been flown by John Romain, who set up the Aircraft Restoration Company in 1989, which is based at Duxford Airfield.

The produce show was re-introduced in 2002 and has again proved popular with local gardeners. The show includes locally grown vegetables, flowers, home-made jams, wines and cakes.

Scout Group

The 1st Datchworth Scout Group originated in 1911 but with its headquarters situated in Welwyn. In 1930, when Reverend Daniels was rector, the headquarters were moved to the old Rectory. This arrangement continued throughout the rest of Reverend Daniels' incumbency and was carried on by his successor, Reverend Shairp. In the 1940s the group was disbanded for a time before being reinstated for a short period in 1960 in the old village hall. However, lack of interest caused the eventual closure of the 1st Datchworth Scout Group in the mid 1960s. Then, in 1985, John and Kath Barnes formed the 2nd Datchworth Scout Group which is still successfully running today.

For a time the new village hall was an acceptable meeting place, but the increasing number of boys in the Scout Group necessitated larger premises. Facilities in other parishes were used for a short time. However, the leaders felt that the boys deserved their own headquarters and so in 1989 it was decided to initiate a series of fundraising activities, over and above the usual ones that financed the day-to-day running of the group.

Figure 180: John Barnes (middle) with the chairman of East Herts Council, Roger Martin and Herts County Commissioner for Scouting, Paul Brenham, at the opening of the Scout Headquarters in October 1990.

Frank Pearman offered land next to the village hall, and this enabled planning to proceed. Initially a pre-fabricated building from the Redlands' redundant works at Woolmer Green was offered to Datchworth, free of charge. Aiming at a target of £16,000 which was the estimated cost of the project, fundraising under Ray Jones and Paul Marshall moved ahead quickly.

Then a blow fell. In the summer of 1989 the promised building went up in flames. Nothing daunted the organising committee and they soon found a replacement. A sixty-foot, timber sectional building was located in Kent and brought to Datchworth in March 1990. By then the scouts and cubs had raised £7,500 and, with a grant from the district council, the erection of the hut was able to commence with the voluntary help from family and friends of the Scout Group. The new headquarters, equipped and decorated by the group, was opened on 20 October 1990 by Paul Brenham, the Herts County Commissioner for Scouting.

The younger branches of Scouts, the Beavers (six to eight-year-olds) and Cubs (eight to eleven-year-olds), also enjoy the use of the Scout Headquarters to pursue the many disciplines which prepare them to become members of the Scout Group.

Brownies & Guides

The 1st Datchworth Guides were formed in 1936 by Mrs Dawson, who remained its captain until it closed for a period in 1947. In 1955 the 1st Datchworth Brownies were formed and, three years later, in 1958, the Guide group was re-formed with Miss Watts as captain assisted by Mrs Shadbolt. Miss Watts was already in the position of Tawny Owl for the Brownies with Mrs Haws as Brown Owl. Despite the commitment of these ladies, the organisations only lasted a few years with the Brownies closing in 1960 and the Guides in 1961.

In 1980 Mrs Grant re-formed the Brownies and was Brown Owl until 1982, when she was succeeded by Christine Hills. In 1983 the 1st Datchworth Guides were re-formed by Sue Hurcus and both these groups have remained active ever since. In 1986 Sue Hurcus left the village and Christine Hills took over as the Guide Leader, who continued as such for a creditable 25 years, stepping down in 2011 when Rachel Arnold took over.

Figure 181: The Guides trefoil bulb display, planted in 2009.

Having re-formed, neither the Brownies nor the Guides had any camping equipment. In order to raise funds for tents and other camping gear, assistant leader, Claire Austin, current director of Austin's Funeral Directors, organised a 'Hertfordshire boundary hike'. This was a great success and all the equipment is still being used today and has allowed the Guides to attend many camping trips over the years, usually in Hertfordshire but also often further afield, including to Austria and Switzerland.

In 2009 the Guides celebrated 100 years of Guiding with many activities, including a visit to the Guiding Centenary Maze at Crystal Palace where, in 1909, a group of girls asked Baden Powell for 'something for the girls'. Datchworth Guides also planted daffodils in the shape of the Guiding trefoil on Datchworth Green, which it is hoped will flower each spring for many years to come.

Parent Teacher Association

The Parent Teacher Association (PTA) has contributed a fair share of social activities and entertainment to the parish. The Association was initially formed in 1970, by the then headmaster of the school, Bob King. Bob was its first chairman and a standard constitution was set up, as provided by the National Confederation of Parent and Teacher Associations (NCPTA), now known as PTA-UK. In 2001, under the chairmanship of Denise Nee, the PTA became a registered charity which helped to boost its income by enabling it to claim gift aid.

The PTA's primary function is to raise funds for the school to purchase items of benefit for the pupils, including educational resources and playground and sports equipment. Fundraising has been carried out in a variety of ways including quiz nights, discos, BBQs, summer fêtes, beer festivals, stage shows and many other activities. In the early days stage shows included productions of Gilbert & Sullivan operas, which were particularly popular. Bob King was the musical director and Rosemary Airey produced and directed the plays. There were five different shows each fully sold out for five nights.

The PTA became an enormous asset to the school by relieving the burden of raising funds from the headmaster and school governors. Fundraising events were being carried out long before the PTA came in to existence. For example, the Reverend Williamson's notebook records a fête that took place on 22 July 1855, where he listed the names of all 79 students that attended. Also, in a 1921 church magazine, an article was written about a summer fête at the school which made a net profit of £50 7s 4d. Today the school summer fête raises about £2,000.

Proceeds from a fête at Datchworth school in 1921 to raise money for the School Improvement Fund:

SALE OF WORK – DATCHWORTH SCHOOL

Receipts -				£	s	d
Gate money				5	6	9
Refreshments				9	7	9
Working Party Stall	£20	1	9			
ditto	0	16	2			
ditto	0	6	6			
	[£21	4	5]	21	4	5
Coconut Shy (cost by Mr J. Little)				5	3	4
Pig Competition (gift of Mr Pearman)				3	17	0
Cigarettes				0	8	4
Cake Competition				1	18	9½
Ices and Bran Tub				1	0	0
Mothers Gifts				0	17	7
Miss Bland	£3	16	0½			
Per the Rev R. Meyer	0	5	0			
	[£4	1	0½]	4	1	0½
[Total receipts]				£53	5	0
Expenses -						
Printing Notices	£0	7	6			
Printing Tickets	0	7	6			
Sundries	0	18	8			
Cigarettes (Prizes)	1	4	0			
[Total expenses]	[£2	17	8]	2	17	8
Nett proceeds				£50	7	4

Figure 182: A summary of income and expenditure of a school fête in 1921 (Parish Magazine)

Datchworth Fairtrade Group

In November 2010 a small group of residents, initiated by Jackie Fowler and Sara Miller, founded the Datchworth Fairtrade Group with the aim of

Figure 183: Datchworth Fairtrade Group (2014)

Back left to right
Anne Charles, Ron Hulman

Front left to right
Mary Poole, Sara Miller, Jackie Fowler

releasing adults and children from slavery in developing countries. Jackie and Sara were soon joined by Mary Poole, Anne Charles and Ron Hulman. The group's ultimate goal was to obtain formal Fairtrade status for the village. Together, the members campaigned to raise awareness of the Fairtrade Foundation's activities with producers and to encourage the residents of Datchworth and local businesses and organisations to purchase Fairtrade goods. Pardy Kumar of Datchworth Stores became a great help to the group by selling Fairtrade products in his shop and the group was successful in involving other village organisations such as the church, parish council and village fête committee. As a result of the campaign, children at the Pre-school and school have also been involved, and as part of a school project they have been learning about Fairtrade. After months of hard work, the group achieved formal Fairtrade status for Datchworth on 30 March 2011, with the additional accomplishment of becoming the first village in the county to do so.

The Millennium and Village Signs

In October 1997 'Datchworth Millennium Fund' was set up. The aim of the group was to provide one or more lasting memorials to mark the turn of the century. It consisted of a chairman (Fizzy Chambers), treasurer (Julian Leach), secretary (Betty Clark) and a maximum of twenty other honorary members, all of whom had to be Datchworth residents over the age of 16 years. The decision was reached that the money would be used to purchase a village sign to be placed on Datchworth Green, a new stained glass window for the church and a Millennium village party. Unfortunately, despite all of the hard work involved, it turned out to be a bit of a wash-out due to rain.

Over the next three years the group organised many fundraising activities, including the first 'open gardens' day, which proved to be so successful that it continues as a biennial event. The open gardens raised £10,500, half of which went towards the fund and the other half was given to the British Red Cross. Other events included a barn dance, 60s Valentine's Day disco and 'jazz on the green', another popular occasion which has become a regular means of fundraising by the sports club. The money raised from these events, including over £2,000 donated by local residents, reached a total of £12,500 of which £1,717 was spent on the village sign that was erected on Datchworth Green. The sign was officially unveiled at a grand village ceremony by the Reverend Richard Syms. After the village sign, church window and party had been paid for, there was a surplus from the fund which was kept in abeyance. This was to be used for a worthy project to be chosen at a later date. It was not until 2010 that a suitable cause was found which resulted in the money being given to the village hall to provide a new front door.

Figure 184: Datchworth Village Sign (2000)

The village sign was designed and made by Brian Gaze, from Bury St Edmunds in Suffolk. After much deliberation over the design, it was finally agreed that the church should be a prominent feature as it is an important part of the village. The 'sporty' nature of Datchworth could be represented by games of cricket and rugby. The third idea was that children should be depicted to acknowledge the part they played in contributing initial designs and ideas for the sign in a school competition. Serious consideration was given to the inclusion of a ghostly horseman riding a headless horse that is said to haunt White Horse Lane but it was decided that this was too blood-thirsty.

At Burnham Green the idea to erect a village sign was first put forward by the villagers before the turn of the Millennium, when the village hall committee was looking for ways to spend money raised from the village festival. However, it wasn't until 2011 that the sign was finally erected. It was officially unveiled by Lord Laming on 29 April 2011, as part of Burnham Green's Royal wedding celebrations, to mark the marriage of Prince William to Kate Middleton. The sign was designed and made by Robin Penstone-Smith of Essendon Forge and the solid oak post was donated by local resident and businessman, Alan Tyler of Lewis Tyler and Sons.

In the centre of the sign is a model of an Ordnance Survey Triangulation Pillar (Trig Point) to represent the theory that Burnham Green is said to be the highest point between it and the Ural Mountains in Russia to the east. Either side of the Trig Point are two oak trees to symbolise 'Two Oaks Drive'. To the left is the village hall (previously Burnham Green School) and to the right a plough depicting the agricultural heritage of the village. Naturally, the plough is being drawn by a white horse to echo the sign of the White Horse public house in White Horse Lane. Beneath the nameplate, the sign is adorned with bullrushes, as prior to the 1950s the green itself was marshy and overgrown. The conditions were ideal for rushes to grow and consequently Burnham Green was allegedly nicknamed 'Rushy Park' in those days.

Royal Coronations and Jubilees

There have been some memorable Jubilee and Coronation celebrations in Datchworth. A social gathering was organised in honour of Queen Victoria's Diamond Jubilee in 1897, which took place in the meadow at the back of Mardleybury pond. Dinner for the old people was provided in an old cart shed next to Mardleybury Manor and an address was read by the chairman of the parish council, the Reverend John Wardale. After dinner, everybody walked to Datchworth Green for sports, greasy pole climbing and a tug-of-war contest.

In 1911, to mark the Coronation of King George V, the parish council set up a fund to arrange 'a meat tea for adults and children, and sports'. George Little offered his 'meadow at Bridgefoot for the sports' and an agreement was made that after all expenses had been paid, any surplus cash was to be donated to a fund for a 'parish room'. The excess amounted to £2 8s and was devoted to this cause.

In 1935 the flowering cherry trees along Datchworth Green were planted to honour the 25th anniversary of King George V and Queen Mary's Coronation, as was the copper beech near the Plough public house, which was planted by Doreen Miller, the daughter of Mark Miller, the blacksmith. The tree now has a semi-circular bench beneath it that was purchased by public subscription and erected in 1996, in memory of Raj Kumar. Raj was the son of the well respected Pardy and Pinky Kumar of Datchworth Stores, who tragically died in a car accident at the age of 18.

Figure 185: Burnham Green village sign (2011).

Figure 186: The copper beech tree planted in 1935 by Doreen Miller (Figure 101). (2013)

During 1935 there were many activities to celebrate the Silver Jubilee, some of which were captured on celluloid. Highlights were produced in a film called 'Recollections of Datchworth's Jubilee Year'. At the end of the Jubilee celebrations the village hall was 'packed to capacity' with members of the parish to watch the film.

Many parishioners were delighted or perhaps astonished to notice themselves appearing in the film, as illustrated in a quotation from the parish magazine of January 1936 which describes the audience reaction, as written by Reverend Shairp:

> For the first time we really had an opportunity to see ourselves as others see us and in settings which all of us recognised... The shouts of delighted laughter that greeted each figure as he or she was recognised in circumstances which were not always flattering testified alike to the popularity of the film and the uncanny flair for 'situation' which the photographer displayed.
>
> The programme included [the] films [such as] Trooping the Colours and Royal Procession, Jubilee Day lent by Lord Dunedin, together with other films of general interest, as well as Pluto and Mickey Mouse cartoons. The hall was full – indeed many were refused admittance.

Figure 187: Clive & Doreen Hodson-Smith joining in the Diamond Jubilee festivities on Datchworth Green (2012)

The Silver Jubilee of Queen Elizabeth II on 2 June 1977 was a celebration of a different nature, in that on this occasion the parish decided to divide itself into several groups. Each group organised its own street party and games. But, of course, people wandered around the village and visited other street parties. In the evening, Datchworth had a special bonfire, one of an organised chain of bonfires across the country. This took place on the old turkey farm site and was attended by residents from all parts of the village.

On the occasion of Queen Elizabeth's Golden Jubilee in June 2002, once again, small groups arranged their own parties to celebrate. Unfortunately the weather was very poor with a lot of rain. However, this did not dissuade a few parishioners from enjoying festive high jinks protected from the weather by their gazebos.

In 2012 Datchworth joined in the national celebrations to mark 60 years of Queen Elizabeth's reign. These took place throughout the country over an extended weekend at the beginning of June and groups of parishioners organised events for villagers in Datchworth, Bulls Green and Burnham Green. With their hard work and voluntary help from other local residents and organisations, successful parties were held on the three village greens on Monday 4 June. The weather was changeable with sunshine and showers but this did not dampen anyone's spirits. It was a day that was full of fun. At Datchworth the tug-of-war made a welcome return appearance and there was a 'cake bake', a dog show and silly games held at Bulls Green and Burnham Green.

The Bulls Green group planted a new English oak tree and put up a plaque on the green to commemorate the occasion. Many local organisations, residents and councils donated sufficient funds to ensure that the parties were free for everybody. Making a profit or loss was not a consideration but in fact, small profits were made. The Datchworth group resolved that their

Figure 188: Datchworth Green's cake. Made by Dawn Williams and donated by Fizzy Chambers.

proceeds should be a special gift to the Elderberries for their enjoyment. Burnham Green gave their profit to the village hall committee to fund future village benefits and Bulls Green put theirs towards a new village sign.

Hertfordshire's Best Kept Village

Datchworth is proud of its village status and is fortunate to have a parish council that continues to fight against unnecessary urbanisation, exemplified by comments like those of author Ruth Stratton, who said 'it's the sort of place where you go and feel that time has stood still'.

In 1965 Datchworth won 'Hertfordshire's Best Kept Village' competition. A sign was erected on Datchworth Green and was unveiled by the Lord Lieutenant of the County, Sir George Burns. Also in attendance were Lord Brocket, Norman Pearman, who was chairman of the parish council, and hundreds of residents. Following the ceremony, refreshments were laid on at the newly built cricket pavilion. Datchworth was also runner-up for the award in 1979 and came third in the preliminary round in 1986, receiving a judge's commendation for 'villages making a special effort'.

The accounts in this chapter have demonstrated the tireless efforts of villagers who, over the years, have given up countless hours of free time to ensure that 'village organisations and entertainment' remain part of the character of Datchworth.

Figure 189: Lord Brocket giving a speech at the 'Hertfordshire's Best Kept Village' ceremony in 1965. (Datchworth Museum)

Residents' Memories

Reg Chalkley: For entertainment we would play at the skittle alley which was in a barn at the White Horse public house, Burnham Green. The skittles and ball were made of very rough wood. Also, in the winter curling would be played on Mardleybury pond when it froze, boys used to clear 'lanes' with twigs for the game.

Jack Nash: We used to skate on the pond in front of Pound House, it was on public land although it had a wall round it. George Shadbolt went through the ice and I saw him come up under it twice, the third time he came up through the hole he made when he fell through, and then got out. At the village hall I attended dancing classes. The old village hall was a wonderful place, it had a billiard table and dartboards.

'Peg' Newman: Manners were rougher. I remember a bare-knuckle fight between two men stripped to the waist. It took place on the green, at the Post Office end. A crowd turned out to watch it. A quarrel had arisen in one of the pubs between a Datchworth man and a Londoner one Saturday night and they agreed to fight it out the next morning in a proper match. They'd had too much beer to fight there and then. The match was fairly conducted. The Datchworth man won pretty quickly. The other man was knocked down several times and agreed he could not go on. They shook hands and made friends.

Mr Tyler (Burnham Green): The Tilbury and White Horse had a skittle alley. We played 'four corners' with a large disc, approximately 9-12 inches diameter, throwing it up to 20 feet at five skittles, one in the middle and one in each corner. In Burnham Green, we had two fairs every year which were held at Burgesses Farm.

Bill Nash: The landlord of the Tilbury used to treat locals to half a pint of beer so as to get their company for a game of skittles played with 'ninepins' and a wooden cheese shaped disc.

Katie Russell: We had a ladies' cricket team in the 1920s.

Norman Pearman: Cricket started in 1921 on ground behind Cherry Tree Cottage adjacent to Bramfield Road.

Phyllis Smalley (Burnham Green): It was a close knit community and nearly everyone was related one way or another. In the summer, there would be a flower show, the exhibits of flowers and vegetables were a sight to be seen; dahlias would be nearly as big as footballs, as would the onions. We had a tug-of-war team as well as a football and cricket team. Every year we were given a party alternately by the British Legion and WI. These parties were really appreciated, we played games and the food was lovely. Bonfire night was a big event, a large bonfire would be built in the middle of the village green and various Guys would be stuck on top. All the village turned out and we all roasted chestnuts and potatoes. The cinema in Welwyn Garden City had a children's matinee on Saturday mornings. We would walk 1½ miles to Welwyn North station. The return fare was 1½d and 3d to go in the cinema. On our way to the station we used to run past Kit Nash's cottage as fast as our legs would carry us, we were scared of her.

Bernard Reynolds: We boys made our own entertainment. We would play cricket using a ball made from tightly bound sacking and bats from scrap timber. We made cars out of fruit boxes, they had makeshift flags on them and imaginary petrol. The pump had been fashioned from a rotten long-case clock. Also, Mark Miller from the forge made blades for our home-made skates so that we could skate on the frozen ponds. Someone once found a discarded coffin which became a car or boat. Once, we also made a boat out of half a beer barrel and challenged the Burnham Green boys to a naval battle. It was not very good so the next vessel was an old tree trunk. That featured in a fight against 'Wormy' Green and all six of the crew fell into the water. We also made a huge brakeless quadricycle and took on Burnham Green in a race down Coltsfoot Lane. The device was as broad as the lane and careered out of control through Gypsy Johnson's fire into a hedge. For the adults, Ernie Farrin held dog races in his field. A rabbit skin was towed from a capstan for the dogs to chase while Will Tyler from the shop took bets in his role of village bookie.

Appendix 1

'We Will Remember Them ... '

The year of this book's publication is significant, as it celebrates the 30th anniversary of the first edition of *Five Hide Village* by T O Beachcroft and W B Emms.

2014 also marks the 100th anniversary of the beginning of the First World War. This was a terrible conflict with disastrous consequences for the whole of Europe and beyond. Millions of soldiers, both volunteers and conscripts, lost their lives, often in the most awful of conditions, from the deadly chlorine gas of Flanders, to the waist deep mud of Passchendaele.

In the spring of 2014 Burnham Green resident Malcolm Tebbutt was approached by the Reverend Susannah Underwood, with the request to investigate the history of the thirteen First World War casualties listed on the Datchworth War Memorial situated in All Saints' churchyard.

Malcolm agreed and began by searching the internet, where he found useful information from the Commonwealth War Graves Commission, censuses, marriage records and military records. He also toured northern France and visited French and Belgian war cemeteries and, where possible, he placed a single rose on each grave or memorial of the Datchworth men. Of the First World War casualties named on the memorial, John Lisles was the only one to have been buried in Datchworth churchyard.

Information was gathered about both First and Second World War Datchworth casualties and the findings were put on display in the church throughout the month of August 2014. The following material has been extracted from this exhibition, as kindly agreed by Malcolm.

Figure 190: Entrance to Hermies Hill British Cemetery

First World War Casualties

Name	Regiment and Number
Stanley William Arnold	7th Battalion, Lincolnshire Regiment (42804)
John Bennett	7th Battalion, Lincolnshire Regiment (42815)
Reginald Campkin	4th Battalion, London Regiment (Royal Fusiliers) (765220)
William Ellis	6th Battalion, Bedfordshire Regiment (15706)
Charles William Francis	1st Battalion, Rifle Brigade (9654)
Thomas George Griffin	4th Battalion, Bedfordshire Regiment (12896)
William Hipgrave	9th Battalion, Norfolk Regiment (39325)
John Lisles	8th Battalion, Bedfordshire Regiment (16930)
Arthur Medhurst	11th Battalion, Rifle Brigade (S/8089)
Herbert Scales	21st Battalion, Manchester Regiment (51530)
Walter Shadbolt	165th Machine Gun Corps (Infantry) (102351)
Albert Tyler	1st Battalion, Bedfordshire Regiment (13633)
Cecil Tyler	7th Battalion, Bedfordshire Regiment (22868)

STANLEY WILLIAM ARNOLD

Stanley was born in 1899 in Datchworth. He was the eldest son of Thomas and Annie Arnold and lived at Bridgefoot Cottages in Brookbridge Lane with his two younger brothers, Arthur and Reginald, and two younger sisters, Evelyn and Dorothy.

He signed up with the Lincolnshire Regiment towards the end of the war along with John Bennett. He went to France and was killed almost immediately 'going over the top'. His death came tragically close to the end of the war on 5 September 1918 when he was only 19. His grave is in the Lebucquière Communal Cemetery in France (only a few miles from the grave of his friend, John Bennett).

Figure 191: Stanley Arnold's gravestone

JOHN BENNETT

Figure 192: John Bennett's gravestone

John was born in 1898 in Datchworth. He was the son of George and Florence Bennett of Burnham Green and had two brothers and two sisters.

He signed up with the Lincolnshire Regiment towards the end of the war along with his school friend, Stanley Arnold. Their regimental numbers are only 11 apart. John lasted even less time in the trenches than his friend, dying on 10 March 1918 aged only 19. His body now lies in the Hermies Hill British Cemetery, just a few miles away from Stanley's grave in Lebucquière. As well as the usual personal details, the gravestone also bears a special message from John's family 'Not lost but gone before'.

REGINALD ERNEST CAMPKIN

Reginald was born on 21 February 1891, in Brixton, London. In the 1901 census, Reggie was living at Jersey Lodge in Bulls Mill on the River Beane, between Waterford and Stapleford, with his parents, Ronald and Minnie Campkin. His grandparents, Thomas and Emily Campkin, lived at the adjoining farm at Waterford Hall.

At the time of the next census, in 1911, Reggie had started work in the theatre and was boarding with a family of theatre workers in Wimbledon. By 1912, at the age of 21, he had become a theatrical manager, probably at the New Wimbledon Theatre, which opened on 26 December 1910. In October of that year Reggie married Hilda Hargreaves in All Souls' Church, Marylebone, and they went on to have two daughters, Joan and Hilda.

Figure 193: Reginald Campkin

Reggie fought with the 4th Battalion of the Royal Fusiliers as a Second Lieutenant. In August 1914 the 4th Battalion was amongst the very first British forces to land in France after the declaration of war and they went on to take up position on the canal bank at Mons in Belgium. Reginald was killed in action on 28 March 1918, at the age of 27. A family story says he was shot by a sharpshooter on the Vimy Ridge, which is just to the north of Arras and the site of several memorials. As he has no known grave, he is remembered on the Arras Memorial in northern France. At the time of Reggie's death, his parents were living at The Limes (now Clibbons, 87 Bramfield Road) in Datchworth so it is thought that they would have asked for his name to be added to the memorial at Datchworth.

WILLIAM ELLIS

Figure 194: William Ellis's gravestone

William was born in 1895 in Welwyn. He was the son of George and Lucy Ellis but in the 1911 census he was listed as a 16-year-old farm labourer living with his Auntie Mary, a widow, and various cousins in Burnham Green. One of the cousins was Joshua Threader, who lived in Bramfield Road, Datchworth, for many years.

He joined the Bedfordshire Regiment and died at the age of 22, on 6 April 1918. His body lies in the Gommecourt British Cemetery No 2, in Hebuterne near Arras in northern France.

CHARLES WILLIAM FRANCIS

Charles was born in 1884 in Bermondsey, London. He was the son of a brewer's drayman, also named Charles. His mother, Elizabeth, died when he was still quite young and at the time of the 1901 census, his father was recorded as a widower. By 1911 his father had remarried and the family moved from Bermondsey to Hooks Cross, where Charles senior was the publican of the Three Horseshoes Public house.

Charles joined the Rifle Brigade well before the war, on 28 January 1903, at the age of 18. His service record shows he measured five feet four inches tall and weighed eight stone at that time. He would have been one of the first to go to war as part of the Expeditionary Force and was the first death amongst all those remembered on the Datchworth War Memorial, having fallen at Ypres on 26 April 1915, aged 31. He is remembered on the Menin Gate at Ypres, no known grave has been identified for him.

Figure 195: Charles' name on the Menin Gate

THOMAS GEORGE GRIFFIN

Figure 196: Arras Memorial

Thomas was born in 1897 in Watton-at-Stone. He was the son of John and Emily Griffin. In the 1901 census, he was living at the Wharfing Cottages in Stapleford with his parents, three older brothers and three older sisters. By the age of 14, in 1911, he was living with his sister, Edith and her husband, Fred, in Essendon, where he worked as a farm labourer.

He joined the Bedfordshire Regiment with his older brother, Fred, whose service number was 12871, only 25 digits before Thomas's. Whilst Fred survived the war, Thomas died, aged 21, on 23 April 1917. His name is listed on the Arras Memorial in northern France, as well as on the Datchworth War Memorial and the Howardsgate War Memorial in Welwyn Garden City.

WILLIAM CHARLES HIPGRAVE

William was born in 1888 in Burnham Green. The 1901 census lists him as the son of Henry, a cowman, and Harriett Hipgrave, with two younger brothers, Robert and Walter, two younger sisters, Mabel and Mary, and an older sister, Emily. The following year, another brother, Herbert, was born, who eventually lived in White Horse Lane, Burnham Green.

William's brother, Walter, served in the Machine Gun Corps and was repatriated to England to hospital on 2 October 1918 while William was still fighting. This must have been a shock to his large family. But worse was to come. William, who had joined the Norfolk Regiment, was killed tragically, at the age of 29, in the 'final push' on 23 October 1918, only two weeks before the end of the war. This news would have come just as the family were concerned about the fate of Walter, whose service record shows he died in hospital of meningitis on 30 August 1919.

Figure 197: William Hipgrave's name on the Vis en Artois Memorial

Whilst Walter's name does not appear on the war memorial in Datchworth, he has a Commonwealth War Graves Commission gravestone in the west part of the graveyard. Both William and Walter were awarded the Victory Medal posthumously. William's name appears on the memorial at Vis en Artois in northern France.

JOHN LISLES

Figure 198: John Lisles' gravestone in Datchworth churchyard.

Jack Lisles, as he was known, was born in 1888 in Datchworth. He was the son of Joseph and Susan Lisles. In the 1911 census, he is listed as a farm labourer living with his widowed mother in Hollybush Cottages, only a few doors away from Bert Scales (another casualty of the war).

He joined the 8th Battalion Bedfordshire Regiment and was near Cecil Tyler when Cecil was killed on 14 August 1916 as, according to Alan Tyler, he wrote a letter of sympathy to Cecil's mother. Tragically, Jack himself died only six weeks later on 28 September 1916, aged 28. He must have returned home wounded, as he is the only one of the thirteen First World War casualties listed on the Datchworth War Memorial, who is actually buried in All Saints' churchyard. His Commonwealth War Graves Commission gravestone is under a tree against the western boundary of the churchyard and bears a special message requested by his family: 'Nothing in my hands I bring. Simply to thy cross I cling'.

ARTHUR MEDHURST

Arthur was born in Islington in 1882 but moved to Datchworth with his mother, Pamela, and brother, Harry. In 1891 he was living in Govers Green with his mother, brother, stepfather, Henry Wray, stepbrothers, Alfred and Frederick, and stepsister, Emily. By 1911 he had moved to New Southgate, aged 30, where he was working as a greengrocer and living with his stepsister, Emily, who was by then married to George Rowe.

Arthur signed up with the 11th Battalion, Rifle Brigade. In 1917 they were in action during the German retreat to the Hindenburg Line, the Battle of Langemarck, the Battle of the Menin Road Ridge, the Battle of Polygon Wood and the Cambrai Operations. Arthur died on 7 April 1917, aged 36, one of the oldest of the Datchworth casualties. He was buried in the Étretat churchyard extension in Étretat near Le Havre, France. British No.1 General Hospital was established in Étretat, so it is likely Arthur was wounded (or sick) before he died, as there was little or no fighting here.

HERBERT SCALES

Herbert (usually known as Bert) was born in Datchworth in 1898. He was the son of ploughman and general farm labourer, Richard Scales and his wife, Ann, and had a younger brother, Fred, an older sister, Beatrice, and older brothers, William, Richard and Alfred. The family lived at Hollybush Cottages in Datchworth.

He joined the 21st Battalion of the Manchester Regiment and died, at the age of just 20, on 4 October 1917. He is one of the many for whom no grave exists, as the body was lost in battle. However his name is remembered on the Tyne Cot Memorial in Flanders as well as the one in Datchworth.

WALTER SHADBOLT

Walter was born in Tewin in 1886, where he lived with his parents, Arthur and Elizabeth, and a large family of brothers and sisters. He had four older brothers, William, Ronald, Henry and Ernest, one older sister, Annie, two younger brothers, Joseph and Bertie, and two younger sisters, Edith and Bessie. Before the war he worked in the watercress fields alongside the B1000 and in 1913, at the age of 24, he married Rosetta Willsher.

He initially joined the Northants Regiment and later moved to the Machine Gun Corps. Walter died on 31 July 1917, aged 30. He is honoured on an elevated panel of the Menin Gate at Ypres and his name appears on a family gravestone in St Peter's churchyard, Tewin where his younger brother, Bertie, is buried after he 'died from wounds received on active service' on 15 July 1916, aged 22. Walter's wife remarried after his death and lived at Bridgefoot Villa in Datchworth and she saw to it that his name was listed on the Datchworth War Memorial.

ALBERT TYLER

Albert Tyler was born in 1881 in Datchworth. He was the son of railway plate-layer, Charles, and his wife, Martha. He had a large family that included four older brothers, Harry, Charles, George and Edward, and six older sisters, Mary, Alice, Harriett, Elizabeth, Ellen and Emily. In 1906 he married Alice Mary Ewington of Burnham Green. They were living in Watton Lane, Datchworth, at the time of the 1911 census with their three children, Albert John, aged five, Ernest William, aged three and Gladys Amy, aged one.

Albert went off to war with the 1st Battalion of the Bedfordshire Regiment and died on 16 March 1917, aged 36. He now lies buried in the Cambrin Military Cemetery in northern France. After his death, he was awarded the Victory Medal, British War Medal and the 1915 Star (for service in France and Flanders).

Figure 199: Albert Tyler's gravestone

Appendix 1

CECIL TYLER

Cecil was born in 1897 at Bulls Green, Datchworth. He was the son of William and Dinah Tyler and had four older brothers, William, Edward, Ernest and Lewis, and two younger brothers, Albert and Philip. He also had one older sister, Elsie, and a younger sister, Florence. By the time the 1911 census was taken, 13-year-old Cecil and his family had moved to Burnham Green Lane where his father was listed as a 'dealer'.

He followed his brothers, Ted and Ernie (who joined the Leicestershire Regiment) and Lewis (who joined the Bedfordshires), and went off to war in the 7th Battalion of the Bedfordshire Regiment. Albert Tyler (also on the memorial) was, in fact, not closely related to them.

There is a story that Lewis met Ted and Ernie in the trenches and allegedly it appeared in the British newspapers but it has not yet been found. Cecil's parents were to receive the terrible news of his death on 14 August 1916, at the age of only 19. John Lisles (also on the Datchworth memorial) wrote to Cecil's mother when Cecil was killed. Cecil now lies in northern France in the Ration Farm Military Cemetery at La Chapelle d'Armentières. His brothers, Ted, Ernie and Lewis, survived the war. Cecil's grave is unusual in that it does not just record the usual bare details of name, rank, regiment number and date of death. His parents selected the following personal message, which is engraved at the foot of his stone: 'Thy will be done. 'Tis hard to say, when those you love are called away. Mother and Dad'.

Figure 200: Cecil Tyler's gravestone

Second World War Casualties

Name	**Regiment and Number**
Robert Francis Brownsell	1st Battalion, East Lancashire Regiment (5950906)
Leonard Cranwell	2nd Battalion, Oxford and Bucks Light Infantry (5961179)
Herbert Mark Miller	Bedfordshire and Hertfordshire Regiment (5950434)
Roy Frederick Benson Temperley	50 Squadron, Royal Air Force Volunteer Reserve (61986)

ROBERT FRANCIS BROWNSELL

Figure 201: Robert Brownsell

Robert was born in 1917 and was the son of Charles and Amy Brownsell of Burnham Green. He was a keen footballer, playing for the renowned Burnham Green Football Club before the war. He is listed in the football club minutes as playing in the 1937/38 season, when they played in the Hertford and District Junior League (1st Division), the Welwyn Garden City Hospital Cup, Knebworth Nursing Cup and the Graphic Cup.

Robert joined the 1st Battalion of the East Lancashire Regiment as a Private. He was the only member of Burnham Green Football Club not to return from the war. He was killed in action in Germany, tragically near to the end of the war on 1 March 1945, aged 27, little knowing that VE Day was just two months away.

Robert is now buried in the Reichswald Forest War Cemetery in Nordrhein-Westfalen, Germany, just the German side of the Dutch border. As well as being remembered on the Datchworth War Memorial, his name is also engraved on a family gravestone in the Datchworth churchyard.

LEONARD CRANWELL

Born in Royston in 1922, Leonard Cranwell was only 16 when the Second World War started. However, he married his sweetheart, Lilian, in Islington early in 1944 before joining the 2nd Battalion of the Oxfordshire and Buckinghamshire Light Infantry. In 1945 his Battalion was posted to the Middle East, when they went to Palestine as Britain's Imperial Strategic Reserve.

Most people think the War ended in 1945 but the tension in the Middle East continued and, even after the VE Day and VJ Day festivities, when most other soldiers were getting back to normal life at home, Leonard, at the age of only 23, was shot by a sniper in Bethlehem Road, Jerusalem, on 29 July 1946. Leonard's wife was never to see him again and he now lies buried in the Ramleh War Cemetery in Gaza, out of reach of all but the most determined relatives.

Without access to census records of the period, it is not known what the Datchworth connection was. However, it seems likely that his parents lived in or near Datchworth and were responsible for getting his name added to the memorial.

HERBERT MARK MILLER

The Commonwealth War Graves Commission, which has extensive and generally reliable records, report that Herbert Miller was a Private in the Bedfordshire and Hertfordshire Regiment, number 5950434, that he died on 2 January 1941, and that he is remembered with honour at Datchworth (All Saints') churchyard.

Research into Herbert Mark Miller has presented a puzzle. According to parish burial registers, there is no-one by the name of Herbert Mark Miller who died during the Second World War. The only person of this name is the son of Mark Miller, listed on the 1911 census as a blacksmith in Tewin, where 13-year-old Herbert Mark Miller lived with his parents Mark and Eva, one younger brother, and three sisters. Herbert Mark Miller, known to locals as Mark, who later became a blacksmith in Datchworth, was born in 1898 and died in 1954, so he was definitely not the Herbert Miller who died in the Second World War.

However, Herbert Mark Miller had a son named Herbert Cecil Miller, who was born on 4 October 1919 and was buried in Datchworth churchyard on 7 January 1941. His death certificate states that Herbert Cecil Miller was a Private, number 5950434, in the Bedfordshire and Hertfordshire Regiment. So far these details match the Commission's record closely, however, according to the death certificate, he died, at the age of 21, in Hertford County Hospital after his pedal bike was hit by a car.

ROY FREDERICK BENSON TEMPERLEY

Roy was born *c.*1920 and lived in Old Pound House in Hollybush Lane with his parents, Frederick and Mary, and joined the Volunteer Reserve of the RAF. He was assigned as a pilot officer to Bomber Command. According to the Bomber Command website, bombing raids were taking place by day at this time over Heligoland. Four out of six Blenheim Bombers failed to return on 26 August 1941 and daylight bombing of Germany was temporarily stopped. Roy was probably in one of these planes.

The newspaper articles below bring to life the anxiety his parents, Frederick and Mary, must have gone through as they learned first that he was missing in action; then that he had been killed.

TEMPERLEY.—Missing in Aug., 1941, in air operations against the enemy, PILOT OFFICER R. F. B. TEMPERLEY, R.A.F.V.R., dearly beloved only son of Mr. and Mrs. F. H. Temperley, Old Pound House, Datchworth, Herts, aged 20. 12·2·1942.

TEMPERLEY.—To the precious memory of ROY, Pilot Officer, R.A.F.V.R. Bomber Command, missing from air operations against the enemy on Aug. 25, 1941. "A most gallant and courageous airman whose devotion to duty was obvious to all." 26.8.1942

Roy's body now lies in the Rheinberg War Cemetery about 85km north of Cologne and a memorial has been placed in the National Arboretum in Staffordshire.

Appendix 2

The Abel Smith family of Woodhall

Members of the Abel Smith family are mentioned frequently in this book, as they were major Datchworth landowners throughout the nineteenth and early twentieth centuries, so a brief history of the family may be of interest.

The Smiths have contributed financially towards many important projects, including the building of the school, the upkeep and improvement of the church, and were also responsible for building many nineteenth century properties.

Samuel Smith (1754-1834), a banker from Nottingham, moved to the area in 1801 when he purchased the Woodhall Estate at Watton-at-Stone. He gradually acquired more land and property in the area, including a substantial amount in Datchworth Parish.

At Samuel's death in 1834, the estate passed to his son, Abel Smith (1788-1859) whose eldest son, also called Abel (1830-1898), inherited the estate in 1859 upon his father's death. For clarity, the two Abel Smiths have been referred to respectively as 'senior' and 'junior' in the text where necessary. Subsequently the estate passed to Abel Henry Smith (1863-1930) in 1898 at the death of Abel Smith (junior). These four successive generations of the family were all Members of Parliament in their time.

In 1920 Abel Henry Smith sold the majority of his land in Datchworth parish, consisting of Datchworth Bury and its lands that stretched north to Bragbury End and south to Datchworth Green and also included Raffin Green Farm. Brothers John and Jeremiah Inns were the purchasers. Other property to the south and west of Datchworth Green was purchased by Robert Wallace, some of which is still owned by his son, John Wallace. By the mid 1940s, John and Jeremiah Inns had died, leaving no heirs to their property. It was in 1947 that Charles Pearman, tenant of Bury Farm since 1913, purchased the freehold of Datchworth Bury and its lands that are still farmed by his grandson, Frank. Over the years both the Wallace and Pearman families have contributed generously to the community in various ways.

Abel Henry Smith died in 1930. As he had no sons, the inheritance of the estate went to his younger brother, Major Edward Pelham Smith. The contents of the mansion at Woodhall were dispersed and the house became a school in 1934 and was subsequently let to Heath Mount School. Meanwhile members of the Abel Smith family lived in a series of smaller houses on the estate. In 1937, at the death of Edward Pelham Smith, the estate was inherited by his son, Thomas Abel Smith (1913-1983). In 1957 Thomas converted the former stables into a large family home which is where his son, the present owner of the estate, Ralph Abel Smith, his wife, Alexandra, and family, reside today. The only land in Datchworth that is still in the ownership of the Woodhall Estate is Moat Farm at Bulls Green.

Figure 202: Samuel Smith
(R M Abel Smith)

Figure 203: Abel Smith, senior
(R M Abel Smith)

Chapter Sources

1. First 1000 years

J E B Gover, A Mawer, F M Stenton, *The Place-names of Hertfordshire* (1938 reprinted 1970)
L Munby, *The Hertfordshire Landscape* (1977)
A Rook, 'Welch's Farm – A Success for the Fieldworker', *Hertfordshire Archaeological Review* (Autumn 1974).
A Rook, 'Part I The discovery' in 'An Iron Age Bronze Mirror from Aston, Hertfordshire'; *Antiquaries Journal* (1982) Vol LXII, Part 1
A Rook, *A History of Hertfordshire* (1984)
T Williamson, *The Origins of Hertfordshire* (2010)
Welwyn Archaeological Society News (various) courtesy of Tony Rook

2. Domesday Book and Datchworth

R W Finn, *An Introduction to Domesday Book* (1963)
J Morris, ed, *Domesday Book Hertfordshire Text* (1976)
W Page, *Victoria County History for Hertfordshire*, Vol III (1908)
D Roffe, *Decoding Domesday* (2007)
A Savage, *The Anglo-Saxon Chronicles* (2002)
F Thorn, *Understanding and interpreting Domesday Book* (1988)
T Williamson, *The Origins of Hertfordshire* (2010)
HALS: DP/33/29/2 1829 survey of Datchworth fields
website: British History Online
website: The National Archives

3. Famine, Plague, Tax and Revolt

N Bowyer, *A Short History of Bramfield* (1970)
J Brooker and S Flood, eds, *Hertfordshire Lay Subsidy Rolls 1307 and 1334* (1998)
J E Cussans, *History of Hertfordshire,* Vol II (1874-78) and Vol III (1879-81) both reprinted 1972
A M Foster, *A Visitors' History of Hitchin* (1992)
A H Thompson, 'The registers of John Gynewell, Bishop of Lincoln, for the years 1349-50' *Archaeological Journal 68* (1911)
M Webley, *The Medieval Manor of Codicote* (1997)

4. Land, Status and the English Civil War

Sir J Clapham, *A Concise Economic History of Britain* (1963)
D Hey, *The Oxford Companion to Local and Family* (1996)
Journal of the House of Commons, vol. 2, (1640-43)
J Richardson, *The Local Historian's Encyclopaedia* (1986)
A Thomson, ed, *The Impact of the First Civil War on Hertfordshire, 1642-47* (2007)
HALS: 96HW55 will & Inventory for Daniel Nash
HALS: QPE/1-4 Poll Book, Knight of Shire Dec 1697
HALS: Quarter Session Books 1619 – 1657; Calendar of Quarter Sessions Rolls 1658 – 1700
website: The National Archives re: State Papers, Charles I
website: History Learning Site; C Trueman, *The Causes of the English Civil War*

5. Law and the Creation of the Parish Council

M Bailey, *The English Manor c.1200 – c.1500* (2002)
D Hey, *Oxford Companion to Local and Family History* (1996)
W Page, *Victoria County History for Hertfordshire*, Vol III (1908)
R Trow-Smith, *The History of Stevenage (1958)*
T O Beachcroft & W B Emms, *Five Hide Village* (1984)
Hertford Mercury and Reformer, 15th Jan 1842
Hertfordshire Constabulary
HALS: CP32/1/1-5 Datchworth Parish Council minutes Dec 1894-1960
HALS: DP33/8/1 Vestry book 1701-1779
HALS: QS/CB/38 Special Petty Sessions 1845-1870; list of constables appointed
HALS: DE/L/2281 Datchworthbury court roll 1768
HALS: Quarter Sessions Books 1619 – 1799
website: *Encyclopaedia Britannica*
website: History of the Judiciary
website: Legal Dictionary

6. Agriculture and Farms

Books, articles and documents

J Andrew, A Museograph originally produced by the Birmingham Museum of Science & Industry; reprint (2008)
re: weights and measures
S Friar, *The Local History Companion* (2001)
D Hey, *The Oxford Companion to Local and Family History* (1996)
B King, *A Brief History of Allotments* (2013)
Paper by J Wallace, *Farming in Hertfordshire Past and Present*
R Whitlock, *The English Farm* (1983)
A Young, *General View of the Agriculture of the County of Hertfordshire* (1804)

HALS: CP32/1/2-3 Parish Council minutes 1895-1924, 1924-37
HALS: DE/K/23114-5 Abel Smith admitted tenant to Smiths Close
HALS: DP33/27/1A &1B tithe award and map, 1838-9
HALS: DP33/29/2 1829 survey of Datchworth fields
HALS: DP33/3/1 W Hawtayne's tithe and glebe accounts 1711-1747
HALS: Ordnance Survey map, 1881; re Shippins Farm

Datchworth farms (HALS documents)

Bragbury End	D/Egr/27; D/ERy/B210; DE/AS/1527-1528A; DE/AS/1531-2; DE/AS/1535; DE/AS/1538-9; DE/AS/1542; DE/AS/1554-5; DE/AS/1561-5; DE/AS/1589-1595; DE/L/2290; DE/L/2307-10
Bridgefoot Farm	DE/AS/4099
Bulls Green Farm	DEGA/3260; DE/P/E66 auction sale 1919
Burnham Green Farm	DE/P/E325; DE/P/E220/7; DE/P/E220/12-14; DE/P/E254/6
Cherry Tree Farm	DE/AS/1443
Coltsfoot Farm	DE/P/E94; DE/P/E325; DE/P/T2837; DE/P/E66/7 sale particulars 1919; DE/P/E66 auction sale 1919; DE/AS/1815 sale particulars 1832
Datchworth Green Farm	DE/AS/1815 sale particulars 1832; DE/Bw/28346
Datchworthbury Farm	DE/AS/1443; DE/AS/1605; DE/AS/1624-5; DE/AS/1628
Green End Farm	DE/AS/1651; DE/AS/1653; DE/AS/1667-8; DE/AS/1673-5; DE/AS/1679-85; DE/L/2276; DE/SH/T21
Hawkins Hall Farm	DE/AS/1980; DE/AS/4099
Hoppers Hall Farm	DE/AS/1753-4; DE/AS/1771-2; DE/AS/1782-3; DE/AS/1785-6; DE/AS/1980; DE/AS/4099
Miles Farm	DE/AS/1521-5; DE/AS/1530; DE/AS/1534; DE/AS/1536-7
Moat Farm	DE/AS/1816; DE/AS/1443; DE/P/E94; DE/P/T2795-816; DE/P/T2837; DE/SH/T17
Painters Green Farm	DE/AS/1739; DE/AS/1753-4; DE/AS/1771-2; DE/AS/1778-9; DE/AS/1782-3; DE/AS/1785-6; DE/AS/1831-2; DE/AS/1980; DE/AS/4099; DE/K1/20586-7
Raffin Green Farm	DE/AS/1605; DE/AS/1610-1; DE/AS/1624-5; DE/AS/1628

7. Services: Gas, Electricity and Water

T O Beachcroft & W B Emms, *Five Hide Village* (1984)
Conveyance between Eastern Gas Board and EH Watson 1954, courtesy of John Wallace
Hertford Mercury and Reformer, Dec 1853

HALS: CP32/1/1-5 Datchworth Parish Council minutes Dec 1894-1960
HALS: DE/L/4141 1912; lease for taking water from Bridgefoot well

8. Two World Wars

T O Beachcroft & W B Emms, *Five Hide Village* (1984)
J Wallace, notes on flying bombs
Datchworth Parish magazine (Datchworth Museum)

HALS: CP32/1/1-5 Datchworth Parish Council minutes Dec 1894-1960
HALS: CP82 & CP83 Hertfordshire County Council 2 Volume 86, 1919-1920
HALS: DP33/3/3 War memorial receipts 1919

website: Herts Memories, J Birch 'Our Hertford and Ware', re: Zeppelin attack on Hertford

9. Population, Employment and Local Business

B Johnson, *Hertfordshire Inns* (1962)
Kelly's Directory for Hertfordshire (various)
L Munby, *Hertfordshire Population Statistics 1563-1801,* (1964)
J Walker, ed, *Datchworth Tithe Accounts 1711-1747* (2010)
Dury and Andrews' map 1766, reprint Hertfordshire Record Society (2004)

HALS: DE/AS/1336 1836 sales particulars Tilbury and Rose Cottage
HALS: DE/AS/1716 1838 Tilbury and poor house; Henry Campkin's declaration
HALS: QS/VAR/16-20 victuallers register
HALS: QS/VAR/129-218 victuallers register
HALS: QS/VAR/2230-2317 victuallers register

website: Find My Past

10. The Church

J Bristow, *The Local Historian's Glossary & Vade Mecum* (1997)
R Clutterbuck, *The History and Antiquities of the County of Hertford*, Volume II (1821)
J E Cussans, *History of Hertfordshire*, Vol II (1874-78 reprinted 1972)
M Harrison, *Victorian Stained Glass*, (1980)
The Hertfordshire Family and Population History Society, *Hertfordshire monumental Inscriptions:* (1982)
W Page, *Victoria County History for Hertfordshire*, Vol III (1908)
Royal Commission on Historical Monuments, *An Inventory of the Historical Monuments in Hertfordshire*, (1910)

HALS: DE/Bg/4/155 Drawing by J C Buckler c 1835-40; All Saints' Church
HALS: DE/Gr Gerish collection; newspaper cutting re Watton-at-Stone church
HALS: DP33/3/2 vestry letters, 1900-05
HALS: DP33/4/1 churchwardens accounts, 1845-80
HALS: DP33/8/1-3 vestry books, 1701-1779, 1777-1829, 1829-1919
HALS: 63615A William Williamson's parish notebook
HALS: *East Hertfordshire Archaeological Transactions* (1902)

website: British History Online

11. Nonconformity and the Baptist Chapels

R Hine, *A History of Hitchin* (1929)
A Ruston, 'Protestant Nonconformity', in D Short, ed, *An Historical Atlas of Hertfordshire* (2011)
A Ruston, *Nonconformity in Hertfordshire* (2005)
W Urwick, *Nonconformity in Hertfordshire* (1884)
D Watts, 'The Work of the Hertfordshire Baptist Union', *The Baptist Quarterly* (c1983)

HALS: DE/AS/1641-2 1718 Meeting house and Pettits
HALS: DE/AS/1643-4 1723 Meeting house and Pettits
HALS: DE/AS/1645 1729 will of Benjamin Chapman
HALS: DE/P/E99 1909 lease land for Burnham Green Baptist Chapel, Countess Cowper
HALS: NQ2F Datchworth Baptist Chapel

12. The Old Houses

Books, articles, websites etc

T O Beachcroft & W B Emms, *Five Hide Village* (1984)
J Broad, ed, *Bishop Wake's Summary of Visitation Returns from the Diocese of Lincoln 1706-1715*, part 2 (The British Academy, Records of Social and Economic History, new series, 50, 2012)
R Clutterbuck, *The History and Antiquities of the County of Hertford*, Volume II (1821)
J E Cussans, *History of Hertfordshire*, Vol II (1874-78 reprinted 1972)
J E B Gover, A Mawer, F M Stenton *The Place-names of Hertfordshire* (1938 reprinted 1970)
A Greening, *Hawkins Hall Farm In the County of Hertfordshire* (1998)
Kelly's Directory for Hertfordshire (various)
L Munby, *Hertfordshire Population Statistics 1563-1801*, (1964)
W Page, *Victoria County History for Hertfordshire*, Vol III (1908)
N Salmon, *The History of Hertfordshire* (1728)
J Walker, ed, *Datchworth Tithe Accounts 1711-1747* (2010)
Deeds of Robert Wallace, courtesy of John Wallace
Deeds of Rose Cottage, courtesy of Peter Hyne
Deeds of the Little House, courtesy of Will & Olek Topping
Copy of will, Thomas Pennyfather,1529 (Datchworth Museum)
Hertford Mercury and Reformer, Dec 1846
Hertfordshire Mercury and County Press, 12 Aug 1977
Welwyn and Hatfield Times 12 Aug 1977

HALS: Land Tax, Datchworth, 'miscellaneous' section contains window tax returns.
Ordnance Survey map, 1881; re: Shippins Farm

website: Find My Past
website: Stevenage Borough council
website: English Heritage

Datchworth houses (HALS documents)

Bragbury End	D/Egr/27; DE/AS/1527-1528A; DE/AS/1531-2; DE/AS/1535; DE/AS/1538-9; DE/AS/1554-5; DE/AS/1561-5; DE/AS/1589-1595; DE/L/2290; DE/L/2307-2310
Bragbury End Hall	DE/AS/1542; D/Ery/B210 sale particulars 1912
Bridgefoot	DE/AS/4099
Bulls Green	DEGA/3260; DE/P/E66 auction sale 1919
Burnham Green Farm	DE/P/E220/7; DE/P/E220/12-14; DE/P/E254/6; DE/P/E325
Cherry Tree Farm	DE/AS/1443 will Dowager Viscountess Townshend 1784
Coltsfoot	DE/P/E94; DE/P/E325; DE/P/T2837; DE/P/E66/7 sale particulars 1919; DE/P/E66 auction sale 1919; DE/AS/1815 sale particulars 1832

Datchworth Green Farm	DE/Bw/28346; DE/AS/1815 sale particulars 1832
Datchworth rectory	DP33/8/4 sale 1933-1944
Datchworthbury	DE/AS/1596; DE/AS/1601-4; DE/AS/1624-5; DE/AS/1628; 40HW12 will Thomas Foster 1614; 40HW25 will Grizell Foster 1617; DE/AS/1621 will Hon W J Townshend 1783; DE/AS/1443 will Dowager Viscountess Townshend 1784; DE/AS/1605 sale particulars 1802
Green End Cottage	DE/L/2277-80; DE/SH/T21
Green End Farm	DE/AS/1679-85; DE/AS/1651; DE/AS/1653; DE/AS/1667-8; DE/AS/1673-5; DE/L/2276
Hawkins Hall	DE/AS/1980; DE/AS/4099; DE/L/P6 manor boundary; DE/AS/1991 marriage settlement Gripper/Williams 1737; DE/AS/1834 will T Gripper 1760; DE/AS/1993 will E Gripper 1765
Hoppers Hall	DE/AS/1753-4; DE/AS/1771-2; DE/AS/1782-3; DE/AS/1785-6; DE/AS/1980; DE/AS/4099
Miles Farm	DE/AS/1521-5; DE/AS/1530; DE/AS/1534; DE/AS/1536-7; DE/AS/1524-5
Moat Farm	DE/AS/1816; DE/P/E94; DE/P/T2795-816; DE/P/T2837; DE/SH/T17; DE/AS/1443 will Dowager Viscountess Townshend 1784
Painters Green Farm	DE/AS/1739; DE/AS/1753-4; DE/AS/1771-2; DE/AS/1778-9; DE/AS/1782-3; DE/AS/1785-6; DE/AS/1831-2; DE/AS/1980; DE/AS/4099; DE/K1/20586-7
Pettits	DE/AS/1638-9; DE/AS/1641-50; DE/L/2276-81; DE/SH/T21; DE/AS/1702 meeting house
Raffin Green Farm	DE/AS/1610-1; DE/AS/1624-5; DE/AS/1628; DE/AS/1605 sale particulars 1802

13. The Schools

M G Jones, *The Charity School Movement* (1938)
Kelly's Directory for Hertfordshire, 1855
F A Richardson, *Knebworth, The Story of a Hertfordshire Village* (1982)
Hertfordshire Mercury and County Press, Sept 1925
School Managers meeting minutes accessed by Mary Poole for *Five Hide Village,* (no longer available)
HALS: 63615A William Williamson's parish notebook
HALS: HED1/229/1 Datchworth School log book 1904-1932
website: Find My Past

14. 20th Century Planning and Building Disputes

T O Beachcroft & W B Emms, *Five Hide Village* (1984)
HALS: CP32/1/1-5 Datchworth Parish Council minutes Dec 1894-1960
website: East Herts Council, re: planning

15. All Saints' Rectors

J Burg, ed, *Religion in Hertfordshire 1847-1851* (1995)
Crockford's Clerical Directory (1884-1950)
J Foster, *Alumni Oxonienses* (1891)
W Page, *Victoria County History for Hertfordshire*, Vol III (1908)
People of Tewin, *The History of Tewin* (2009)
W Urwick, *Nonconformity in Hertfordshire* (1884)
J & J A Venn, *Alumni Cantabrigienses* (1922)
J Walker, ed, *Datchworth Tithe Accounts 1711-1747* (2010)
Datchworth Parish magazines, 1932-36 (Datchworth Museum)
HALS: ACC 3252 1976-1990 12 All Saints' Parish Magazine
HALS: D/P33/1/24 Parson's fees 1785
HALS: DP33/8/1-3 vestry books, 1701-1779, 1777-1829, 1829-1919
HALS: DP33/27/1A &1B, Tithe award and map, 1838-9
website: England Football Online
website: The National Archives, re:1936 Tithe Act
website: History of the Church of England, re: Church commissioners
website: Hertfordshire reference library; *Dictionary of National Biography* C S Knighton re: William Downham

16. The Poor Law

T O Beachcroft & W B Emms, *Five Hide Village* (1984)
C R Cheney & M Jones, *A Handbook of Dates* (2000)
S Friar, *The Local History Companion* (2001)
D Hey, *The Oxford Companion to Local and Family History* (1996)
S Shave, 'The welfare of the vulnerable in the late 18th and early 19th centuries: Gilbert's Act of 1782', *History in Focus*, 14 (2008).
C W Sutton, 'Philip Thicknesse', *Dictionary of National Biography*
P Thicknesse, *An Account of the Four Persons Found Starved to Death at Datchworth in Hertfordshire* (1769)
Hertford Museum: Hertford Union Workhouse information and photograph
Hertford Mercury and Reformer, 2nd Feb 1856

Hertfordshire Mercury and County Press, 7th May 1910

HALS: BG/HER/27-38; BG/HER/39; BG/HER/40-41 Hertford Union Workhouse: Admissions and Discharges (1873-1916), Births 1847-1918), Deaths (1847-1914)
HALS: DE/AS/1512, DE/AS/1710-15, conveyance and sale of Datchworth Green poor house
HALS: DE/AS/1679-85 re: Green End Farm and Philip Thicknesse
HALS: DE/AS/1716-19, DE/P/T2963-8 sale of old Tilbury and poor house (1837-8)
HALS: DE/L/2277-81 re: Green End, Pettits, Thicknesse, meeting house
HALS: DP33/8/1-3 vestry books, 1701-1779, 1777-1829, 1829-1919
HALS: DP33/18/1-2, poor in the parish
HALS: DP/33/14/1, apprenticeship indentures

website: The National Archives
website: Hertfordshire Names

17. Troublemakers

W B Johnson, *'Memorandoms For ...' The Carrington Diary* (1973)
W E Tate, *The Parish Chest* (1969)
Herts Guardian, Agricultural Journal and General Advertiser, 1852-67
Hertford Mercury and Reformer, 1834-68
Information re: Shadbolts in New Zealand, courtesy of Pauline Conolly
Ken Griffin: convict information from *Transported Beyond the Seas* and Herts Assize

HALS: DP106/1/3 Tewin Parish baptism register 1813-71
HALS: DP33/1/4 Datchworth Parish baptism register 1854-92
HALS: Quarter Sessions Books from the 18th and 19th centuries

website: Convict Records; transportation

18. Colourful Characters

People of Tewin, *The History of Tewin* (2009)
Essex Newsman, 5th November 1887
Grantham Journal, 8th March 1873
Hertfordshire Constabulary
Reynolds Newspaper, 6th November 1887
The Blackburn Standard, 14th January 1893

website: 'The Witches Collective', witchcraft in Hertfordshire
website: Find My Past re: Home Office prison registers etc
website: Luton Paranormal Society

19. The Most Haunted Village in Hertfordshire

R Stratton and N Connell, *Haunted Hertfordshire* (2006)

website: Herts memories
website: Luton Paranormal Society

20. Village Organisations and Entertainment

T O Beachcroft & W B Emms, *Five Hide Village* (1984)
W Johnson, *'Memorandoms for ...': The Carrington Diary* (1973)
Campaign to Protect Rural England (Hertfordshire)
Datchworth Museum, photographs and other information
Datchworth Parish Council conveyances
Datchworth Parish Magazine (Datchworth Museum)
Information from the Hertfordshire Girlguiding records office, courtesy of Mary Underwood
The Boy Scouts Association (registration returns 1921 to 1990); courtesy of Frank Brittain, Herts Scouts Archivist
Village Hall committee AGM minutes, 1957 to 1972

HALS: CP32/1/1-5 Datchworth Parish Council minutes Dec 1894-1960

website: East Herts Council, re: planning

Bibliography

BOOKS

M Bailey, *The English Manor c.1200 – c.1500* (2002)
T O Beachcroft & W B Emms, *Five Hide Village* (1984)
N Bowyer, *A Short History of Bramfield* (1970)
J Bristow, *The Local Historian's Glossary & Vade Mecum* (1997)
J Broad, ed, *Bishop Wake's Summary of Visitation Returns from the Diocese of Lincoln 1706-1715*, part 2 (The British Academy, Records of Social and Economic History, new series, 50, 2012)
J Brooker and S Flood, eds, *Hertfordshire Lay Subsidy Rolls 1307 and 1334* (1998)
J Burg, ed, *Religion in Hertfordshire 1847-1851* (1995)
C R Cheney & M Jones, *A Handbook of Dates* (2000)
Sir J Clapham, *A Concise Economic History of Britain* (1963)
R Clutterbuck, *The History and Antiquities of the County of Hertford*, Volume II (1821)
Crockford's Clerical Directory (1884-1950)
J E Cussans, *History of Hertfordshire,* Vol II (1874-78) and Vol III (1879-81) both reprinted 1972
R W Finn, *An Introduction to Domesday Book* (1963)
A M Foster, *A Visitors' History of Hitchin* (1992)
J Foster, *Alumni Oxonienses* (1891)
S Friar, *The Local History Companion* (2001)
J E B Gover, A Mawer, F M Stenton *The Place-names of Hertfordshire* (1938 reprinted 1970)
K Griffin, *Transported Beyond the Seas*
M Harrison, *Victorian Stained Glass*, (1980)
D Hey, *The Oxford Companion to Local and Family History* (1996)
The Hertfordshire Family and Population History Society, *Hertfordshire monumental Inscriptions:* (1982)
R Hine, *A History of Hitchin* (1929)
B Johnson, *Hertfordshire Inns* (1962)
W B Johnson, *'Memorandoms For ...' The Carrington Diary* (1973)
M G Jones, *The Charity School Movement* (1938)
Journal of the House of Commons, vol. 2, (1640-43)
Kelly's Directory for Hertfordshire (various)
J Morris, ed, *Domesday Book Hertfordshire Text* (1976)
L Munby, *Hertfordshire Population Statistics 1563-1801,* (1964)
L Munby, *The Hertfordshire Landscape* (1977)
W Page, *Victoria County History for Hertfordshire*, Vol III (1908)
People of Tewin, *The History of Tewin* (2009)
F A Richardson, *Knebworth, The Story of a Hertfordshire Village* (1982)
J Richardson, *The Local Historian's Encyclopaedia* (1986)
D Roffe, *Decoding Domesday* (2007)
A Rook, *A History of Hertfordshire* (1984)
Royal Commission on Historical Monuments, *An Inventory of the Historical Monuments in Hertfordshire*, (1910)
A Ruston, 'Protestant Nonconformity', in D Short, ed, *An Historical Atlas of Hertfordshire* (2011)
A Ruston, *Nonconformity in Hertfordshire* (2005)
N Salmon, *The History of Hertfordshire* (1728)
A Savage, *The Anglo-Saxon Chronicles* (2002)
R Stratton and N Connell, *Haunted Hertfordshire* (2006)
W E Tate, *The Parish Chest* (1969)
P Thicknesse, *An Account of the Four Persons Found Starved to Death at Datchworth in Hertfordshire* (1769)
A Thomson, ed, *The Impact of the First Civil War on Hertfordshire, 1642-47* (2007)
F Thorn, *Understanding and interpreting Domesday Book* (1988)
R Trow-Smith, *The History of Stevenage (1958)*
W Urwick, *Nonconformity in Hertfordshire* (1884)
J & J A Venn, *Alumni Cantabrigienses* (1922)
J Walker, ed, *Datchworth Tithe Accounts 1711-1747* (2010)
M Webley, *The Medieval Manor of Codicote* (1997)
R Whitlock, *The English Farm* (1983)
T Williamson, *The Origins of Hertfordshire* (2010)
A Young, *General View of the Agriculture of the County of Hertfordshire* (1804)

JOURNALS AND ARTICLES

Datchworth Parish magazines, 1932-36 (Datchworth Museum)
East Hertfordshire Archaeological Transactions (1902) (HALS)
Welwyn Archaeological Society News (various) courtesy of Tony Rook
J Andrew, A Museograph originally produced by the Birmingham Museum of Science & Industry; reprint (2008) re: weights and measures (website)
A Greening, *Hawkins Hall Farm In the County of Hertfordshire* (1998)
B King, *A Brief History of Allotments* (2013) (website)
A Rook, 'Part I The discovery' in 'An Iron Age Bronze Mirror from Aston, Hertfordshire'; *Antiquaries Journal* (1982) Vol LXII, Part 1

Bibliography

A Rook, 'Welch's Farm – A Success for the Fieldworker', *Hertfordshire Archaeological Review* (Autumn 1974).
S Shave, 'The welfare of the vulnerable in the late 18th and early 19th centuries: Gilbert's Act of 1782', *History in Focus*, 14 (2008).
A H Thompson, 'The registers of John Gynewell, Bishop of Lincoln, for the years 1349-50', *Archaeological Journal 68* (1911)
J Wallace, *Farming in Hertfordshire Past and Present*
J Wallace, notes on flying bombs
D Watts, 'The Work of the Hertfordshire Baptist Union', *The Baptist Quarterly* (c1983)

NEWSPAPERS

Access: those dated 1834-68, from 'Find My Past' website, otherwise from HALS
Essex Newsman, 5th November 1887
Grantham Journal, 8th March 1873
Hertford Mercury, in its various forms from 1842-1977
Herts Guardian, Agricultural Journal and General Advertiser, 1852-1867
Reynolds Newspaper, 6th November 1887
The Blackburn Standard, 14th January 1893
Welwyn and Hatfield Times 12th August 1977

MISCELLANEOUS SOURCES OF INFORMATION

Campaign to Protect Rural England (Hertfordshire)
Conveyance between Eastern Gas Board and EH Watson 1954, courtesy of John Wallace
Datchworth Museum: copy of will, Thomas Pennyfather,
Datchworth Museum: photographs and general information
Datchworth Parish Council conveyances
Deeds of Robert Wallace, courtesy of John Wallace
Deeds of Rose Cottage, courtesy of Peter Hyne
Deeds of the Little House, courtesy of Will & Olek Topping
Dury and Andrews' map 1766, reprint Hertfordshire Record Society (2004)
Hertford Museum: Hertford Union Workhouse information and photograph
Hertfordshire Archives and Local Studies (HALS): many documents accessed, references listed in 'Chapter Sources'
Hertfordshire Constabulary
Information re: Shadbolts, courtesy of Pauline Conolly in New Zealand
Information re: the Hertfordshire Girlguiding records, courtesy of Mary Underwood
Information re: Datchworth convicts, courtesy of Ken Griffin
School Managers meeting minutes accessed by Mary Poole for *Five Hide Village,* (no longer available)
The Boy Scouts Association (registration returns 1921 to 1990)
Village Hall committee AGM minutes, 1957 to 1972

WEBSITES

website: British History Online
website: Convict Records; transportation
website: East Herts Council, re: planning
website: England Football Online
website: English Heritage
website: Find My Past; Parish registers, censuses 1841 to 1911
website: Hertfordshire Names
website: Hertfordshire reference library; *Dictionary of National Biography*
website: Hertfordshire reference library; *Encyclopaedia Britannica*
website: Hertfordshire reference library; *Oxford English Dictionary*
website: Herts Memories
website: History Learning Site, C Trueman, *The Causes of the English Civil War*
website: History of the Church of England, re: Church commissioners
website: History of the Judiciary
website: Legal Dictionary
website: Luton Paranormal Society
website: Stevenage Borough council
website: The National Archives
website: The Witches Collective; witchcraft in Hertfordshire

Index

Abbreviations: JP, Justice of the Peace; MC, Military Cross; MP, Member of Parliament; PC, Police Constable; jnr, junior; snr, senior.

Authors names are **not** in the index but have been included in 'Chapter Sources'.

Farms have been listed under 'Farm', **not** under their individual names.

Occupations from census data, 1841-1911, pages 74-5, have **not** been included.

Offences, punishments and other details on pages 178-80 have **not** been included although the names of the offenders are in the index.

Datchworth parish in 1839 based on the tithe map
(HALS: DSA4/34/2)